MODERN LEGAL

CU00691177

Copyright and the Public Interest

AUSTRALIA
Law Book Co.
Sydney

CANADA and USA
Carswell
Toronto

HONG KONG
Sweet & Maxwell Asia

NEW ZEALAND
Brookers
Wellington

SINGAPORE and MALAYSIA
Sweet & Maxwell Asia
Singapore and Kuala Lumpur

MODERN LEGAL STUDIES

COPYRIGHT AND THE PUBLIC INTEREST

Gillian Davies, Ph.D., DL, of Lincoln's Inn, Barrister
Honorary Professor, University of Wales, Aberystwyth
Chairman of a Technical Board of Appeal and
Member of the Enlarged Board, European Patent Office

London
Sweet & Maxwell
2002

Published in 2002 by
Sweet & Maxwell Limited of
100 Avenue Road London NW3 3PE
www.sweetandmaxwell.co.uk
Typeset by YHT Ltd, London
Printed in Great Britain by Creative Print and Design Wales

A CIP catalogue record for this book
is available from the British Library.

ISBN 0421 74209

No natural forests were destroyed to make this product,
only farmed timber was used and re-planted.

The chief glory of every people
arises from its authors

Samuel Johnson

Preface to the First Edition

At a time when within the Berne Union and in the European Community there are plans for the further international harmonisation of copyright laws, it is timely to re-examine the basic justifications for copyright. The first two legislative texts on copyright, the UK Statute of Anne 1709 and the Copyright Clause of the US Constitution 1787, embodied the concept that providing copyright protection for authors for a limited time would encourage and promote learning and progress and thus act for the public good.

This study discusses the proposition that copyright is a just and proper concept, established and developed in the public interest, and explores the extent to which the notion of the public interest has influenced the copyright laws of a few major jurisdictions, namely, France, Germany, the United Kingdom and the United States of America.

The proposition that copyright is in the public interest has been taken for granted in the past but, in recent years, it has been questioned within the context of the challenges to the copyright system posed by technical developments. In this debate, the underlying philosophy of copyright and its basic functions have been called into question and the public interest has been invoked, not in favour of better protection for copyright owners, but in favour of free and unfettered access by the public to copyright works.

By examining the underlying principles which have governed the copyright system from its origins, the study also draws attention to the fact that the roots of European and US copyright shared a common approach and that, contrary to the prevailing opinion that the Continental European and Anglo-American approaches to copyright are diametrically opposed, historical analysis shows that there is in fact a rich tradition of consensus as regards the justifications for and legislative solutions to copyright on which to draw during the harmonisation process.

The study is presented in three parts. Part I provides an introduction to the concept of the public interest in the copyright system and explores the underlying principles governing copyright legislation, as well as its origins in Western Europe. Part II reviews the concept of the public interest in the history of copyright in the United Kingdom, the United States of America, France and Germany. Part III deals with copyright and public policy, considering the moral and economic functions of copyright in relation to the alternatives thereto, the limitations imposed on copyright in the public interest and, finally, draws some conclusions in relation to the role of the state.

The author wishes to thank the Max Planck Institute for Foreign and International Patent, Copyright and Competition Law, Munich, which provided her with the opportunity to research and publish this study, and, in particular, Professor Friedrich-Karl Beier and Dr. Adolf Dietz for their encouragement. Thanks are also due to the International Federation of the Phonographic Industry (IFPI), which gave her leave of absence in the summer of 1990 to begin work on this study. Finally, the author is indebted to Raph Lunzer for his careful reading of the text and to Catriona Thomas for her help with preparing the manuscript for publication.

Gillian Davies
Munich
September 30, 1993

Preface to the Second Edition

The first edition of this book had as its aims to re-examine the basic justifications for copyright in the context of the challenges to the copyright system posed by technical developments in the early 1990s and to contribute to the debate on public policy in relation to copyright reform and harmonisation.

Throughout its near 300-year history, the law of copyright has been closely linked to developments in technology. First introduced in England in 1709 in response to the invention of printing, copyright law has been adapted continually to technological change, as new works and new uses of works have resulted from technical progress. In the course of the twentieth century, this process accelerated to accommodate the advent of the film, sound recording, radio, television, cable and satellite broadcasting, computer technology and advances in copying techniques. Over the past 10 years, these developments have been compounded by the use of computer technology to digitise works in combination with new digital distribution and communication technologies. The distribution of copyright-protected works on a global scale over the internet is now a reality and is the latest technical, legal and economic challenge facing the copyright system.

The first edition of this book was published in 1994 and in the interim the pace of change in national laws and at the international and European Union levels in the field of copyright and related rights has been unprecedented. The development of the internet has also prompted much academic and intergovernmental discussion about copyright policy and the cultural and economic importance of both copyright and, more generally, the law of intellectual property. The eight years since the first edition have seen the adoption of three important new international instruments in the field of copyright and related rights: the Agreement on Trade-Related Intellectual Property Rights (TRIPs) in 1994; the World Copyright Treaty (WCT) and the World Performances and Phonograms Treaty (WPPT), both adopted in 1996 under the auspices of the World Intellectual Property Organisation (WIPO), with the aim of regulating the copyright problems posed by the internet. The world of copyright has also been transformed by the ambitious programme for the harmonisation of copyright and related rights undertaken by the European Union, a comparatively recent player on the copyright scene. When the first edition of this book appeared, only one EC Directive in the copyright field had entered into force, the Directive on the Legal Protection of Computer Programs. Meanwhile, no less than six more Directives concerned with copyright and related rights have been adopted, including that concerned with the problems of the internet, the European Directive on the Harmonisation of Certain Aspects of Copyright and Related Rights in the Information Society, 2001. As a result, the copyright laws of the three major European Union Member States discussed in this book have required substantial amendment at intervals to bring them into line with the Directives and continue to do so.

In all these developments, the public interest in the copyright system has attracted the attention of legislators and commentators to a much greater extent than in the past. The literature on the subject at the time of writing the first edition of this book was comparatively scarce. Today, the subject attracts a great deal of interest and, indeed, debate. Both aspects of the public interest in copyright are now generally recognised. On the one hand, copyright is acknowledged to be a motor for stimulating creative activity, thereby promoting learning and progress for the benefit of the public; on the other, limitations and exceptions to copyright answer to the public interest in the widest possible availability of copyright material. A successful copyright law must find a balance between these two goals of public policy.

The purpose of this new edition is to update the text to reflect the changes in national legislation and case law of the past eight years and to take account of the developments in international and European Union law over the same period, in so far as these changes and developments are relevant to the public interest. The very rich literature on the subject has also been taken into account. The text is based on information available to the author on June 30, 2002.

The second edition contains a completely new Part, Part IV, entitled "The Future of Copyright—Obstacles and Perspectives". The new Part IV discusses the impact that digital technology is having on copyright and the legal frameworks required for appropriate protection of copyright works. The solutions found in the new international instruments and EU and US legislation are discussed, as well as the promise of technical solutions. Finally, the need for and obstacles to the improved international protection of copyright are reviewed.

The first edition of this study[1] was published under the auspices of the Max Planck Institute for Foreign and International Patent, Copyright and Competition Law, Munich, which provided the author with the opportunity to begin research on the topic. My thanks are due to Professor Dr Gerhardt Schricker of the Max Planck Institute for encouraging me to embark on a new edition and agreeing to its publication.

This book would not have appeared without the support and encouragement of many colleagues in the field. I wish especially to thank Professor William R. Cornish and Professor Gerald Dworkin for their interest and advice and Dr Martin Vogel for his careful reading of Chapter 7 on Germany and most helpful suggestions. My thanks are also due, in particular, to Christophe Geiger, member of the research staff of the Max Planck Institute, who provided me with invaluable research assistance, constructive criticism and suggestions concerning the structure and contents of this new edition. His contribution was especially important with respect to Chapters 6 and 7 on France and Germany and Parts III and IV. Due to his keen interest in the subject, as well as his enthusiasm for the project, I have greatly benefited from our many discussions. I should like to thank also Elisabeth Iles, Head of Library Services at the International Federation of the Phonographic Industry (IFPI) in London, for her willing and indefatigable assistance in tracking down research material and references, as well as all who have helped to make the completion of this book possible.

Gillian Davies
Munich
August 31, 2002

---

[1] G. Davies, *Copyright and the Public Interest*, (Vol. 14 IIC Studies in Industrial Property and Copyright Law, Max Planck Institute for Foreign and International Patent, Copyright and Competition Law, Munich, Weinheim, New York, NY; VCH 1994).

Contents

PART II THE CONCEPT OF THE PUBLIC INTEREST IN THE HISTORY OF COPYRIGHT—NATIONAL EXAMPLES

Table of Cases

Table of UK Statutes

Table of Statutory Instruments

Table of USA Statutes

Table of French Statutes

Table of German Statutes

Table of EC Legislation

Table of International Conventions

xliii

PART I

THE PUBLIC INTEREST IN THE COPYRIGHT SYSTEM

Chapter 1

Introduction

> The system of copyright has great advantages and great disadvantages, and it is our business to ascertain what these are, and then to make an arrangement under which the advantages may be as far as possible secured, and the disadvantages as far as possible excluded.[1] *T. Macaulay*

The purpose of this study is to discuss the proposition that copyright[2] **1–001** is a just and proper concept, established and developed in the public interest and to explore the extent to which the notion of the "public interest" has influenced the copyright laws of a few major jurisdictions from their origins in the eighteenth century to date. In this context,

---

[1] *Hansard*, Vol. 56, February 5, 1841, at 346 (T. Macaulay).

[2] Throughout this study, the word "*copyright*" is used in its widest sense as a generic term to describe the various systems of law, which in 2002 protect authors of literary, artistic and musical works and other right owners, such as performers, film producers, producers of phonograms (sound recordings) and broadcasting organisations. Evidently, in the discussion of the history of copyright it is authors of literary, artistic and musical works, as well as publishers, with whom we are mainly concerned. There are two basic approaches to the protection of the various categories of copyright owners. The system of "*droit d'auteur*" (author's rights), based on the protection of the individual author, and that of "*copyright*", which admits protection both of individuals and of corporate bodies and thus permits a wide variety of creative endeavour to share the umbrella of copyright. The "*droit d'auteur*" system as a general rule affords protection only to individual authors; others, such as performers, producers of phonograms and broadcasting organisations, are protected by means of related, sometimes called neighbouring rights ("*droits voisins*"). Copyright systems do not make the same distinction. This study does not deal in any detail with these distinctions, being concerned with the broad concept of copyright (see, however, Ch.13, where these distinctions are addressed in the context of the international harmonisation of copyright law.) However, for the sake of clarity, where in this study author's rights, in particular, as opposed to copyrights in general, are referred to, the term "author's rights" is used. Likewise, the term "*droit d'auteur*" is translated as author's right.

the basic justifications for copyright and the public policy role of the state in relation to copyright are examined, with particular reference to the challenges to the modern copyright system posed by the technical revolution brought about by digital technology and the world of the internet.

"When considering the public interest ... it is to be remembered that one feature ... is that justice should always be done and should be seen to be done."[3] The concept of *pro bono publico* is Roman: according to Cicero, "The good of the people is the chief law."[4]

Whether a particular act is "in the public interest" is probably not subject to any objective tests. Inherent in the noble motive of the public good is the notion that, in certain circumstances, the needs of the majority override those of the individual, and that the citizen should relinquish any thoughts of self-interest in favour of the common good of society as a whole. Milton expressed this principle cogently:

"That grounded maxim
So rife and celebrated in the mouths
Of wisest men; that to the public good
Private respects must yield."[5]

The first two important legislative statements on copyright, the English Statute of Anne 1709[6] and the copyright clause of the American Constitution, framed in 1787, both address the public interest issue.

1–002   The Statute of Anne is described as "an Act for the encouragement of learning, by vesting the copies of printed books in the authors or purchasers of such copies, during the times therein mentioned". The Preamble gives three main motivations for the legislation. First, to prevent for the future the printing and publication of "books and other writings, without the consent of the authors or proprietors of such books and writings", that is, to outlaw the pirate trade in books. Second, by preventing piracy to remedy a practice seen as being to the "very great detriment" of authors, leading "too often to the ruin of

---

[3] *per* Morris, L.J., *Ellis v Home Office* [1953], 2 QB 135.
[4] De Legibus III, iii.8.
[5] Samson Agonistes, line 865.
[6] The Statute of Queen Anne, 1709, Ch. XIX (see Appendix 1). This was the first parliamentary English Copyright Act and the first without provision for censorship.

them and their families". Third, "for the encouragement of learned men to compose and write useful books".

The Statute of Anne is the direct ancestor of American copyright law. The copyright clause of the US Constitution retains the fundamental ideas of the full title of the Statute of Anne and vests Congress with the power "to promote the progress of science and useful arts, by securing for limited times to authors and inventors the exclusive right to their respective writings and discoveries".[7] The word "science" in this context retains its eighteenth-century meaning of "knowledge or learning".[8]

The language of both statements embodies the concept that providing protection for the author against unauthorised publication for a limited period will encourage and promote learning and progress, and preserve the public domain, thus acting for the public good.

The copyright system as we know it today is still built on these early foundations. The premise is accepted that creating is worthwhile and that copyright provides a means of giving creators what is properly due to them, thereby stimulating cultural activity and the production and distribution of new works for the public, a result which cannot be other than for the common good.

National laws are only enacted if they are in the public interest, or at least it must be assumed that the enacting body so regards them, since it is the task of the legislator to make laws for society as a whole. "Those who govern must act as if they were defending the public good, the general interest; it is even useful that they should believe it, because faith strengthens conviction."[9] Moreover, "Copyright is an instance in which the public good fully coincides with the claims of individuals."[10] Certainly, this has been the consistent view of the British throughout the past 200 years, as the following quotations from Macaulay speaking in 1841 and from the Whitford Committee's report in 1977 demonstrate.

1–003

"The advantages arising from a system of copyright are obvious. It is desirable that we should have a supply of good books; we cannot have such a supply unless men of letters are liberally remunerated and

---

[7] Constitution of the United States of America, Art.I, 8, cl.8.

[8] L.R. Patterson and S.W. Lindberg, *The Nature of Copyright—A Law of Users' Rights*, (The University of Georgia Press, Athens and London, 1991), p.40.

[9] P. Recht, *Copyright, a New Form of Property*, [1969] Copyright 94.

[10] J. Madison, quoted in P. Goldstein, *Copyright Principles, Law and Practice*, Little Brown and Company, Boston, Toronto, London 1989, at 5, n.2.

the least objectionable way of remunerating them is by way of copyright."[11]

"The exclusive rights which are granted by national copyright, patent, trademark and design laws are granted because it is in the public interest to grant them."[12]

Over 150 countries have enacted copyright laws[13] and the Berne Convention for the Protection of Literary and Artistic Works has 150 Member States (as of June 30, 2002). This confirms the fact that there is virtually universal agreement that the copyright system is indeed in the public interest. In the course of the twentieth century, many nations have subscribed to the Universal Declaration of Human Rights (United Nations 1948) and/or the International Covenant on Human Rights (League of Nations 1919). These two documents provide, *inter alia*, for the protection of authors' rights.[14] They confirm the consensus that the copyright system has a significant part to play in stimulating world-wide cultural activities for the mutual benefit of those who create, and those who enjoy the fruits of that labour.

1–004 The proposition that copyright is in the public interest is mostly taken for granted. References to the issue have been scarce in the literature in Europe in the past. However, in recent years, the subject has attracted a great deal of interest and controversy and the proposition that copyright is in the public interest has been questioned in the context of the challenges posed to the copyright system by technical developments. These challenges are proliferating year by year in the present period of rapid technological change and the digital environment. In the 1970s and 1980s they included: advances in copying techniques which led to unauthorised reproduction of copyright works on an unprecedented scale; new uses of works made possible by new technology such as video production, satellite transmission and cable distribution; the creation and production of new categories of works such as computer programs, data bases and multi-media works. In the 1990s these developments have been compounded by the use

---

[11] T. Macaulay, in *Hansard, loc. cit.*, above, n.1.

[12] Copyright and Designs Law, Report of the Committee to consider the Law on Copyright and Designs, Chairman—The Honourable Mr Justice Whitford, March 1977, HMSO, Cmnd 6732, para.84.

[13] K. Garnett and G. Davies, *Copinger and Skone James on Copyright, Supplement to the 14th ed.*, Sweet and Maxwell, London, 2002, Ch. 26.

[14] Art. 27(2), Universal Declaration of Human Rights; Art. 5(1), International Covenant on Human Rights.

of computer technology to digitise works in combination with new digital distribution and communication technologies. The distribution of copyright-protected works has been transformed by the scientific revolution wrought by digital technology. In 2002, digitally recorded words, sounds and images are copied, stored and distributed virtually instantaneously over the internet on a global scale. This is the latest technical, legal and economic challenge facing our close to 300-year-old copyright system.

As a result, the copyright system has been labouring for the past three decades under considerable strain and has attracted the attention not only of legislators, called upon by the interested parties to update and improve the level of protection provided to right owners in their national laws in order to keep pace with the new technologies, but also of economists and academics. In this debate, the underlying philosophy of copyright and its basic functions have been called into question. The public interest has been invoked, not in favour of strengthening the protection afforded to authors and other right owners to protect them against piracy in cyberspace, but in favour of free and unfettered access by the public to copyright works combined with the means of copying them for personal use.

The copyright system as it has developed over the past nearly 300 years, has created, in the public interest, a balance between the rights of the authors, on the one hand, and the interest of the public in access to protected works, on the other. From the inception of copyright law, rights have been subject to limitations of duration and exemptions for personal and scientific use. This balance has been expressed in Article 27 of the Universal Declaration of Human Rights which provides:

(i) everyone has the right freely to participate in the cultural life of the Community, to enjoy the arts and to share in scientific advancement and its benefits;

(ii) everyone has the right to the protection of the moral and material interests resulting from any scientific, literary or artistic production of which he is an author.

Thus, copyright systems are recognised as having a two-fold purpose: to accord exploitation rights to those engaged in literary and artistic production and to answer to the general public interest in the widest possible availability of copyright material.

7

1–005   In assessing the balance between these two apparently conflicting purposes, so as to ensure the protection of the individual and the public, different governments have adopted varying approaches to the questions: "What is fair?" and "What rights and limitations are required?"

These differences reflect the varying emphases placed in diverse parts of the world on the several basic principles underlying copyright. "The very concept of copyright from a philosophical, theoretical and pragmatic point of view differs country by country, since each has its own legal framework influenced by social and economic factors."[15]

The emphasis placed on the relationship between copyright law and the public interest also differs.

This study explores, firstly, the underlying principles governing copyright legislation internationally and the origins of copyright law in Western Europe; second, the importance attributed to the concept of the public interest in the history of the copyright laws of the United Kingdom, the United States of America, France and Germany, in that order. As a matter of history, that is the order in which the respective States first legislated on copyright. In Part III, issues related to copyright and public policy are examined, including the moral and economic functions of copyright, the alternatives to copyright and the nature and extent of the limitations and exceptions imposed on copyright. Part IV addresses the future of copyright, discussing firstly the impact of digital technology on copyright and second the international protection thereof and the perspectives for achieving further convergence of copyright laws and universal solutions to the problems of the digital revolution through the harmonising effect of international treaties. In the discussion of these issues, the various arguments and theories are tested against the yardstick of the principles laid down in the six ideals of copyright law postulated by Professor Zechariah Chafee in his seminal article published in 1945 and entitled "Reflexions on the Law of Copyright".[16] In conclusion, the public policy role of the state in maintaining the copyright system is considered.

---

[15] C. Masouyé, *Guide to the Berne Convention*, WIPO, 1978, para.1.15.
[16] Z. Chafee, *Reflexions on the Law of Copyright*, [1945] 45 Columbia Law Rev. 503 and 719.

Chapter 2

The Underlying Principles Governing Copyright Legislation

"What is its history—its judicial history? It is wrapt in obscurity and uncertainty." *Judge Joseph Hopkinson*[1]

The development of the modern copyright system has been referred to as being

> due in no small measure to the confusion of ideas resulting from the events in eighteenth century England, ... The ideas—that copyright is a monopoly; that copyright is primarily an author's right; that the author has natural rights in his works which must be limited by statute—once stated by the courts, became a fixed part of the heritage of copyright.[2]

2–001

It is important to begin an examination of the underlying principles governing copyright legislation with the eighteenth-century English Statute of Anne because it is the foundation upon which the modern concept of copyright in the Western World was built. Historical analysis provides a framework to serve as a basis for interpreting and evaluating modern copyright laws. It is of contemporary relevance. The Statute of Anne was the product of a new communications technology, the printing press, and modern copyright laws have to be

---

[1] *per* Joseph Hopkinson J. in the lower court opinion in the landmark US case of *Wheaton v Peters*, 29 Fed. Cas. 862, 871 (n.17486) (C.C.E.D.Pa 1832).

[2] L.R. Patterson, "The Statute of Anne: Copyright Misconstrued", [1966] 3 Harv. J. Legis 223. See also on the history of copyright law in England and the USA, L.R. Patterson and S.W. Lindberg, *The Nature of Copyright—A Law of Users' Rights*, The University of Georgia Press, Athens and London, 1991.

regularly fine-tuned to adapt to the new communications technologies of the day. "In changing the conceptual nature of copyright, it became the most important single event in copyright history. Two of the principles on which the Statute of Anne rests were revolutionary: recognition of the individual author as the fountainhead of protection and adoption of the principle of a limited term of protection for published works."[3] Or as Barbara Ringer has put it more colourfully, the Statute of Anne is "the mother of us all and a very possessive mother at that".[4] It is important also to note that it was not the first English statute to deal with copyright but the first to be adopted by Parliament as opposed to royal decree and the first to be unconnected with censorship.[5]

Prior to the Statute of Anne, from the early sixteenth century onwards, in England and elsewhere in Europe, "privileges" had been granted by the sovereign to booksellers following the invention of printing, to regulate the book trade and to protect printers against piracy. These privileges were in time used as an instrument of censorship by the authorities. From 1557, in England, privileges were the monopoly of members of the Stationers' Company. The royal interest in granting the monopoly was not to provide protection to the stationers' property rights but to satisfy the desire of the crown for an effective control over the publishing trade and the press so as to outlaw the publishing of seditious and heretical books.[6]

2–002 The system of privileges was abolished with the Cromwellian Revolution. Privileges had derived their authority from the Crown and, along with the King's authority, were set at nought. They were replaced by a series of Parliamentary ordinances. These prohibited printing unless the book was first licensed. Printing was prohibited *without the consent of the owner*. In 1662, the Licensing Act[7] was passed

---

[3] *Halsbury's Laws of England*, 4th. ed., Lord Hailsham of St. Marylebone, Vol. 9, Butterworths, London, 1974.

[4] Paper delivered at WIPO seminar, Montreux, 1971.

[5] Earlier Star Chamber Decrees, censorship ordinances during the Interregnum and the Licensing Act of 1662 were copyright as well as censorship Acts.

[6] The preamble of the Stationers' Company charter reads as follows: "Know ye that we, considering and manifestly perceiving that certain seditious and heretical books rhymes and treatises are daily published and printed by divers scandalous malicious schismatical and heretical persons, not only moving our subjects and leiges to sedition and disobedience against us, our crown and dignity, but also to renew and move very great and detestable heresies against the faith and sound catholic doctrine of Holy Mother Church, and wishing to provide a suitable remedy in this behalf."

[7] Licensing Act 1662 (13 & 14 Car. 2 c.33).

which prohibited the printing of any book unless first licensed and entered in the register of the Stationers' Company. It also prescribed regulations as to printing and outlawed books suspected of containing matters hostile to the church or government. The Act further prohibited any person from printing or importing, *without the consent of the owner*, any book which any person had the sole right to print. The penalty for piracy was forfeiture of the books and a fine to be paid half to the King and half to the owner. Thus, "The sole property of the owner is here acknowledged in express terms as a common law right".[8] The Act of 1662 was continued by several Acts of Parliament but expired in 1679. The system had fallen into disrepute because the power of members of the Stationers' Company to claim copyright in perpetuity had led to high prices and a lack of availability of books. The control of the book trade exercised by the Stationers' Company was broken with the result that book piracy flourished.

Parliament was regularly petitioned, therefore, for a new Licensing Act. The booksellers argued that failure to continue exclusive rights of printing had resulted in disincentives to writers. Without some form of protection to encourage authors, the public interest would be harmed by the decreased flow of works.[9] To the entreaties of members of the Stationers' Company was added in 1690 the voice of the philosopher, John Locke, who, although opposed to licensing as leading to unreasonable monopolies injurious to learning, "demanded a copyright for authors which he justified by the time and effort expended in the writing of the work which should be rewarded like any other work". He also advocated limiting the term of protection to a period of from 50 to 70 years after the death of the author.[10]

In response, the Statute of Anne was passed in 1709 and came into force on April 10, 1710. The Act, adopted, as we have seen from the Preamble, for the encouragement of learning, simultaneously sought to satisfy:

(i) the demands of the Stationers' Company by restoring to them

---

[8] K. Garnett, J. Rayner James and G. Davies, *Copinger and Skone James on Copyright*, 14th ed., Sweet & Maxwell, London 1999, para.2–11.

[9] L.R. Patterson, *Copyright in Historical Perspective*, Nashville, Vanderbilt University Press, 1968, at 142.

[10] J. Locke, *Two Treatises of Government* [1690], edited by P. Laslett, Cambridge University Press, 1988, para. 27. And see J. Locke, *Memorandum to Edward Clark*, cited in M. Rose, *Authors' and Owners, the Invention of Copyright*, Harvard University Press, 1994, at 32, 33.

the sole right to print books then printed for a period of 21 years;

(ii) the demands of authors and their assigns for recognition of their sole right to print books not yet printed, published or "that shall hereafter be composed" for a term of 14 years from the date of publication. After the expiration of the 14-year term, the sole right of printing or disposing of copies returned to the author, if living, for another term of fourteen years. Thus the statutory copyright was not to be limited to the members of the Guild, and it was not to exist in perpetuity;

(iii) the public interest in the supply of cheap books by providing that "if any bookseller or booksellers, printer or printers, shall ... set a price upon, or sell, or expose to sale, any book or books at such a price or rate as shall be conceived by any person or persons to be too high and unreasonable; it shall be and may be lawful for any person or persons, to make complaint thereof" to the Archbishop of Canterbury, Lord Chancellor (or to a number of specified dignitaries of church and bench) who were given powers to enquire into the price and "to limit or settle the price of every such printed book ... according to the best of their judgements".[11]

2–003   Title to the copy of a book had to be registered before publication with the Stationers' Company and nine copies had to be delivered for the use of certain libraries. This latter provision responded to the motivation of the Statute to promote learning and progress in the public interest.[12]

Penalties for infringement were severe: infringing books were subject to forfeiture and a fine of a penny for every sheet copied. This resulted in a steep fine when many copies of a substantial book were pirated. The fine was divided equally between the Crown and the complainant.

An interesting additional feature is that the Act expressly provided that the importation and sale of books in Greek and other foreign languages printed "beyond the seas" should remain unaffected by its provisions.

---

[11] The Statute of Queen Anne, 1709, Ch. XIX, s.IV (see Appendix s.s.)
[12] It is of interest to note that the deposit of books in certain libraries is still required in the United Kingdom (see K. Garnett, J. Rayner James and G. Davies, *Copinger and Skone James on Copyright, op. cit.,* n.8, above, paras 27–65, *et seq.*

It is apparent then that this, in historical terms, first copyright law, responded to several objectives. Its stated purposes were to be for the encouragement of learning, for preventing the practice of piracy for the future, and for the encouragement of learned men to compose and write useful books.

To achieve these objectives, it sought to break the perpetual mono- **2–004** poly of the booksellers and printers of the Stationers' Company over the book trade. It recognised for the first time a right of the author to control the publishing and printing of his work and the interest of the author himself, as well as his assigns, to be protected against piracy. It gave a nod to the natural rights of authors by recognising that piracy was not only "to their very great detriment" but also "too often to the ruin of them and their families". Yet it also sought to provide the public with a supply of "useful" books at cheap prices.

> The Act was a compromise between the demands of the publishers and what Parliament considered the public interest ... the legal monopoly which the printers had in perpetuity was broken but they were still left in a strong position. The character of the Act is that of a Trade Regulation, but the law nevertheless recognised that the source of the copyright is the work created by the author.[13]

In this Act, therefore, are found the seeds of the underlying principles on which the modern international copyright system is founded.

These principles may be described under four main headings[14]:

(i) natural law

(ii) just reward for labour

(iii) stimulus to creativity

(iv) social requirements

---

[13] L.R. Patterson, "The Statute of Anne", *op. cit.*, n.2 above, at 13.

[14] Stewart describes these principles under the following headings: the principle of natural justice; the economic argument; the cultural argument; the social argument; S.M. Stewart, *International Copyright and Neighbouring Rights*, 2nd. ed., Butterworths, London, 1989, paras 1.02–1.05.

(i) Natural Law

2–005   The rights of the author over his work are considered as embodied in natural law, inherent in the "very nature of things".[15] He is the creator of the work; it is an expression of his personality and the fruit of his mind. The natural law of property was propounded by Locke.[16] Starting from the premise that people had a natural right of property in their bodies, he argued that people also owned the labour of their bodies and the results of that labour. It followed that the author has an exclusive natural right of property in the results of his labour and should have control over the publication of his work as well as the right to object to any unauthorised modification or other attack on the integrity of his work. "It is just, that an author should reap the pecuniary profits of his own ingenuity and labour. It is just, that another should not use his name, without his consent. It is fit that he should judge when to publish, or whether he ever will publish."[17]

(ii) Just Reward for Labour

"It is certainly not agreeable to natural justice, that a stranger should reap the beneficial pecuniary produce of another man's work."[18]

2–006   If it is accepted that creating is worthwhile, be it art, music, literature or other work and that the fruits of such labour enrich our lives, then

---

[15] F.J. Kase, *Copyright Thought in Continental Europe*, South Hackensack, N.J., Fred B. Rothman, 1967, at 8.

[16] J. Locke, The Second Treatise of Civil Government s.27, in *Two Treatises of Government, op.cit.*: "Whatsoever then he removes out of the State that Nature hath provided, and left it in, he hath mixed his *Labour* with, and joyned to it something that is his own, and thereby makes it his *Property*. It being by him removed from the common state Nature placed it in, it hath by his *Labour* something annexed to it, that excludes the common right of other Men. For this *Labour* being the unquestionable Property of the Labourer, no Man but he can have a right to what that is once joyned to, at least where there is enough, and as good left in common for others." On the natural law and copyright, see A.C. Yen "Restoring the Natural Law: Copyright as Labor and Possession", [1990] 51 Ohio State Law Journal, No.2. For a discussion of the purpose of copyright including the Lockean justification therefore, see also B. Friedman, "From Deontology to Dialogue: The Cultural Consequences of Copyright", [1994] 13 Cardozo Arts and Entertainment 157.

[17] *Millar v Taylor, per* Lord Mansfield, 4 Burr. 2334, at 252.

[18] *ibid., per* Willis J., at 218.

the authors deserve to be remunerated when their work is exploited. Remunerating a creator for the use of his work enables him to continue working and is natural justice in accord with the maxim that the labourer is worthy of his hire. After all, in Dr Johnson's view, "no man but a blockhead ever wrote except for money".[19]

The author is thus entitled to economic rewards. As the US Supreme Court stated in 1954, "Sacrificial days devoted to ... creative activities deserve rewards commensurate with the services rendered".[20]

Moreover, today, copyright provides the economic basis for investment by the cultural industries in the creation, production and dissemination of works and other protected subject matter.

In the modern world considerable investment is needed to make the creation of some works, such as works of architecture or films, possible. As the purpose of the creation of practically all works is to make them available to the public, that process too, such as publication and distribution of books or records, is expensive. These investments will not be made unless there is a reasonable expectation of recouping them and making a reasonable profit.[21]

(iii) Stimulus to Creativity

Just reward for labour provides a stimulus to creativity; thus, these two basic principles of copyright are inextricably linked.   **2–007**

As we have seen, the UK Statute of Anne and the copyright clause in the American Constitution both laid emphasis on the role of copyright protection in the stimulation of creativity. A stated aim of the English law was the "encouragement of learned men to compose and write useful books". The US Constitutional clause aimed "to promote the progress of science", in the sense of knowledge and learning.

"Copyright law presupposes that, absent subsidy, authors and publishers will invest sufficient resources in producing and publishing original works only if they are promised property rights that will

---

[19] J. Boswell, *Life of Johnson* (L.F. Powell's revision of G.B. Hill's ed.), at 19, April 5, 1776.
[20] *Mazer v Stein*, 347 US 201, 219.
[21] S.M. Stewart, *op. cit.*, para.1.03.

enable them to control and profit from their work's dissemination in the marketplace."[22]

"Take away from English authors their copyrights, and you would very soon take away from England her authors."[23]

"It is important to emphasise that the main purpose of copyright protection must be to stimulate the production of intellectual works."[24]

Like most other observers, I am irrevocably convinced that the facilities which copyright affords for the remuneration of intellectual creativity *stimulates* creatively gifted people to go in for activities of this kind. As far as I can judge, the thesis of all creativity being the exclusive result of inward compulsion is untenable. Very often a person has to choose between artistic activity and some other means of gaining a livelihood. If the economic proceeds of artistic activity were not assured, the choice would often fall in the other direction.[25]

(iv) Social Requirements

2-008   "The social usefulness of copyright consists in providing an economic basis for creation."[26]

It is a social requirement in the public interest that authors and other right owners should be encouraged to publish their works so as to permit the widest possible dissemination of works to the public at large. "If the ideas and experiences of creators can be shared by a wide public within a short space of time they contribute to the advance of society."[27]

"The sole interest of the United States and the primary object in conferring the monopoly lie in the general benefits derived by the public from the labors of authors."[28]

---

[22] P. Goldstein, *Copyright Principles, Law and Practice*, Little Brown and Company, Boston, Toronto, London, 1989, para.1.1.
[23] A. Trollope, *Autobiography*, Ch.6.
[24] S. Ljungman, "Nogot om Verkshöjd", [1972] NIR 35.
[25] S. Ljungman, "The Function of Copyright in Present Day Society: Some Reflections with Reference to the Nordic Situation", [1976] 88 R.I.D.A. 51, 65.
[26] A. Kerever, "Is Copyright an Anachronism?", [1983] Copyright 368.
[27] S.M. Stewart, *op. cit.*, para.1.05.
[28] Hughes C. J. in *Fox Film Corp. v Doyal*, 286 US 123, 127.

One has come to realise that in the final analysis the protection of copyright leads to the enrichment of the national cultural patrimony; that the higher the level of protection the more authors are encouraged to create and, in consequence, to expand the literary and artistic influence of their respective countries; that the more intellectual creations there are, the greater the extent to which the entertainment industry, and the book and recording industries, etc., which are the essential partners of authors, are encouraged to establish themselves and grow.[29]

These four fundamental principles are, of course, cumulative and interdependent. They are applied in the justification of copyright in all countries, although different countries give varying emphasis to each of them. To generalise, it is true to say that, in the development of modern copyright laws, the economic and social arguments are given more weight in the countries of the common law tradition, whereas, in the countries of the continental civil law tradition, the natural law argument is to the fore.

These differences in approach, between common law copyright, with its emphasis on protection of the work with a view to encouraging authors to create and disseminate their works, and the civil law author's right, which puts the protection of the author in relation to his rightful property in the first place, are illustrated by the national accounts of the development of the copyright laws in Part II with respect to the United Kingdom, the United States of America, France and Germany. The natural law justification for copyright has had particular influence on the concept and development of moral rights. The differences should not however be exaggerated and as this study shows there is much common ground in the historical and present-day justifications for copyright in the common law and civil law countries.[30]

---

[29] C. Masouyé, "Droit d'auteur: Horizon 2000", [1979] "Il Diritto di Autore" 163 (author's translation).

[30] On the nature and extent of these divergencies and the impact of international harmonisation measures thereon, see Ch.13, below. See also G. Davies, "The Convergence of Copyright and Authors' Rights—Reality or Chimera?", [1995] 26 IIC 964.

Chapter 3

Origins of Copyright Law in Europe

"Copyright is a beast of substantial historical ancestry." *Sheldon N. Light*[1]

Thus far, we have looked primarily at the origins of copyright law in England for the reason that England was the first country to legislate on the subject. Before examining the legislative history in relation to the public interest of individual countries, it may be useful briefly to contrast the origins of copyright law in Continental European countries with the situation in England.[2]

3–001

The invention of the printing press led to the introduction of printing in Europe in the late fifteenth and early sixteenth centuries. The possibility to print multiple copies of books cheaply resulted in a new market for books for a public who previously had not had access to the manuscripts, which in the past had had to be copied laboriously by hand and had been available only to the most privileged members of society. Printers and publishers made substantial investments; they

---

[1] S.N. Light, "Parody, Burlesque and the Economic Rationale for Copyright", [1979] 11 Connecticut Law Review, No.4, 615.

[2] This brief summary relies particularly on: S.M. Stewart, *International Copyright and Neighbouring Rights* (London, Butterworths, 2nd ed. 1989); S. Ricketson, *The Berne Convention for the Protection of Literary and Artistic Works: 1886–1986,* (London, Centre for Commercial Law Studies, Queen Mary College, 1987); W.R. Cornish, *Intellectual Property: Patents, Copyright, Trade Marks and Allied Rights,* (London, Sweet & Maxwell, 4th ed. 1999); P. Wittenberg, *The Protection of Literary Property* (Boston, The Writer Inc, 1986–1978, revised ed. 1978); L.R. Patterson, *The Statute of Anne: Copyright Misconstrued,* [1966] 3 Harv. J. Legis 223 and *Copyright in Historical Perspective* (Nashville, Vanderbilt University Press, 1968); A. Birrell, *Seven Lectures on the Law and History of Copyright in Books* (London, Cassell, 1899), M.-C. Dock, *Etude sur le droit d'auteur,* Libraire générale de droit et de jurisprudence, Paris, 1963; E. Pouillet, *Traité théorique et pratique de la propriété littéraire et artistique,* Paris, Marchal et Billard, 3rd ed. 1908.

acquired works from authors (or republished classics which they edited or translated anew) and presses and paper were expensive. "These first printers were and had to be men of great learning and ingenuity. They either wrote or translated most of the material they produced. They built their own presses, cut their own type, made the incidental parts and bound their own works."[3] With later improvements in printing technology, the cost of printing declined and cheaper books resulted in ever larger audiences to the advantage of authors, publishers and printers as well as the general public.

The printers and publishers soon formed themselves into powerful guilds and petitioned the authorities for protection against unfair competition from printers who copied their editions. Unfettered competition, with freedom for any printer to copy anothers' editions, led in all the major European countries to a situation in which "piracy was born, so to speak, with the art itself."[4]

3–002 In this situation, a pattern emerged all over Europe. Exclusive privileges were granted for limited times to printers and publishers by national authorities to print certain works or a number of works.[5] In every country, the authorities' interest was the same: to control the book trade, which represented a new method of making information available to the people, and to encourage a new industry. Moreover,

> It did not take the authorities long to realise that by restricting the rights to privileges, which were granted only to a small number of people, they could control all publications quite easily . . . and this gave the Governments an easy and effective weapon allowing them to exercise a very tight censorship over this new medium.[6]

The period of privileges lasted longer on the Continent than in England. In Germany, the first privilege was granted in 1501 (the

---

[3] P. Wittenberg, *op. cit.* at 10.

[4] M.-C. Dock, "Genèse et évolution de la notion de propriété littéraire", [1974] LXXIX R.I.D.A. 165.

[5] The first recorded grant appears to have been that made in 1469 by the Venetian Senate to John of Speyer, a German printer who had settled in Venice, for a period of five years. The grant actually afforded him a complete monopoly of printing in Venice. Perhaps fortunately for the Venetian printing trade he died soon after. F.D.A. Prager, "History of Intellectual Property From 1545 to 1787", [1944] 26 Journal of the Patent Office Society, No. 11 at 715 (full text of grant at 750). See also, M.-C. Dock, *Etude sur le droit d'auteur, op. cit.*, n.2, above, at 63.

[6] S.M. Stewart, *op. cit.*, para. 2.04.

earliest privilege in England dated from 1518) and the system was not entirely abolished until the first German copyright law was adopted following the creation of the German *Reich* in 1871. From 1832, the Alliance of German States had provided for reciprocity in respect of the protection of privileges, and certain minimum standards were agreed upon in 1837. Privileges were granted originally by the Heads of the *Länder* with effect for the various German states and by the Emperor with effect for the Holy Roman Empire. They were awarded to printers and publishers as in England but, according to Ulmer and von Rauscher: "It has become apparent from more recent research into copyright law that they were also granted in a number of cases to authors".[7]

In France, privileges dated from the early sixteenth century and the system continued until abolished in the Revolution of 1789. The first privileges were granted by the King to printers in 1507 and 1508; as elsewhere they aimed at encouraging the printing trade and were granted for a limited time to printers for individual works, prohibiting all others from printing the works in question.[8] Very soon, however, the Crown saw the danger of the free dissemination of ideas in print and "the Crown found the further advantage of censorship in the exclusive right to print and publish, but no interest was shown in the rights of the author".[9] Privileges became an instrument for maintaining public order and in all the regulations and edicts concerning them, there was no mention of authors.[10]

Modern copyright systems derive three basic features from the privileges: the exclusive rights of reproduction (printing) and distribution (publication) and the fact that privileges were limited in time.[11] Remedies included seizure and forfeiture of infringing copies as well as fines. In some cases, remedies were more drastic. In France, under an Ordinance of 1566, the penalty for infringement was death by hanging or strangling.

"In all of this, the role and status of the author was minimal".[12]

3–003

---

[7] S.M. Stewart, *op. cit.*, para. 15.01, by Eugen Ulmer and Hans Hugo von Rauscher auf Weeg. For a detailed history of German Copyright see M. Vogel, *Deutsche Urheber- und Verlagsrechtsgeschichte zwischen 1450 und 1850*, AGB XIX, Frankfurt a.m., 1978.

[8] M.C. Dock, *Etude sur le droit d'auteur, op. cit.*, p. 64.

[9] S.M. Stewart, *op. cit.*, para. 14.01, by P. Chesnais.

[10] M.C. Dock, *Etude sur le droit d'auteur, op. cit.*, pp. 70 and 71.

[11] Privileges from the Crown were limited in time. The UK stationers' copyright, regulated by company ordinances, was deemed to exist in perpetuity.

[12] S. Ricketson, *op. cit.*, n. 2, above, para. 1.1.

Ricketson suggests two main reasons for this: first, that in the early days of printing, most of the books published were old or classical texts; secondly, that authors still looked to patronage for their chief source of income.

The author owned the manuscript, but was dependent on the printers and booksellers if he wished to communicate his work to the new reading public. The printers bought manuscripts outright. However, from 1642 onwards in England, the publisher had to have the author's consent to print and to use his name.[13] However,

> right of copy was the stationer's not the author's. Living authors furnished some of the material for the printing mills, and, increasingly, these manuscripts had to be purchased in a business way (usually payment was made in a lump sum); but upon entry the author dropped away and it was the stationer who had the right of multiplication of copies...[14]

Authors complained, but by all accounts were more concerned with what are now called moral rights (a late nineteenth-century concept introduced into the Berne Convention at the Rome Revision Conference in 1928[15] and only gradually incorporated in national legislation subsequently), objecting to publication without consent, false attribution of authorship and modifications to the text which were harmful to their reputation. Wittenberg gives a number of examples of such complaints from English authors, including the following heartfelt attack by one George Wither, an English author, in 1625:

> For many of our moderne booksellers are but needlesse excrements, or rather vermine, ... yea, since they take upon them to publish bookes contrived, altered and mangled at their own pleasures, without consent of the writers; and to change the name

---

[13] Venice had introduced such a rule in 1545, providing that "no printer of this city shall dare to print ... any works ... unless ... the author or his heirs ... have declared their consent and requested the printing". Quoted in F.D.A. Prager, n. 5, above, at 719 and 750.

[14] B. Kaplan, *An Unhurried View of Copyright*, Columbia University Press, New York and London, 1967, at 5.

[15] Berne Convention for the Protection of Literary and Artistic Works 1883, Paris Act 1971, Art. 6[bis].

sometymes, both of booke and author (after they have been imprinted).[16]

Stewart also gives examples of the concern of authors with their moral **3–004** rights, including that of Martin Luther's complaint to the Council of Nuremberg that his works had been published in altered and amended form.[17]

The transition from the system of privileges to copyright in Western Europe took over a century. The gradual end of absolute monarchy led inexorably to the end of privileges. As Kerever tells us:

> All the States of Western Europe experienced a changeover in that the effect of the law was to replace the sovereign by the author himself as the source of the right to prohibit unlawful copies, whereby the right was transferred to the publisher under a contract. This changeover was far from simultaneous.[18]

The English Statute of Anne came first in 1709. Denmark and Norway adopted an ordinance in 1741 and Spain a law in 1762. The French revolutionary decrees of 1791 and 1793 came next. Copyright for publishers was first recognised in the Prussian Code of 1794 but authors were not to obtain rights of their own in Prussia until 1837. Privileges were not replaced by copyright in the various Italian States until early in the nineteenth century, for example, Milan in 1810 and the Two Sicilies in 1811. Following the unification of Italy, a law on copyright was adopted in 1865.[19]

---

[16] P. Wittenberg, *op. cit.*, (2nd ed.) at 25.

[17] S.M. Stewart, *op. cit.*, para. 2.06.

[18] A. Kerever, "The Achievements and Future Development of European Legal Culture", [1990] Copyright 131.

[19] V. and V. De Sanctis, in Stewart, *op. cit.* at 448.

PART II

THE CONCEPT OF THE PUBLIC INTEREST IN THE HISTORY OF COPYRIGHT— NATIONAL EXAMPLES

Chapter 4

United Kingdom

The Eighteenth Century Debate on the Nature of Copyright

4–001   The historical evolution of the copyright system in England up to and including the entry into force of the Statute of Queen Anne on April 10, 1710, has been described in Chapter 2. This Statute remained in force, virtually unchanged, until superseded by the Copyright Act of 1842.[1] The Statute was amended in 1814[2] when the two contingent 14-year periods of protection were replaced by a single term of 28 years, calculated from the day of first publication, or the natural life of the author, if he was still living at the expiration of that period. In the meantime, however, the Statute of Anne had given rise to an impassioned debate about the nature of copyright, often referred to as "The Question of Literary Property",[3] or "The Battle of the Booksellers", which was fought out in the Courts.

In 1731, 21 years after the Statute of Anne came into force, the stationers' monopoly on printing books already in print when the Statute had come into force expired. Printers in Scotland and in the provinces issued new editions of old books and the London booksellers sought means to prevent this in a series of cases brought before both the English and Scottish courts. The booksellers argued that, at common law, and regardless of the expiry of the statutory period of protection, authors had a perpetual right to authorise printing, rights which had been assigned to them.[4]

It was not disputed that the manuscript of a work was the property of the author and that prior to publication his right to it could exist indefinitely. The question was posed only with regard to published works. As Kaplan puts it: "Did the copyright in published works cease at the expiration of the limited periods specified in the statute, or was there a non-statutory, common law copyright of perpetual duration, with the Statute merely furnishing accumulative special remedies

---

[1] Copyright Act 1842 (5 & 6 Vict., c.4).
[2] Sculpture Copyright Act 1814 (54 Geo., 3., c.56).
[3] B. Kaplan, *An Unhurried View of Copyright* (New York, Columbia University Press, 1967), at 12. See also M. Rose, "Author as Proprietor: Donaldson v. Beckett and the Genealogy of Modern Authorship", in *Of Authors and Origins, Essays on Copyright Law*, eds. B. Sherman and A. Strowel, (Oxford, Clarendon Press, 1994).
[4] *ibid.*

during the limited periods?".[5] The argument thus raged over whether copyright was an inalienable form of property arising from the act of creation or a limited right of control or monopoly bestowed by Statute in the public interest.

The debate is interesting for the purpose of this study because it opposed squarely the "public interest" theory of copyright with that of "natural rights".

The issue was first decided in favour of the perpetual right by a **4–002** majority of the Court of King's Bench in the case of *Millar v Taylor* in 1769.[6] The Court held that there was a common law right of an author to his copy stemming from the act of creation and that that right was not taken away by the Statute of Anne. The decision was subsequently overturned, however, by the House of Lords in *Donaldson v Beckett* in 1774,[7] "a case which decided that copyright was the deliberate creation of the Statute of Anne and thereafter treated as statutory property. Thus, the effect of the Statute of Anne was to extinguish the common law copyright in published works, while leaving the common law copyright in unpublished works unaffected".[8]

The arguments put forward on both sides are as fresh today as in the eighteenth century.

Finding in favour of the common law right on grounds of natural law, Mr Justice Willis said:

> It is certainly not agreeable to natural justice, that a stranger should reap the beneficial pecuniary produce of another man's work. . . . It is wise, in any State, to encourage letters, and the painful research of learned men. The easiest and most equal way of doing it, is by securing to them the property of their own works. . . . A writer's

---

[5] For an account of English cases in the mid-18th century see D. Saunders, "Purposes or Principle? Early Copyright and the Court of Chancery", [1993] EIPR 452. The Scottish cases are described in H.L. MacQueen, *Copyright, Competition and Industrial Design*, 2nd. ed., Hume Papers on Public Policy: Vol.3, No.2, (Edinburgh University Press, 1995). See also R.S. Tompson, "Scottish Judges and the Birth of British Copyright", *The Juridical Review*, Pt 1 [1992] 1.

[6] *Millar v Taylor*, 4 BURR. 2301.

[7] *Donaldson v Beckett*, 4 BURR. 2407. The previous year, the Court of Session in Scotland had already ruled against the common law copyright in the case of *Hinton v Donaldson* (1773) Mor 8307. Lord Kames rejected common law copyright as "contrary to law, as ruinous to the public interest, and as prohibited by statute".

[8] K. Garnett, J. Rayner James and G. Davies, *Copinger and Skone James on Copyright*,(London, Sweet & Maxwell, 14th ed. 1999), para.2.16.

fame will not be the less, that he has bread, without being under the necessity of prostituting his pen to flattery or party, to get it...[9]

Lord Mansfield's eloquent expression of the author's natural right is famous:

Because it is just, that an author should reap the pecuniary benefits of his own ingenuity and labour. It is just, that another should not use his name, without his consent. It is fit that he should judge when to publish, or whether he ever will publish. It is fit he should not only choose the time, but the manner of publication; how many; what volume; what print. It is fit, he should choose to whose care he will trust the accuracy and correctness of the impression; in whose honesty he will confide, not to foist in additions....[10]

4–003 In Lord Mansfield's opinion, the same reasons held after publication and, therefore, it seemed to him "just and fit" to protect the copy after publication.

Mr Justice Yates, in a dissenting opinion, was against a perpetual common law copyright. For him:

all property has its proper limit, extent and bounds ... the legislature had no notion of any such things as copyrights as existing for ever at common law: ... on the contrary, they understood that authors could have no right in their copies after they had made their works public; and meant to give them a security which they supposed them not to have had before...[11]

He went on to address "the inconvenient consequences the public may feel" if perpetual copyright were to be established. "Instead of tending to the advancement and the propagation of literature, I think it would stop it; or at least might be attended with great disadvantages to it."

An exclusive perpetual property in authors would be dangerous; it would give them the right to suppress as well as publish; it would lead

---

[9] *Millar v Taylor*, above n.6, at 2334.
[10] *ibid.*, at 2398.
[11] *ibid.*, at 2391.

to uncertainty and litigation if the author abandoned his copy; could lead to the fixing of such an exorbitant price upon a book as to "lock it up" "from the general bulk of mankind"; it would lead to restraints on trade. He concluded, therefore:

> The legislatures have provided the proper encouragements for authors; and, at the same time, have guarded against all these mischiefs. To give that legislative encouragement a liberal construction, is my duty as a judge; and will ever be my own most willing inclination. But it is equally my duty, not only as a judge, but as a member of society, and even as a friend to the cause of learning, to support the limitations of the statute.[12]

The issue did not rest there. According to Birrell: "The question of literary property was discussed everywhere and by everybody".[13]
In his views, Mr Justice Yates was in distinguished company. Boswell reports Dr Johnson as having been against perpetual copyright and as having the following opinion, expressed in 1773:

> There seems [said he] to be in authors a stronger right of property than that by occupancy; a metaphysical right, a right, as it were, of creation which should from its nature be perpetual, but the consent of nations is against it; for were it to be perpetual, no book, however useful, could be universally diffused amongst mankind should the proprietor take it into his head to restrain its circulation. No book could have the advantage of being edited with notes, however necessary to its elucidation, should the proprietor perversely oppose it. For the general good of the world, therefore, whatever valuable work has once been created by an author, and issued out by him should be understood as no longer in his power, but as belonging to the public; at the same time the author is entitled to an adequate reward. This he should have by an exclusive right to his work for a considerable number of years.[14]

Furthermore, when the issue came for a final resolution to the House **4–004** of Lords some years later in *Donaldson v Beckett* (1774), the opinions of

---

[12] *ibid.*, at 2394.
[13] A. Birrell, *Seven Lectures on the Law and History of Copyright in Books* (London, Cassell, 1899), at 122.
[14] *ibid.*

all the judges were solicited by the House of Lords to assist it in reaching its decision. These opinions were not decisive but advisory. A majority[15] of judges found there had been a common law copyright but that it had been taken away by the Statute of Anne so that an author was "precluded from every remedy, except on the foundation of the said statute, and on the terms and conditions prescribed thereby".

The House of Lords debated the case in the light of the opinions of the judges and, according to the report of the case in the Parliamentary History of England, the Lords voted against the existence of common law copyright by a vote of 22 to 11.[16] Thus, copyright was found to be the deliberate creation of the Statute of Anne and thereafter treated as statutory property. The principal opponent of common law copyright was Lord Camden, who saw in it a monopoly which would be damaging to the public at large.

> Some authors are careless about profit as others are rapacious of it; and what a situation would the public be in with regard to literature, if there were no means of compelling a second impression of a useful work. . . . All our learning will be locked up in the hands of the Tonsons and Lintons of the age, who will set what price upon it their avarice chuses to demand, till the public become as much their slaves, as their own hackney compilers are.[17]

The fascinating aspect of these cases is the fact that they focused with such passion and eloquence on issues which are still relevant to copyright today. In *Millar v Taylor*, the spotlight was fixed for the first time on the rights of the author. In both cases, the question of the need for a balance to be found between the rights of the author, on

---

[15] There is some evidence that the vote was actually 6 to 5 in favour of the author's common law right not being taken away by the Statute of Anne: see M. Rose, *Authors and Owners—The Invention of Copyright*, (Harvard University Press, 1993), at 98 and Appendix B. This did not affect the outcome of the case, however, since the role of the judges in the case was advisory and the decision was taken by the Lords.

[16] See H.B. Abrams, "Historic Foundation of Copyright Law", [1983] 29 Wayne Law Review 1119; and see 17 Parl. Hist. Eng. 953 [HL 1774]. Abrams argues that *Donaldson v Beckett* has been consistently misinterpreted by the Courts in the USA and UK ever since. He points out that the usual interpretation that a common law copyright had existed but was overriden by the Statute of Anne is incorrect. In fact, the House of Lords decided there had never been a common law copyright. For a further discussion of the case, see M. Rose, *op. cit.*, see n.3 above.

[17] 17 Parl. Hist. Eng., [HL 1774], at 1000.

the one hand, and the interests of the general public, on the other, came strongly into focus. And it is the constant need to balance these two interests that has remained the principal challenge to the legislator on copyright ever since.

Between 1709 and the major copyright revision Act of 1842, the Statute of Anne was amended from time to time to add to the list of protected works. The 1709 Act protected only "books and other writings" and gradually engravings, prints, lithographs and works of sculpture were added. In 1777, musical and dramatic compositions were held to be books within the meaning of the Statute of Anne[18] and in 1833 the Dramatic Copyright Act provided for a public performance right in dramatic works.[19]

The Revision Act of 1842

The passage of the 1842 Copyright Act[20] provided the occasion for a **4–005** further battle royal, this time in Parliament, on the nature of copyright; particularly controversial was the issue of the period of protection. Once again, the natural rights of the author and the public interest were at issue. The principal proponents in the debate were Sergeant Talfourd, a barrister, who had been putting forward bills for a new Copyright Act annually since 1837, and Lord Macaulay, the famous historian, who opposed the bill. "The bill became hugely controversial, and provoked great public interest."[21] In the end, the Act extended the period of copyright to the life of the author and seven years after his death or a term of 42 years from publication, whichever should be the longer. Posthumous works were protected for 42 years from publication.

Talfourd brought all his eloquence to bear on the issue in the face of his great opponent. Arguing for extension of protection beyond the death of the author he said:

... at the moment when his name is invested with the solemn

---

[18] *Bach v Longman* [1777], 2 COWP 623.
[19] Dramatic Literary Property Act 1833 (3 & 4 Will,, 4, c,15),
[20] Copyright Act 1842 (5 & 6 Vict., c.45).
[21] C. Seville, *Literary Copyright Reform in Early Victorian England (the Framing of the 1842 Copyright Act)*, (Cambridge University Press, 1999), p.6.

interest of the grave—when his eccentricity or frailties excite a smile or a shrug no longer—when the last seal is set upon his earthly course, and his works assume their place among the classics of his country—your law declares that his works shall become your property, and you requite him by seizing the patrimony of his children.[22]

In making his proposal he said "he had regard to what was expedient to authors, to publishers, and to the public ...". Prior to the increase in the term of protection in 1814

precisely the same arguments were then urged as against the present bill, that books would become dearer, there would be fewer written, fewer published, and fewer sold. Now, since the year 1814, books had greatly increased in number, and diminished in price, and, therefore, had he not a strong and unanswerable proof that extensions of copyright, by no means implied dearness of books.

He did not, he said, rest the "right of this bill merely on the ground of some natural right, without regard to expediency ...".[23]

Macaulay opposed extending the period of protection beyond the life of the author, being satisfied that the measure would "inflict grievous injury on the public, without conferring any compensating advantage on men of letters".[24] He emphasised that the legislature must be free to legislate for the public good and that "no natural right of property" could survive the original proprietor. The speech contains his most famous passages about copyright, including the following:

The system of copyright has great advantages, and great disadvantages, and it is our business to ascertain what these are, and then to make an arrangement under which the advantages may be as far as possible secured, and the disadvantages as far as possible excluded. ...

The advantages arising from a system of copyright are obvious. It is desirable that we should have a supply of good books; we cannot

---

[22] Quoted by S.M. Stewart, "Two Hundred Years of English Copyright Law", [1977] Copyright 228.
[23] Hansard, vol.56, 1841, at 342–3.
[24] *ibid.*, at 344 *et seq.*

have such a supply unless men of letters are liberally remunerated: and the least objectionable way of remunerating them is by means of copyright. . . .

It is good that authors should be remunerated; and the least exceptionable way of remunerating them is by a monopoly. Yet monopoly is an evil. For the sake of the good we must submit to the evil; but the evil ought not to last a day longer than is necessary for the purpose of securing the good.

He did not think that authors would be stimulated to produce more **4–006** by the knowledge that their heirs would benefit from a copyright *post mortem*: "Now would the knowledge, that this copyright would exist in 1841, have been a gratification to Johnson? Would it have stimulated his exertions? Would it have once drawn him out of his bed before noon?"

Macaulay was also of the opinion that if heirs had a copyright they would misuse it to the detriment of the public, seriously fearing, "that if such a measure as this should be adopted, many valuable works will be either totally suppressed or grievously mutilated."

As was to be expected, the debate resulted in a compromise. The principle of copyright protection continuing after the death of the author was accepted but, instead of the 60 years called for by Sergeant Talfourd, a period of only seven years after death, or 42 years from publication, whichever should be the longer, was adopted.

The Preamble to the Act echoed the sentiments of that of the Statute of Anne: "Whereas it is expedient to amend the law relating to copyright and to afford greater encouragement to the production of literary works of lasting benefit to the world". "The Act formed the basis of modern copyright law: it provided the groundwork for the domestic aspects of the 1911 Act, and this foundation was to a significant extent carried forward in the 1956 and 1988 Acts".[25] The Act repealed the 1709 and 1814 Acts, restating the existing law of copyright and maintained the system of registration at Stationers' Hall. Registration was no longer mandatory but was required before any action could be brought against infringers. The Act also extended the performing right, previously confined to dramatic works, to musical works.

Between 1842 and 1911, there were only minor legislative

---

[25] C. Seville, *op. cit.*, p.6–7.

adjustments made: to extend protection to paintings, drawings and photographs in 1862[26] and to regulate performance rights in musical works (1882 and 1888).[27] However, an important change in the law was brought about by the International Copyright Act 1844, which introduced into domestic law the opportunity for foreign works to be protected in the United Kingdom by bilateral agreements with foreign governments. Without such Agreements, the House of Lords decided in 1854 no foreigner could own a copyright in England.[28]

The 1878 Royal Commission Report

4–007   In 1875, a Royal Commission was set up to examine the laws relating to "Home, Colonial, and International Copyright", which reported in 1878.[29] It concluded that the form of the copyright law, as opposed to its substance, was badly in need of revision, it being "in many parts so ill-expressed that no one who does not give much study to it can expect to understand it." Recommending a codification and clarification of the law, the Commission entertained "no doubt that the interest of authors and the public alike requires that some specific protection should be afforded by legislation to owners of copyright."

Of particular interest is the fact that the Commission responded to a proposal put forward for the exclusive rights of the copyright owner to be replaced by "a system of royalty": the first proposal for a compulsory or statutory licence. The "royalty" lobby had urged "the benefit that it is supposed would arise to the public from the early publication of cheap editions." The Commission was unconvinced and concluded "that copyright should continue to be treated as a proprietary right."

The public interest is a recurring theme in the report. A major recommendation was that the duration of copyright should in no case be calculated from the date of publication but should last for the life of the author and a fixed number of years after his death, in order "to

---

[26] Fine Arts Copyright Act 1862 (25 & 26 Vict., c.68)

[27] Copyright (Musical Compositions) Act 1882 (45 & 46 Vict., c.40) and Copyright (Musical Compositions) Act 1888 (51 & 52 Vict., c.17).

[28] Bilateral Agreements were entered into thereafter with Prussia (1846), Hanover (1847), France (1851), Belgium (1848), Spain (1857) and Italy (1861). The UK failed to reach an agreement with the USA where there was widespread piracy of the works of British nationals. cf. Jeffreys (C.) v Boosey (T.) (1855) 4 H.L.C. 815.

[29] Report of the Commissioners of the Copyright Commission, 1878 [C–2036].

secure that adequate encouragement and protection to authors which the interests of literature, and therefore of the public, alike demand from the State." The Commission's recommendation was to follow the example of Germany and adopt a term of life plus 30 years.

A continuing preoccupation with the need for the public to have **4–008** access to cheap books is reflected in the evidence given by the Permanent Secretary to the Board of Trade, the department whose successor, the Department of Trade and Industry, is still responsible for copyright in the United Kingdom. He argued in favour of the importation into Britain without the consent of the author of colonial reprints, based on consideration of the public interest. Prices of books were allegedly very high and "altogether prohibitory to the great mass of the reading public". Colonial reprints would be cheaper and authors would not lose because they would benefit from an extended market. The Commission was again not persuaded, recommending that colonial imports should be subject to the author's consent.

Important in the history of British copyright also is the strong recommendation to the Government of the day to enter into a bilateral copyright agreement with the United States of America in order to provide for reciprocal protection for British and US authors.

The recommendations of the Commission remained a dead letter. It was Britain's involvement in the preparatory work on the Berne Convention which finally gave the necessary impetus for reform. Britain was active in the conferences leading to the adoption of the Convention in 1886 and ratified it the following year. However, following the revision conference in Berlin in 1908, the law had to be revised if Britain was to be able to give foreign copyright owners the level of protection required by the new Berlin Act of the Convention, including protection without compliance with any formalities and a period of protection of life and 50 years thereafter.

The Twentieth Century

In 1909, therefore, a new Committee was appointed to consider and **4–009** make recommendations for changes to the copyright law required by the Berlin Act. The Committee examined the Berlin Act Article by Article to see what, if any, amendments were required to the UK Act.

The report echoed the concern of the 1878 report at the confusion prevailing from the plethora of legislative provisions governing copyright, saying: "It would be a great advantage if the British law were placed on a plain and uniform basis, and that basis were one which is common so far as practicable to the nations which join in the [Berne] Convention". [30]

The public interest arose as an issue in relation to adopting the new term of protection recommended by the Berlin Act, namely the life of the author and 50 years after his death (hereinafter referred to as "p.m.a." (*post mortem auctoris*)). The Committee concluded: "We do not consider that it would be prejudicial to the public interests to adopt the proposed term, and we think that it would tend to beneficial assistance in the development and progress of literature and art". [31]

The 1911 Act

4–010 The Copyright Act 1911[32] brought about several major reforms, many of which were required to comply with the Berlin Act of 1908. As well as codifying the law,[33] it abolished common law copyright in unpublished works, and the requirement for registration, that leftover from the days of the Stationers' Company, altogether. This was necessary since the Berne Convention no longer permitted formalities. It also extended the term of protection to the international standard set by the Berne Convention of 50 years p.m.a. As regards new technologies, it provided protection for photographs and sound recordings for a period of 50 years from the making thereof. Works of architecture were protected as artistic works and choreographic works as dramatic works.

The Act introduced into the law the requirement that for copyright to subsist in a literary, dramatic, musical and artistic work, the work must be "original".

The adoption of a period of protection of 50 years p.m.a. with respect to literary, musical and artistic works to conform with international practice was subject to an important proviso. At any time after the expiration of 25 years from the death of the author of a

---

[30] Report of the Committee on the Law of Copyright, 1909, Cmnd 4976, at 7.
[31] *ibid.*, at 16.
[32] Copyright Act 1911 (1 & 2 Geo.5, c.46).
[33] The Copyright Act 1911 repealed no less than 21 enactments, (s.36, Second Schedule).

published work, a compulsory licence permitted reproduction subject to payment by the publisher to the author's heirs of a 10 per cent royalty.[34] It had been argued that the interest of the public was in securing the utmost cheapening of books at the earliest possible moment. There was a similar provision under which at any time after the death of the author of a literary, dramatic or musical work which had been published or performed in public, application could be made to the Judicial Committee of the Privy Council to require the owner of the copyright to grant a licence allowing reproduction or performance of the work in public if he had refused consent.[35]

Films were not specifically protected but that gap was remedied by the courts in 1912 when it was held that each photograph in the film was an artistic work.[36] The author was given new rights with respect to the use of his work in the making of cinematographic films and sound recordings. At the same time, a statutory licence for the reproduction of musical works by "mechanical contrivances" was introduced, known thereafter in the United Kingdom as "the mechanical licence". Finally, certain doubtful areas of the law were clarified, the author being given a translation right, a dramatisation right and, in the case of a novel or non-dramatic work or of an artistic work, the right to convert it into a dramatic work by way of performance in public or otherwise. In 1934, the courts held that the copyright in sound recordings, of which the maker or producer was the author, also included a performance right separate from that in the works recorded.[37]

1912–1955

The influence of the Berne Convention continued to make itself felt; it was revised twice in subsequent years, in 1928 at Rome and in 1948 at Brussels. The United Kingdom was able to ratify the Rome Act on the basis of the Copyright Act 1911. As this was not possible with the Brussels Act of the Berne Convention, following the Revision Conference, a new Committee was appointed in 1951:

4–011

---

[34] Copyright Act 1911, s.3.
[35] ibid., s.4.
[36] Barker v Hutton, 1912, 28 TLR 496.
[37] Gramophone Co Ltd v Stephen Cawardine & Co, [1934] Ch.450.

to consider and report whether any, and if so what, changes are desirable in the law relating to copyright in literary, dramatic, musical and artistic works with particular regard to technical developments and to the revised International Convention for the Protection of Literary and Artistic Works signed at Brussels in June 1948, and to consider and report on related matters.

The Committee in its report[38] noted that the field of activity covered by its terms of reference "affects the general public to a far greater extent than would appear at first sight". It recommended that the law should be amended so as to allow accession to the Brussels Act of the Berne Convention:

> We believe that it is in the interests alike of the general public and of authors, composers and artists, that the rights of the latter in the works of their brain should not merely enjoy protection in the country of origin, but also that wider protection to be gained only in association with other countries. The protection of intellectual property is not a matter which should be restricted to national boundaries.[39]

The perennial issue of perpetual copyright was raised, the case for it having been argued before the Committee; the latter rejected the case observing: "the public at large has an overwhelming interest in the reproduction of literary, dramatic and musical works, and we are satisfied that it would be quite impossible to justify a right in perpetuity".[40]

The Committee further recommended the repeal of the compulsory licence provisions of the 1911 Act referred to above, stating:

> For the great bulk of published works the question of a period of copyright, so far as it affects the general public, is of no importance after the first 25 years have expired. But as to the exceptional book which remains in demand at, say, the end of the first 25 years, the general public are interested in two ways. Firstly, they are concerned that authors and publishers alike should secure adequate

---

[38] Report of the Copyright Committee, October 1952, HMSO, Cmnd 8662.
[39] ibid., at 3 para.3.
[40] ibid., at 7 para.17.

returns for their labours, so as to ensure that these exceptional works continue to be written and published. Secondly, they are also concerned that the copyright period should not be so long that the copyright owner can indefinitely maintain prices at too high a level.[41]

Having assessed the evidence, the Committee concluded that the compulsory licences were not "decisive to secure the publication of books in cheap editions which would not otherwise be available to the public at, or at about, the same prices".[42] Moreover, no applications had ever been made to the Judicial Committee of the Privy Council for their authority to issue works of deceased authors. **4–012**

Voices were raised in protest at the Committee's recommendation and called for the Government to reject it in the name of the public interest. The compulsory licences were regarded by some as a safeguard to historians and other students requiring ready access to works of past generations.

Plant considered the safeguard to have "served as a reminder to copyright owners that there is a public interest in the exercise of the privilege which will, if necessary, be protected".[43]

The Committee also proposed a number of specific amendments to the law to bring it up-to-date *to take account of new technical advances and to permit the United Kingdom to ratify the Brussels Act of the Berne Convention, signed in 1948, and the Universal Copyright Convention, signed in 1952.* In 1956, a new Copyright Act was adopted. This Act repealed the 1911 Act and all outstanding copyright legislation.

The 1956 Act

The 1956 Act duly repealed the compulsory licence provisions of the 1911 Act.[44] It introduced for the first time copyright for 50 years from publication in films (cinematographic works), in radio and television broadcasts and in published editions of works. The performance right in sound recordings recognised by the Courts in the 1934 *Cawardine* **4–013**

---

[41] *ibid.*, at 8 para.20.

[42] *ibid.*, at 9 para.23.

[43] A. Plant, *The New Commerce in Ideas and Intellectual Property*, Stamp Memorial Lecture, (Athlone Press, London, 1953).

[44] Copyright Act 1956 (4 & 5 Eliz., 2, c.74); ss.3 and 4 of the 1911 Act were repealed.

case was confirmed and the mechanical licence retained.

To comply with the Brussels Act, it introduced a specific right to object to false attribution of authorship.

The Act also established the Performing Right Tribunal to which disputes over the terms of broadcasting and public performance licences for the use of musical works and sound recordings by broadcasters and others could be referred.

Performers were not protected by the 1956 Act. Protection under the criminal law against misappropriation of their performances was first introduced in 1925. A series of statutes—the Performers' Protection Acts 1958–72—subsequently extended the protection available to them, establishing summary offences against making recordings or films of performances, performing them in public and broadcasting performances without the written consent of the performer.

The Public Interest in the Debate for Reform and the 1988 Act

The Whitford Committee

4–014   The pace of technical development, allied to the continuing evolution of the Berne Convention, which was revised in Stockholm in 1967 and again in Paris in 1971, prompted the setting up of a new departmental Committee in 1973, under the Chairmanship of Mr Justice Whitford. The Committee's terms of reference were, *inter alia*: "to consider and report whether any, and if so what, changes are desirable in the law relating to copyright as provided in particular by the Copyright Act 1956..."[45]

The Whitford Committee's report was published in 1977.[46] It proposed simplification of the general structure of the Copyright Act 1956 and a whole series of reforms aimed at rationalising and updating the law, including such changes as were necessary to enable the

---

[45] There was a specific exclusion from the terms of reference of "any consideration of the merits of lending to the public as one of the acts restricted by copyright in a work". In fact, the Public Lending Right Act 1979 established a public lending right in respect of books in an entirely separate legislative process.

[46] Report of the Committee to consider the Law on Copyright and Designs, Chairman, the Hon. Mr Justice Whitford, Cmnd 6732, HMSO, March 1977.

United Kingdom to ratify the 1971 Paris Acts of the Berne and Universal Copyright Conventions. The report was acclaimed as a highly valuable contribution to the copyright debate but legislation did not follow for over a decade. During this period, the Government legislated on an *ad hoc* basis to deal with such urgent matters as improved remedies against piracy and the protection of computer software and cable programmes, and produced a series of consultative documents.[47] These culminated only in 1986 with a White Paper outlining the Government's legislative intentions.[48] The intervening debate, described by Cornish as "a ferment of proposition and counter-proposition",[49] is relevant to the subject of this study and it is instructive to examine the extent to which the Whitford Committee's report and the Government's Green and White Papers on the reform of the copyright law specifically addressed the issue of the public interest.

The Whitford Committee made clear its commitment to the pro- **4–015** position that copyright is in the public interest, within the context of the relationship between national intellectual property rights and the principle anchored in EC law of free flow of goods and services:

> ... There is a danger that the rights may be whittled down to an extent that makes them insufficiently rewarding to achieve their object. It is always hard for those brought up to believe in competition as the most beneficent market force, to realise that the exclusive rights which are granted by national copyright ... laws are granted because it is in the public interest to grant them. And the greater the extent to which these rights are devalued the less the benefit to the public interest.[50]

In relation to the problem of reprography, the Committee expressed the view "that the fact that 'education' is a good cause is not

---

[47] Reform of the Law relating to Copyright, Designs and Performers' Protection, Cmnd 8302, HMSO, July 1981. Intellectual Property Rights and Innovation, Cmnd 9117, HMSO, December 1983. The Recording and Rental of Audio and Video Copyright Material, Cmnd 9445, HMSO, February 1985.

[48] Intellectual Property and Innovation, Cmnd 9712, HMSO, 1986.

[49] W.R. Cornish, *Intellectual Property: Patents, Copyright, Trade Marks and Allied Rights* (London, Sweet & Maxwell, 4th ed. 1999), para. 9–17.

[50] Whitford Committee report, above n.46, para.84.

in itself a reason for depriving copyright owners of remuneration".[51] Stressing the need for action to ensure remuneration for photo-copying, the Committee drew attention to the economic justification for copyright:

> Unless something is done there is a serious danger that, in some fields at least, publication will cease. We can envisage a vicious circle: the increase in library and other copying means smaller circulations; which means higher costs; which in its turn means more copying. In the end publication ceases.

And that, clearly, would not be in the public interest.

The Committee considered the public interest also in relation to the term of protection. It considered that "the main purpose of any copyright law must be the protection of the proper interests of the creators of works ... which are the subject of copyright".[52] It heard arguments for an increase in the term of protection of literary and artistic works and from "voices which are raised in support of a drastic reduction in term ... upon the basis that at present insufficient attention is given to the public interest in as widespread and unfettered a dissemination as possible of works of all categories".[53] It concluded that the term of protection of 50 years p.m.a. in the case of literary and artistic works and from publication in the case of works produced by legal entities should remain unchanged, finding that these terms "appear to be adequate to ensure a proper return to copyright owners". The Committee also heard evidence in favour of a perpetual copyright in certain works "which, on expiry of the original term, should vest in Trustees, who would be obliged to exploit the works for the benefit of the public and to use the proceeds of exploitation for cultural purposes", that is, a public paying domain.[54]

4–016 The question posed by the Committee was "whether it is right in principle to establish any extended term or perpetual copyright, and more particularly any extended term or perpetual copyright with this particular aim in mind". The Committee saw the issue as a question of public interest:

---

[51] *ibid.*, para.268.
[52] *ibid.*, para.627.
[53] *ibid.*, para.636.
[54] *ibid.*, para.643.

Those in favour say that the public interest is best served by financing the country's cultural projects through the exploitation of the works of its dead authors. Those against say that copyright protection is only acceptable, and then only in the relatively short term, in order to resolve the conflict of public interest between a fair return to the creator and the desirability of the public having an unrestricted right of use.[55]

The Committee concluded that a perpetual copyright to provide a public paying domain was not in the public interest.

The Committee also considered the public interest with respect to exceptions, *i.e.* uses of copyright works which are considered as non-infringing. Newspaper interests had proposed that publication "in the public interest" should be admitted as a defence to infringement of copyright and it called for it to be made clear, in the area of fair dealing, that extensive quotation or, indeed, in some cases, reproduction in full, could be justified on this ground.[56]

The Committee recommended a general exception in respect of fair **4–017** dealing which, in accordance with Article 9(2) of the Berne Convention, does not conflict with a normal exploitation of the work and does not unreasonably prejudice the legitimate interests of copyright owners. It took the view that:

> Any sort of work is likely to be of public interest, and the freedom to comment and criticise, to discuss and to debate, ought not, in principle, to be restricted. ... There must, however, be some protection for the interests of copyright owners and ... a copyright owner is surely entitled to complain if his market is being cut into, in the sense that other people are selling the work rather than their views on the work.[57]

This proposal was not taken up by the Government which adopted the view that this definition could "enlarge the freedom available to users".[58]

The Whitford Committee put forward two proposals which were subsequently the subject of fierce debate and ultimately rejected by

---

[55] *ibid.*, para.646.
[56] *ibid.*, para.667.
[57] *ibid.*, para.676.
[58] Cmnd 8302, *op. cit.*, n.47, above, Chap. 13, para.4.

the Government. These are of particular interest in the context of the public interest. The first was for a statutory blanket licensing scheme for reprography, removing photocopying from the scope of the "fair dealing" and library exceptions. The second was for a royalty system or levy on the sale of recording machines for audio and video private copying, coupled with a supplemental blanket licensing scheme for educational recording.

4–018 The report made the case as follows:

> Complete freedom for individuals and education establishments to record for nothing from any source would not only weaken the record industry but also harm the interests of composers, writers, publishers, performers and others who are dependent on that industry, to the ultimate detriment of the whole community.[59]

The latter proposal was subsequently the subject of heated discussion and deliberation. The Government's policy on the issue and view of the public interest in relation thereto vacillated; first it called for further and convincing evidence that a levy system would provide an acceptable solution[60]; subsequently, it supported the introduction of such a scheme for audio and video home taping in a Green Paper[61] and put forward detailed recommendations for legislation in a White Paper in 1986[62]; finally, it dropped the matter in the Bill introduced to Parliament in 1987,[63] and vigorously opposed all efforts to include it during the Bill's subsequent passage through Parliament. In this debate, the Government appeared to identify the public interest only with the interest of consumers.

For example, in its 1985 Green Paper outlining Government proposals for the introduction of a levy on the sale of blank audio and video tapes, the Government proposed setting the maximum level of the levy by legislation to safeguard the public, there being "a strong public interest element entailed, with consumers likely to bear the ultimate cost".[64] The fact that, as the Government admitted "a fun-

---

[59] Whitford Committee report, Cmnd 6732, *op. cit.*, n.46, above, para. 320.

[60] Cmnd 8302, *op. cit.*, n.47, above, para.23.

[61] *The Recording and Rental of Audio and Video Copyright Material. A Consultative Document.* (Green Paper, February 1985, HMSO), Cmnd 9445.

[62] *Intellectual Property and Innovation*, (April 1986, HMSO), Cmnd 9712.

[63] Copyright, Designs and Patents Bill (House of Lords, 1987).

[64] Cmnd 9445, *op. cit.*, n.61, above, s.VII.

damental right conferred by copyright law cannot be used in present conditions for the purpose intended by the statute, and that home taping is a major use of copyright material for which copyright owners receive no payment", appeared to weigh less in the balance.[65]

When in 1986, the Government set out its legislative intentions in a **4–019** White Paper, it recalled that "Intellectual property is about creative ideas—... widespread dissemination of these ideas benefits society as a whole and stimulates further creative activity".[66] In concluding that a levy on audio blank tape would be the best solution to the home recording problem, the Government stated it had taken account of the need to balance the interests of copyright owners and performers with those of the public at large. When the Government subsequently dropped the levy, it said it had reconsidered the balance between those interests, announcing that it had concluded that any financial benefit to copyright owners and performers would be outweighed by the adverse effects the levy would have had on consumers, especially handicapped people, concluding this time: "It is a question of balance, and on this question we have come down on the side of the consumer".[67]

In its 1981 Green Paper, the Government stated that: "Copyright plays a significant role in commercial life and has a considerable impact in areas such as education where there is also a public interest" and acknowledged that "consideration has to be given to its evolution in response to changing economic conditions, social requirements and technical developments".[68]

In relation to the duration of copyright, the Government concurred with the recommendation of the Whitford report that the normal term of copyright should remain unchanged, recalling that: "The term of life plus 50 years is a compromise between on the one hand the economic interests of authors and their direct descendants and on the other hand the public interest in widespread and unfettered dissemination of works".[69]

The Government also agreed with Whitford that perpetual copyright in unpublished works should be abolished, holding "that it is

---

[65] *ibid.*, s.II.
[66] Cmnd 9712, *op. cit.*, n.62, above, para.1.
[67] *Hansard*, House of Lords Official Report, Vol.489, No.34, Thursday, November 12, 1987, at 1532.
[68] Cmnd 8302, *op. cit.*, n.47, above, Introduction, para.4.
[69] *ibid.*, Chap.12, para.5.

wrong for any material of possible public interest and importance to be protected by copyright in perpetuity".[70] Thus unpublished works would attract a term of life plus 50 years, as for published works.

4–020 The public interest was also addressed in the 1981 Green Paper in relation to exceptions to the right of reproduction: "The public interest demands that not every unauthorised reproduction of copyright material should constitute an infringement of copyright". [71] The aim of such exceptions is "to avoid copyright acting as an impediment to the use of copyright material for certain defined purposes, while ensuring the economic interests of copyright owners are not thereby damaged". The Government rejected Whitford's suggestion to define fair dealing as use which "does not unreasonably prejudice the economic interests of the author" because it considered it might unjustifiably result in "further encroachment into the basic copyright".

In 1983, the Chief Scientific Adviser in the Cabinet Office, who had been asked by the Prime Minister to examine whether the existing system of intellectual property was best suited to the national interest, published a report which *inter alia* put the case for intellectual property rights including copyright in the United Kingdom.

> A system of intellectual property rights should encourage new products and processes to reach the market and bolster trade in ideas ... For a nation which produces proportionately more good ideas than most countries but has a relatively small home market and has been less successful in the application of technology, the public good lies in trading products and ideas. It is therefore in the overall national interest that a strong world-wide system of protecting intellectual property should exist.[72]

The 1988 Act

4–021 When finally, out of all the controversy, the Copyright, Designs and Patents Act 1988 was enacted,[73] it represented a major reform. As we have seen, it aimed to take account of the technological developments

---

[70] *ibid.*, Chap.12, para.8; Cmnd 9712, *op. cit.*, n.62, above, Chap. 15, paras.15.2 and 15.7.

[71] Cmnd 8302, *op. cit.*, n.47, above, Chap.3, para.1.

[72] *Intellectual Property Rights and Innovation*, December 1983, HMSO, Cmnd 9117, para.1.8.

[73] 1988 Copyright, Designs and Patents Act, Chap.48, HMSO.

of the 30 years since the 1956 Act as well as to enable the United Kingdom to ratify the 1971 Paris Act of the Berne Convention. It dealt not only with copyright but also revised the law relating to industrial designs, patents and trademarks. The Act has one major advantage over that of 1956; it restates the law on a more logical and consistent basis and in much clearer language and, thus, is more readily intelligible to the layman. It incorporated the previous *ad hoc* amendments to the 1956 Act which had dealt with remedies against piracy and protection with respect to computer software and cable programmes. Other measures included: the introduction of specific protection with respect to satellite broadcasting and cable programmes for their operators as well as for right owners; the grant of the right to control rental to the authors of films and phonograms (under UK law at the time in both cases the producers) and computer programs; the introduction of the moral rights to be identified and to object to derogatory treatment of their works for authors and film directors to enable the UK to ratify the Paris Act of the Berne Convention; the replacement of the Performing Right Tribunal with a Copyright Tribunal with extended powers over collecting societies; and the provision of civil rights of action for performers and producers of phonograms against unauthorised exploitation of performances (previously performances had enjoyed only the protection of criminal law sanctions).

In one aspect, the 1988 Act was ahead of its time. When the passage of the Act was being discussed, the film, music and computer industries faced growing concerns about the potential for piracy and uncontrolled private copying by means of the new digital reproduction technology being introduced on the market. To meet the threat, the use of spoiler or copy-protection systems were being developed. In support of these trends, the 1988 Act led the field internationally by providing right owners with protection against devices designed to circumvent copy-protection devices. Rights and remedies were introduced to protect copyright works lawfully issued to the public in copy-protected electronic form against devices designed to circumvent such copy-protection systems. This legislation predated the equivalent provisions of the WIPO Copyright Treaty (WCT) and the WIPO Performances and Phonograms Treaty (WPPT) by eight years and those of the Information Society Directive by 13.[74] The Infor-

---

[74] CDPA 1988, s.296; see also *Sony Computer Entertainment v Paul Owen and Others*, [2002] EWHC 45(CH); [2002] E.C.D.R. 27 for a recent case where s.296 was applied.

mation Society Directive contains more comprehensive legal protection for copy-protection systems and also provides for protection of electronic rights management information.[75] The 1988 Act will no doubt require amendment in this regard.

Post-1988 Act Developments: The Influence of the European Union

4–022   Since the 1988 Act came into force, its provisions have been amended regularly in order to implement a number of European Community Directives in the field of copyright and related rights. The 1988 Act will no doubt come to be seen as the last copyright legislation to be passed in the United Kingdom substantially free of influence from the European Commission's programme of harmonisation of the laws in this field. This programme was launched in 1988, with the publication of the Commission's Green Paper entitled "Copyright and the Challenge of Technology: Copyright Issues Requiring Immediate Action".[76] Since 1990, four statutory instruments amending the Act have been adopted in order to comply with five Directives and public consultation on the implementation of the latest EC Directive on the Harmonisation of Certain Aspects of Copyright and Related Rights in the Information Society (the Information Society Directive) is expected to start shortly.[77]

---

[75] See Ch.12, below.

[76] COM.(88) 172 final.

[77] Directive 91/250/EEC on the legal protection of **computer programs**, implemented by the Copyright (Computer Programs) Regulations 1992 (SI 1992/3233), which came into force on January 1, 1993; Directive 92/100/EEC on **rental, lending and other rights** in the copyright field, and Directive 93/83/EEC on copyright and related rights in relation to **cable and satellite broadcasting** both implemented by the Copyright and Related Rights Regulations 1996 (SI 1996/2967), which came into force on December 1, 1996; Directive 93/98/EEC on the **duration of copyright and related rights** implemented (with the exception of Art.4) by the Duration of Copyright and Rights in Performances Regulations 1995 (SI 1995/3297), which came into force on January 1, 1996. Art.4 of the Directive is implemented by SI 1996/2967; Directive 96/9/EC on the **legal protection of databases**, implemented by the Copyright and Rights in Databases Regulations 1997 SI/3032, which came into force on January 1, 1998. The awaited consultation paper on the implementation of EC Directive 2001/29/EC (the "Information Society Directive") had not been published by the Patent Office by June 30, 2002. It was issued on August 7, 2002, and is available on the Office's website, *www.patent.gov.uk*.

Implementation of the EC Directives has already had and undoubtedly will continue to have a considerable impact on UK copyright legislation. Since the copyright approach of the United Kingdom is in a minority within the European Union, certain concepts of the Continental-European civil law author's right approach have inevitably found their way into UK law and this trend is bound to continue. This is despite the fact that, as Cornish has noted, "the Directives do not exist to eliminate differences at this level" being mostly concerned, apart from harmonising the duration of protection, to address problems arising from new technology.[78]

For example, the Rental Right Directive has obliged the United Kingdom notably to treat the principal director of a film as an author in addition to the producer, who was considered the sole author under the previous law. The term of protection of films is no longer 50 years calculated from the date of its making but 70 years from the death of a group of persons, including the principal director, the authors of the screenplay and dialogue and the composer.[79] Similarly, rental rights, which were previously granted only to producers of films and phonograms and to authors of computer programs, have had to be accorded to all authors and also to performers. The rental right did not previously apply to the lending of books because authors already benefited from the Public Lending Right Scheme.[80] The inalienability of certain rights of remuneration secured to authors and performers under the Directive is also a new concept impinging as it does on the usual UK freedom of contract approach.[81] Again, to comply with the Database Directive, the 1988 Act required amendment. Databases had previously been considered to be compilations but are now a separate category of literary work with a specific definition of "originality"; a database is original if, and only if, by reason of the selection or arrangement of the contents of the database the database

4–023

---

[78] W.R. Cornish, "Recent Changes in British Copyright Law", [1997] 172 R.I.D.A. 151 at 157.

[79] CDPA 1988, s.13B.

[80] This is a non-copyright system entitling eligible authors of books lent out by public libraries, and who register their works, to share in a central government fund. Public Lending Right Act, 1979; amended by the CDPA 1988, ss.18A and 40A, in order to comply with the Rental Rights Directive. See also J. Griffiths, "Copyright and Public Lending in the United Kingdom", [1997] E.I.P.R. 499.

[81] On the Rental Right Directive, see *inter alia*: A. Mosawi, "Some Implications of the New Regulations Regarding Rental Rights", [1995] 8 ENT.LR 307; R. Fry, "Rental Rights Derailed: Performers and Authors Lose out on Rental Income for Old Productions", [1997] 2 ENT.LR 31.

constitutes the author's own intellectual creation.[82] This is the first time that "originality" has been explicitly defined in UK copyright law and has given rise to controversy over the meaning of originality under the revised 1988 Act.[83]

The influence of Community legislation on the copyright law of the United Kingdom is set to continue inexorably as the Commission has the intention to legislate on a number of other issues in the future. One area where plans for Community legislation are well advanced is enforcement of rights. A Green Paper on Combating Counterfeiting and Piracy in the Single Market was published in 1998 and consultations are continuing.[84] Further issues to be addressed by the Commission's future copyright programme, which are likely to have a considerable impact on UK law, include the collective management of copyright and related rights, collecting societies and moral rights.[85]

Of immediate interest to the subject of this study is the Duration Directive, which provides for a uniform period of protection for authors of 70 years p.m.a., thus harmonising upwards to the longest period of protection in any state, that of Germany, and affecting the public interest. The rationale for this directive is discussed below in Chapter 10. Protection for holders of so-called related rights under the directive, including film and phonogram producers, broadcasting organisations and performers is to last for 50 years. The impact of the

---

[82] CDPA 1988, s.3A(2).

[83] On the Database Directive, see *inter alia*: C. Garrigues, "Databases: A Subject-Matter for Copyright or for a Neighbouring Rights Régime?", [1997] E.I.P.R. 3; S. Lai, "Database Protection in the United Kingdom: The New Deal and Its Effects on Software Protection", [1998] E.I.P.R. 32; J. Adams, " 'Small Earthquake in Venezuela': The Database Regulations 1997", [1998] E.I.P.R. 129; S. Chalton, "The Effect of the EC Database Directive on United Kingdom Law in relation to Databases: A Comparison of Features", [1997] E.I.P.R. 278, and "The Copyright and Rights in Databases Regulations 1997: Some Outstanding Issues on Implementation of the Database Directive", [1998] E.I.P.R. 178.

[84] COM(98) 569 final of October 15, 1998. The UK Government issued a consultation paper on possible changes to the criminal provisions in intellectual property law early in the year 2000. In March 2001, with the support of the Government, a private member's bill, The Copyright, etc. and Trade Marks (Offences and Enforcement) Bill, was introduced in the House of Commons.

[85] The harmonisation of national copyright and related rights laws in the European Union is discussed in K. Garnett, J. Rayner James and G. Davies, *Copinger and Skone James on Copyright, op. cit.*, n.8, above, and the Supplement thereto, Ch.25E. On the impact of the harmonisation programme on the CDPA 1988, see also W.R. Cornish, *op. cit.*, n.78, above.

implementation of the directive in the United Kingdom is discussed below.[86]

The Public Interest and Limitations on Copyright

"In Britain or any other Berne Convention State, copyright arises   **4–024**
upon the creation of a literary or artistic work and is enforceable
without formalities: its potency is accordingly the greater and the need
to qualify it in the public interest may be more pressing".[87]

Thus, the public interest guides the legislator in determining the
term for which copyright protection is accorded and the extent of the
statutory defences and exemptions or permitted acts in relation to
copyright. It is the legislator's task to achieve a proper balance
between the protection of copyright and the wider public interest and
the 1988 Act provides a wide range of acts which do not infringe
copyright.

A new element to be taken into account in relation to the permitted act provisions of the 1988 Act is the impact of the Human
Rights Act 1998, implementing the European Convention of Human
Rights (ECHR), and, in particular, Article 10 thereof guaranteeing
the right to freedom of expression. The relationship between the
defences of fair dealing and the public interest, on the one hand, and
the right of freedom of expression, on the other, has been addressed in
recent case law and is referred to below in the discussion of these
defences.[88]

A further consideration is the likely impact on the permitted acts
provisions of the 1988 Act of the EC Information Society Directive.[89]

---

[86] See also J.N. Adams and M. Edenborough, "The Duration of Copyright in the United Kingdom after the 1995 Regulations", [1996] E.I.P.R. 590; J.N. Adams, "The Reporting Exception: Does it Still Exist", [1999] E.I.P.R. 383; J. Griffiths, "Copyright in English Literature: Denying the Public Domain", [2000] E.I.P.R. 150.

[87] W.R. Cornish, *Intellectual Property: Patents, Copyright, Trade Marks and Allied Rights* (London, Sweet & Maxwell, 4th ed. 1999), para.13–03.

[88] *Newspaper Licensing Agency Ltd. v Marks and Spencer plc*, [2001] R.P.C. 76, CA; House of Lords decision [2001] E.C.D.R. 28; *Ashdown v Telegraph Group Ltd.*, [2001] EWCA Civ 1142; [2002] E.C.D.R. 32 at 337. On this subject, see K. Garnett and G. Davies, *Copinger and Skone James on Copyright,* Supplement to the 14th. ed., p.66 and paras 9 05D, *et seq.*

[89] Directive 2001/29/EC of the European Parliament and the Council of May 22, 2001, [2001] O.J. L167/10; *cf.* n.77, above; see also Ch.12, below.

The Directive limits the type and scope of permitted exceptions by laying down an exhaustive list of exceptions which Member States may include in their national legislation. The permitted exceptions are not mandatory and Member States are free to pick and choose among them. Thus, the Directive does not seek to impose harmonisation in the area of permitted acts, except in so far as no additional exceptions are permitted. This poses problems for the United Kingdom since there is no general exception in the Directive permitting fair dealing for the purposes of research or private study, although there are general exceptions for criticism and review, and for the reporting of current events. The 1988 Act will no doubt require some amendment to comply with the Directive.

Term of Protection

4–025   As we have seen, the question of term has been central to the evolution of the debate in the United Kingdom related to maintaining the balance between the public interest in stimulating creativity by means of protecting right owners and the public interest in dissemination of and access to works protected by copyright. The case for perpetual copyright and that for a drastic reduction in the term of protection were argued, as noted above, as recently as before the Whitford Committee.

Macaulay called copyright "a tax upon the public ... [which should] not last a day longer than is necessary for the purpose of securing the good".[90]

As Cornish states, this "tax" "should be broadly commensurate with the objectives of conferring copyright. The obvious economic test of this is: what measure of protection is needed to bring about the creation and production of new works and other material within the copyright sphere? ... the issue is largely a matter of the duration of copyright".[91]

Duration has ever been and will surely remain a controversial matter.[92] However, the 1988 Act term of protection for authors of 50 years p.m.a., in force in the United Kingdom since 1909, had attracted

---

[90] *Hansard, op. cit.*, Vol.56, at 348.
[91] W.R. Cornish, *op. cit.*, at 9–46.
[92] On the history of duration in the UK, see A. Robinson, "The Life and Terms of U.K. Copyright in Original Works", [1997] 2 ENT.LR 60.

a wide consensus and followed the standard set by the Berne Convention. It was, of course, an arbitrary standard. As the Whitford Committee pointed out: "The development of copyright law in this and other countries and the acceptance of obligations under international conventions has made it virtually impossible to deal with term on a logical basis".[93]

Whitford also considered whether a shorter term was justified in the case of photographs, sound recordings, cinematograph films, published editions and broadcasts. It had been suggested that there was an element of industrial activity in the creation of these works which made them less worthy of a long term of protection than literature and the arts. The Committee rejected the suggestion, pointing out that "merit, literary or artistic, has got nothing to do with copyright. Copyright can subsist in a work involving no creative ability".[94] It concluded that the term of protection for these works—50 years from publication—should remain unchanged. Whitford finally commented, "if there are to be major changes in term it should, we think, be on the basis of international agreement".[95]

As mentioned above, the duration of copyright in literary, dramatic, **4–026** musical and artistic works has recently been increased to 70 years p.m.a. to comply with the EC Directive on duration. Likewise individual contributors to the making of a film benefit from 70 years p.m.a. Introducing the legislation in the House of Commons, the Minister stated that the increase was necessary because harmonisation at 50 years would have been difficult because it would have meant protection reductions in three Member States, Germany (life plus 70), France (life plus 70 for musical works) and Spain (life plus 60 years). "The directive was, moreover, subject to qualified majority voting, and it became clear that most other member states were willing to accept harmonisation at life plus 70 years. In those circumstances, the UK agreed, albeit reluctantly, to accept the increased term."[96] The debates in both Houses of Parliament on the matter demonstrated almost total aquiescence in what amounted in fact to a *fait accompli* and the public interest was scarcely mentioned. Only one peer complained

---

[93] Whitford Committee Report, Cmnd 6732, *op. cit.*, n.46, above, para. 41.
[94] *ibid.*, para.633.
[95] *ibid.*, para.637.
[96] *per* the Minister for Science and Technology, I. Taylor, introducing the statutory instrument to the House of Commons, December 16, 1995, reproduced in [1995] 43, No.2, Journal, Copyright Soc. of the USA, at 199.

that "To add twenty years to what is a generous form of law is extraordinary".[97] The public interest was invoked by the Government spokesman in the Lords only in relation to the balance to be achieved between the interests of the public and those of right owners in safeguarding the interests of users affected by the revival of copyright by means of the introduction of a licence of right in consideration of reasonable remuneration.[98]

The increase in the term of protection has been subject to strong criticism in the United Kingdom. Laddie has described the increase as providing "an over-abundance of protection to the monopoly right owner" and posed the question:

> ... what justification is there for a period of monopoly of such proportions? It surely cannot be based on the principle of encouraging artistic creativity by increasing the size of the carrot. No one is going to be more inclined to write computer programs or speeches, compose music or design buildings because 50, 60 or 70 years after his death a distant relative whom he has never met might still be getting royalties.[99]

Another commentator, Parrinder, points out that "Dead authors already enjoy an ample period of copyright protection in this country. Will a further increase in the term of protection benefit anyone but the copyright holders? Nobody has said that it will, and the public have never been asked".[1]

Statutory Defences Against Infringement

Fair dealing

4–027   Since the 1911 Act, certain statutory defences have been available in relation to infringement of copyright, the most important of which is fair dealing, a defence similar but not equivalent to that of "fair use" in

---

[97] Lord Peston, *ibid.*, at 230.

[98] SI 1995/3297, Regulation 24.

[99] H. Laddie, (The Hon. Mr Justice Laddie), "Copyright: Over-strength, Over-regulated, Over-rated?", [1996] EIPR 253.

[1] P. Parrinder, "The Dead Hand of European Copyright", [1993] EIPR 391. See also W.R. Cornish, "Intellectual Property", in [1994] 13 *Yearbook of European Law*, p.485.

the United States of America.[2] The 1988 Act [3] permits fair dealing for three purposes, as did the 1956 Act: research or private study; criticism or review; and reporting current events. The defence only applies within these bounds. Unlike the US defence of "fair use", fair dealing is not an open-ended defence of general application. Moreover, fair dealing with a literary, musical or artistic work for the purpose of criticism or review or the reporting of current events is conditional upon sufficient acknowledgment of the identity of the author of the work.

The exception for research or private study applies only to literary, dramatic, musical and artistic works and (new in the 1988 Act) to the typographical arrangement of published editions. Only the production of single copies is allowed.[4] It does not apply to sound recordings, films, broadcasts and cable programmes.

Prior to the 1911 Act, this defence had been recognised in the case law.[5] According to the Government's Green Paper: "These exceptions are of obvious importance in that they seek to establish a proper balance between the legitimate interests of copyright owners and the legitimate desires of users of copyright material".[6]

The question of infringement only arises if the whole or a substantial part of a work is taken. The quality of what is copied has been held to be more important than quantity[7] and, in this respect, the courts have approved the test that "what is worth copying is *prima facie* worth protecting".[8] Moreover, the "part" which is regarded as

---

[2] G. Dworkin and R.D. Taylor state that the government resisted attempts to change the term to "fair use" because the meaning of the term was well established: Dworkin & Taylor, *Blackstone's Guide to the Copyright, Designs and Patents Act, 1988* (London, Blackstone Press Limited, 1989), p. 72.

[3] CDPA 1988, s.29 and 30. On fair dealing generally, see K. Garnett, J. Rayner James and G. Davies, *Copinger and Skone James on Copyright, op. cit.*, n.8, above, paras 9–06, *et seq.* D. Bradshaw, "Fair Dealing and the Clockwork Orange Case: A Thieves' Charter?" [1994] ENT.L.R. 6; C. Colston, "Fair Dealing: What is Fair?" [1995] Denning Law Journal, 91; J. Griffiths, "Preserving Judicial Freedom of Movement—Intepretating Fair Dealing in Copyright Law" [2000] I.P.Q.: No.2, 164.

[4] *ibid.*, s.29(b).

[5] *Bradbury v Hotten*, [1872] L.R.8 Ex.1; and see E.P. Skone James, J.F. Mummery and J. Rayner James, *Copinger and Skone James on Copyright* (London, Sweet & Maxwell, 1980), paras 467, 468 and 512.

[6] Cmnd 8302, *op. cit.*, n.47, above, Chap.13, para.2.

[7] *Hawkes & Son (London) Ltd v Paramount Film Service Ltd*, [1934] Ch.593. *Ladbroke (Football) Ltd v William Hill (Football) Ltd.*, [1964] 1 W.L.R. 273.

[8] *University of London Press Ltd v University Tutorial Press Ltd*, [1916] 2 Ch.601, 610; *Ladbroke (Football) Ltd v William Hill (Football) Ltd.*, [1964] 1 W.L.R. 273; see also K. Garnett, J. Rayner James and G. Davies, *Copinger and Skone James on Copyright, op. cit.*, n.8, above, paras 7.25 to 7.34.

substantial can be a feature or combination of features of the work, abstracted from it rather than forming a discrete part.

4–028 The House of Lords has considered the "substantial part" test in two recent cases. In *Designers Guild Limited v Russell Williams (Textiles) Limited (Trading as Washington DC)*[9] (Designers Guild), the case concerned fabric designs. The House of Lords held that there are two situations in which there is copying of a substantial part. The first is where an identifiable part of the whole of the original work has been copied. The second is where the copying was copying of the original work, taken as a whole, but with modifications, or "altered copying". The test to be applied in determining whether "altered copying" has taken place is whether the infringer incorporated a substantial part of the independent skill, labour etc. contributed by the original author in creating the copyright work. The test was based on the underlying premise of copyright law that a person was not at liberty to appropriate the benefit of another's skill and labour. In another case, concerning the copying of the typographical arrangement of newspapers, the House of Lords held that the test of substantiality is quantitative in the sense that, as there could only be infringement by making a copy, the question would always be whether enough of the published edition had been copied to amount to a substantial part. But the question of a substantial part was also qualitative and the quality relevant for the purposes of substantiality is the originality of that which has been copied. In the case in question, it depended not on the proportion which the copied part bore to the whole but upon whether the copy could be said to have appropriated the presentation and layout of the edition.[10]

4–029 In the long process of deliberation leading up to the passage of the 1988 Act, there was much argument both in favour and against permitting wider exceptions. The balance of interests in the 1988 Act has not shifted substantially in one or the other direction.

Whitford made a recommendation,[11] which the Government accepted,[12] to restrict the scope of the term "research or private study" so as to exclude research carried out for the business ends of a

---

[9] [2001] E.C.D.R.10 at 123.

[10] *Newspaper Licensing Agency v Marks and Spencer*, n.88, above. *Cf.* CDPA 1988, s.8. The majority of the Court considered s.8 to protect not the format of each article published in newspapers, but the typographical arrangement of the whole newspaper.

[11] Whitford Committee report, Cmnd 6732, *op. cit.*, n.46, above, para. 291.

[12] Cmnd 8302, *op. cit.*, n. 47, above, Chap. 2, para. 8.

commercial organisation. This became the subject of controversy when the Bill was introduced in Parliament. The Government was persuaded by British industrial interests to drop the restriction. They argued "that to exclude commercial research would impose additional costs on industry which would decrease its world-wide competitiveness and that any revenue raised would be swallowed up by the administrative costs of collecting it".[13] However, following the implementation of the Database Directive, the law now provides that the doing of anything in relation to a database for the purposes of research for a commercial purpose is not fair dealing with a database.[14] Fair dealing for purposes of criticism and review is permitted in respect of all books. Multiple copies may be made provided sufficient acknowledgment is given. The same applies with respect to reporting current events except that photographs may not be copied and no acknowledgment is required if the reporting is done by means of a sound recording, film, broadcast or cable programme. **4–030**

Whether a particular use has been "fair" is for the courts to determine. Lord Denning MR stated the test to be applied, as follows:

> It is impossible to define what is "fair dealing". It must be a question of degree. You must consider first the number and extent of the quotations and extracts. Are they altogether too many and too long to be fair? Then you must consider the use made of them. If they are used as a basis for comment, criticism or review, that may be fair dealing. If they are used to convey the same information as the author, for a rival purpose, that may be unfair. Next, you must consider the proportions. To take long extracts and attach short comments may be unfair. But, short extracts and long comments may be fair. Other considerations may come to mind also. But after all is said and done, it must be a matter of impression.[15]

Other factors to be taken into account are whether the work is unpublished—an unpublished work is not automatically outside the provisions of the fair dealing defence but appropriation of *unpublished*

---

[13] G. Dworkin & R.D. Taylor, *op. cit.* at 73.
[14] CDPA 1988, s.29(5).
[15] *Hubbard v Vosper*, [1972] 2 WLR 394.

material is a more substantial breach of copyright, if unjustified, than publication of an extract from a *published work.*

Recent Case Law on Fair Dealing

4–031   There have been several important decisions of the Court of Appeal involving fair dealing in recent years, where the Court has reviewed the principles to be applied in fair dealing cases and which illustrate the scope of the defence.

In 1998, in *Pro Sieben Media AG v Carlton UK Television Ltd*[16] (*Pro Sieben*), the defendant had broadcast a current affairs programme which examined in critical fashion the issue of chequebook journalism and the sale to the media of stories about people's private lives. The programme included a 30-second sequence taken from an interview, broadcast by the plaintiff *Pro Sieben*, with Mandy Allwood, a woman who was notorious at the time for being pregnant with eight foetuses and making money out of her situation. The plaintiff brought an action for copyright infringement and the defendant relied on the fair dealing defence for criticism or review. At first instance, the judge decided that the defence failed principally for lack of sufficient acknowledgment of the author of the original programme and did not decide whether the use was fair dealing.

The Court of Appeal, however, reversed that decision finding there had been sufficient acknowledgment and that the defence of fair dealing did apply to the use of the 30-second extract. In reaching its decision, the Court recalled that the permitted acts under the 1988 Act are all directed to achieving a proper balance between protection of the rights of a creative author and the wider public interest and that free speech is a very important part of that wider public interest. It stated that the general principles applicable to the issue of fair dealing are the following: it is a question of degree or of fact and impression. The degree to which the challenged use competes with exploitation of copyright by the copyright owner is a very important consideration, but not the only consideration. The extent of the use is also relevant, but its relevance depends very much on the particular cir-

---

[16] [1999] 1 WLR 605. See also M. Haftke, "Pro Sieben Media AG v. Carlton UK Television Ltd. and Twenty-Twenty Vision Ltd.", [1999] ENT.L.R. 118; J. Phillips, "Fair Stealing and the Teddy Bear's Picnic", [1999] ENT.L.R. 57; and R. Burrell, "Reining in Copyright Law: Is Fair Use the Answer", [2001] 4 I.P.Q. 361.

cumstances. If the fair dealing is for the purpose of criticism, that criticism may be strongly expressed and unbalanced without forfeiting the fair dealing defence. The words "for the purpose of criticism or review" and "for the purpose of reporting current events" should be construed as composite phrases. The intentions and motives of the user of copyright material were highly relevant in relation to fair dealing. A sincere but misguided belief that the use was criticising a work or reporting current events was not enough for the defence to be made out. As regards criticism, this could include criticism of the ideas to be found in a work and its social or moral implications, as well as criticism of style. The critic's purpose is important but the court should also focus on the likely impact on the audience. The Court found the defence of fair dealing made out because the appellant's programme was made for the purpose of criticism of works of cheque-book journalism in general, and the treatment by the media of the Allwood story in particular. Moreover, the events were clearly current; the use of the extract was short; it did not represent any unfair competition with *Pro Sieben*'s exploitation of the rights it had acquired in the interview and was not seeking to disguise an infringing purpose or act.

The Court of Appeal also reviewed the cases where guidance has been given as to the way fair dealing should be applied in *Hyde Park Residence Ltd. v Yelland* (*Hyde Park*).[17] The case concerned the publication by a newspaper of still photographs, taken on a security camera, of a visit by Diana, Princess of Wales, and Dodi Fayed, to Villa Windsor in Paris, on the day prior to their deaths in a car accident. The stills had been stolen by a security guard and sold to the newspaper, which published them more than a year later. *Hyde Park* had sought summary judgment at first instance relying on breach of copyright. The defendant relied *inter alia* on the defence of fair dealing for the purpose of reporting current events, which was upheld by the judge. On appeal, the Court overturned that decision concluding that the defence of fair dealing could not succeed.

4–032

> Thus the cases establish, and I believe it right, that it is appropriate to take into account the motives of the alleged infringer, the extent and purpose of the use, and whether that extent was necessary for the purpose of reporting the current events in question. Further if

[17] [2001] Ch.143.

the work had not been published or circulated to the public that is an important indication that the dealing was not fair ... The Court must judge the fairness by the objective standard of whether a fair minded and honest person would have dealt with the copyright work, in the manner [in question], for the purpose of reporting the relevant current events ... I do not believe that a fair minded and honest person would pay for the dishonestly taken driveway stills and publish them in a newspaper knowing that they had not been published or circulated ... Further the extent of the use was excessive.[18]

Fair dealing was also considered by the Court of Appeal in *Ashdown v Telegraph Group Limited*,[19] (*Ashdown*). The case concerned a claim for infringement of copyright and summary judgment in relation to the unauthorised publication by a newspaper of extracts of a confidential diary minute concerning a secret meeting between the former leader of the liberal party and the Prime Minister. The Court considered the relationship between freedom of expression and fair dealing, finding that the fair dealing provisions of the 1988 Act reflect freedom of expression in that, in the specific circumstances set out and provided there is fair dealing, freedom of expression displaces the protection that would otherwise be afforded to copyright. Thus, where part of a work is copied in the course of a report on current events, the "fair dealing" defence will normally afford the Court all the scope that it needs properly to reflect the public interest in freedom of expression and, in particular, the freedom of the press. The fair dealing defence should lie where the public interest in learning of the very words written by the owner of the copyright is such that publication should not be inhibited by the chilling factor of having to pay damages or account for profits. In finding that the defence of fair dealing was not made out in the case in suit and upholding the decision of the judge at first instance on this point, the Court referred to the factors to be taken into account in balancing the public interest in freedom of expression against the interests of owners of copyright and stressed that, following the entry into force of the Human Rights Act 1998, considerations of public interest are paramount. The factors

---

[18] *ibid.*, *per* Aldous L.J., para.3.7.
[19] *Ashdown v Telegraph Group Limited*, [2001] EWCA Civ 1142; [2002] E.C.D.R. 32 at 337.

cited were commercial competition (to what extent did the reproduction compete with the market for the work?); prior publication
(had the material been published already?); and the amount and
importance of the work taken. The Court found that the facts of the
case were not such that the importance of freedom of expression
outweighed the application of the established tests of fair dealing.

Public Interest Defence

The common law defence of public interest "is a defence outside and   **4–033**
independent of statutes, is not limited to copyright cases and is based
upon a general principle of common law".[20] It has, however, been
given statutory recognition in the 1988 Act: "Nothing in this part
affects any rule of law preventing or restricting the enforcement of
copyright, on grounds of public interest or otherwise".[21] The scope of
the defence remains a matter for the courts and there is a growing
body of case law on the subject.

The courts have found that

> public interest, as a defence in law, operates to override the rights
> of the individual, (including copyright), which would otherwise
> prevail and which the law is also concerned to protect. Such public
> interest as now recognised by the law, does not extend beyond
> misdeeds of a serious nature and importance to the country.[22]

However, as Lord Denning has stated, "The information must be
such that it is a proper subject for protection", that is, not obscene,
blasphemous or seriously deceptive of the public, and "there are some
things which may be required to be disclosed in the public interest, in
which event no confidence can be prayed in aid to keep them
secret".[23]

In the mid-1980s,[24] the Court stressed the need to differentiate
between what is interesting to the public (no defence) from what it is

---

[20] *Beloff v Pressdram*, [1973] RPC 783. See also M. Sayal, "Copyright and Freedom of
the Media: A Balancing Exercise?" [1995] 7 ENT.LR 263; and R. Burrell, *op. cit.*, n.16,
above.

[21] CDPA 1988, o.171(3).

[22] *per* Ungoed-Thomas J., in *Beloff v Pressdram*, above, n.20.

[23] *Op. cit.*, *Hubbard v Vosper*, at 395–6.

[24] *Lion Laboratories Ltd v Evans*, [1985] QB 526.

in the public interest to be made known (defence available). The defence was said to exist "to protect the community from destruction, damage or harm". This principle was illustrated in a 1991 case, where the Court held that the defence of public interest allowed the publication of secret information which, in the public interest, should be known. The fact that the information may interest the public is not sufficient. Once the information has been published, there is no additional public interest requirement for further publication.[25]

4–034 An interesting example of the application of the public interest defence arose in 1988 in a case before the House of Lords. It was held that the United Kingdom courts have a general equitable jurisdiction to decline to enforce copyright claims in certain cases; two examples of such circumstances were where a work contained false statements calculated to deceive the public; and where the work was of a grossly immoral tendency. In the case in question, the publication was held to have been against the public interest and in breach of the duty of confidence which the author had owed to the crown. This being so "it was inconceivable that a United Kingdom court would afford to him or his publishers any protection in relation to any copyright which either of them may possess in the book".[26]

More recently, the public interest defence has been the subject of consideration and somewhat conflicting decisions in two cases before the Court of Appeal. In *Hyde Park Residence v Yelland & others* (*Hyde Park*),[27] the Court of Appeal in a majority decision circumscribed the public interest defence. The facts of the case have been set out briefly above in connection with the defence of fair dealing. *Hyde Park* relied on a number of causes of action, including breach of contract, breach of confidence and infringement of copyright and sought summary judgment in respect of the allegations of breach of copyright. The defendant relied *inter alia* on the public interest defence to justify publication of the photographs in question. A majority of the Court of Appeal (Aldous and Stuart-Smith LJJ) rejected the submission that there was a general defence of public interest to an action for infringement of copyright. They argued that copyright is an intel-

---

[25] *Newspapers v News (UK) Ltd*, [1991] F.S.R. 37.

[26] per Lord Jauncey in *Attorney General v Guardian Newspapers; same v Observer; same v Times Newspapers* (No.2), [1990] A.C. 109, at 293.

[27] [2001] Ch.143. For commentaries on the case, see *inter alia*, R. Burrell, "Defending the Public Interest", [2000] E.I.P.R. 394; and J. Phillips, "When is a Fact", [2000] ENT.L.R. 116.

lectual property right provided for by the 1988 Act. That Act contains detailed provisions of the types of acts that are permitted to be carried out by persons without the copyright owner's consent.

> They range from fair dealing to use for education, by libraries and for public administration. They are ... provisions directed towards achieving a proper balance between the protection of copyright, and the wider public interest. They ... set out in detail the extent to which the public interest overrides copyright ... The 1988 Act does not give a court general power to enable an infringer to use another's property, namely his copyright, in the public interest. Thus a defence of public interest outside ... the 1988 Act, if such exists, must arise by some other route.[28]

The Court acknowledged that the courts have inherent jurisdiction to refuse to allow their process to be used in certain circumstances and that this is made clear by section 171(3) of the 1988 Act, quoted above. A court therefore has the right to refuse to enforce an action for infringement of copyright just as it can refuse to enforce a contract or other cause of action which offends against the policy of the law, but such jurisdiction is limited to cases where enforcement of the copyright would offend against the policy of the law. Public interest does not extend beyond misdeeds of a serious nature and importance to the country. The Court also found that the 1988 Act gives effect to the United Kingdom's obligations pursuant to the Berne Convention and certain European Union Directives and that a general defence of public interest would be contrary to these international obligations.

In conclusion, the Court held that the circumstances in which a court would be entitled to refuse to enforce copyright on the basis of the public interest defence include those where the work:

(i) is immoral, scandalous or contrary to family life;

(ii) is injurious to public life, public health and safety or the administration of justice;

(iii) incites or encourages others to act in a way referred to in (ii).[29]

4–035   These conclusions of the Court of Appeal on the public interest defence were not fully endorsed by another decision of the Court of Appeal, sitting in a different composition, in the case of *Ashdown v Telegraph Group Ltd. (Ashdown).*[30] Again, the facts of the case have been set out above in relation to the defence of fair dealing. The newspaper contended *inter alia* that the right to freedom of expression came within the public interest defence of the 1988 Act. It argued that the principles laid down by the Court of Appeal in *Hyde Park* in relation to that defence were not binding because the decision of the Court of Appeal had been given prior to the coming into force of the Human Rights Act 1998, implementing the European Convention on Human Rights (ECHR). It contended that the question whether the restriction on the right of freedom of expression imposed by the 1988 Act was necessary in a democratic society had to be considered in every case in order to comply with Article 10, ECHR. The trial judge held that Ashdown was entitled to summary judgment and the newspaper appealed.

The Court of Appeal dismissed the appeal but put a different interpretation on the scope of the public interest defence to that of its majority colleagues in *Hyde Park*. As regards the EHCR arguments, the Court held that restriction of the right of freedom of expression can be justified where necessary in a democratic society to protect copyright and that the infringement of copyright constitutes interference with the peaceful enjoyment of possessions[31] and with rights recognised under international Conventions and harmonised under European law. Since copyright protection itself was subject to exceptions, it followed that both the right of freedom of expression and copyright were qualified. The fair dealing exceptions under the 1988 Act had the effect of displacing protection in the interest of freedom of expression. Since copyright protected only expression and not ideas, the principle of freedom of expression would normally be sufficiently protected by the right to publish information and ideas contained in another's work without copying the words themselves. However, unlike the majority in *Hyde Park*, the Court envisaged circumstances where the right to freedom of expression could not be accommodated within the exceptions provided for by the 1988 Act

---

[30] *Ashdown v Telegraph Group Limited*, [2001] EWCA Civ 1142; [2002] E.C.D.R. 32 at 337.

[31] *cf.* ECHR, First Protocol, Art.1.

and it would be justified to use the actual words of another. "On occasions, indeed, it is the form and not the content of a document which is of interest".[32] It held that the public interest defence was not as restricted as suggested in *Hyde Park* and, in rare circumstances, the right of freedom of expression could override the rights conferred by the 1988 Act as a matter of public interest. The Court endorsed the observations made by Mance LJ in his partially-dissenting minority judgment in the *Hyde Park* case, where he said "the circumstances in which the public interest may override copyright are probably not capable of precise categorisation or definition" but apparently accepted that the courts do have a discretion to refuse to enforce copyright on public interest grounds. However, the public interest defence could not succeed in *Ashdown* because the extensive reproduction of Ashdown's own words in the minute was not justified by reference to Article 10 of the ECHR.

The case is of particular interest because it was the first reported case in England in which the interaction between the right to freedom of expression guaranteed by Article 10 of the ECHR and the property rights conferred by intellectual property legislation was considered and confirms a trend towards the application of the ECHR to copyright cases by courts in Europe.[33]

Other Statutory Defences

Other statutory defences to infringement include: the incidental **4–036** inclusion of any work in an artistic work, sound recording, film, broadcast or cable programme[34]; the use of copyright material by the public administration, *e.g.* in parliamentary or judicial proceedings, etc[35]; abstracts of scientific and technical articles[36]; exemptions concerning artistic works to permit photography or sketching of a publicly exhibited sculpture or building[37]; playing sound recordings for purposes of non-profit-making clubs[38]; public showing or playing of

---

[32] *Ashdown*, n.30, above, para.43.
[33] *c.f.* Ch.6, para.6.041.
[34] CDPA 1988, s.31.
[35] *ibid.*, s.45–50.
[36] *ibid.*, s.60.
[37] *ibid.*, s.62–65.
[38] *ibid.*, s.67.

broadcasts or cable programmes where no admission charge is made[39]; time-shift recording of television and radio broadcasts for private and domestic use.[40]

Statutory Exemptions in Favour of Education and Libraries

4–037   The 1956 Act allowed certain libraries to copy at the request of those engaged in research or private study. The development of photo-copying technology "has placed on this exception a weight which it was never designed to bear".[41] It was considered inappropriate, therefore, by Whitford, who proposed that a blanket licensing system should be imposed by statute, and that photocopying should be removed from the scope of the fair dealing and library exceptions. In its 1981 and 1986 Green Papers, the government rejected these proposals, concluding that voluntary blanket licensing was the appropriate solution in most cases. It recognised that, for example, music publishers believe that licensing of photocopying is not in their best interests and considered "that copyright owners should not in general be obliged to join blanket licensing schemes and should in general retain their exclusive rights".[42] It proposed a derogation from this principle, however, for education. It proposed providing legis-lation "to facilitate the establishment of licensing schemes for pho-tocopying, and to ensure the right balance of interest between copyright owners and users of copyright materials".[43]

The 1988 Act has made it clear that the making of multiple copies by libraries for the purposes of research and private study is not fair dealing. The Act also gives the Copyright Tribunal jurisdiction over general licensing schemes for reprographic copying. A number of such schemes have come into existence since the 1981 Green Paper under the aegis of the Copyright Licensing Agency (CLA), representing authors and publishers.

In the field of education, a blanket licensing scheme has been in existence between the CLA and local education authorities, repre-senting schools, since 1986. In return for a lump sum fee, multiple

---

[39] *ibid.*, s.72.
[40] *ibid.*, s.70.
[41] G. Dworkin & R.D. Taylor, *op. cit.* at 169.
[42] Cmnd 9712, *op. cit.*, n.48, above, Chap.8, para. 8.3.
[43] *ibid.*, para.8.6.

copies of up to 5 per cent of a book published in the UK or the whole of an article in a periodical are permitted. Certain types of work are excluded, such as printed music, newspapers, maps, etc. All copying outside the terms of the licence is an infringement. A similar agreement is in force with independent schools and, since 1988, an experimental scheme is operated with certain universities. This differs from the schools scheme in that the licence fee is not a lump sum but is related to the actual number of copies made. The university scheme also preserves the fair dealing exception with respect to single copies. The 1988 Act sets out to promote such schemes. As noted above, the **4–038** Copyright Tribunal has power to arbitrate in any disputes arising therefrom but the Government has also provided a statutory licence to cover the case where no blanket licensing scheme exists. Section 36 permits photocopying by an educational establishment for the purposes of instruction of up to 1 per cent of any work in any quarter of the year. Moreover, no blanket licence system may restrict the proportion of a work which may be copied to less than that amount, although payment may be required.

The terms of any licensing scheme for reprographic copying may be referred to the Copyright Tribunal in the case of dispute. The 1988 Act requires the Tribunal to have regard to: "(a) the extent to which published editions of the works in question are otherwise available, (b) the proportion of the work to be copied, and (c) the nature of the use to which the copies are likely to be put".[44]

The Government has also taken powers, subject to certain procedures, to extend the coverage of a licensing scheme for reprographic copying by an educational establishment for the purposes of instruction to similar works "unreasonably excluded" from the scheme, provided that such extension would not conflict with the normal exploitation of the works or unreasonably prejudice the legitimate interests of the copyright owners.[45]

The Act permits a number of other acts for the purpose of education including: certain things done for the purpose of instruction or examination[46]; the inclusion of short passages of literary or dramatic works in anthologies for educational use[47]; performing, playing or

---

[44] CDPA 1988, s. 130.
[45] ibid., s.137.
[46] ibid., s.32.
[47] ibid., s.33.

sharing a work in educational activities[48]; and educational recording of broadcasts and cable programmes in the absence of a licensing scheme.[49]

Special Regulations Concerning Libraries and Archives

4–039 There are a number of special provisions in the 1988 Act regulating copying of works by prescribed libraries and archives and the Government is given power to set out more detailed conditions in regulations,[50] including the definition of prescribed libraries. Non-profit making (local authority and educational) libraries are intended and single copies may be made and supplied to people requiring them for research or private study of one article from any periodical and parts of published works, subject to payment of the cost of producing the copy and an overhead charge. There are specific restrictions prohibiting the making of multiple copies[51] and rules governing, *inter alia*, the supply of copies to other libraries, preservation or replacement copies, etc. It should also be noted that the new right to control rental of sound recordings, films and computer programs applies to library lending whether or not a charge is made by the library. However, the Government again has powers to grant compulsory licences if the copyright owners refuse unreasonably to grant licences.[52]

Conclusion

4–040 Introducing the Copyright, Designs and Patents Bill to the House of Lords in 1988, the Secretary of State for Trade and Industry gave expression to the view of the Government of the day with respect to copyright, saying:

It has been observed that nothing can be more properly described as a man's property than the products of his mind, and over the years a system of law has been established to protect ideas—patents

---

[48] *ibid.*, s.34.
[49] *ibid.*, s.35.
[50] *ibid.*, s.37–44.
[51] *ibid.*, s.40.
[52] *ibid.*, Sch.7, ss.6, 8 and 34.

for inventions, copyright for literature and art, and so on. The intellectual property system has served us well by encouraging creativity and innovation and the spread of ideas. Intellectual property is of substantial economic significance. It forms the foundations of major industries. Without copyright law, the publishing and record industries would scarcely operate. The entertainment world would be in chaos.[53]

On the question of the balance of interest between the creator and the public, he observed: "In drawing up the Bill, we have sought to provide a fair return for creative talent and those who develop and use their work, while ensuring that ideas are not locked away but are accessible to society as a whole."[54]

He went on to suggest that the Bill would encourage creativity and enterprise and the growth of fair competition.

It will be seen, therefore, that the justifications for copyright legislation in the United Kingdom have remained constant over the years. On the one hand, there is the aim to protect the natural rights of the author by protecting the products of his mind; at the same time, the copyright system aims to encourage creativity and the dissemination of ideas and knowledge to the general public. There has been a concern to balance the interest of the author in protection, on the one hand, with the interest of the public in access to works, on the other. There has been also a consistent policy on the part of successive British Governments to bring the law up-to-date regularly in order to deal with the latest technical developments. Finally, throughout the nearly 300 years of copyright law in the United Kingdom, there has been a continual concern for copyright legislation to be adapted to the public interest.

4–041 In the Government's White Paper, "Intellectual Property and Innovation", published in April 1986,[55] the Government stressed that the protection of intellectual property benefits society as a whole and stimulates further creative activity. In order to keep intellectual property law abreast of changing conditions, it suggested that there were three aims to be achieved: first, new technical developments should be accommodated (and a review of the historical development

---

[53] *Op. cit.*, n.67, above, at 1476.
[54] *ibid.*
[55] Cmnd 9712, *op. cit.*, n 48, above.

of copyright law shows that each new major revision was prompted by such technical developments); secondly, the Government has to ensure that intellectual property rights strike the appropriate balance between, on the one hand, protection which ensures an adequate reward for authors and creators and, on the other hand, access to creative ideas in ways which stimulate competition and allow for the use of modern technology; thirdly, there must be an efficient system for the enforcement of intellectual property rights. The report further summed up the United Kingdom's attitude to intellectual property, saying:

> The United Kingdom relies heavily on getting value from its intellectual property. To this end, it is vital that the intellectual property system should strike the right balance between protection and exploitation; it should provide protection and reward as incentives to innovation but not at the expense of stifling competition or preventing the wider use of technology.[56]

As regards copyright, it stated that the broad aims of the Government in the revision of copyright law "are to ensure continued protection for those who create copyright works, while at the same time recognising that the public has a substantial interest in the availability of their works".[57]

In December 1983, the Chief Scientific Adviser to the Cabinet Office concluded that: "While the Government devotes considerable resources to encouraging innovation generally, it does not give adequate priority to providing the system of intellectual property rights that British business requires . . ." and suggested that, as a nation and compared to the UK's main trading partners, "there is insufficient awareness of the importance and value of intellectual property rights".[58]

4–042 That situation has changed and the Government has come to realise that copyright plays a vital role in the British economy. Following the publication of the Cabinet Office report in 1983, the Common Law Institute of Intellectual Property (CLIP) undertook a series of studies into the economic value of intellectual property in order to encourage

---

[56] *ibid.*, at 3 para.3.
[57] *ibid.*, at 35 para.4.
[58] Cmnd 9117, *op. cit.*, n.47, above, summary, para.3.

the Government to give adequate priority to the subject. Its first report, *The Economic Importance of Copyright*, was published in 1985[59] and a further study, *The Export Performance of the Copyright-Dependent Industries*, was published in 1988.[60] In 1993, CLIP followed these studies up with an updated and expanded version of its 1985 study on the economic importance of copyright.[61] This showed that in 1990 the copyright industries with primary direct dependence on copyright accounted for 3.6 per cent of GDP (Gross Domestic Product), up from 2.6 per cent in 1982, and employed more than 800,000 people, an increase of 200,000 over 1982. Industries "substantially dependent" on copyright accounted for a further 1.8 per cent, bringing the total to 5.4 per cent of GDP and employment of 1.3 million.

Most recently, in 2001, the Department for Culture, Media and Sport published a report on the economic contribution of the creative industries to the United Kingdom.[62] This shows that the creative industries that are substantially dependent on copyright generate revenues of around £112.5 billion and employ over 1.3 million people. Exports contribute around £10.3 billion to the balance of trade and the industries account for up to 6 per cent of GDP. In the period 1997–98, output grew by 16 per cent, compared to under 6 per cent for the economy as a whole.

These studies have underscored the economic value of the copyright industries and their growth potential as well as the importance of copyright to the national economy.

The rationale for copyright and related rights in the United Kingdom continues to be that such rights play a vital role in protecting and promoting creativity and that "the knowledge economy depends on strong intellectual property rights".[63] The Government is concerned to raise the general public's awareness of the value of intellectual property rights and knowledge of the contribution made

---

[59] J. Phillips, *The Economic Importance of Copyright* (CLIP, 1985).

[60] J. Skilbeck, *The Export Performance of the Copyright-Dependent Industries* (CLIP, 1988).

[61] T. Price, *The Economic Importance of Copyright*, (Common Law Institute of Intellectual Property, (CLIP), London, 1993). Unlike the 1985 study, the 1993 one includes computer software for the first time among the industries totally dependent on copyright.

[62] *Creative Industries Mapping Document 2001*, (Department for Culture, Media and Sport (DCMS), March 2001).

[63] Dr Kim Howells, Consumer Affairs Minister, Chairman of the Intellectual Property Group of the Creative Industries Task Force, UK Patent Office Press release, March 31, 2000.

by such rights to the development and success of the creative industries for the benefit of the wider community.[64]

---

[64] cf. *Report from the Intellectual Property Group of the Government's Creative Industries Task Force,* March 2000.

Chapter 5

The United States of America

Origins of the 1790 Act

5–001   The British Colonies in America had no separate copyright statute. Immediately following the War of Independence (1775–1783)[1] and the establishment of the United States of America, Congress passed a resolution recommending to the several States that they secure to authors or publishers of any books not before printed the copyright of such books for a term of not less than 14 years.[2] During the next two or three years, 12 of the 13 States passed Copyright Acts.[3] These were variously entitled. Seven had as their object the "encouragement" or "promotion of literature and genius". Four were described as having the purpose of "securing to authors the exclusive right and benefit of publishing literary productions".

The preambles to these early laws show that the legislators in question justified copyright under both natural law and economic principles and also had regard to the public interest. This is well illustrated by the preamble to the Connecticut statute which provided:

---

[1]   The independence of the new nation was recognised by Great Britain in the Treaty of Paris (1783).

[2]   Resolution of May 2, 1783 on the reports of Mr Williamson, Mr Izard and Mr Madison, see P. Wittenberg, *The Protection of Literary Property* (Boston, The Writers Inc Publishers, rev. ed. 1978), at 32.

[3]   Wittenberg, *op. cit.*, at 33.

Connecticut, 1783, January session: An act for the encouragement of literature and genius;

Massachusetts, March 17, 1783: An act for the purpose of securing to authors the exclusive right and benefit of publishing their literary productions for 21 years;

Maryland, April 21, 1783: An act respecting literary property;

New Jersey, May 27, 1783: An act for the promotion and encouragement of literature;

New Hampshire, November 7, 1783: An act for the encouragement of literature and genius, and for securing to authors the exclusive right and benefit of publishing their literary productions for 20 years;

Rhode Island, 1783, December session: An act for the purpose of securing to authors the exclusive right and benefit of publishing their literary productions for 21 years;

Pennsylvania, March 15, 1784: An act for the encouragement and promotion of learning by vesting a right to the copies of printed books in the authors or purchasers of such copies during the time therein mentioned;

South Carolina, March 26, 1784: An act for the encouragement of arts and sciences;

Virginia, October 1785: An act for securing to the authors of literary works an exclusive property therein for a limited time;

North Carolina, November 19, 1785: An act for securing literary property;

Georgia, February 3, 1786: An act for the encouragement of literature and genius;

New York, April 29, 1786: An act to promote literature.

Whereas it is perfectly agreeable to the Principles of natural Equity and Justice, that every Author should be secured in receiving the Profits that may arise from the Sale of his Works, and such Security may encourage Men of Learning and Genius to Publish their Writings; which may do Honor to their Country, and Service to Mankind.

The term of protection varied, the longest period being 21 years. While the contents of these laws were not identical, they were all clearly modelled on the Statute of Anne.

Printing in the American colonies was run on purely commercial lines.

Perhaps the most important difference between colonial America and Europe in the seventeenth and eighteenth centuries was that literature did not rely as much on patronage in America as it did in Europe and therefore American writers looked to the general public rather than wealthy or influential individuals for their financial rewards.[4]

Newspapers and periodicals published most of the output of American writers in serialised form. **5–002**

With 12 State copyright statutes, it was not surprising that when the Constitution was drafted it should include provision for copyright. "The constitutional clause empowering Congress to enact a copyright statute reflects the belief that property rights, properly limited, will serve the general public interest in an abounding national culture."[5] The copyright clause authorises Congress to legislate: "to promote the progress of Science . . . by securing for limited times to authors . . . the exclusive right to their respective writings." Legislation followed rapidly. Congress passed the original Copyright Act on May 31, 1790.[6] The Act was entitled: "An Act for the encouragement of learning by securing the copies of maps, charts and books, to the authors and proprietors of such copies, during the times therein mentioned". It provided for "a term of 14 years and if the author be living at the expiration of the term, an extension for a further term of

---

[4] S.M. Stewart, *International Copyright and Neighbouring Rights* (London, Butter-worths, 2nd ed. 1989), para.2.17.

[5] J. Madison, see Introduction, above n.10.

[6] Laws of the First Congress, Second Session, Chap.XV (see Appendix 2).

14 years, or if not, to his executors, administrators or assigns".

In the State Statutes, the copyright clause of the Constitution and in the 1790 Act, the same basic ideas as to the functions of copyright were apparent as those which prevailed in England and the English Statute of Anne clearly served as the model for the 1790 Act. These basic ideas were that copyright is for the promotion of learning; for the benefit of the author; to prevent harmful monopoly (by imposing a limited term); and is granted by the State to provide order in the book trade.

> The dominant idea in the minds of the framers of the Constitution appears to have been the promotion of learning. The proposals submitted [to the Constitutional Convention] by Madison and Pinckney, apparently arrived at independently, are instructive on this point. Both manifest an interest in having the Federal Government promote knowledge, and provide for the author's copyright in addition to other provisions for this specific purpose. The idea next in importance seems to have been protection for the author.[7]

As the Supreme Court said in 1954:

> "The copyright law, like the patent statutes, makes reward to the owner a secondary consideration." *United States v Paramount Pictures*, 334 US 131 68 S Ct 915, 929, 92 L.Ed 1260. However, it is "intended definitely to grant valuable, enforceable rights to authors, publishers, etc., without burdensome requirements; 'to afford greater encouragement to the production of literary [or artistic] works of lasting benefit to the world.'" *Washingtonian Pub. Co v Pearson*, 306 US 30, 36, 59 S. Ct. 397, 400, 83 L. ED 470.

The economic philosophy behind the clause empowering Congress to grant patents and copyrights is the conviction that encouragement of individual effort by personal gain is the best way to advance public welfare through the talents of authors and

---

[7] L.R. Patterson, *Copyright in Historical Perspective* (Nashville, Vanderbilt University Press, 1968), at 193. On the nature and history of U.S. copyright law generally, see L.R. Patterson & S.W. Lindberg, *The Nature of Copyright—A Law of Users' Rights*, (The University of Georgia Press, Athens and London, 1991); and P. Goldstein, *Copyright's Highway-The Law and Lore of Copyright from Gutenberg to the Celestial Jukebox*, (New York, Hill and Wang, 1994).

inventors in "Science and useful Arts." Sacrificial days devoted to such creative activities deserve rewards commensurate with the services rendered.[8]

Nimmer refers to "the philosophical issue as to whether copyright **5–003** should be regarded as properly based upon the 'natural right' concept fundamental (at least in origin) to the theory of private property". In his view:

> there is nothing to indicate that the Framers, in recognising copyright, intended any higher standard of creation in terms of serving the public interest than that required for other forms of personal property. We may assume that the men who wrote the Constitution regarded the system of private property *per se* as in the public interest. In according a property status to copyright they merely extended a recognition of this public interest into a new sector.[9]

The 1790 Act provided protection only to the author of maps, charts and books. Only citizens or residents of the US were protected as well as their executors, administrators or assigns. Protection was afforded against the following acts done without authorisation: printing, reprinting or publishing copyrighted works; importing copies of a protected work and selling infringing copies knowingly. Penalties included delivering up of the infringing copies to the author for destruction and a fine of 50 cents for every infringing sheet. Only half of the fine was paid to the author, the other to the US Government. The pirating of foreign works was expressly allowed and, in this, the US Statute differed from the Statute of Anne. However, as regards *unpublished* manuscripts, the author was specifically protected against unauthorised publication.

The question whether a common law copyright in published works had existed in the US prior to the adoption of State and Federal legislation arose. As we have seen, the question whether a perpetual common law copyright existed had been settled in Great Britain in the case of *Donaldson v Beckett* in 1774. The House of Lords had rejected

---

[8] *Mazer v Stein*, 347 US 201, 74 S. Ct. 460.
[9] M.B. Nimmer, *Nimmer on Copyright. A Treatise on the Law of Literary, Musical and Artistic Property and the Protection of Ideas*, (New York, Matthew Bender, 2001 ed.), para.1.03A.

the concept of a common law property in literary works; copyright had been established by the Statute of Anne. In 1834, the question was considered in the case of *Wheaton v Peters* by the US Supreme Court. It was decided that there had been no common law copyright in published works in the United States but that copyright had been created by the 1790 Act.

> That Congress, in passing the Act of 1790 did not legislate in reference to existing rights, appears clear, from the provision that the author & c. "shall have the sole right of printing," & c. Now if this exclusive right existed at common law, and Congress were about to adopt legislative provisions for its protection, would they have used this language? Could they have deemed it necessary to vest a right already vested? Such a presumption is refuted by the words above quoted, and their force is not lessened by any other part of the act. Congress, then, by this act, instead of sanctioning an existing right, as contended for, created it.[10]

5–004   So far as manuscripts were concerned, however, the Court found: "that an author, at common law, has a property in his manuscript ... cannot be doubted; but this is a very different right from that which asserts a perpetual and exclusive property in the future publication of the work, after the author shall have published to the world ... That every man is entitled to the fruits of his own labor, must be admitted; but he can enjoy them only, except by statutory provision, under the rules of property which regulate society, and which define the rights of things in general".

The combined result of the 1790 Act and the case of *Wheaton v Peters* was to lead to a rejection of the natural rights theory as a premise for copyright protection. As Goldstein states:

> The US Supreme Court expressly rejected a natural rights basis to copyright in its landmark decision *Wheaton v Peters*, where it observed that Congress, "instead of sanctioning an existing right, ... created it" when it enacted the 1790 Act. The House Report on the 1909 Copyright Act emphazized that "the enactment of copyright legislation by Congress under the terms of the Constitution is not based upon any natural right that the author has in

---

[10] 33 US (8 Peters) 591.

his writings... but upon the ground that the welfare of the public will be served and progress of science and useful arts will be promoted by securing to authors for limited periods the exclusive rights to their writings."[11]

Patterson describes the decision of the Court in *Wheaton v Peters* in which there were dissenting judgments, as follows:

The striking point about the premises of the majority and the dissenters is that they are polar, one proceeding from the interest of the public, the other from the interest of the individual creator. This is not to say that both views did not take into account the interest of both the public and the individual author; it is to say that their premises brought the justices to different conclusions as to how best to resolve the conflict between the public's interest in learning and the author's interest in his property. The majority, viewing copyright as a monopoly, were content to protect the author's property for a limited period under the conditions prescribed by the Statute. To do otherwise would be contrary to the public interest.[12]

Thenceforth, the justification for copyright law in the USA was based primarily on the social benefits derived therefrom and not on reward for the author. Copyright was held to exist primarily to benefit the public interest and only secondarily to benefit the author.

Legislative Developments Between 1790 and 1976

1790–1909

The 1790 Act was followed by a series of amending legislation **5–005** extending the scope of copyright protection. Between 1789 and 1905 there were altogether 25 laws dealing with copyright. In 1802, protection was extended to prints; in 1831 musical compositions were granted protection and the term was prolonged to a first term of 28

---

[11] P. Goldstein, *Copyright Principles, Law and Practice* 3 Vols. (Boston, Little, Brown & Co. 1989), para.1.1.

[12] L.R. Patterson. *Copyright in Historical Perspective, op. cit.*, n.7, above, 211.

years with a renewal term of 14 years. In 1856, the protection afforded to dramatic compositions was extended to include a public performance right. In 1865, photographs and negatives were protected. In 1870, a general revision of the copyright law took place and protection was extended to paintings, drawings, statues, etc. and to translations and dramatisations of existing works. In 1882, "designs for moulded decorative articles, tiles, plaques, or articles of pottery or metal" were added. A further general revision of the law took place in 1891. That Act for the first time provided protection for non-US citizens from countries party to an international agreement to which the United States of America belonged and which provided reciprocal protection for US works. However, the effect of this was limited by the notorious manufacturing clause which provided that foreign works were protected only if printed in the United States of America, a clause which was only repealed by the 1976 Copyright Act.

The Copyright Act of 1909, which codified the law and extended the renewal period to 28 years, remained in force until January 1, 1978, when the 1976 Act took effect. The 1909 Act made three important changes to the law: the creation of a compulsory licence for making recordings of musical works; the grant to the copyright owner of a specific right to authorise reproduction of the work, and the enactment of the work-for-hire doctrine, which led to the development of the corporate copyright of legal entities as opposed to that of natural persons. In 1912, the 1909 Act was amended to provide protection for motion pictures.

The Long Road to Reform and the 1976 Act

5–006   From 1924 until the outbreak of the 1939–45 Second World War, many efforts were made to revise the 1909 Copyright Act. A number of revision bills were introduced mainly with a view to bringing US law into conformity with the Berne Convention. "In the end, however, all these efforts bogged down in controversy among the various private interests, particularly over the fundamental differences between the Berne Convention and the US Law."[13]

After the war, legislative efforts aimed at US membership of the Berne Convention were abandoned and the US participated in the

---

[13] Report of the Register of Copyrights on the General Revision of the US Copyright Law, 87th Congress, 1st session, July 1961, at x.

work leading to the adoption of the Universal Copyright Convention (UCC) in 1952. Only minor amendments to US law passed in 1954 were needed to conform with the UCC, to which the US became a party when it entered into force in 1955.

In 1955, Congress asked the Copyright Office to undertake a series of studies to provide the groundwork for a general revision. "The studies were designed to present, as objectively as possible, the history and provisions of the [1909] present law, the problems it raises, past proposals for revision, comparable provisions in foreign laws and international conventions, and an analysis of the issues and alternative solutions."[14] Using the resulting 34 studies as a basis for debate, the Register of Copyrights presented comprehensive recommendations for revision of the law to Congress in July 1961.[15] In doing so, he stated:

> In arriving at our recommendations we have given consideration to all the views expressed on a particular problem. . . . The needs of all groups must be taken into account. But these needs must also be weighed in the light of the paramount public interest. We have tried to find practical solutions that will afford a balance between the various private interests and at the same time safeguard the welfare of the public.[16]

As regards the purpose of copyright, the report concluded:

> The primary purpose of copyright is to stimulate the creation and dissemination of intellectual works, thus advancing "the progress of science and useful arts". The grant of exclusive rights to authors is a means of achieving this end, and of compensating authors for their labors and their contributions to society. Within limits, the author's interests coincide with those of the public. Where they conflict, the public interest must prevail. The ultimate task of the copyright law is to strike a fair balance between the author's right to control the dissemination of his works and the public interest in fostering their widest dissemination.[17]

---

[14] ibid.
[15] ibid.
[16] ibid. at xi.
[17] ibid. at 6.

5–007 Throughout the 1960s and 1970s, a series of bills for general revision of the 1909 Act were introduced at regular intervals in both Houses of Congress. The revision process was dogged by controversy, notably with respect to cable television, and action was delayed pending the adoption by the Federal Communications Commission of new cable television rules. Revision represented a huge task. As the House Report on the 1976 bill stated, since the 1909 Act was passed:

> ... significant changes in technology have affected the operation of the copyright law. Motion pictures and sound recordings had just made their appearance in 1909, and radio and television were still in the early stages of their development. During the past half century a wide range of new techniques for capturing and communicating printed matter, visual images, and recorded sounds have come into use, and the increasing use of information storage and retrieval devices, communications satellites, and laser technology promises even greater changes in the near future. The technical advances have generated new industries and new methods for the reproduction and dissemination of copyrighted works, and the business relations between authors and users have evolved new patterns.[18]

In 1971, however, special legislation[19] was passed to create a limited copyright in sound recordings to tackle what had become the widespread problem of unauthorised reproduction (commonly known as piracy).

Following extensive hearings, the 1976 revision Act was finally adopted on October 19, 1976. It represented a comprehensive revision of the copyright law and was the result of more than 20 years of deliberation. The legislation was described as representing a "tension between the monopoly controls of copyright and the broad needs of the public for access to information; between the Constitution's aim—"to promote the progress of science and useful arts"—and its chosen means—a limited monopoly in individual "Authors and Inventors"[20]. It abolished the previous dual system of common law

---

[18] House of Representatives Report No. 94–1476 to the 94th Congress, 2nd session, dated September 3, 1976, at 47.

[19] Public Law, 92–140 (92nd Congress s.646) of October 15, 1971.

[20] B. Ringer, "First Thoughts on the Copyright Act of 1976", [1977] *Copyright* 187, n. 2, quoting Rep. R. Drinan.

and statutory copyright, establishing in its place a single Federal system of copyright protection for both published and unpublished works. It specifically prohibited the application of State law to the subject-matter of copyright specified in the Act.[21]

The Act gives protection to a broad variety of works, including the following categories: literary works; musical works, including any accompanying words; dramatic works, including any accompanying music; pantomimes and choreographic works; pictorial, graphic, and sculptural works; motion pictures and other audiovisual works; and sound recordings[22].

The legislative history of the 1976 Act makes clear that it was intended to cover everything that had previously been subject to statutory protection, to add some new classes of copyrightable material, and to leave the door open for the courts to expand statutory coverage in step with technological advances.[23]

As the House Report stated: 5–008

Authors are continually finding new ways of expressing themselves, but it is impossible to foresee the forms that these new expressive methods will take. The bill does not intend either to freeze the scope of copyrightable technology or to allow unlimited expansion into areas completely outside the present congressional intent.[24]

The Act maintained the 1971 amendment of the 1909 statute making sound recordings copyrightable subject-matter, but limited protection thereof to the reproduction right, providing no broadcasting or public performance right. It also recognised computer programs and compilations and derivative works as subject-matter of copyright.

Three fundamental criteria for protection are required: originality, authorship and fixation. Thus, copyright subsists in original works of authorship fixed in any tangible medium of expression, now known or later developed, from which they can be perceived, reproduced or

---

[21] Copyright Act 1976, Title 17 US Code, s. 301.
[22] ibid., s.102.
[23] B. Ringer and H. Sandison in S.M. Stewart, op. cit., para.21.05.
[24] House Report, op. cit., above, n.18, at 51.

otherwise communicated, either directly or with the aid of a machine or device. Traditionally, the criterion of originality had a low threshold, protecting works under the "sweat of the brow" doctrine, according to which the investment of labour was sufficient to obtain protection. In 1991, however, the Supreme Court in a landmark decision[25] found that telephone directory white pages did not pass the originality test. It rejected the sweat of the the brow basis for protection and held that a work must display some minimal creativity, finding that "originality is a constitutionally mandated prerequisite for copyright protection ... and the essence of copyright". Thus, for a compilation to be original there must be a minimum of judgment underlying the collection's selection or arrangement of information.

5–009 A major reform was brought about as regards duration of protection, which, in line with the international copyright norm of the Berne Convention, was set at 50 years from the death of the author. The reform had consequential effects on the duration of pre-existing copyrights. Works made for hire, anonymous and pseudonymous works and sound recordings created after January 1, 1978 were protected for 75 years from the date of publication.

Exclusive rights in copyright works comprised the rights to do or authorise reproduction, the preparation of derivative works, distribution of copies of works by sale or by rental, lease or lending, and, in the case of certain works, to perform or display the work publicly.[26] Limitations and exceptions to these rights were spelled out in detail.[27] For the first time, a general statutory provision recognising the venerable doctrine of fair use, developed by the courts since the mid-nineteenth century, was enacted. This permits fair use for purposes such as criticism, comment, news reporting, teaching, scholarship or research and lays down certain factors to be considered in determining whether a certain use is fair.[28] Other limitations on exclusive rights included detailed provisions concerning reproduction by libraries and archives[29]; specific exceptions to public performance rights and

---

[25] *Feist Publications v Rural Telephone Service Co.*, 499 U.S. 340, 111 S. Ct. 1282, 113 L. Ed. 2d 358 (1991). For commentaries on the case see M. Schwarz, "Copyright in Compilations of Facts: Feist Publications, Inc. v. Rural Telephone Service Co., Inc.", [1991] E.I.P.R. 178; P.E. Geller, "Case Note", [1991] 150 R.I.D.A. 99.

[26] Copyright Act 1976, s.106.

[27] *ibid.*, s.s.107–118; for a discussion of the statutory limitations on copyright, see para.5–022 *et seq.*, below.

[28] *ibid.*, s.107 (for a discussion of fair use see also para.5–028 *et seq.*, below).

[29] *ibid.*, s.108.

compulsory licensing in the case of certain cable transmissions, jukebox performances, and non-commercial (i.e. public) broadcasts.[30] The 1909 compulsory licence for mechanical reproduction of music was retained.[31] A Copyright Royalty Tribunal was established to settle disputes concerning all four compulsory licences.[32]

The Supreme Court has recently drawn attention to the fact that two Registers of Copyright have observed that the 1976 revision of the Copyright Act represented "a break with the 200-year-old tradition that has identified copyright more closely with the publisher than with the author." ... The Court noted also that the intent to enhance the author's position *vis-à-vis* the patron was evident from the 1976 Act's work-for-hire provisions. These retained the provision making the employer the author of a work made for hire but defined the term to prevent converting commissioned works into "works made for hire" by agreement save in limited situations. "Congress' adjustment of the author/publisher balance is a permissible expression of the economic philosophy behind the Copyright Clause of the Constitution, *i.e.* 'the conviction that encouragement of individual effort [motivated] by personal gain is the best way to advance public welfare' ".[33] Nevertheless, according to Patterson and Lindberg, "the 1976 Act clearly moves toward resolving the philosophical debate by strongly reflecting the statutory-grant theory of copyright and implicitly rejecting the natural-law property theory". At the same time, in their view, "the 1976 Act comes nearer than any of the prior statutes ... to implementing the constitutional policy of advancing the progress of knowledge by protecting authors".[34]

Post–1976 Act Developments

The 1976 Copyright Act still provides the basic framework for the current copyright law and related laws contained in Title 17 of the United States Code. However, over the last quarter century it has been continuously amended, principally to meet the new treaty

5–010

---

[30] *ibid.*, s.110, s.111, s.116 and s.118.

[31] *ibid.*, s.115(c)(2).

[32] *ibid.*, s.801(b)(1) and (2).

[33] *New York Times Co v Tasini*, 533 U.S. 483(2001), p.9, n.3, quoting *inter alia* B. Ringer, *op. cit.*, n.20, above, and *Mazer v Stein*, 347 U.S. 201, 219 (1954).

[34] L.R. Patterson and S.W. Lindberg, *op. cit.*, n.7, above, at 92 and 99.

obligations resulting from the Berne Convention, the Agreement on Trade-Related Aspects of Intellectual Property (the TRIPs Agreement) 1994, the WIPO Copyright Treaty (WCT) and the WIPO Performers and Phonograms Treaty (WPPT), both adopted in 1996,[35] and to deal with the challenges to copyright posed by digital technology and the internet. Amendments subsequent to the 1976 Act number no less than 48 statutory enactments now contained in Title 17, US Code.[36] This is not the place for a comprehensive overview of all this amending legislation. Of particular relevance to the digital environment and the public interest, however, are the following: the 1988 Berne Convention Implementation Act[37]; the 1990 Visual Artists Rights Act[38]; the 1990 Computer Software Rental Amendments Act[39]; the 1992 Audio Home Recording Act[40]; the 1994 Uruguay Round Agreements Act[41]; the 1995 Digital Performance Right in Sound Recordings Act[42]; the 1998 Sonny Bono Copyright Term Extension Act[43]; the 1998 Fairness in Music Licensing Act[44]; and the 1998 Digital Millenium Copyright Act, which embodied also the WIPO Copyright and Performances and Phonograms Treaties Implementation Act and the Online Copyright Infringement Liability Limitation Act[45].

5–011 **The Berne Convention Implementation Act 1988** paved the way for the US adherence to the Berne Convention on March 1, 1989, "an epochal event"[46] bringing the United States of America into the

---

[35] See Ch.12, below.

[36] Subsequent amendments to the copyright law are listed in chronological order in the preface to the text of Title 17 of the United States Code published by the US Copyright Office on its website: *www.loc.gov/copyright/title_17*. See also J.C. Ginsburg, "Recent Developments in U.S. Copyright Law", [1987] 133 R.I.D.A. 111; "Developments in U.S. Copyright Law Since 1990", [1993] 158 R.I.D.A. 133; and "News from US (I)", [1999] 179 R.I.D.A. 143.

[37] Pub. L. No.100–568, 102 Stat.2853, October 31, 1988. See also J. Ginsburg and J.M. Kernochan, "One Hundred and Two Years Later: the United States Adhere to the Berne Convention", [1989] 141 R.I.D.A. 57.

[38] Pub. L. No.101–650, 104 Stat.5089, 5128, December 1, 1990.

[39] Pub. L. No.101–650, 104 Stat.5089, 5134, December 1, 1990.

[40] Pub. L. No.102–563, 106 Stat.4237, October 28, 1992.

[41] Pub. L. No.103–465, 108 Stat.4809, 4973, December 8, 1994.

[42] Pub. L. No.104–39, 109 Stat.336, November 1, 1995.

[43] Pub. L. No.105–298, 112 Stat.2827, October 27, 1998.

[44] Pub. L. No.105–298, 112 Stat.2827, 2830, October 27, 1998.

[45] Pub. L. No.105–304, 112 Stat.2860, 2887, October 28, 1998.

[46] B. Ringer and H. Sandison in S.M. Stewart, *op. cit.* n.23, above, at 21.01.

major multilateral copyright Convention. Moral rights, which had never gained statutory recognition in the United States of America but which Member States of the Berne Convention are bound to respect, were stated to be provided for "under the confirmation of a great many common law precedents, several state statutes, and federal laws".[47] In 1990, however, Congress enacted the Visual Artists' Rights Act, which affords limited rights of attribution and integrity to a narrowly defined class of visual artists with respect to certain artistic works and photographs. In the same year, the Computer Software Rental Amendments Act was adopted, granting authors or producers of software the right to authorise or prohibit the rental of copies, even after sale.

The Audio Home Recording Act 1992 dealt with the problem of private copying (the non-commercial copying of recordings for personal, domestic use) by digital means. The Act combined a royalty payment system on digital audio recording devices and media for the benefit of copyright owners with the obligation to incorporate a technical control mechanism to prevent unauthorised serial copying of copyright works in digital audio recording and interface devices.[48] The Act also prohibited distribution of devices "the primary purpose or effect of which is to avoid, bypass, remove, deactivate or otherwise circumvent" the "Serial Copy Management System" (SCMS). The Act only tackled digital audio private copying, leaving aside the problem of video private copying and copying by analogue means. The obligation to incorporate technical controls means that any digital audio recording device or audio interface device manufactured, imported or distributed on the US market must be fitted with SCMS, which is a device controlling copying. This system does not prevent copying altogether. It allows individuals to make copies directly from original digital audio recordings; however, no further copies can then be made from those copies, thus preventing what is known as "serial copying". Thus the consumer's right to make copies is preserved, but

5–012

---

[47] *ibid*. at 21.27.

[48] In *Recording Industry Association of America v Diamond Multi-media System Inc.* (180F.3d 1072 (9th Cir. 1999), the court found that the defendant's *Rio* device, a portable MP3 player, was not a "digital audio recording device" under the AHRA and therefore was not subject to the equipment levy. The Rio is a handheld playback device that can store up to 60 minutes of compressed music files downloaded from the internet to a personal computer and then transferred to the Rio's memory (or to a removable memory card which extends its capacity). The Rio cannot itself make further copies.

the proliferation of copies which would displace sales and harm investment is avoided.[49]

Introducing the Act in the US House of Representatives, Congressman William J. Hughes said that it represented a compromise between the interests of "record companies, hardware manufacturers, and musical interests, while protecting the broader public interest".[50]

5–013 **The Uruguay Round Agreements Act (URAA) 1994** implementing the successful outcome to the Uruguay Round of the General Agreement on Tariffs and Trade took effect on January 1, 1996.[51] This included changes in domestic law arising from the TRIPs Agreement, signed on April 15, 1994. The URAA contains several significant amendments to the copyright law. It creates civil and criminal remedies to protect performers against unauthorised fixation and trafficking in sound recordings and music videos of live musical performances (bootlegging). It also provided for copyright in certain foreign works that had fallen into the public domain in the United States of America but not in their country of origin, being a member of the World Trade Organisation or the Berne Convention, to be restored with effect from January 1, 1996.

5–014 **The Digital Performance Rights in Sound Recordings Act (DPRA) 1995**[52] provided owners of copyright in sound recordings, producers and performers, with limited public performance rights in sound recordings. The Act established a statutory licence with respect to subscription service digital transmissions complying with certain limitations and conferred on producers and performers full control over interactive digital transmissions and over other subscription services. The Act is notable for its restricted scope: it does not apply to traditional radio and TV broadcasts, or to background music services such as Muzak. Nor does it apply to music transmitted at public venues, such as restaurants, hotels and night clubs.[53]

---

[49] For further information see G. Davies & M.E. Hung, *Music and Video Private Copying, An International Survey of the Problem and the Law* (London, Sweet & Maxwell, 1993), at 201 *et seq.*

[50] Statement of Congressman W.J. Hughes on the floor of the US House of Representatives on H.R.3204, The Audio Home Recording Act of 1992, September 22, 1992. The Act came into force on October 28, 1992.

[51] P.L. No.103–465, 108 Stat.4809 of December 8, 1994.

[52] S 227, P.L. No.104–39, of November 1, 1995.

[53] This Act was the result of a compromise hammered out in smoke-filled rooms by the interested parties. Evidence for this statement can be found in *BNA's Patent, Trademark & Copyright Journal, Vol. 51, 1995*, at 46: "The creation of a sound recording performance right was proposed in the last Congress ... but was stalled by a clash

1998 saw the adoption of several important new and controversial **5–015**
copyright statutes: **The Sonny Bono Copyright Term Extension
Act**, extending by an additional twenty years the term of protection
for existing copyright works, including works made for hire; **The
Fairness in Music Licensing Act**, exempting certain restaurants and
other retail establishments from the requirement of paying royalties
for the use of music to the performing rights societies; and, finally,
The Digital Millenium Copyright Act, the main goal of which
was to make the necessary changes to the US copyright law to enable
the United States of America to ratify the WCT and WPPT and to
update the law to meet the needs of the Internet era.

These new provisions resulted from a legislative process set in train
following the recommendations of the Working Group on Intellectual Property Rights of the National Information Infrastructure Task
Force in order to adapt the law of copyright to the digital, networked
environment of the National Information Infrastructure (NII). The
rationale for the changes remain of particular interest.[54] The role of
the Working Group was to examine the intellectual property implications of the NII and make recommendations on any appropriate
changes to US intellectual property law and policy.[55] The Group
envisaged that the NII of the future will be an advanced high-speed,
interactive, broadband, digital communications system connected up
to a Global Information Infrastructure (GII) that will allow the world
to share information, to connect, and to communicate as a global
community.[56] The Working Group's conclusions may be summarised
as follows: the NII represents significant changes in technology that
upset the balance that currently exists under the Copyright Act; its
goal therefore is to accommodate and adapt the law to technological
change so that the intended balance is maintained and the Constitutional purpose is served.[57]

> Copyright protection is not an obstacle in the way of the success of
> the NII; it is an essential component. Effective copyright protec-

---

between the recording and publishing industries ... An industry accord was finally
reached in June and incorporated into the Senate bill...".

[54] *Report of the Working Group on Intellectual Property Rights (NII Report)*, B.A. Lehman, Assistant Secretary of Commerce and Commissioner of Patents and Trademarks,
Chair, Washington, September 1995.

[55] *ibid.* at 2.

[56] *ibid.* at 8.

[57] *ibid.* at 212.

tion is a fundamental way to promote the availability of works to the public.[58]

...weakening copyright owners' rights in the NII is not in the public interest; nor would a dramatic increase in their rights be justified.

With no more than minor clarification and limited amendment, the Copyright Act will provide the necessary balance of protection of rights—and limitations on those rights—to promote the progress of science and the useful arts. Existing copyright law needs only the fine tuning that technological advances necessitate, in order to maintain the balance of the law in the face of onrushing technology.[59]

5–016 **The Sonny Bono Copyright Term Extension Act 1998** had the aim of bringing the period of protection in the United States of America into line with other countries, in particular, the Member States of the European Union, which, following the adoption in 1993 of a Directive establishing an EU-wide copyright term, already provided for a term of protection of 70 years *post mortem auctoris* (*pma*)[60]. For works made for hire, the term was extended from 75 to 95 years from first publication or 120 years from the year of creation, whichever expires first. For pre-1978 works still in their original or renewal term of copyright, the total term was extended to 95 years from the date that copyright was originally secured. The extension of term was considered necessary to avoid discrimination against US works abroad, since, according to the Berne Convention and the Universal Copyright Convention,[61] Contracting States with longer periods of protection may limit protection of foreign works to the shorter period of protection prevailing in the country of origin of a work; thus, without the extension, US works could end up being afforded less protection abroad than their foreign counterparts. The main justification for the extension was therefore the need to harmonise US law with the European Union standard. It was also argued

---

[58] *ibid.* at 16.

[59] *ibid.* at 17.

[60] Directive 93/83/EEC Harmonising the Term of Protection of Copyright and Certain Related Rights, October 29, 1993. Member States were required to implement the Directive by July 1, 1995.

[61] Berne Convention, Art.7(8); UCC, Art.IV(4).

that the extension would provide further economic incentives to stimulate creativity.

> The additional value of a longer term will, therefore, be reflected in the money received by the author for the transfer of her copyright, leading again to increased incentives to create ... Extended protection for existing works will provide added income with which to subsidize the creation of new works. This is particularly important in the case of corporate copyright owners, such as motion picture studios and publishers...[62]

The extension of term has been met with a chorus of disapproval from US and foreign commentators, culminating in a constitutional challenge to the Sonny Bono Term Extension Act before the Supreme Court.[63] These issues are discussed below in the section "The Public Interest and Limitations on Copyright, Term of Protection".

The Fairness in Music Licensing Act 1998 was included in Title II   5–017
of the same Act. This provided a new statutory exemption for a broad range of restaurants and other retail establishments from the requirement to pay licensing fees to the performing rights societies for the public performance of non-dramatic musical works by means of radio and TV transmissions. This Act proved also to be controversial. The European Union, prompted by the Irish Performing Rights Society, took action against the United States for non-compliance with its obligations under Article 13 of the TRIPs Agreement before the WTO Dispute Resolution Panels. The complaint was that the exceptions did not "confine limitations or exceptions to exclusive rights to certain special cases which do not conflict with the normal exploitation of the work and do not unreasonably prejudice the legitimate interests of the right holder" and did not therefore meet the three-step test of Article

---

[62] Senate Judiciary Committee Report, S. Rep. No.104–315, 104th Cong. 2d Sess. (1996).

[63] The Supreme Court granted certiorari in the case *Eldred v Ashcroft* on February 19, 2002 (U.S. SupCt, No.01–618. On this subject, see Ch.10, below, and *inter alia*: Hon. Hank Brown and David Miller, "Copyright Term Extension: Sapping American Creativity", [1996] 44 Journal, Copyright Soc. of the USA, 94 at 99, quoting the decision in *Sony Corp. v Universal City Studios, Inc.*, 464 U.S. 417, 429 (1984); P. Alberstat, "Copyright Extension in the United States: The Mouse that Roared", [1999] ENT.L.R., 61; J.C. Ginsberg, "The Last Ten Years in US Copyright: Overreaching or Reaching Out?", paper presented at Fordham University School of Law, 10th Annual International Intellectual Property Conference, New York, April 4–5, 2002.

9(2) of the Berne Convention, incorporated by reference in the TRIPs Agreement.[64] The World Trade Organisation Dispute Resolution Panel found for the European Union and the United States was asked to remedy the violation by July 27, 2001.[65]

5–018　**The Digital Millenium Copyright Act** (DMCA), signed into law in October 1998,[66] is undoubtedly the most important and far-reaching legislation to be adopted since the 1976 Act. The immediate objectives of the Act were to implement US treaty obligations resulting from the WCT and WPPT 1996, "to move the nation's copyright law into the digital age"[67] and to facilitate the robust development and world-wide expansion of electronic commerce, communications, research, development, and education in the digital age.[68] According to the Register of Copyrights, "the congressional determination to promote electronic commerce and the distribution of digital works by providing copyright owners with legal tools to prevent widespread piracy was tempered with concern for main-taining the integrity of the statutory limitations on the exclusive rights of copyright owners".[69] Thus, the DMCA establishes both new rights and some new statutory exemptions, while seeking to preserve the right of fair use.

The DMCA comprises five titles, of which four are relevant here. Title I implements the WIPO treaties; Title II creates limitations on the liability of online service providers for copyright infringement under certain circumstances; Title III creates an exception for making

---

[64] WTO Panel Report (WT/DS160/R), June 15, 2000. See also J.C. Ginsburg, "Toward Supranational Copyright Law? The WTO Panel Decision and the "Three-Step Test" for Copyright Exceptions", [2001] 187 R.I.D.A. 3; B.C. Goldmann, "Victory for Songwriters in WTO Music-Royalties Dispute Between U.S. and EU", [2001] 4 IIC 412. See also Ch.10, below, on the "Three-Step Test"; and Y. Gaubiac, "Les exceptions au droit d'auteur: un nouvel avenir", [2001] 6 *Communication Commerce Electronique*, 12.

[65] This deadline was not met, nor has legislation to amend the law been introduced to date. In October 2001, arbitrators appointed by the WTO ruled that the financial losses incurred by the EU copyright owners as a result of The Fairness in Music Licensing Act was €1,219,000 ($1.1 m.) per year. The USA has agreed to pay this amount for a period of three years pending amendment of the US copyright law.

[66] Pub. L. No.105–304, 112 Stat.2860, October 28, 1998.

[67] Executive Summary, Digital Millenium Copyright Act, Section 104 Report, p.1.

[68] Report of the Committee, US Senate, 105th. Congress, 2d. Session, May 11, 1998, p.1.

[69] Statement of Marybeth Peters, Register of Copyrights, before the Subcommittee on Courts, the Internet, and Intellectual Property, of the Committee on the Judiciary, US House of Representatives, 107th Congress, 1st session, December 12–13, 2001.

a copy of a computer program by activating a computer for purposes of maintenance or repair; Title IV contains six miscellaneous provisions relating to: the functions of the Copyright Office; distance education; the exceptions in the Copyright Act for libraries and for making ephemeral recordings; "webcasting" of sound recordings on the internet; and the applicability of collective bargaining obligations in the case of transfers of rights in motion pictures.[70]

Title I creates two new copyright prohibitions; one prohibits circumvention of technological measures used by copyright owners to protect their works and the other tampering with copyright management information. These obligations provide legal protection deemed critical to the safe and efficient exploitation of works on digital networks. The prohibition on tampering with copyright management information promotes reliable information, thus facilitating e-commerce and is clearly in the interests of both right owners and the general public.

Technological measures are divided into two categories: measures that prevent unauthorised *access* to a copyright work[71] and measures that prevent unauthorised *copying* of a work, once access has been lawfully obtained. Making or selling devices, such as black box de-scramblers, or services used to circumvent either category of technological measure is prohibited also in certain circumstances: if the device was primarily designed to circumvent access controls, or has only limited commercially significant purpose or use other than to circumvent; and is marketed as a circumvention device. **5–019**

As to the act of circumvention, circumventing the first category of technological measures controlling access to a work is prohibited, but not the second, controlling copying. This distinction was employed to give the public the continued ability to make fair use of copyright works by copying in appropriate circumstances.[72] There is a funda-

---

[70] For detailed analyses of the DMCA, see "The Digital Millenium Copyright Act of 1998", US Copyright Office Summary, December 1998. See also J.C. Ginsburg, "News from US(I)", [1999] 179 R.I.D.A. 143.

[71] The prohibition on the act of circumvention of access control measures did not come into force until October 28, 2000. See J.C. Ginsburg, "From Having Copies to Experiencing Works: the Development of an Access Right in U.S. Copyright Law", in *U.S. Intellectual Property: Law and Policy*, H. Hanson, ed., (Sweet and Maxwell, London, 2000).

[72] As regards copying, note that s.1201(k) mandates that all analogue videocassette recorders must be designed to conform to certain defined technologies, commonly known as Macrovision, currently in use for preventing unauthorised copying of analogue videocassettes and certain analogue signals.

mental issue here. If access to works is controlled in the digital environment and they are copy-protected by technological means, fair use would normally not come into play until after access to the work has been obtained. Otherwise, the copyright owner of an exclusive reproduction right would be obliged to make the work available in a copiable format to facilitate fair use. In such a case, the purpose of the copy-protection technology would be defeated. It is suggested that on this point Ginsburg must be right when she asserts: "In the past, if low technology imposed a tolerance for widespread copying, that state of affairs should not be confused with a legal *right* to engage in widespread convenience copying".[73]

5–020   There are a number of exemptions from prohibition on circumvention of technological measures that control access to copyrighted works. The broadest such exemption establishes an ongoing administrative rule-making procedure to evaluate the impact on the exercise of fair use of the prohibition against the act of circumventing such access-control measures[74]. There are six additional exceptions, which appear to be responses to interest-group lobbying rather than principle: non-profit libraries, archives and educational institutions are permitted to circumvent solely for the purpose of making a good faith determination as to whether they wish to obtain authorised access to a work; circumvention to enable reverse engineering of computer programs to achieve permitted operability with other programs; circumvention in order to identify flaws and vulnerability of encryption technologies; and circumvention in situations concerning the protection of minors, personal privacy and authorised security testing. Title I also provides for civil remedies and criminal penalties for violation of the prohibitions. These provisions are discussed in greater detail in Chapter 12, below.

---

[73] J.C. Ginsburg, "News from US (I)", *op. cit.* n.70, above, at 205. The Court of Appeal in *Universal City Studios v Corley,* 273 F.3d 429 (2d. Cir. 2001) addressed this point directly, stating that fair use does not guarantee copying by the optimum method or in the identical format of the original (see also para.5–034, below).

[74] Pursuant to this procedure, two classes of works have been announced by the Librarian of Congress to be subject to the exemption: compilations consisting of lists of websites blocked by filtering software applications; and literary works, including computer programs and databases, protected by access control mechanisms that fail to permit access because of malfunction, damage or obsolescence. Recommendation of the Register of Copyright and Determination of the Librarian of Congress, 65 FR 64555, October 27, 2000.

To comply with the WCT and WPPT, restoration of copyright protection is ensured in respect of works from WCT and WPPT member countries that are still protected in the country of origin, but fell into the public domain in the United States in the past because of a failure to comply with formalities that then existed in US law, or due to a lack of treaty relations.

The DCMA also creates four new limitations on liability for copyright infringement by online service providers, covering: transitory communications, where the provider merely acts as a data conduit, transmitting digital information from one point on a network to another at someone else's request; system caching, *i.e.* retaining copies, for a limited time, of material made available online by a person other than the provider, and then transmitted to a subscriber; storage of information including infringing material on systems or networks at direction of users, subject to certain conditions; and information location tools such as hyperlinks, online directories, search engines and the like; in this case, liability is limited for the acts of referring or linking users to a site containing infringing material using such tools. Each limitation entails a complete bar on monetary damages, and restricts the availability of injunctive relief in various respects. A party seeking the benefits of the limitations must qualify as a service provider and meet two overall conditions: (1) it must adopt and reasonably implement a policy of terminating in appropriate circumstances the accounts of subscribers who are repeat infringers; and, (2) it must accommodate and not interfere with standard technical measures. Such measures are defined as measures that copyright owners use to identify or protect copyright works, that have been developed pursuant to a broad consensus of copyright owners and service providers in an open, fair and voluntary multi-industry process, are available to anyone on reasonably non-discriminatory terms, and do not impose substantial costs or burdens on service providers.

The DMCA also expands the previous exemption for "ephemeral recordings" made by broadcasters to cover digital audio services that pay royalties for public performances under a statutory licence. In addition, a statutory licence is created to allow a webcaster to make more than one ephemeral copy.[75]

Furthermore, the DMCA amends the Digital Performance Right in Sound Recordings Act 1995 to provide for licensing of sound recordings for webcasters and other digital audio services. A new **5–021**

---

[75] DMCA, s.402, amending s.112, Copyright Act 1976.

statutory licence has been created for public performances by certain non-interactive, non-subscription digital audio services.[76] Copyright owners retain control over interactive, on-demand delivery of sound recordings. The statutory licence only applies to services with the primary purpose of providing audio or other entertainment programming and not the sale or promotion of products. The royalty rates are to be set at fair market value by arbitration panels, subject to review by the Copyright Office.

As the above survey illustrates, the past 10 years have seen unprecedented activity on the legislative front in the United States of America. Much of this, as Ginsburg has noted:

> appropriately reaches out to address new problems prompted by new technologies, so as to strike a happier balance of copyright owner, intermediary, and end-user interests, so that our legal system may continue to afford a hospitable environment for the creation and dissemination of works of authorship, to the ultimate enrichment of the public.[77]

In the development of the law, Congress has borne a heavy responsibility in dealing with the load of copyright legislation and endeavoring to maintain the delicate balance between the competing interests of various right owners, users and those of the public. During the 1990s, there was an increasing tendency in Congress to refer contentious issues "to off-the-record negotiations among interested parties" to develop a compromise they can all support.[78] This represents an abdication of responsibility. Congress should be a leader in the development of intellectual property policy and not merely a reactive force, encouraging parties to resolve their differences and

---

[76] DMCA, s.405, amending the DPRA 1995.

[77] J.C. Ginsburg, "The Last Ten Years in U.S. Copyright: Overreaching or Reaching Out?" *op. cit.*, p.1.

[78] See above nn.50 and 53. This occurred with respect to the music licensing bill S 1628, since overtaken by the Fairness in Music Licensing Act 1998, which when introduced in the Senate "was offered as a compromise measure, worked out through hours of negotiations with the interested parties". See BNA's Patent, Trademark & Copyright Journal, Vol.51, No.1271 of March 28, 1996. The same happened over the adoption of the fair use bill H R 4263 in 1992 (P.L.102–492, 106 Stat.3145, 102d. Cong. 2d. sess. (1992). See comment by J. Litman, "Copyright and Information Policy", (1992) 55 Law and Contemporary Problems, p.185 at 196. See also T.P. Olson, "The Iron Law of Consensus: Congressional Responses to Proposed Copyright Reforms since the 1909 Act", (1989) 36 Journal, Copyright Soc. of the USA, p.109.

then codifying the off-the-hill agreement. To react only:

> is an abdication of Congress's constitutional responsibility. If Congress fails to act in the face of changing circumstances, it lets others decide by default how the constitutional goal of promoting the progress of science should be achieved ... Our responsibility is first and foremost to make *policy*: policies, which in our judgement will best further the Article 1 [of the Constitution] goal.[79]

The Public Interest and Limitations on Copyright

The public interest, as we have seen, has played a determining role **5–022** and continues to do so in the justification for copyright protection in the USA and in determining the subject-matter of such protection. This emphasis on taking the public interest into account may be said to have played a positive role in striking the balance between authors and other right owners and the general public. In particular, it has also had an important impact on the duration of protection afforded to right owners and on the exceptions permitted under US copyright law by means of the application of the doctrine of fair use and pursuant to specific statutory limitations in the Copyright Act itself.

Term of Protection

The copyright clause of the Constitution empowered Congress to **5–023** legislate to secure authors an exclusive right "for limited times". As Nimmer notes: "This phrase creates a very real limitation upon Congressional power ..." and "seems to represent an attempt to strike a balance between two competing interests: the interest of authors in the fruits of their labour on the one hand, and on the other, the interest of the public in ultimately claiming free access to the materials essential to the development of society".[80]

There could be no question in the USA of a perpetual copyright because it would be unconstitutional. Congress, nevertheless, has to

---

[79] Speech of Rep. W. Hughes (D-NJ) to Copyright Society of the USA, October 7, 1993.
[80] M.B. Nimmer, *op. cit.*, n.9, above, para.1.05.

date had an unfettered discretion when it comes to fixing the term.

As we have seen, the 1790 Act originally followed the Statute of Anne on duration, providing for a term of 14 years from registration of the title prior to publication; this term was renewable by the author, if still alive, for a further 14 years. When in 1831 the original term was lengthened to 28 years, the purpose of the amendment was said to be "to enlarge the period for the enjoyment of copyright, and thereby to place authors in this country more nearly upon an equality with authors of other countries".[81]

In 1909, the starting point of the period of protection was changed so that it was measured from the date of publication; the renewal period was also extended to 28 years, bringing the total possible term of protection to 56 years. The 1909 Act remained in force and the period of protection unchanged until January 1, 1978 although, throughout the intervening period, numerous bills were introduced to Congress which included proposals to change the period of protection.

5–024 According to a study on the duration of copyright prepared for a Congressional Committee and published in 1961,[82] in the various proposals put forward in these bills:

> Generally speaking, the individual creators and their publishers supported a longer term and favored the life of the author plus 50 years, although they were willing to agree to a term of 60 or 56 years from creation or publication if some of their other aims could be achieved. ... On the other side, favoring no extension of the term were such users as radio broadcasters and record manufacturers.

The same study considered the length of the term in the light of the limitation imposed on Congress by the copyright clause in the Constitution and stated that:

> The basic consideration, therefore, is to determine what duration of limited time will best promote the progress of science and useful arts.

---

[81] Report of the Committee on the Judiciary of the House of Representatives, 7 Register of Debates, Appendix CXIX.

[82] Study 30—Duration of Copyright, prepared for the Subcommittee on Patents, Trade Marks and Copyrights of the Committee on the Judiciary, US Senate, 86th Congress, 2nd ed., Washington 1961.

The term should be long enough to provide an incentive for the author, *i.e.*, to encourage him to create by giving him the assurance that, if successful, his economic reward will be adequate. ... It is not only the author who must be considered but also the members of his immediate family whom he may be obliged to support. Further, it is to the author's advantage and to the advantage of the public, to provide an adequate term of protection to make it commercially feasible for publishers and other distributors to aid him in exploiting his work. The period of protection should be sufficient to provide an adequate economic return to all of these interests, if it is true, as seems to be assumed in the Constitution, that it is to the benefit of the public to promote the creation and dissemination of intellectual works.

That statement reflects the principles of one of Professor Chafee's proposed six ideals of copyright law,[83] according to which the term of protection should not exceed the purpose of protection. As the study pointed out:

The theory of the Constitution seems to be that after a period of protection sufficient to provide incentive by assuring to the successful authors and distributors an economic return adequate to take care of their legitimate interests, it is to the benefit of the public to have the work fall into the public domain.[84]

The basic term decided on in the 1976 Act, namely the life of the **5–025** author plus 50 years, calculated from the "creation" of the work, brought the United States of America into line with the international standard of the Berne Convention and raised no problems with regard to the "limited times" proviso. This reform represented a major departure from the US tradition. The arguments for the change put forward by the House Committee Report in 1976 may be summarised as follows:

(1) The 56-year term under the 1909 Act was not long enough to ensure an author and his dependents the fair economic benefits from his works. Life expectancy had increased substantially.

---

[83] Z. Chafee Jr., "Reflexions on the Law of Copyright", I & II, [1945] 45 *Columbia Law Rev.* 503 and 719.
[84] Study 30, *op. cit.*, n.82, above, at 80.

(2) The tremendous growth in communications media has substantially lengthened the commercial life of a great many works.

(3) Too short a term harms the author without giving any substantial benefit to the public. The public frequently pays the same for works in the public domain as it does for copyrighted works, and the only result is a commercial windfall to certain users.

(4) A system based on the life of the author would provide a clearer method of computing term than a system based on "publication".

(5) The burden and expense of the renewal procedure would be removed.

(6) The perpetual, unlimited common law rights in unpublished works were to be abolished; the statutory term of 50 years p.m.a. would represent a fair recompense for that loss.

(7) The need for the USA to conform with a generally recognised world standard.[85]

The House Report concluded that "the advantages of a basic term of copyright enduring for the life of the author and for 50 years after the author's death outweigh any possible disadvantages".[86]

The reform also satisfied Chafee's test; for him 50 years p.m.a. had four merits. It satisfies the ideal of international protection; with the abandonment of formalities, publication ceases to be a good starting-point for the copyright period; it comes closer to the ideal of just protection—the author's life is a natural measure to which the lives of his children are related; it ceases at one and the same time for the whole of an author's life work.[87]

5–026 Meanwhile, as discussed above, the Sonny Bono Copyright Term Extension Act 1998 has lengthened the term of copyright protection to life plus 70 years for individual authors and to 95 years for authors with legal personality and works made for hire. Prior to the adoption of the extension, the US Copyright Office held hearings and more

---

[85] House of Representatives Report, *op. cit.* n.18, above, at 134.
[86] *ibid.* at 136.
[87] Z. Chafee, *op. cit.* at 731.

than one bill was introduced in Congress.[88] The extension when proposed was a response to the adoption in the European Union of the EC Directive harmonising the term of protection of copyright and certain related rights; this set the term of protection for individual authors at life plus 70 years. The Directive, adopted in 1993 had to be implemented in the Member States by July 1, 1995. The primary rationale for the Sonny Bono Act extension was therefore to bring US law into line with the standard of the European Union and to avoid US creators having 20 years less protection than their European counterparts, 20 years when Europeans would not be paying for the use of US copyright works. It was argued that this situation would be unfair to authors and harmful economically to the country. The United States of America exports many works to the European Union and, it was argued, had an important commercial interest to advance by extending the copyright term.

The proposal to extend the term of protection had mixed reactions from the start. Opponents argued that it would benefit corporate copyright owners rather than individual authors and the public, and would threaten access to and preservation of works that would otherwise fall into the public domain. A cogent adverse comment on the proposal from a group of professors of law at US law schools, questioned the justification for the proposed extension and suggested that its proponents had not presented any evidence to show that the public interest in such an extended term outweighed its costs. They pointed out:

> We do not recognise new intellectual property rights, or strengthen old ones, simply because it appears that a worthy person may benefit; rather we do so only for a public purpose and where it appears that there will be a public benefit ... the Copyright Act of 1976 is itself the product of lengthy debate and represents innumerable compromises that seek to achieve the proper balance between private returns to authors and public benefit, including a broad public domain ... A natural corollary is that this delicate balance can easily be upset by a series of *ad hoc* changes.[89]

---

[88] Term extension bills HR 989 and S 483. These bills died with the adjournment of the 104th Congress in October 1996.

[89] D.S. Karjala, *et al.*, "Comment of US Copyright Law Professors on the Copyright Office Term of Protection Study", [1994] 12 EIPR 531.

The professors also rejected the idea that the United States should follow the European lead: "that should not cause us to change our underlying intellectual property philosophy, nor does it provide a reason for avoiding the careful cost/benefit analysis called for by that philosophy . . . The United States should be leading the world toward a coherent intellectual property policy for the digital age and not simply following what takes place in Europe."[90]

5–027 Now that the proposal has become law, as already mentioned above, the constitutionality of the extension has been challenged and the Supreme Court has granted certiorari and will consider the case in the near future.[91] It is argued that the constitutional power respecting copyright charges Congress to strike a balance between creators and the public benefit and that the extension imposes substantial costs on the general public without supplying any such public benefit. Moreover, under the constitutional power to enact copyright legislation, rights may only be secured for limited times; 70 years pma or 95 years from publication cannot be considered limited.

The Constitution erects at least three boundaries around copyright policy: first, the duration of the copyright term must be "limited"; secondly, Congress must secure the right to authors; thirdly, the copyright policy must promote the "useful arts". In 1984, the Supreme Court highlighted this special charge when it noted that, "as the text of the Constitution makes plain, it is congress that has been assigned the task of defining the scope of the limited monopoly that should be granted to authors or to inventors in order to give the public appropriate access to their work product". Congress may fail that task by passing copyright term extension since it seems to run afoul of all three constitutional limitations on copyright policy.[92]

Commentators take the view that the new terms cannot be considered "limited" times and that to meet that criterion any term should comply with international norms; it is argued that the 70 years pma of the European Union does not represent an international norm, unlike the Berne Convention or the TRIPs Agreement, both of which set a term of 50 years pma for authors' rights. It is also objected that the extended terms do not benefit authors, as such, but copyright

---

[90] *ibid.* at 532.

[91] See n.63, above.

[92] The Hon. H. Brown and D. Miller, "Copyright Term Extension: Sapping American Creativity", [1996] 44 *Journal of the Cop. Soc. of the USA*, 94, quoting from the decision in *Sony Corp. v Universal City Studios, Inc.*, 464 U.S. 417, 429 (1984).

owners who have acquired the rights. In the case of films, which are of particular commercial importance to the United States, the 20-year extension to 95 years from publication may yield an extra 20 years in the European Union, but the EU term will normally be still longer because it is calculated as 70 years from the death of the last surviving co-author of the film. Moreover, it is suggested that the extension cannot represent a meaningful incentive for future creation for an author embarking on a new work. Finally, it is pointed out that it is against the public interest to deprive the public of access to works for an additional 20 years, limiting the public domain, and that the increased term of protection is anti-competitive and will make works more expensive during that period. The overall result in the long run may be to weaken copyright:

One may fear that "user rights" advocates will contend, and courts will agree, that copyright now endures for so long a time, that the subsisting (and excessive) period of exclusivity must be tempered by more vigorous exceptions to copyright protection. The cost of delaying the public domain therefore may be to compromise the scope and force of copyright coverage throughout the term of protection.[93]

Fair Use

The doctrine of fair use

Since the mid-nineteenth century, the fair use defence has represented **5–028** the most frequently invoked defence to actions for infringement of copyright. "From the infancy of copyright protection, some opportunity for fair use of copyrighted materials has been thought necessary to fulfil copyright's very purpose, 'to promote the Progress of Science and useful Arts ...' ".[94] The Supreme Court in 1985 stated that fair use was traditionally defined as "a privilege in others than the owner of the copyright to use the copyrighted material in a reasonable manner without his consent, "and that the statutory formulation of the defence of fair use in the Copyright Act 1976 reflects the intent of Congress to codify the common-law doctrine".[95]

---

[93] J.C. Ginsburg, "News from US (I), *op. cit.*, n.70 above, at 279.
[94] *Campbell and Acuff-Rose Music, Inc.*, 510 U.S. 569 (1994) at 575.
[95] *Harper & Row Publishers Inc. v Nation Enterprises*, 225 USPQ 1073 (1985) at 1076. See also H. Ball, *The Law of Copyright and Literary Property*, Albany, N.Y., Banks, 1944, at 260.

The earliest judicial recognition of the doctrine of fair use was given by Justice Story in a decision of 1841 in a case concerning the letters of President George Washington:

> The question, then, is, whether this is a justifiable use of the original materials, such as the law recognizes as no infringement of the copyright of the plaintiffs. ... It is certainly not necessary, to constitute an invasion of copyright, that the whole of a work should be copied, or even a large portion of it, in form or in substance. If so much is taken, that the value of the original is sensibly diminished, or the labors of the original author are substantially to an injurious extent appropriated by another, that is sufficient, in point of law, to constitute a piracy pro tanto. ... In short, we must often, in deciding questions of this sort, look to the nature and objects of the selections made, the quantity and value of the materials used, and the degree in which the use may prejudice the sale, or diminish the profits or supersede the objects, of the original work.[96]

Expanding on the rationale for fair use, Justice Story some years later explained, "in truth, in literature, in science and in art, there are, and can be, few, if any, things, which in an abstract sense, are strictly new and original throughout. Every book in literature, science and art, borrows, and must necessarily borrow, and use much which was well known and used before.[97]

5–029   For over a century, the Courts developed this theory, excusing certain otherwise infringing acts on the ground of fair use. The common-law doctrine was not codified until the Copyright Act 1976. However, the House Report on the 1976 Act made it clear that the intention of the legislature was not to change the doctrine as it had evolved over the years. Stating that, "the endless variety of situations and combinations of circumstances that can arise in particular cases precludes the formulation of exact rules in the statute", the report emphasised: "Section 107 is intended to restate the present judicial doctrine of fair use, not to change, narrow, or enlarge it in any way".[98] Furthermore,

---

[96] *Folsom v Marsh*, 9F Cas. 342, at 348.
[97] *Emerson v Davies*, 8 F. Cas. 615, 619 (No.4,436) (CCD Mass. 1845).
[98] House of Representatives Report No.94, at 66.

the statute left the Courts freedom to consider additional factors[99] and provided no guidance as to the relative weight to be given to each of the factors.

Section 107 of the 1976 Copyright Act lays down the principle that "the fair use of a copyrighted work ... for purposes such as criticism, comment, news reporting, teaching (including multiple copies for classroom use), scholarship, or research, is not an infringement of copyright". It then gives a non-exhaustive list of four factors which the Courts should take into account in determining whether the use made of a work in any particular case is fair. These are:

(1) the purpose and character of the use, including whether such use is of a commercial nature or is for non-profit educational purposes;

(2) the nature of the copyrighted work;

(3) the amount and substantiality of the portion used in relation to the copyrighted work as a whole; and

(4) the effect of the use upon the potential market for or value of the copyrighted work.

The Supreme Court in 1994 stated that the statutory examples of permissible uses provide only general guidance. The four statutory factors are not meant to be exclusive and are to be explored and weighed together in the light of copyright's purpose of promoting science and the useful arts.[1]

The law was amended in 1991 to make it clear that the fact that a **5–030** work is unpublished shall not itself bar a finding of fair use, if such finding is made upon consideration of all the above factors.[2]

According to Ball, "The author's consent to a reasonable use of his copyrighted works had always been implied by the courts as a necessary incident of the constitutional policy of promoting the progress of science and the useful arts".[3]

For Goldstein, "Section 107 and its decisional and legislative his-

---

[99] *DC Comics, Inc. v Unlimited Monkey Business, Inc*, 598 F Supp. 110, 224 U.S.P.Q. (N.D. Ga.1984).

[1] *Campbell v Acuff-Rose Music, Inc.*, 510 U.S. 569 (1994). See also J.C. Ginsburg, Case note [1994] 162 R.I.D.A. 349.

[2] P.L. 102–492, 106 Stat. 3145, 102d. Cong. 2d. Sess. (1992).

[3] H. Ball, *loc. cit.*, n.95, above.

tory leave no doubt that the object of the fair use defense is to confirm, not contradict, copyright law's basic goal—to put copyrighted works to their most beneficial use so that 'the public good fully coincides ... with the claims of individuals' ".[4]

The fair use doctrine has also been described as having "evolved to guard against the possibility that the author's right of control over his works could defeat rather than serve the public interest in dissemination."[5]

5–031 The factors enumerated in section 107, were based on criteria evolved from case law. Nimmer cites the following as a typical example of factors taken account of by the courts:

> Fair use is to be determined by a consideration of all of the evidence, and among other elements entering into the determination of the issue, are the extent and relative value of copyrighted material, and the effect upon the distribution of objects of the original work. Whether a particular use of a copyrighted article, without permission of the owner, is a fair use, depends upon the circumstances of the particular case, and the court must look to the nature and objects of the selections made, the quantity and value of material used, and the degree in which the use may prejudice the sale, diminish the profits, or supersede the objects of the original work ... fair use is to be determined by a consideration of all the evidence in the case....[6]

Goldstein states that Congress and the courts have reconciled the public good with the claims of individuals through two, overlapping, approaches to the fair use doctrine. These approaches he describes as a private benefit approach and a public benefit approach. The former excuses uses that the copyright owner would have licensed but for insurmountable transaction costs. The latter excuses the use, even in the absence of transaction costs, "if the social benefit of the use outweighs the loss to the copyright owner".[7] The private benefit approach to fair use allows use that would have been made under

---

[4] P. Goldstein, *op. cit.*, para.10.1.

[5] W. Gordon, "Fair Use as Market Failure: A Structural and Economic Analysis of the *Betamax* Case and its Predecessors", [1982] 82 Colum. L. Rev. 1600.

[6] M.B. Nimmer, *op. cit.* para.13–102.9, citing *Mathews Conveyor Co. v Palmer-Bee Co.*, 135 F 2d 73, 85 (6th Cir. 1943).

[7] P. Goldstein, *op. cit.*, para.10.1.2.

licence if transaction costs (costs of user in searching out and nego-tiating a licence with the copyright owner) had not precluded licence negotiations; in other words where there has been market failure. This approach requires also that the benefits conferred by the use will exceed the losses its use will inflict on the copyright owner.

However, as the Supreme Court noted in *Harper v Row*: "It is fundamentally at odds with the scheme of copyright to accord lesser rights in those works that are of greatest importance to the public. Such a notion ignores the major premise of copyright and injures author and public alike."[8] For the public benefit approach to allow fair use an overriding public need must be conclusively demon-strated.[9] But

> where a claim of fair use is made, a balance must sometimes be struck between the benefit the public will derive if the use is permitted and the personal gain the copyright owner will receive if the use is denied. The less the adverse effect that an alleged infringing use has on the copyright owner's expectation of gain, the less public benefit needs to be shown to justify the use.[10]

Major Developments in Fair Use Case Law Since the 1976 Act

Fair use has been the subject of a number of important decisions **5–032** interpreting the four factors which the Courts have to take into account in deciding whether a particular use is fair. Some of these cases have concerned new uses made possible by new technology.[11]

In the first of these, the *Sony*[12] decision of 1984, the Supreme Court held by a majority that home taping off-air for time-shifting purposes of broadcast television programmes was fair use. It took the view that the sale of copying equipment such as video cassette recorders did not constitute contributory infringement, if the equip-ment was capable of substantial, commercially significant, non-

---

[8] *Harper v Row*, above n.95, at 1080.
[9] Supplementary Report of the Register of Copyright on the General Revision of the US Copyright Law, 89th Congress, 1st session, May 1965, at 27–28.
[10] *MCA Inc. v Wilson*, 677 F 2d 180, 211 U.S.P.Q. 577 (2d Cir. 1981).
[11] See also, R.L. Zissu, "Fair Use: From Harper and Row to Acuff Rose", [1994] 42, 1 Journal, Copyright Soc. of the USA, 7.
[12] *Sony Corp. of America v. Universal City Studios, Inc.*, 464 U.S. 417, 104 S.Ct. 774, 78 L. Ed. 2d 574 (1984).

infringing uses; in its opinion, time shifting for private use in the home was plainly a substantial non-commercial use and even when unauthorised constituted legitimate fair use. Thus, regarding the first factor, the purpose and character of the use, it found time shifting to be non-commercial. As regards the fourth factor, the Court recognised that private copying might infringe the copyright owner's rights in some circumstances but considered time shifting to be a use that "had no demonstrable effect upon the potential market for or value of the copyrighted work". The case appeared to set an important precedent, characterising non-commercial, home copying as fair use, a precedent which could be applied to copying by means of many other kinds of technological devices in the future. It should be noted, however, that in its discussion of the first fair use factor the Court also stated that "... every commercial use of copyrighted material is presumptively an unfair exploitation of the monopoly privilege that belongs to the copyright owner" and that, if the intended use by a defendant was for commercial gain, this required a conclusion that the first fair use factor be weighed against the defendant; further, the likelihood of injury for the potential market for or value of the copyrighted work could be presumed, with respect to the fourth factor.

The Court also addressed the public interest in the copyright system:

> The monopoly privileges that Congress may authorise are neither unlimited nor primarily designed to provide a special private benefit. Rather, the limited grant is a means by which an important public purpose may be achieved. It is intended to motivate the creative activity of authors and inventors by the provision of a special reward, and to allow the public access to the products of their genius after the limited period of exclusive control has expired...
>
> As the text of the Constitution makes plain, it is Congress that has been assigned the task of defining the scope of the limited monopoly that should be granted to authors or to inventors in order to give the public appropriate access to their work product. Because this task involves a difficult balance between the interests of authors and inventors in the control and exploitation of their writings and discoveries on the one hand, and society's competing interest in the free flow of ideas, information, and commerce on the other hand, our patent and copyright statutes have been amended repeatedly...

The Supreme Court the following year considered to what extent fair **5–033** use sanctions the unauthorized use of quotations from a public figure's unpublished manuscript.[13] Here, the second and fourth fair use factors, the nature of the copyrighted work and the effect of the use on the potential market for the work, were at issue. The Court found that the fact that a work is unpublished is a critical element of its nature and that the scope of fair use is narrower with respect to unpublished works. The unpublished status of the work inevitably impacts on the potential market for the work. The Court characterised the fourth factor as the single most important element of fair use. It also stressed the relevance of the quality of expression copied, in evaluating the third factor, the amount and substantiality of the portion copied, describing it as the heart or essence of the plaintiff's work.[14] Of interest too is the Court's finding that the use of the copyrighted material was not excused by the public's interest in the subject–matter.

Fair use was held to apply in a controversial case involving reverse engineering of computer programs. The defendant wished to make videogames which would be compatible with the plaintiff's game console but was unable to do so without reverse engineering the plaintiff's operating system and making copies thereof in the process. The Court found that the fair use doctrine applied because there was no other way to discover the ideas and principles of the plaintiff's programme and the copying was done solely to discover unprotected aspects of the plaintiff's work. In its decision the Court stated:

"... the fact that computer programs are distributed for public use in object code form often precludes public access to the ideas and functional concepts contained in those programs, and thus confers on the copyright owner a *de facto* monopoly over those ideas and functional concepts. That result defeats the fundamental purpose of the Copyright Act—to encourage the production of original works by protecting the expressive elements of those works while leaving the ideas, facts, and functional concepts in the public domain for others to build on".[15]

---

[13] *Harper & Row, loc. cit.*, n.95, above.
[14] Note that legislation has since made it clear that fair use of unpublished works is not *per se* excluded (see para.5–030 and n.1, above).
[15] *Sega Enterprises, Ltd. v Accolade, Inc.* 977 F.2d 1510 (9th Cir. 1992) at 1527.

In a second case involving videogames, the Court came to a similar conclusion but emphasised that the fair use exception did not justify piracy: "fair use in intermediate copying does not extend to commercial exploitation of protected expression. The fair use reproductions of a computer program must not exceed what is necessary to understand the unprotected elements of the work".[16]

In 1994, in *Campbell v Acuff-Rose Music, Inc*, the Supreme Court was concerned with parody in a case where, but for a finding of fair use, the rights in the plaintiff's song would have been infringed.[17] The Supreme Court for the first time held that parody, like other comment or criticism may claim fair use, arguing that parody has an obvious claim to transformative value and stating that "the goal of copyright, to promote science and the arts, is generally furthered by the creation of transformative works". Moreover, "the more transformative the new work, the less will be the significance of other factors, like commercialism, that may weigh against a finding of fair use". In its judgment, the Court departed from its previous *Sony* decision by emphasising that the commercial nature of a defendant's use, which it had previously stated in *Sony* to be the single most important element to be taken into account in cases of fair use, is only one of many considerations to be addressed.[18] No single consideration should be taken in isolation; all the criteria should be analysed together. "The task is not to be simplified with bright-line rules, for the statute, like the doctrine it recognises, calls for case-by-case analysis."

5–034 More recently, new digital uses and markets have given rise to litigation in which the fair use defence has been invoked unsuccessfully to justify making available music files and films for copying over the Internet. In *UMG Recordings, Inc. v MP3.com, Inc.*,[19] the Court found MP3.com liable for infringement for making unauthorised copies of sound recordings, loading them on to its system of file servers and

---

[16] *Atari Games Corp. v Nintendo of America*, 975 F. 2d 832 (Fed.Cir. 1992).

[17] cf n.1, above.

[18] In *Sony Corp. of America v Universal City Studios*, (464 U.S. 417 (1984) and *Harper & Row*, n.95, above, the Court had emphasised the commercial nature of defendant's use, declaring in *Sony* that "every commercial use is presumptively unfair," and in *Harper & Row* that the impact on the potential market for the plaintiff's works was "undoubtedly the single most important element of fair use".

[19] *UMG Recordings Inc. v MP3.com, Inc*, 92 F. Supp. 2d 349 (S.D.N.Y. 2000). For a commentary on this case and the cases mentioned in nn.20 and 21, see M. Landau, "Digital downloads, copy code and U.S. Copyright Law", paper delivered at the Ninth Annual Conference on International Intellectual Property Law and Policy, Fordham University School of Law, New York, April 19 and 20, 2001.

permitting internet users to download the copies, and rejected MP3's fair use defence. As regards the four fair use factors, it was not disputed that the use was commercial, but MP3 argued that its use was transformative because it provided a space shift by which subscribers could listen to sound recordings they already owned copies of on CD without requiring the actual physical discs. The Court stated that merely repackaging or republishing the original is not sufficient to establish fair use because such services are not transformative. Moreover, the entire copyrighted works at issue were copied; this weighed against a finding of fair use and a copyright owner has the right to curb the development of a market such as that in issue by refusing to license a copyrighted work or by doing so on terms it finds acceptable.

In *Universal City Studios v Reimerdes* (the so-called *DeCSS* case, heard in 2000 and confirmed on appeal in 2001), an access control and copy prevention system known as Content Scramble System (CSS), developed by the film industry to protect its films in digital versatile disc (DVD) format, was hacked.[20] The system permitted movies on CSS-protected DVDs to be viewed only on players and DVD-ROM drives equipped with licensed technology, permitting the films to be decrypted and played, but not copied. The CSS encryption algorithm and keys were reverse-engineered by the defendant and used to create DeCSS, a computer program that decoded the scrambled signals on encrypted DVDs. DeCSS was then made widely available on the internet, enabling films to be posted on the internet, distributed, viewed and copied. Action for injunctive relief was brought against the hackers under the Digital Millenium Copyright Act (DMCA, s.1201(a)(1)), alleging violation of the anti-circumvention provisions of the Act, which prohibits unauthorised offering of products that circumvent technological measures which effectively control access to copyrighted works. The defendants *inter alia* challenged the constitutionality of s.1201(a)(1) on the ground that by foreclosing a fair use defence to unauthorised circumvention of technological measures protecting access to copyrighted works, Congress was in breach of the First Amendment, the Constitutional guarantee of free speech. The District Court entered a permanent injunction barring the defendant

---

[20] *Universal City Studios, Inc., v Reimerdes*, 111 F. Supp. 2d 294 (S.D.N.Y. 2000), affirmed in *Universal Studios, Inc., v Corley*, 273 F.3d 429 (2d. Cir. 2001); for a comment on the decision of the first instance District Court, see D. Goldberg and R.J. Bernstein, "The Prohibition on Circumvention and the Attack on the DVD", [2001] E.I.P.R. 160.

from posting DeCSS on his web site or from knowingly linking via a hyperlink to any other website containing DeCSS; in so doing, it rejected the constitutional attacks on the statute and the injunction. The Court of Appeals upheld the District Court's judgment. The defendant was found to be in violation of s.1201(a)(1) DMCA and DeCSS was held to be a means of circumventing an access control under the statute; DeCSS was primarily designed for the purpose of circumvention and had limited commercial purpose other than to circumvent. As regards fair use, it was pointed out that the prohibition of s.1201(a)(1) DMCA was limited to the act of circumvention itself, leaving intact all traditional defences to copyright infringement, including fair use, so long as access is authorised or the use falls under one of the statutory exceptions established by s.1201(a)(1) DMCA. The Courts declined to find a conflict with Constitutional free speech guarantees or to accept the constitutional challenge based on claimed restriction of fair use. As the Court of Appeals stated, would-be users could still engage in reasonable copying from the audiovisual works, albeit not by decrypting DVDs. It pointed out that there is no constitutional requirement that fair use of DVD films must be made by copying the original work in its original format, saying:

> We know of no authority for the proposition that fair use, as protected by the Copyright Act, much less the Constitution, guarantees copying by the optimum method or in the identical format of the original ... The fact that the resulting copy will not be as perfect or as manipulable as a digital copy obtained by having direct access to the DVD movie in its digital form, provides no basis for a claim of unconstitutional limitation of fair use ... Fair use has never been held to be a guarantee of access to copyrighted material in order to copy it by the fair user's preferred technique or in the format of the original.

In the Napster case, a file-swapping service for collectors of MP3 music files was concerned, which enabled computer users to post and search for MP3 music files on the internet and to copy them from one hard disc to another via the internet.[21] Napster itself did not maintain

---

[21] *A & M Records v Napster Inc.*, 239 F.3d 1004 (9th Cir. 2001). Digital MP3 files are created through a process known as "ripping". Ripping software allows a computer burner to copy an audio compact disc directly onto a computer's hard drive by compressing the audio information on the CD into the MP3 format, which allows for rapid

the files on its equipment; these remained on the hard discs of users. However, Napster provided "Musicshare" software and maintained an index facility which allowed one user to access another's hard disc directly and search for and download the music files of their choice, thus facilitating the transmission of MP3 files between and among users. The plaintiffs, owners of copyrighted sound recordings, alleged that Napster was a contributory and vicarious copyright infringer. At both first instance and on appeal, the Court rejected Napster's asser-tion that its subscribers were engaged in non-commercial personal fair use copying because, *inter alia*, end-users' widespread and systematic copying could not be deemed non-commercial and unpaid file sharing had a deleterious effect on the present and future digital download market for the plaintiffs' protected sound recordings. Napster was found liable for infringement and for facilitating wide-spread infringement by end-users. The Court of Appeals concluded that the activity of the end-users was not fair use and had been rightfully enjoined by the first instance. The Court, stating that the case required the application of well-established doctrines of copyright law to a new technology, in considering the four fair use factors, found the use to be commercial rather than personal and that the use was not transformative. Moreover, the creative nature of the musical compositions and sound recordings copied "cut against" a finding of fair use. In Napster, the end-users were taking copies of the entire song, so the "taking" was both quantitatively and qualitatively sub-stantial. The Court also affirmed the first instance's finding that Napster harmed the market for the works in two ways: by reducing audio CD sales among college students and raising barriers to plaintiffs entry into the market for the digital downloading of music.[22] The injunction barring Napster from offering copyright protected sound recordings was therefore maintained.

Statutory Exceptions to Protection

The public interest also dictates the decisions of Congress with regard **5–035** to the express limitations imposed in the Copyright Act itself on the

---

transmission of digital audio files from one computer to another by email. On this case, see also D. Lefranc, "Le nouveau public (réflexions comparatistes sur les décisions "Napster" et "MP3.com"), [2001] 1 D. 107.

[22] *A & M Records, Inc. v Napster, loc. cit*, Opinion of the Court of Appeals at 1016.

exercise of the exclusive rights granted to right owners. Section 106 of the Copyright Act grants copyright owners the exclusive right to do and to authorise five uses of their works, subject to the general limitation for fair use (section 107), already discussed, and subject also to certain specific limitations.

The five exclusive rights granted are the rights to reproduce; to prepare derivative works; to distribute copies to the public; to perform the work publicly and to display the work publicly. "The five fundamental rights that the bill gives to copyright owners—the exclusive rights of reproduction, adaptation, publication, performance, and display—are stated generally in section 106. These exclusive rights, which comprise the so-called 'bundle of rights' that is a copyright, are cumulative and may overlap in some cases."[23]

These five rights are expressed in broad language and together cover nearly all economically important uses of copyright works. However, limitations are imposed on these all-encompassing rights in subsequent sections which narrow the scope of the rights to meet what are considered to be the needs of the general public. The limitations include exemptions (*e.g.* certain reproductions by libraries for archives and for non-profit and charitable uses), compulsory and statutory licences, as well as the defence of fair use, discussed above.

The 1909 Copyright Act contained only one compulsory licence, the mechanical licence for recording musical works. The 1976 Act added compulsory licensing in the case of certain cable transmissions of wireless broadcast signals, jukebox performances of music and the use of published musical works and published pictorial, graphic and sculptural works by non-commercial educational broadcasters. At that time, the Copyright Royalty Tribunal was established with power to adjust the rates of the statutory royalties payable and to distribute certain funds. Meanwhile, further statutory licences have been created and, in 1990, in order to comply with the Berne Convention, the jukebox compulsory licence was eliminated and replaced by private licence agreements.

5–036 At present, the following compulsory and statutory licences are provided for in the Copyright Act 1976, as amended: statutory licence for secondary transmissions by cable systems[24]; statutory licence for

---

[23] See House of Representatives Report No.94–1476, *op. cit.*, see n.18, above, at 61.

[24] Copyright Act 1976, as amended (Title 17, U.S. Code), s.111.

making ephemeral recordings[25]; compulsory licence for the public performance of sound recordings by means of digital audio transmission[26]; compulsory licence for making and distributing phonorecords (sound recordings)[27]; compulsory licence for the use of certain works in connection with non-commercial broadcasting[28]; statutory licences for secondary transmissions by satellite carriers for private home viewing and for local transmissions[29]; statutory obligation for distribution of digital audio recording devices and media.[30]

In 1993, the Copyright Royalty Tribunal was abolished[31] and replaced by *ad hoc* Copyright Arbitration Royalty Panels (CARPs) under the supervision of the Librarian of Congress.[32] The panels adjust the copyright compulsory licence royalty rates and distribute the royalties to the appropriate copyright owners.

The proliferation of compulsory and statutory licences is problematic. Major rights of copyright owners are subject to conditions that effectively deny them the right to control the use of the work, replacing exclusive rights by a mere right to remuneration. The actual amounts of remuneration to be paid are also laid down by statute in some cases. As Ringer pointed out following the introduction of new compulsory licences in the 1976 Act:

> the interweaving of four full-scale compulsory licensing schemes into the main fabric of the U.S. copyright system may have ominous implications for the future. Copyright has heretofore been considered a bundle of exclusive rights that can be withheld or sold as the owner sees fit. Does our experience in the development of the 1976 Act suggest that in the future, whenever a new right is granted by Congress, it will necessarily be subject to compulsory licensing rather than exclusive?[33]

---

[25] *ibid.*, s.112.
[26] *ibid.*, s.114.
[27] *ibid.*, s.115.
[28] *ibid.*, s.118.
[29] *ibid.*, s.s.119 and 122.
[30] *ibid.*, Ch.10.
[31] Copyright Royalty Tribunal Reform Act, 1993, Public Law 103–198.
[32] The CARP system is currently under review by the Subcommittee on Courts, the Internet, and Intellectual Property Committee on the Judiciary, US House of Representives (107th Congress, 2nd Session, 2002).
[33] B. Ringer, *op. cit.*, n.20, above, at 193.

As already noted above in the discussion of post-1976 legislation, there has been a proliferation of new limitations and statutory exceptions both to existing and new rights in legislation such as the Fairness in Music Licensing Act 1998 and the Digital Millennium Copyright Act 1998.

5–037 The rationale for the limitations and exceptions of the 1976 Act were described at the time as follows:

> The principle that guided Congress in deciding whether to leave a particular exclusive right intact or to subject it to an exemption, compulsory license or defense is the long-standing precept that rights should be so adjusted that the public good fully coincides ... with the claims of individuals. ... Either or both of two judgements, one economic, the other political, underlie Congress' decision in any case to subject an exclusive right to an exception, compulsory license or defense.[34]

Goldstein gives various examples of how these principles have been applied in the law. He suggests that the exemption for performance or display of a work by instructors or pupils in the course of face-to-face teaching activities (section 110(1))

> reflects the economic judgment that search and negotiation costs will systematically prevent classroom teachers from obtaining licenses to perform copyrighted works in classroom settings. ... The exemption for classroom performances also reflects a political judgment that educational uses are more socially productive than certain other uses of copyrighted works and thus should enjoy added weight in the copyright balance between private claims and the public good.[35]

Similar considerations prompted Congress in establishing the compulsory licence system in favour of cable operators. As is stated in the House Report:

> In general, the Committee believes that cable systems are commercial enterprises whose basic retransmission operations are based

---

[34] P. Goldstein, *Copyright*, *op. cit.* at 515.
[35] *ibid.*, at 516.

on the carriage of copyrighted program material and that copyright royalties should be paid by cable operators to the creators of such programs. The Committee recognizes, however, that it would be impractical and unduly burdensome to require every cable system to negotiate with every copyright owner whose work was retransmitted by a cable system. Accordingly, the Committee has determined to maintain the basic principle of the Senate bill to establish a compulsory copyright license for the retransmission of those over-the-air broadcast signals that a cable system is authorized to carry pursuant to the rules and regulations of the FCC.[36]

An important limitation on the rights of copyright owners is provided for in section 108 with respect to reproduction by libraries and archives. In this provision, Congress sought to establish a balance between the interests of right owners and users by allowing libraries and archives or their employees to reproduce or distribute no more than one copy of a protected work, under certain conditions.[37] To ensure that this balance was fairly struck and would continue to be so, Congress directed the Register of Copyrights to submit to Congress, at five-year intervals, "a report setting forth the extent to which this section has achieved the intended statutory balancing of the rights of creators and the needs of users."

The Underlying Philosophy in the US Law of Copyright

As this study has amply illustrated, the public interest has been an essential factor in the development of US copyright law in the positive sense that it is regarded as a mechanism for the stimulation of creativity for the ultimate benefit of the public. "The sole interest of the United States and the primary object in conferring the monopoly lie in the general benefits derived by the public from the labours of authors."[38]   **5–038**

---

[36] House Report No.94–1476, *op. cit.* n.18, above, at 90.

[37] Copyright Act 1976, Title 17 US Code, s.108(i). S.108(i) was subsequently deleted by the Copyright Amendment Acts of 1992, Pub. No.102–307, 106 Stat.262, 272, enacted June 26, 1992.

[38] *Film Fox Corp v Doyal*, 286 US 123,127 [1932].

The US Supreme Court has on a number of occasions interpreted the scope of the Constitutional clause and its impact on legislation enacted under it. It has frequently drawn attention to the positive aspect in which copyright serves the public interest.

> The [constitutional] clause thus describes both the objective which Congress may seek and the means to achieve it. The objective is to promote the progress of science and the arts. As employed, the terms "to promote" are synonymous with the words "to stimulate", "to encourage", or "to induce". To accomplish its purpose, Congress may grant to authors the exclusive right to the fruits of their respective works. An author who possesses an unlimited copyright may preclude others from copying his creation for commercial purposes without permission. In other words, to encourage people to devote themselves to intellectual and artistic creation, Congress may guarantee to authors and inventors a reward in the form of control over the sale or commercial use of copies of their works.[39]

"Congress thus seeks to define the rights included in copyright so as to serve the public welfare and not necessarily so as to maximize an author's control over his or her product."[40]

> We have often recognized that the monopoly privileges that Congress has authorized, while intended to motivate the creative activity of authors and inventors by the provision of a special award, are limited in nature and must ultimately serve the public good.[41]
>
> The monopoly privileges that Congress may authorise are neither limited nor primarily designed to provide a special private benefit. Rather, the limited grant is a means by which an important public purpose may be achieved. It is intended to motivate the creative activity of authors and inventors by the provision of a special reward, and to allow the public access to the products of their genius after the limited period of exclusive control has expired.[42]

---

[39] *Goldstein v California*, 412 US 546, 37 [1973].

[40] *Harper & Row, op. cit*, n.95, above, at 1089.

[41] *Fogerty v Fantasy, Inc.*, 114 S. Ct. 1023 [1994].

[42] *Sony Corp of America v Universal City Studios*, 220 US PQ 673 [1984].

The limited scope of the copyright holder's statutory monopoly, like the limited copyright duration required by the Constitution, reflects a balance of competing claims upon the public interest: creative work is to be encouraged and rewarded, but private motivation must ultimately serve the cause of promoting broad public availability of literature, music, and other arts. The immediate effect of our copyright law is to secure a fair return for an "author's" creative labour. But the ultimate aim is, by this incentive, to stimulate artistic creativity for the general public good.[43]

This same concern for the public interest is exhibited by Congress **5–039** when considering amendments to the Copyright Act. Attention has been drawn *inter alia* to the importance attached to the public interest by the House Reports on the 1909 and 1976 Acts, by the Register of Copyrights' Report of 1961 and by the Supreme Court on many occasions. According to Goldstein:

The premise of social benefit imports a value judgement and an empirical judgement. Everytime Congress amends the Copyright Act it makes a value judgement about the quantity and quality of literary, musical and artistic works that are socially desirable and an empirical judgement about the amendment's probable efficiency in achieving that end.[44]

"But the touchstone for decision in all these cases is the same: copyright law's overarching ambition to encourage the widest possible production and dissemination of literary, musical and artistic works. Each of copyright law's principal features reveals a particular accommodation of the competing demands of incentives and access."[45]

In expanding the scope of copyright protection over the years to new classes of copyright subject-matter, these principles have been applied by Congress. The constitutional notions of "writings" and "authors" have been interpreted liberally to accommodate new classes

---

[43] *Twentieth Century Music Corp v Aiken*, 186 US PQ 67 [1974].

[44] Goldstein, *Copyright, op. cit.*, para.1.1.

[45] *ibid.*, para.1.2.1.

of works deriving from new technology. As the Supreme Court has pointed out:

> These terms [the "writings" of "authors"] have not been construed in their narrow literal sense but rather, with the reach necessary to reflect the broad scope of constitutional principles ... the congressional determination to consider specific classes of writings is dependent, not only on the character of the writing, but also on the commercial importance of the product to the national economy. As our technology has expanded the means available for creative activity and has provided economical means for reproducing manifestations of such activity, new areas of federal protection have been initiated.[46]

"Sound policy, as well as history, supports our consistent deference to Congress when major technological innovations alter the market for copyrighted materials. Congress has the constitutional authority and the institutional ability to accommodate fully the varied permutations of competing interests that are inevitably implicated by such new technology."[47]

5–040 These principles were most recently applied in the enactment of the Digital Millenium Copyright Act (DMCA) 1998. As Senator Leahy stated at the time:

> The DMCA is a product of the Senate Judiciary Committee's recognition that ours is a time of unprecedented challenge to copyright protection. Copyright has been the engine that has traditionally converted the energy of artistic creativity into publicly available arts and entertainment. Historically, the Government's role has been to encourage creativity and innovation by protecting copyrights that create incentives for the dissemination to the public of new works and forms of expression ... This bill is a well-balanced package of proposals that address the needs of creators, consumers and commerce in the digital age and well into the next century.[48]

---

[46] *Goldstein v California*, 412 US 546, 37 at 177 [1973].
[47] *Sony Corp of America v Universal City Studios*, 220 US PQ 675 [1984].
[48] Senate Report, *op. cit.*, n.68, above, at 69.

As the Supreme Court pointed out in *New York Times Co v Tasini*, a certain shift in the philosophical basis for the US copyright law may, however, be detected. As noted above, the 1976 Act has been seen as marking a break with the 200-year tradition that has identified copyright more closely with the publisher than with the author.[49] Since then the duration of protection for many works rests on the identity and existence of the individual author rather than on the act of publication of copies by a publisher or producer. The protection newly afforded to unpublished works means that "Creation (something the author does) will supersede publication (something the publisher or producer does) as the pivotal copyright act".[50] The shift can also be seen in the provisions of the law on ownership of copyright and on works made for hire; for example, the author is the first owner of all rights under copyright and any rights not expressly transferred in writing are retained. A more personalist approach to copyright may also be seen in the Supreme Court's decision in *Feist Publications v Rural Telephone Service Co.*, where the Court referred to the Constitution, explaining that the copyright clause's reference to authors and writings "made it unmistakenly clear that these terms presuppose a degree of originality" and that a modicum of creativity is required for any work to be eligible for copyright protection.[51]

In Chapter 13, below, we discuss further the extent to which the Berne Convention and other international agreements on copyright are bringing about a gradual convergence between the personalist approach of the *droit d'auteur* and the common law approach of copyright. In this chapter, we have seen how the United States has adapted its law to the Berne Convention and been affected by international and EU developments in matters such as the term of protection and the WTO dispute over the Fairness in Music Licensing Act 1998. The US copyright law will no doubt be increasingly influenced by the globalisation of the market for copyright works and the compromises imposed by international copyright treaties.

---

[49] See para.5–009, and n.33, above; see also B. Ringer, "First Thoughts on the Copyright Act of 1976", *op. cit.*, n.20, above.

[50] B. Ringer, *ibid.*, at 192.

[51] See para.5–008 and n.25, above.

Conclusion

5–041 As we have seen, in the United States of America the underlying purpose and philosophy of copyright legislation has traditionally been to foster the growth of learning and culture by encouraging creators to produce works for the public welfare. The grant of exclusive rights to authors for a limited time is seen to be a means to that end. These principles were stated cogently in the House Report on the Copyright Act of 1909[52]:

> The enactment of copyright legislation by Congress under the terms of the Constitution is not based upon any natural right that the author has in his writings, for the Supreme Court has held that such rights as he has are purely statutory rights, but upon the ground that the welfare of the public will be served and progress of science and useful arts will be promoted by securing to authors for limited periods the exclusive rights to their writings. The Constitution does not establish copyrights, but provides that Congress shall have the power to grant such rights if it thinks best. Not primarily for the benefit of the author, but primarily for the benefit of the public, such rights are given. Not that any particular class of citizens, however worthy, may benefit, but because the policy is believed to be for the benefit of the great body of people, in that it will stimulate writing and invention to give some bonus to authors and inventors.
>
> In enacting a copyright law, Congress must consider ... two questions: First, how much will the legislation stimulate the producer and so benefit the public, and, second, how much will the monopoly granted be detrimental to the public? The granting of such exclusive rights, under the proper terms and conditions, confers a benefit upon the public that outweighs the evils of the temporary monopoly.[53]

Protection for authors and other right owners is therefore granted because it is deemed to be in the public interest to stimulate creativity and to ensure the widest possible dissemination of works. Similar

---

[52] House of Representatives Report No.2222, 60th Congress, 2nd session, (1909) p.7.
[53] *ibid.*

considerations determine the extent of limitations on authors' rights. The principles governing the establishment of such limitations were described in the Register's report on the general revision of the US Copyright Law of July 1961.

> Within reasonable limits, the interests of authors coincide with those of the public. Both will usually benefit from the widest possible dissemination of the author's works. But it is often cumbersome for would-be users to seek out the copyright owner and get his permission. There are many situations in which copyright restrictions would inhibit dissemination, with little or no benefit to the author. And the interests of authors must yield to the public welfare where they conflict.
>
> While some limitations and conditions on copyright are essential in the public interest, they should not be so burdensome and strict as to deprive authors of their just reward. Authors wishing copyright protection should be able to secure it readily and simply. And their rights should be broad enough to give them a fair share of the revenue to be derived from the market for their works.[54]

In recent years, there has been an increasing recognition on the part of the US Government of the economic and cultural importance of copyright. As regards its cultural impact, the Register in a supplementary report published in 1965 emphasised:

> The inter-relation between copyright and the communications revolution is fully as important to our age as the inter-relation between copyright and the revolution brought on by the printing press was to an earlier one. Somehow people must be made to realise that the copyright statute of a country not only shapes its cultural and intellectual development, but actually penetrates into the lives and thinking of every citizen.[55]

As regards the economic significance of copyright, in 1983, the **5–042** Copyright Office was requested by the Chairman of the Subcommittee on Patents, Copyrights and Trade Marks of the Senate Committee on the Judiciary, to prepare biennial reports concerning

---

[54] Register's Report, *op. cit.*, n.13, above, at 6.
[55] Supplementary Report of the Register of Copyrights on the General Revision of the US Copyright Law, 89th Congress, 1st session, May 1965, at XIV.

the economic scope of the copyright industries and their impact on the US economy. The first of these reports was published in 1984.[56] Due to budget cuts, no subsequent reports were issued by the Copyright Office but since 1990 surveys on the economic contribution of the copyright industries to the US economy have been published at regular intervals by the International Intellectual Property Alliance.[57] These surveys have consistently shown that the copyright industries are one of the United States' largest and fastest-growing economic assets. The most recent report published in 2002 showed that, in 2001, the US copyright industries accounted for 5.24 per cent of US Gross Domestic Product (GDP) or US$535.1 billion (thousand million), an increase of over $75 billion from 1999 and exceeding 5.0 per cent of the economy for the first time.

According to the 2002 report, in the 24 years from 1977 to 2001, the copyright industries'[58] share of GDP grew more than twice as fast as the remainder of the US economy (7.0 per cent as against 3.0 per cent) Between 1977 and 2001, employment in the US copyright industries more than doubled to 4.7 million people or 3.5 per cent of the total workforce. Over the period 1977–2001, employment in these industries had grown more than three times as fast as the remainder of the US economy (5 per cent as against 1.5 per cent). The report also drew attention to the fact that the copyright industries of the United States had large foreign markets, estimating that in 2001 the US copyright industries generated revenues from foreign sales and

---

[56] Report of the US Copyright Office to the Subcommittee on Patents, Copyright and Trademarks of the Committee on the Judiciary, US Senate, on the size of the Copyright Industries in the United States, December 1984. The major findings of the report, which was based on 1977 statistics, was that the copyright industries in the United States of America contributed some US$55 billion to the US economy, which amounted to approximately 2.8% of the Gross National Product. It also showed that the copyright industries employed 2.2 million people, that is, approximately 2.2% at the time of the civilian labour force of the United States of America.

[57] S.E. Siwek, & H. Furchtgott-Roth, *Copyright Industries in the U.S. Economy*, Reports prepared for the International Intellectual Property Alliance (IIPA), November 1990, September 1992, October 1993 and January 1995; S.E. Siwek & G. Mosteller, 1996 and 1998; S.E. Siwek, 1999, 2000 and 2002.

[58] The US copyright-based industries are defined as including the producers of all types of computer software, including business software and entertainment software (such as videogame CD ROMs and cartridges, personal computer CD ROMs and multi-media products); theatrical films, television programs, DVDs and home video and digital representations of audiovisual works; music: records, CDs and audiocassettes; and textbooks, tradebooks, reference and professional publications and journals (in electronic and print media). *Cf* Foreword to the 2002 Report by the President of the IIPA.

exports of over US$88.97 billion (thousand million), representing a 9.4 per cent annual gain over the 1999 figure, leading all major industry sectors.

Copyright in the United States of America has become, therefore, an **5–043** increasingly important issue in national policy debates. It also plays a prominent role in US diplomatic and trade policy. Obtaining improved protection for intellectual property, including copyright, abroad has become a major objective of the US administration's efforts in its bilateral relations with other countries. This was demonstrated, in particular, in the Uruguay Round negotiations of the General Agreement on Tariffs and Trade (GATT), which *inter alia* resulted in the adoption of the Agreement on Trade-Related Aspects of Intellectual Property Rights (the TRIPs Agreement), signed on April 15, 1994.

In 1988, the then US trade representative, Mr Clayton Yeutter, remarked:

> No country benefits from the theft of another's intellectual property. The United States is not the only country with inventors. We want to encourage innovative people everywhere to bring their creativity to the international market place. If countries throughout the world were to provide incentives to foster technological invention and innovation, rather than to steal it, we would all be vastly better off. We cannot build a sound international trading system on a foundation of piracy.[59]

The constancy of the copyright policy of the United States of America was reiterated in the September 1995 Report of the Working Group on Intellectual Property Rights "Intellectual Property and the National Information Infrastructure" already referred to, as follows:

> The copyright law should also serve the public interest—and it does. While, at first, blush, it may appear to be in the public interest to reduce the protection granted works and to allow unfettered use by the public, such an analysis is incomplete. Protection of works of authorship provides the stimulus for creativity, thus leading to the availability of works of literature, culture, art

---

[59] Press Release, Office of the US Trade Representative, February 26, 1988.

and entertainment that the public desires and that form the back-
bone of our economy and political discourse. If these works are not
protected, then the marketplace will not support their creation and
dissemination, and the public will not receive the benefit of their
existence, or be able to have unrestricted use of the ideas and
information they convey.[60]

---

[60] NII Report, *op. cit.*, n.54, above, at 16.

Chapter 6

France*

Origins of the Law

In France, as elsewhere in Europe, the history of copyright, or to be **6–001** more precise of authors' rights, has its origins in the development of the printing trade. The first printing press began operating in Paris in 1470 and, by 1510, there were more than 50 in use.[1] The grant of the first privileges to printers took place in 1507 and 1508. Their aim, according to Pouillet, was, "by the grant of a monopoly to the publisher, to protect him against the disastrous competition which other printers could have subjected him to by profiting from his work and thereby to enable him to recover the costs invested by him in the operation".[2]

The first privileges were granted with respect to religious texts, such as, for example, the epistles of St. Paul. Even before the age of printing, new books could not be published without permission of the Theology Faculty of the University of Paris, and such permission continued to be required before a new book could be printed. This was a mere licence to print, which conferred no exclusivity on the holder, but certified that there was nothing in the book contrary to

---

* In this chapter, the quotations from French texts have been translated by the author except where an English translation of the text has already been published, as is the case, for example, with articles published in the *Revue internationale du droit d'auteur* (*R.I.D.A.*), which is published in French, English and Spanish. Passages cited from R.I.D.A. are taken from the published English version.

[1] A.-C. Renouard, *Traité des droits d'auteur dans la littérature, les sciences et les beaux-arts* (Paris, Jules Renouard et Cie. Libraires, 1838), Vol.1, p.27.

[2] E. Pouillet, *Traité théorique et pratique de la propriété littéraire et artistique* (Paris, Marchal et Billard, 3rd ed. 1908), p.6.

the faith or state security. This system of censorship was confirmed by an edict of François I in 1521[3] and in 1537 the requirement to obtain permission to print any book was again confirmed, at the same time as an obligation on the printer to deposit one copy thereof in the King's Library at Blois was introduced.[4] Originally, permission to print was separate from the privilege and had to be obtained before a request for a privilege was made. In time, permission to print and a request for a privilege were sought and granted simultaneously from the crown. The privilege did not recognise authors' rights and was not intended to reward the creation of the work. By granting the beneficiary the exclusive right to print and sell the work in question, the privilege was intended to enable the publisher to recoup his printing costs and obtain some reward for his commercial risk.

In the early days, privileges were not granted to authors themselves.[5] Privileges served the crown as a means of encouraging the publication of such works as it considered to be in its interest. To facilitate censorship control, privileges were only granted on condition the book would be published by a Parisian bookseller. This led in due course to protests from booksellers in the provinces but throughout the sixteenth century enabled the monarchy to keep strict control of the book trade. Penalties for failure to obey the law were draconian. An Order of 1566 forbade the printing of any book without permission on pain of being hanged or strangled.[6]

6–002 Privileges were originally temporary and granted for a certain number of years. Like in England, however, the printers sought perpetual privileges on the ground that short-term privileges did not enable them to recover their costs. The Parliament opposed perpetual privileges since the monopolies they represented, by eliminating all competition, meant that the price of books was too high. Thus, in a series of Decrees adopted by Parliament between 1551 and 1586, and subsequently confirmed by letters patent of the King in 1618, the following principles were established:

— privileges could only be granted in respect of new works;

[3] *ibid.*, p.7.
[4] M.-C. Dock, *Etude sur le droit d'auteur* (Paris, Librairie générale de droit et de jurisprudence, 1963), p.68.
[5] E. Pouillet, *op. cit.*, p.7; see also M.-C. Dock, *op. cit.*, p.65.
[6] M.-C. Dock, *ibid.*, p.68.

— they could not be renewed unless the existing work had had new material added to it.

Thus, at the start of the seventeenth century, privileges for old works were no longer available and such works had entered the public domain. It was considered that prolongation of privileges was damaging to freedom and industry and that privileges for new works would encourage creativity[7]. This was not the end of the story, however. In 1649, in response to the demands of the booksellers, the crown reintroduced both privileges and prolongations for old books. The booksellers had successfully argued that the fact that these were no longer available caused great harm to the public, because without them it was uneconomic to publish old books. However, Parliament refused to ratify the royal edict. This confused and unsatisfactory situation continued throughout the seventeenth and well into the eighteenth centuries, but the crown held the upper hand. Privileges continued to be granted only to Parisian booksellers and renewals continued to be granted for "new" books, although from 1671 on renewals were not granted for "old" books, defined as having been written by authors dead before 1470. These were considered to have fallen into the public domain.

Throughout this period, authors, as such, remained unprotected by the law. Their rights did not remain totally unrecognised, however, and from an early stage privileges were sometimes granted to authors themselves. Dock gives a number of examples, including those granted by François I and Henry II to Rabelais and by Charles IX to Ronsard.[8] However, the author had no right to print or sell his work and was therefore obliged to cede exploitation to a bookseller and, as a matter of practice, manuscripts of books were sold outright. Nevertheless, the special nature of the connection between the author and his work was not wholly overlooked. As early as 1586, in a dispute over the grant of a privilege, Marion stated: "The author of a book is fully the master thereof, and as such may freely dispose thereof. . . . The reason for this is that men, by common instinct, recognise one towards the other that each individual is lord of what he makes, invents and composes."[9]

---

[7] A. and H.-J. Lucas, *Traité de la Propriété littéraire et artistique*, (Paris, Litec, 2nd ed. 2001), para.6.

[8] M.-C. Dock, *op. cit.*, p.82.

[9] Cited by E. Pouillet, *op. cit.*, p.9 .

131

6—003 The authors themselves did not claim rights. Dock suggests that this was because they felt it to be beneath their dignity to concern themselves with material matters and because financially they were supported by the booksellers, by payments in return for dedicating books to patrons, and by pensions received from patrons.

As in England, it was the booksellers who first invoked the rights of the authors in a dispute which pitted the booksellers of Paris against those of the provinces, who argued that prolongations of privileges were contrary to the public interest.[10] In 1725, Louis d'Héricourt, the advocate who defended the monopoly of the Paris booksellers, based his case on the following arguments: the author creates, and his creation is his own; it is his property; his right is independent of the privilege accorded to the bookseller; he is the absolute master thereof and, therefore, he is free to dispose of it to whom he pleases. The booksellers of Paris hold their rights, not from the King and his privileges, but from the authors and the agreements concluded with them; they may not, therefore, have their rights taken away. He went so far as to say: "Thus, the King has no right thereto, so long as the author is alive or represented by his heirs or beneficiaries; he may not transfer it to anyone by means of a privilege without the permission of he to whom the work belongs" [*i.e.* the bookseller].[11]

D'Héricourt suggested that the property right of the author was a perpetual right. Conceding that works "must be communicated to the public in the public interest", this meant that the authors should be in a position to sell or transfer their works to others in order to bring such communication about. Thus, a bookseller who had obtained a privilege to print the work should remain the owner of the text in perpetuity, and be able to pass it on to his descendants like a piece of land or a house.[12]

As Pouillet pointed out, the principle of the property right of authors, first invoked by the booksellers in their own interest, was a double-edged sword, which inevitably came to be turned against them.[13] Thus, in the course of time, the authors and, in particular, their heirs claimed the prolongation of expired privileges for themselves, arguing that privileges could not be renewed in favour of

---

[10] M.-C. Dock, *op. cit.*, p.116.

[11] E. Pouillet, *op. cit.*, p.10.

[12] See extracts from d'Héricourt's *Mémoire*, reproduced in M.-C. Dock, *op. cit.*, p.115 *et seq.*

[13] E. Pouillet, *op. cit.*, p.11.

booksellers without the consent of the author or his heirs. In 1761, the grand-daughters of La Fontaine obtained a new privilege, on the expiration of that of the original publisher. It was granted to them by the King's Council on the ground that "the works of their grandfather belonged to them by right of heredity".[14] Recognition that authors had certain rights dates from this time, although such rights as they had were by common consent transferred to the bookseller contracted to print and publish the work.[15] It was not until 1777 that the rights of the author were formally recognised within the system of privileges. Provincial booksellers continued to petition the crown in opposition to the *de facto* monopoly over the new-book market of the Parisian booksellers. In support of their case, they invoked the public interest. A petition addressed to the King by the booksellers and printers of Lyon is typical of their claims:

6–004

> What is a privilege? It is a prerogative or advantage accorded by the Sovereign to a person who benefits therefrom to the exclusion of all others, contrary to the common law. ... Once an inventor or author has been compensated for his costs and expenses, his arrangements and his efforts, whether financially or as regards his reputation, everybody should have the right to enjoy the gift of his work. Society owes gratitude and recompense, but both have their limit and measure. If this were not so, every invention would represent a tax on each individual, which would hinder industry and would necessarily destroy competition and trade.[16]

On August 30, 1777, six regulations were promulgated by the Council of State concerning the printing and book trade, of which two are relevant, those concerning privileges and counterfeiting.[17]

The Regulation on Privileges, as amended in 1778, provided that a bookseller who had obtained a privilege would enjoy its benefit for the specific duration granted or for the life of the author, if the latter survived the term of the privilege. After the expiration of a privilege,

---

[14] E. Pouillet, *ibid*.

[15] M.-C. Dock, *op. cit.*, p.123.

[16] *ibid.*, pp.124 and 125, citing "Mss. F.f.22073, No.144".

[17] The texts of these regulations (*les Arrêts du Conseil d'Etat*) dated August 30, 1777, are published in A.-C. Renouard, *op. cit.*, p. 167 *et seq*. For an account of developments in France during this period see C. Hesse, "Enlightenment Epistemology and the Laws of Authorship in Revolutionary France", 1777–1793, [1990] 30 *Representations* 109.

or the death of the author, the holder of the privilege could obtain a licence to reprint the work but without prejudice to the right of third parties also to obtain a licence to print the same work. An author who obtained a privilege in his own name had the right to print and sell his own work himself and in such case could benefit from the privilege for himself and his heirs in perpetuity. However, if he sold the right to exploit his book to a bookseller he lost all rights in the work and the duration of the privilege was reduced to the life of the author.

The King's Council defined the nature of a privilege from the Crown as follows:

> His Majesty has recognised that a privilege for a text is a grace founded in Justice ... The perfection of the work requires that the publisher be allowed to enjoy this exclusive claim during the lifetime of the author ... but to grant a longer term than this, would be to convert the enjoyment of a grace into a property right.[18]

6–005   Dock described the effect of these regulations as follows: "[The privileges] of publishers were real, temporary monopolies, granted in the interest of the general public and which sacrificed freedom to publish works for a period in order to encourage publishers with the incentive of short-term exclusivity".[19]

The Regulation on Counterfeiting prohibited the reproduction of books for which privileges had been given and the printing of such books without permission after expiry of a privilege and the death of the author. Remedies for infringement of the law included seizure and destruction of the offending copies and damages for the holder of the privilege.

This was the position at the start of the Revolution in 1789.

As seen above, the system of privileges concerned published editions of literary works. The authors of dramatic works had different problems. Their plays were performed in the years running up to the Revolution by the *Comédie française*, which by that time had established itself as a complete monopoly, being the only licensed theatre in France. The authors of dramatic works in principle enjoyed the right to be paid royalties for the public performance of their works.

---

[18] C. Hesse, *ibid.*, p.113.
[19] M.-C. Dock, *op. cit.*, p.129.

However, their position was precarious and they were exploited by the actors. Any right to royalties also ended with the death of the playwright. It was the playwrights who in 1790 led the cause of all authors, when they petitioned the Constitutive Assembly for the abolition of the monopoly of the *Comédie française* and for the exclusive right to control the performance of their works during their lifetime and for five years thereafter.

The Revolution and the Decrees of 1791 and 1793

The system of privileges was abolished on August 4, 1789 and the **6–006** Royal Administration of the Book Trade was disbanded in August 1790.[20] The following year, the commercial monopoly of the Publishers' and Printers' Guild was abolished.[21] As Hesse explains: "The revolutionaries wanted to free the minds of citizens from censorship and to liberate the means of spreading and exchanging thoughts—literally, the presses and bookshops".[22] All this left a vacuum soon to be filled.

At first the vacuum was filled by a burgeoning pirate trade, which put the book publishers at risk and led them to petition the National Assembly to provide them with relief by way of a new regulation of the book trade. It was also filled by a proliferation of seditious and libellous pamphlets.

The National Assembly itself was in the throes of a conservative backlash against the collapse of all regulation of the printed word. In the face of a flood of anonymous, libellous and seditious pamphlet literature, the assembly heard repeated demands for laws requiring authors to sign published works and holding authors accountable for their publications. Thus the economic complaints from publishers converged with the political outcry...[23]

A number of proposals for legislation to control the press and

---

[20] Decree of August 10, 1790, Art.13; *Archives nationales*, F 17, 1258, *doss.* 2.

[21] Decree of March 17, 1791; *Collection générale des décrets rendus par l'Assemblée nationale* (Paris, 1791).

[22] C. Hesse, *op. cit.*, p.117.

[23] *ibid.*, p.118.

publishing followed,[24] leading eventually to the adoption of the so-called Revolutionary Decrees of 1791 and 1793.

The Performance Right

6–007 The Decree of January 13–19, 1791 concerning performances was the first law in France to grant an exclusive right to authors. However, as pointed out by Ginsburg, "the author's concerns clearly [did] not occupy centre stage".[25] The main goal of the Decree was to introduce the freedom for any citizen to establish a theatre and there to perform the plays of his choice, thus breaking the *Comédie française*'s monopoly over the works of Corneille, Molière and Racine. The abolition of that monopoly would also lead to competition between theatres, thus making it easier for playwrights to have their new plays performed. At the same time, the Decree provided that the works of living authors could not be performed in France without their express consent in writing. The penalty for failure to observe this right of the author was forfeiture to him of any revenue derived from the performance. The right of the author lasted for his life and accrued to his heirs for five years thereafter. All works of authors dead for more than five years fell into the public domain.[26]

Le Chapelier introduced the draft Decree in a speech much quoted for the eloquence with which he espoused the rights of authors. The fact that he also considered the public interest in connection with these rights has attracted less attention. He began his report by saying that the law should be decided according to the principles of liberty and public property. He said that, in seeking rights for themselves, the dramatic authors recognised the rights of the public and accepted without hesitation that five years after the death of the author works should become public property.

He defined the rights of authors and their rights in relation to those of the public, adding that this was the system operating in England, as follows:

---

[24] *ibid.*, pp.118–125 for an account of these proposals.

[25] J.C. Ginsburg, "A Tale of Two Copyrights: Literary Property in Revolutionary France and America", [1991] 147 R.I.D.A. 131 at 157. See also A. Lucas, *op.cit.*, para.8.

[26] *Décret relatif aux spectacles*, No. 27, January 13–19, 1791 (see Appendix 3 of this study).

The most sacred, most legitimate, most unassailable, and if I may put it this way, the most personal of all properties, is a work which is the fruit of the imagination of a writer; *however, it is a property of a kind quite different from other properties.* When an author has delivered his work to the public, when the work is in the hands of the public at large, so that all educated men may come to know it, assimilate the beauties contained therein and commit to memory the most pleasing passages, *it seems that from that moment on the writer has associated the public with his property, or rather has transmitted it to the public outright;* however, during the lifetime of the author and for a few years after his death nobody may dispose of the product of his genius without consent. *But also, after that fixed period, the property of the public begins, and everybody should be able to print and publish the works which have helped to enlighten the human spirit.*[27] [Emphasis added]

"Thus, there are two requirements, namely that 'such men derive **6–008** some fruit from their labour', but also that after the set period, public property commences'..."

"Hence, disclosure represents the ultimate manifestation of the authors' sovereignty; the relationship of creation which bound him to the *work* gives way to a relationship of *communication* between the *author* and the *public* ... there is a dual imperative ... namely the *joint protection* of the *author* and his *work*, in the interest of the public itself for whom the *work* is naturally intended".[28]

A proposal to increase the term of protection p.m.a. to 10 years was rejected.[29]

A subsequent Decree of August 30, 1792 concerning the rights of dramatic authors made these rights subject to compliance with formalities; the author was obliged to notify the public, at the time of publication of the play, that he had retained the public performance rights. The notice had to be printed at the head of the text of the play and deposited with a notary (Articles 4–6). Otherwise the author lost his rights. The Decree also reduced the term of protection of plays to

---

[27] For the full text of Le Chapelier's report see *Archives Parlementaires de 1787 à 1860, Première Série, Tome xxii,* January 13, 1791, p.210 *et seq.; Le Moniteur Universel,* January 15, 1791.

[28] D. Becourt, "La Révolution française et le droit d'auteur pour un nouvel universalisme", [1990] 143 R.I.D.A. 231 at 236 and 250.

[29] Le Chapelier's report, *op. cit.,* no. 27, above; proposal of M. Delandine, p.216.

ten years following publication (Article 8), as opposed to the period of life plus five years provided for by the 1791 Decree. This revolutionary Decree cannot be said to have advanced the cause of authors' rights; on the contrary, the potential term of protection was greatly reduced.

The Reproduction Right

6–009 The reproduction right of the author obtained recognition with the adoption by the Convention of the Decree of July 19–24, 1793. It was agreed upon without discussion following a report of de Lakanal as eloquent as that of Le Chapelier, describing the rights of authors as "of all properties the least subject to dispute, the increase of which can neither harm republican equality, nor offend liberty".[30]

The Decree provided that authors of writings of all kinds, composers of music, painters and makers of drawings who make engravings of paintings and drawings, should enjoy during their lifetime the exclusive right to sell, have sold and distribute their works in France and to assign their property therein in whole or in part. Their heirs enjoyed the same rights for a period of 10 years after the death of the author. Provision was also made for the deposit of two copies of works of literature and engravings with the national library and, as Ginsburg has observed, several early court decisions under the 1793 law held that it was the required deposit that gave rise to the copyright.[31]

Penalties for infringement included seizure of unauthorised copies and damages of up to the equivalent of the price of 3,000 copies of the original edition.

6–010 The two texts of 1791 and 1793 remained the basic legislation in force in France in the field of authors' rights until 1957, complemented only by case law and a series of legislative texts which modified those of the Revolution as regards term of protection and on matters of detail.

On the occasion of the second centenary of the French Revolution, the revolutionary Decrees on authors' rights were commemorated *inter alia* in an article by the distinguished French copyright

---

[30] Report of M. de Lakanal on behalf of the Committee of Public Instruction, *Le Moniteur Universel*, July 21, 1793, p.176.
[31] J. C. Ginsburg, *op.cit.*, p.167.

expert, André Kerever.[32] He drew attention to the following:

> There is often a misconception about Le Chapelier's report which refers to authors' rights as "the most sacred and the most legitimate, the most unassailable and the most personal of all properties", which terms are echoed in Lakanal's report introducing the 1793 Decree where a relationship is established between authors' rights and "natural law". This absolute character of the property right merely concerns non-disclosed[33] works, for once they have been disclosed, *i.e.* "when an author has handed his work over to the public, he (the author) has made it (the public) a party to his property or, rather, *he has transferred his property to it in full*".
>
> This was because the Revolutionary legislators, men of law and order, were bent on providing "stationers" [publishers] or "theatrical companies [disseminators] with a legitimate legal basis against piracy or infringement...."
>
> Thus, far from being personalist in nature, authors' rights as they emerged from the French Revolution were inspired above all by legal and economic considerations. It was the 19th Century which, through the case law endorsed by the law of March 11, 1957, was to begin to shape out the personalist aspect of authors' rights....
>
> In other words, authors' rights as sketched out by the French Revolution differ very little from English or American copyright. It could even perhaps be held that the copyright recognised by the American Consitution of 1787 is more personalist than the one stemming from the Decrees of 1791 and 1793 since the American text recognises the authors' exclusive right without restriction whereas the Le Chapelier report insists on the fact that a work which has been disclosed belongs to the "public"....
>
> Thus the French Revolution's "droit d'auteur" was perfectly in line with the corresponding English and American copyrights. At the end of the 18th Century, the right's "continental drift"—creators' rights and right over the copy—had not yet occurred.[34] It

---

[32] A. Kerever, "The French Revolution and Authors' Rights", [1989] 141 R.I.D.A. 9 *et seq.* See also A. Kerever, "Copyright: The Achievements and Future Development of European Legal Culture", [1990] *Copyright* 130.

[33] *i.e.* unpublished works (author's note).

[34] R.I.D.A. translation: the French text reads "*La 'dérive des continents' du droit d'auteur—droit du créateur et droit sur l'exemplaire*". In the context, what is meant seems rather to be: "the drifting apart of the continents—the right of the creator on the one hand and copyright on the other".

was the 19th century that was to witness this drift, this separation between an author's right as a right of the person of the creator over the work, considered to be an extension of that person, and the system of copyright which dissociates the right of the person, governed by common law, from the economic right of exploitation of the work.

Kerever's viewpoint is shared by Ginsburg:

> While traditional comparisons of French to Anglo-American law assert that France rejected intrumentalist theories in favor of copyright as the just and fair prerogative of creators, research in primary sources prompts a different conclusion. The various legislative texts reveal a hesitating and uneven progress toward protection of authors' rights. Authors are not securely at the core of the new literary property régime; rather, the public plays a major role. The 1791 text appears predominantly preoccupied with the recognition and enlargement of the public domain. [Lakanal's] speech made in favor of the 1793 law emphasizes that protecting authors will not prove detrimental to society.[35]

The Development of the Law Between 1793 and 1957

6–011 In the following section of this Chapter, the development of legislation on authors' rights during the next 150 years will be briefly traced. As will be seen, the changes in the law brought about by legislation during this period were not significant. As Plaisant noted, referring to the Law of 1793: "for 163 years, with just seven articles, [it] had been enough to protect the whole right of authors in the most extensive manner and in relation to the most unexpected matters".[36] That this was so is a tribute both to the law itself and to the courts which developed the law of copyright through case law.

---

[35] J. C. Ginsburg, *op. cit.* pp.156–157. See also C. Hesse, *op. cit.*, p.131.
[36] M. Plaisant, "Welcome to the Law", [1958] XIX R.I.D.A. 9.

Legislation

The number and importance of the legislative texts adopted between **6–012** 1793 and 1956 relevant to authors' rights and the book trade is not substantial. It is interesting to note, however, that in several of these texts the object appears to be more to control the book trade than to protect the rights of authors.[37]

A Decree of June 15, 1795 (25 prairial, year III) provided that the Commissioners of police and justices of the peace were responsible for enforcing the rights of authors granted by the 1793 Decree.

Two Decrees of March 22, 1805 (1 germinal, year XIII) and of June 8, 1806 regulated the rights of the owners of posthumous works and prohibited publishing such works together with works already in the public domain in order to prevent such owners obtaining "in their favour a sort of privilege for the sale of works which have become the property of the public".

A Decree of February 5, 1810 guaranteed the property rights of an author for himself and his wife for their lifetimes and for his children for 20 years after his death. Other heirs only benefitted for 10 years. It also contained provisions regulating the printing and book trade in response to a report from the Police Minister which stated: the aim to be achieved by a law on the book trade, is: (1) to prevent counterfeits which attack property, discourage industry and ruin commerce; (2) to prevent the publication of writings which could disturb public order or corrupt morals.

The Penal Code of 1810 made counterfeiting a misdemeanour and set **6–013** the level of fines to be paid by those found guilty thereof.

A Law of May 6, 1841 and an Order of December 13, 1842, concerning customs, regulated the importation of books into France. Where there was a presumption that copies of a book were pirated, importation was suspended and the matter referred to the Interior Ministry for decision within 40 days.

A Law of August 3, 1844 guaranteed the widows and children of authors of dramatic works the right to authorise the public performance thereof for 20 years p.m.a. in conformity with the Decree of February 5, 1810.

A Decree of March 28 and 30, 1852 conferred protection on works

---

[37] The sources for the material in this section are E. Pouillet, *op. cit.* p.879 *et seq.*; and M.-C. Dock, *op. cit.*, "Epilogue".

published abroad, making it a misdemeanor to counterfeit such works in France. Thus, the protection of the law was extended to foreign authors unconditionally. Similarly, the importation of pirated copies of French works from abroad was prohibited. This Decree was abrogated by the 1957 Law, when the French legislature decided to bring to an end this period of unilateral generosity.

A Law of April 8–19, 1854 gave widows of authors, composers and artists the rights in their deceased husband's works for the rest of their own lives. Children were entitled to enjoy these rights for 30 years after the death of the last surviving parent.

6–014 Decrees of December 9, 1857 and October 29, 1887 extended the laws on literary property to the colonies.

A Law of May 16, 1866 gave a special exemption for the reproduction without authorisation of music by mechanical musical instruments. This was subsequently revoked on November 10, 1917.

On July 14, 1866, the duration of the rights of authors, their heirs and successors-in-title was set at 50 years p.m.a. A widow lost her rights in her late husband's works, if legally separated at the time of his death or on remarriage.

A Law of July 29, 1881 provided for the deposit of two copies of all books and other printed publications with the national collections as well as of three copies of prints, engravings, sheet music and of all reproductions of works expressed otherwise than in the printed word.

The Law of March 11, 1902 extended the protection of the Law of July 19–24, 1793 to the works of sculptors and designers, "whatever the merit and purpose of the work".

6–015 A Law of April 9, 1910 regarding the rights of authors of artistic works provided that: "Subject to agreement to the contrary, the disposal of a work of art does not result in the disposal of the right of reproduction".

On May 20, 1920, artists were granted a "*droit de suite*" (artists' resale right) meaning that they became entitled to receive a percentage of the sales price of works of art sold at public auctions.

On May 19, 1925, the protection afforded to authors' rights was dissociated from the formality requiring legal deposit of copies of works.

On February 25, 1956, the National Fund for Letters (*Caisse nationale des lettres*) was established and a public paying domain introduced.

As Dock has pointed out: "On the whole, the legislation on authors' rights remained laconic. The upheavals which affected the dissemination of creative works as a result of the advent of records, films, radio and television were not the subject of any legislation for a long time".[38]

Case Law

A number of important principles emerged from the case law over the years. The merit or literary importance of a work was held to have no influence on rights. Thus, all works were protected, regardless of their quality. The courts also took a broad view of what could be considered a literary or artistic work; it had only to be the result of personal effort and work of the mind. Thus case law afforded protection *inter alia* to translations, theatrical adaptations, ballet scenarios, atlases, maps, plans, newspaper articles, compilations, dictionaries, guides, catalogues, prospectuses, etc. The form of the work, not the ideas contained therein, was protected. The same rules applied to musical works; arrangements and variations on works in the public domain were protected. As regards artistic works, the courts applied the 1793 Law "to all works of the graphic and plastic arts without distinction, provided it was the result of personal effort, however minimal the effort and however modest the personality".[39]

    6–016

The protection of photographs was much disputed. The courts were divided. According to one view, propounded in a series of cases beginning in 1863, a photograph was not an artistic work because it resulted from a mechanical process without recourse to the talent of an artist. According to a second line of cases, beginning also in 1863, photographs were considered to be productions of the mind within the meaning of the law. The photographer was responsible for deciding how the subject should be photographed and exposed to the light; in so doing he exercised taste, discernment and skill and therefore the resulting photograph represented a work of the mind.[40] According to a third approach, the court should decide case by case whether a particular photograph for which protection was sought merited protection as an artistic work. This was evidently the least

---

[38] M.-C. Dock, *op. cit.* p.160.

[39] E. Pouillet, *op. cit.* p.103; see E. Pouillet, *ibid.*, Chap.III, for a complete account of the case law and legislation in France as they developed between the Revolutionary Laws and 1908.

[40] Civil Court of the Seine, December 11, 1863, cited by E. Pouillet, *op. cit.*, p.130; Paris, June 12, 1863, cited by E. Pouillet, *op. cit.* p.133.

satisfactory approach, introducing as it did subjective, artistic criteria for protection, contrary to the spirit of the 1793 Law, which as seen above protected works without regard to their literary or artistic merit.

In 1905, it was held that a cinematographic film was an artistic work protected under the 1793 Law.[41]

Exceptions

6–017   The making of manuscript copies for the personal use of the individual making the copy was not considered an infringement of copyright, whereas a manuscript copy made for commercial purposes was. In 1928, it was held that the copying of extracts of works for use in schools was not an infringement (Paris, March 22, 1928). Quotation for the purpose of literary criticism or in support of or against an argument was permitted (Civil Court of the Seine, March 11, 1897), as was quotation for the purpose of historical documentation, teaching and information.

Moral Rights

6–018   The concept of the moral rights of authors developed in France in the last quarter of the nineteenth century and the first half of the twentieth century. Pouillet described these rights as being:

> the right, for the writer and artist, to create and to have his work respected. ... Differences of opinion exist as to its basis. Some consider it to be the very heart of the right of the author, others see in it only one aspect of that right; others distinguish it from the right of reproduction and give it a different basis, arguing that it is derived from the right that every man has to respect for his personality.[42]

Desbois described the moral right as it had developed through case law prior to the 1957 Law, as follows:

---

[41] Civil Court of the Seine, February 10, 1905, cited by E. Pouillet, *op. cit.*, p.140.
[42] E. Pouillet, *op. cit.*, p.256.

In a word, on first publication, the work enters the community, and *a fortiori*, the national heritage, but the economic exploitation thereof will be submitted to the influence or rather the supremacy of the moral right: the exercise of the latter will temper the effect of the transfer, in order to ensure respect for the links which unite the work to the personality of the creator.[43]

Moral rights were to find their apotheosis in the 1957 Law.

Proposals for Reform in the Nineteenth Century—Perpetual Rights versus the Public Interest

In the course of the nineteenth century, the French government **6–019** appointed a number of committees to look into and propose reform of the revolutionary laws on authors' rights. An account of the work of these committees by Jean Matthyssens published in 1954 relates that these committees all paid attention to the public interest,[44] as a study of the sources confirms.

In 1825, a committee was set up under the Chairmanship of the Vicomte de la Rochefoucault. According to Matthyssens: "The King insisted that this Committee should make every effort to reconcile the interests of authors and artists, and equally those of the public and trade".

The question of making authors' rights perpetual arose once more. In its report to the King dated 1828, the Committee rejected perpetual rights for the following reasons:

Such a privilege existed nowhere else; it would harm education by a monopoly lasting too long; it would become either onerous for the public, or illusory for the families; it would often falsely interpret the intentions of the author himself, who by publishing his work, had hoped that editions would increase and multiply easily after him. It therefore appeared to us, Sire, that while the present term of the exclusive right should be extended there should be a limit thereto.

---

[43] H. Desbois, *Le Droit d'auteur en France* (Paris, Dalloz, 3rd ed. 1978), p.265.
[44] J. Matthyssens, "Copyright Law Schemes in France during the Last Century", [1954] IV R.I.D.A. 15.

The Committee recommended a period of protection of 50 years p.m.a., commenting that "the provisions of the draft are the most favourable to their authors and their families that have ever been made in any country. They will stimulate talented men to compose great and serious works, in the certainty that their families will enjoy an honourable patrimony for many years".[45]

Nothing came of the proposals of the Committee.

6–020 A further Committee, this time under the chairmanship of the Comte de Ségur, was appointed in 1836. Again the question of perpetual rights was discussed. Although it seems the Committee "leaned towards perpetuity", it rejected it, expressing:

> fears that such a system would establish to the advantage of the authors' heirs or his assigns, a kind of everlasting tax on publishers, thus increasing the mercenary value of the books and putting a premium on foreign pirating, finally creating costly difficulties, awkward for trade and almost insurmountable as to assessment and the collection of this new tax. ... It was then a question for the Committee of fixing fair limits in the interests of all to the right of ownership of the various heirs of the authors.

The Committee settled in the end for 50 years p.m.a. but was concerned to reconcile the rights of an authors' heirs with the rights of the public to the enjoyment of works. The Committee proposed that, in the public interest, if an heir refused to authorise publication of a work, 15 years after the death of the author the matter could be referred to the courts for an auction of the rights.

Again, nothing came of the Committee's report.

6–021 Early in 1839, the Minister of Education, M. de Salvandy, was charged with making a report to the *Chambre des Pairs*. "The public interest seems to have been the first care of the Minister".[46]

Recommending a period of protection of 30 years p.m.a., M. de Salvandy said:

> Is there not another interest than that of the author and his children? Is there not another acquired right than theirs? Does the

---

[45] *Commission de la propriété littéraire, collection des procès-verbaux*, chairman, le Vicomte de la Rochefoucauld (Paris, Imprimerie de Pillet Aîné, 1826), p.326.

[46] J. Matthyssens, *op. cit.* p.34.

book really belong to them only? Can the verses of Racine be the exclusive property of a family, do they not belong to us all? ... Manifestly, literary ownership has its particular character inasmuch as it is indivisible between the parties entitled of the author [*sic: i.e.* heirs] and the community itself; that besides the right of some to exploit, there is the right of all to enjoy.

In May 1839, the Vicomte Siméon presented a draft Law relating to the rights of authors in their production in letters and arts. He also proposed a period of protection of 30 years p.m.a., giving the following reasons: **6–022**

The government found the duration of 50 years proposed by the Committees of 1825 and 1836 too long. They consider that the exclusive right of publishing thus prolonged, instead of serving the interests of the authors' descendants, would encourage pirating, just as prohibition in trade matters encourages smuggling. The sale of books is a trade that must not be over-shackled if it is to prosper.

In addition, it is of interest to note that Siméon also stated that "the right guaranteed to authors was not a natural right, but a privilege resulting from a benevolent concession of the law".

This draft was never submitted to the Chamber of Deputies.

In 1841, M. Villemain, Minister of Education, was asked to take up the matter once more. M. de Lamartine took part in the debate and persuaded his colleagues to propose a period of protection of 50 years p.m.a. Again, nothing came of the proposals for reform.

It was not until 1861 that a new Committee was set up of which M. Walewski was rapporteur and which reported to the Emperor in 1863.[47] This Committee favoured perpetual rights: "the Committee does not limit itself to adding as a new favour a few years to those that the present legislation grants as a benevolent remuneration, it grants perpetuity without which there is no true ownership".[48] However, referring to the need to reconcile the interests of authors and their families with the requirements of the public interest, the Committee recommended 50 years protection p.m.a. "as a major concession to **6–023**

---

[47] *Commission de la propriété littéraire et artistique, Rapports à l'Empereur, Décrets, Collection des procès-verbaux* (Paris, Imprimerie Impériale, 1863).

[48] *ibid.*, p.252.

the public interest", followed by a right to a royalty of 5 per cent on the sales price of reproductions of works and, in the case of dramatic works, half the amount of royalties paid to living authors.[49]

The question of duration was finally settled in 1866 by the Law of July 14 of that year, which fixed the duration of authors' rights at 50 years p.m.a. The argument for perpetual rights was lost for the moment only to be revived a century later in the perpetual moral rights granted by the 1957 Law. Unlike all the preceding drafts, which had aimed at a general revision of the law, the 1866 Law dealt only with the question of duration.

The Evolution of French Concepts of Authors' Rights

6-024   Case law solved some of the problems posed by new technology but, when a new Law on authors' rights was finally adopted on March 11, 1957, the legislator failed to address many of these problems. Desbois described the philosophy of the 1957 Law as having respected the French tradition of authors' rights, "since the primary concern of the legislator was to maintain the permanent and valid principles of the law in the future as in the present".[50]

The question may be posed, "What were the traditional principles of the French concepts of authors' rights" evoked by Desbois in 1957? How had these concepts evolved in the 150 years between the revolutionary laws of 1791 and 1793 and the Law on authors' rights of 1957?

As we have seen, the aims and objectives of the revolutionary laws did not differ greatly from the pre-existing copyright laws of England and the United States of America. What Kerever has called the authors' rights "continental drift—creator's right and right over the copy"—did not emerge from the legislative texts briefly described above but from case law and out of the development of the theory of moral rights by the courts from the last quarter of the nineteenth century onwards. The only clue the legislation described above gives to the drift lies in the laws which steadily increased the period of protection of the author and, after his death, of his widow and children.[51]

---

[49] *ibid.*, p.255.

[50] H. Desbois, "La loi française du 11 mars 1957", [1957] *Le droit d'auteur* 84.

[51] R. Plaisant, "La Durée du droit pécuniaire de l'auteur et de son évolution", *Mélanges A. Françon*, Paris, Dalloz (1995), p.351.

Indeed, as seen above, until the Law of 1866 introduced a period of **6–025** protection of 50 years p.m.a., so ending the controversy, there were continual voices calling for authors' rights to be perpetual, a demand which caused attention to be given to the nature of authors' rights.

The Rochefoucauld Committee on Literary Property in its 1826 report observed that there was no unanimous view of the nature of authors' rights:

> Two different ways of considering these rights have given rise to two opposed views. Some consider the creation of a literary work as establishing in favour of the author a property right which confers on him, together with the freedom to dispose of his work, the exclusive and perpetual benefit of the profits derived from its publication. Others see in this publication of ideas a hommage to society, which therefore becomes the owner of the published work, but has an obligation to indemnify the author for his work by the grant to him of certain advantages.[52]

Renouard, whose personal opinion was that a balance should be struck between the interests of authors and those of the public, and who feared that a property right would tip the balance too far in favour of authors,[53] described the state of the law in 1838 as follows: "Our legislation concerning intellectual property is incoherent and, above all, incomplete; however, at least it has a stable basis, and the establishment of rights limited in time has resolved the problem of conciliating the rights of authors with those of society".[54]

In 1881, the *Cour de Cassation* stated: "literary and artistic property, which is essentially personal property, has the same characteristics and should be treated in the same way as any other kind of property, with the exception of the limit which the public interest has imposed on its duration".[55]

In relation to this definition, Desbois noted that, at that time, the **6–026** analysis of moral rights had not been developed sufficiently for the Supreme Court to take account of it in parallel with economic rights.[56]

---

[52] Rochefoucauld Committee proceedings, above n.45, p.32.

[53] A.-C. Renouard, *op. cit.*, Vol.I, p.435 *et seq.*

[54] *ibid.*, p.6.

[55] Cited by H. Desbois, in: *Le Droit d'auteur en France, op. cit.*, p.265.

[56] *ibid.*

Pouillet, writing in 1908, gave the following definition of author's rights:

> The right of the author is the privilege recognised by the law to exploit his work, and reap all the benefits which the work admits of, to the exclusion of all others for a certain period. Once that period has expired, the work falls into the public domain and everybody is free to exploit it without restriction.[57]

For Pouillet, the right was a property right, albeit one of a special character, subject to special regulation. While having its source in natural law, it required different treatment to other types of property. As regards the argument that, since the author's right was a property right, it should be perpetual, Pouillet remarked the following:

> Did the legislator not have the the right, when for the first time he recognised and afforded protection to this property right, to lay down the conditions to which he considered it necessary to subject that protection, *in the general interest*. ... Is it not natural, therefore, for thelegislator, *in the general interest, in order to safeguard the right of the public to the intellectual enjoyment of the work*, to refuse to endorse perpetual authors' rights?[58] [Emphasis added]

Thus, at the turn of the twentieth century, it would seem that authors' rights were regarded as special property rights, granted by the State, *i.e.* not arising automatically out of natural law, and limited in duration in the public interest.

The Twentieth Century

The Road to Reform: The Draft Law of 1945

6–027   In August 1945, a Committee on Intellectual Property established under the chairmanship of Professor Jean Escarra, submitted draft legislation to the government. The draft was accompanied by a letter which stated the aims of the Committee:

---

[57] E. Pouillet, *op. cit.*, p.24.
[58] *ibid.*, p.30.

Thus the present draft is first of all a codification of the right of literary and artistic ownership: it is constantly inspired in the final reading of each text, by the concern to use the copyright as a means of favouring literary and artistic creation and of insuring the integrity of works each of which has its share of originality.[59]

This was the first draft of what in due course became the 1957 Law. In the meantime, successive drafts were considered by the various government departments concerned and discussed with interested parties. It was not until June 9, 1954 that a bill was finally tabled at the National Assembly and that the work of the Committee came to an end.

The 1957 Law on Literary and Artistic Property

The Parliamentary debates which led to the adoption of the new Law **6–028** on March 11, 1957 thus lasted three years. The preamble of the bill had stated its object as being:

To codify the case law that has been created in the last century and a half concerning authors' rights and to lay down in a definitive text the latest state of French doctrine in this field; to answer also to the need felt by intellectual creators to be protected, taking into account the new economic and technical conditions and also the new forms of art which have come into being since the legislation of the French Revolution.[60]

The Vice-President and Rapporteur of the Intellectual Property Committee of the Government, Marcel Boutet, stated in a commentary on the new Law: "French law had from the beginning to choose between two intellectual tendencies; the one which attributed the pre-eminence to the person of the author and the other that envisaged above all the purpose of the book, that is to say its communication to the public".

According to him, the author's right:

---

[59] Cited by J. Vilbois in: "Historical Account", [1958] XIX R.I.D.A. 41.
[60] See *Exposé des motifs du projet de Loi sur la propriété littéraire et artistique*, annexed to the Minutes of the session of the *Assemblée nationale*, held on June 9, 1954 (doc. no.8612) [1954] V R.I.D.A. 150.

Born during the French Revolution which proclaimed the eminent dignity of the human person ... the texts of 1791 and 1793 could not fail to give precedence to the creator. It is the creation, intellectual manifestation of the personality, that invests the author with a number of rights, without inasmuch injuring public interests.

The aim of the legislation was:

less to seek to innovate than to codify the existing law. ... Effectively, the new law presents no modification in structure with respect to the old texts and to the case law built up over a century and a half; it is still the spirit of the original doctrine of copyright that goes on living.

It is thus that the legislation of 1957 carries into effect the synthesis of the author's rights and the interests of the public, in the preeminence of the creator.[61]

6–029 The references to the interests of the public in the passages cited above are among the very few such references that the author has found in the reports on the preparatory work leading to the adoption of the 1957 Law and in the commentaries which followed on from its adoption. A lone voice in the Council of the Republic (the equivalent of the present Senate under the 1946 Constitution) spoke briefly during the parliamentary debate of the public interest and the role of copyright in the dissemination of works to the public.[62] Even where reference is made to the interests of the public, these are not defined and there is no discussion of the need to establish a balance between the rights of authors and the interests of the public. In assessing the new Law, most commentators took as their starting point the question posed by Alphonse Tournier "whether in the interests of authors it has conserved the achievements of the old law and the so-called legacy

---

[61] M. Boutet, "General Considerations", [1958] XIX R.I.D.A. 13.

[62] Speech of M. Jacques Debû-Bridel, *Conseil de la République* session of October 30, 1956, JO October 31, 1956: "In a law such as this, whatever the interests of the authors, which we must defend, whatever the perfectly legitimate interests of producers, which we must respect, the real interested party, not to say the only interested party, is the national community, in other words the public ... we must not forget that our main aim should be to defend the possibility of wider dissemination of works of the mind."

of the past".[63] Tournier, however, also considered whether, and to what extent, it had taken into account new ideas and new facts which had emerged in the modern world. Tournier refers to the public interest only in relation to certain limitations imposed by the law on the rights of authors:

> Whereas the legislator showed the utmost concern for the author, he was obliged to take account of "the author's social role", and, therefore, to limit him in the exercise of his rights. The diffusive power of modern technical devices is such that literary and artistic productions have become an integral part of the daily life of the masses, and the author must therefore make certain concessions in the public interest.

According to Desbois, the 1957 Law raised the moral right "to the first place because, on the juridical level, its mission is to protect the personality of the author through the work."

Hence the new Law in its Article 1 put the emphasis on moral rights, providing that:

> The author of a work of the mind shall enjoy in that work, by the mere fact of its creation an exclusive incorporeal property right which shall be enforceable against all persons.[64] The legislator does not intervene to attribute to the writer, the artist, the composer, an arbitrary monopoly, under the influence of considerations of expediency, in order to stimulate the activity of men of letters and artists in the interest of the collectivity; the author's rights exist independently of his [the legislator's] intervention.[65]

It will be seen that, in Desbois' opinion, the 1957 Law by giving pride of place to moral rights had recognised that authors' rights exist independently of the intervention of the legislator. *This was a new approach in French copyright law.* As seen above, up to and including the early part of the present century authors' rights were regarded as special property rights, granted by the State.

In other respects, the 1957 Law consolidated the existing legislation   **6–030**

---

[63] A. Tournier, "An Appraisal of the Law", [1958] XIX R.I.D.A. 79.

[64] *cf.* Intellectual Property Code 1992, Art.L.111–1, first sentence.

[65] H. Desbois, "The Moral Right", [1958] XIX R.I.D.A. 121 at 125; see also H. Desbois, "La loi française du 11 mars 1957", *op. cit.*, n.50, above, pp.184, 185.

and case law. Its provisions remain the basis of the present provisions on literary and artistic property contained in the Intellectual Property Code, 1992.[66]

As discussed above, moral rights were introduced here for the first time in French legislation, the author enjoying the right to respect for his name, his authorship and his work. The right was attached to his person and was to be perpetual, inalienable and imprescriptible (Article 6 (L.121–1)). The non-limitative list of protected works embraced all those works previously recognised by the courts as protected by the revolutionary laws and included cinematographic works and works produced by a process analogous to cinematography.[67] Photographic works were protected to the extent that they were of an artistic or documentary character as were other works of a like character produced by a process analogous to photography (Article 3 (L.122–2)). Authorship was confined to physical persons. Legal entities could not be regarded as authors except in the case of a collective work. Thus authorship of a cinematographic work vested in the co-authors (of the script, adaptation, dialogue, music and the director), although the Law introduced a legal presumption of assignment to the producer of the right to exploitation of the work (Article 17 (L.132–23)). Case law had previously recognised the producer as the author.[68]

The economic rights of the author, which continued to subsist for 50 years p.m.a. (Article 21),[69] included the performance right and the right of reproduction. Performance was defined as consisting in the direct communication of the work to the public by means of public recitation, musical and dramatic performance, public presentation, dissemination by any method of words, sounds or images, public projection and broadcast transmission (Articles 26 and 27 (L.122–1 and L.122–2)). The principle that the author should benefit from a proportional participation in the receipts resulting from the sale or

---

[66] To illustrate the continuity of the law, where Arts of the 1957 Law are referred to hereafter, the equivalent Arts of the Intellectual Property Code 1992 are cited in brackets.

[67] There was one exception to the rule that all works recognised by the courts were protected under the new Law. On March 13, 1957, the Civil Court of Paris had found that a producer of sound recordings was entitled to protection with respect to his original recording and that such recordings had to be assimilated in all respects to original literary and artistic works. [1957] XVII R.I.D.A. 162.

[68] E. Pouillet, op. cit. p.140.

[69] Calculated from the end of the year of the authors' death.

exploitation of a work was laid down (Article 35 (L.131–4)). Detailed rules were established with regard to performance and publishing contracts for the protection of authors.

As mentioned above, in the public interest, a number of limitations on the rights of authors were laid down in the Law. Permitted uses included: private and gratuitous performances carried out exclusively within the family circle; copies or reproductions reserved strictly for the private use of the copier and not intended for collective use. Furthermore, provided that the name of the author and the source were clearly stated, the following uses were permitted: analyses and short quotations justified by the critical, polemic, educational, scientific, or informatory nature of the work in which they are incorporated; press reviews; dissemination of public speeches through the press or by broadcast programmes; parody, pastiche and caricature, observing the rules of the genre (Article 41 (L.122–5)). Certain recordings of broadcasts were also permitted "by reason of the national interest which they may represent or of their documentary character" for preservation in official archives (Article 45 (L.132–20)). These limitations are still to be found in the present Intellectual Property Code 1992 and are discussed below in the context of the statutory exceptions permitted under the present law, as interpreted by the Courts in case law.

The Public Interest in the Debate for Reform and the 1985 Law

Commenting on the adoption of the 1985 Law on Authors' Rights **6–031** and on the Rights of Performers, Producers of Phonograms and Videograms and Audiovisual Communication Enterprises, the Minister of Culture, Jack Lang, set out the philosophy of the Government of the day with regard to these rights, saying *inter alia*:

> This reform is one of the essential juridical aspects of an overall strategy aimed at endowing France with the material and intellectual means of meeting the challenges confronting it in the cultural sphere. It behoves the national community to apply itself to fostering the creation of intellectual works. The State does so by appropriating considerable resources and by organising suitable institutions to provide for needs that the market alone cannot meet.

It does so also by providing its partners in the private sector with rules of the game that are clear and adapted to technological and social developments. Such is the purpose of the law....

In order to do this, the technical upheavals that have occurred during the past thirty years had to be taken into account and the economic and financial conditions required to foster creation had to be established....

This draft law drew its inspiration from three principles:

— to facilitate concerted action among those participating in the creation of intellectual works;

— to provide them with one of the most advanced systems of legal protection in the world;

— to foster the dissemination of works to the public.[70]

M. Lang had introduced the bill into Parliament with the same words in his *exposé des motifs*. He made therein a number of other points relevant to the public interest. In respect of Part II of the bill concerning related rights he remarked:

It is in this field that there is the most acute need to legislate. It is a question of conferring rights [on performers, producers and audiovisual communication enterprises] in order to enable them to master the economic and social consequences of the rapid development of new means of communication without however obstructing their use.

With reference to Part IV, which established rules governing the operation of collecting societies for the first time, subjecting their activities to the approval of the Ministry of Culture, he observed that this was "necessary in order to guard the authors, performers and producers as well as the broadcasters and the public against possible abuses in the exercise of their rights by the societies".[71]

---

[70] J. Lang, "The law of 3 July 1985", [1986] 127 R.I.D.A. 6 *et seq.* The *travaux préparatoires* relating to the adoption of the new law were published in French in [1986] 127 R.I.D.A. 167, *et seq.*

[71] *Exposé des motifs* of the draft law on the rights of authors and the rights of performers, producers of phonograms and videograms and audiovisual communication enterprises, presented to parliament in the name of M. Pierre Mauroy, Prime Minister, by M. Jack Lang. French text in [1986] 127 R.I.D.A. 168.

During a debate in the Senate in April 1985, M. Lang expressed the belief that the bill represented a balance between the needs of the various interested parties, including those of the public interest.[72]

The rapporteur of the Committee of the National Assembly, M. Alain Richard, in his report on the bill said: **6–032**

> The main purpose of the bill (no.2169) is to adapt the legislation on literary and artistic property to technical, economic and social developments, recognising moreover specific rights in favour of those auxiliaries of creation, the performers and producers. ... It is incumbent on the State to fix the respective rights of the various partners in intellectual creation, with the aim of promoting a large measure of cooperation, ensuring that the interested parties obtain appropriate legal protection and finally of encouraging the exploitation of the national heritage.[73]

Reference may also be made to the Report of M. Charles Jolibois, rapporteur of the responsible Senate Committee on the occasion of the second reading of the bill. He stated that:

> The Senate, throughout its consideration of the draft law, has endeavoured never to lose sight of the fact that authors' rights and the rights related thereto should be applied within a competitive French production. It is of course a question of being in a position to produce works competitively as against competitors abroad and, moreover, to avoid blockages in the mechanism of production.[74]

Likewise, the report of M. Charles Metzinger, on behalf of the Committee for Cultural, Family and Social Affairs, stressed the fact that the bill aimed to ensure a favourable environment for creativity by adapting "our legislation to the technological upheavals which

---

[72] *Journal officiel*, session of April 2, 1985.

[73] Report by A. Richard in the name of the *Commission des lois constitutionelles de la Législation et de l'Administration générale de la République sur le projet de loi relatif aux droits d'auteur et aux droits des artistes-interprètes, des producteurs de phonogrammes et de videogrammes et des entreprises de communication audiovisuelle.* See document of the *Assemblée nationale* no.2235 (Annex to the minutes of the session of June 26, 1984), [1986] 127 R.I.D.A. 176 *et seq.*

[74] Report of C. Jolibois in the name of the Special Committee of the Senate on the draft Law adopted with amendments by the National Assembly on second reading. Doc. *Sénat* No.350. French text in [1986] 127 R.I.D.A. 278 *et seq.* at 279.

have taken place over the past thirty years and by creating the economic and financial conditions which are essential for the furtherance of creativity".[75]

6–033 It is important to note that the 1985 Law did not replace the 1957 Law but amended it. It extended the definition of cinematographic works to include "other works consisting of moving sequences of images, with or without sound, together referred to as audiovisual works". The limitation on the protection of photographs to those "of an artistic or documentary character" was removed. Graphical and typographical works and computer programs were protected. Producers of audiovisual works were given protection and their rights defined (the presumption of assignment to the producer of the exclusive exploitation rights in the audiovisual work was confirmed). The term of protection for musical compositions was extended to 70 years. Part II of the Law dealt with so-called neighbouring or related rights, introducing for the first time protection for performers and producers of phonograms and videograms. Moral rights were recognised for performers as well as the right to authorise the fixation, reproduction and communication to the public of performances. The authorisation of producers of phonograms and videograms was required for reproduction, making available to the public by way of sale, exchange or rental, or communication to the public of their phonograms or videograms.

However, neither the producer nor the performer could oppose the broadcasting or public performance of a phonogram, such use entitling them only to remuneration. These rights were granted for a period of 50 years from publication or performance, respectively, whereas the moral rights of performers were made perpetual. The Law also introduced remuneration to be paid to authors, performers and producers for the private copying of phonograms and videograms (Part III). Part IV introduced rules governing the administration of collection and distribution societies. All activities in respect of videograms intended for the private use of the general public were made subject to supervision by the National Cinematographic Centre (Part VI). Finally, the sanctions and penalties for infringement in the Penal Code were updated and strengthened.

---

[75] *Observations de la commission des Affaires culturelles, familiales et sociales présentées par M. Charles Metzinger, rapporteur pour avis*, No.2235, p.105.

The increase in the period of protection of musical works to 70 years p.m.a. was, as reported by Kerever,

> introduced during parliamentary discussion of the government bill without eliciting any major theoretical debate. The Parliament appeared to be more sensitive to publishers' problems than to the author's situation. The idea was to enable publishers to amortize investments, larger for certain works than for others, by lengthening the term of protection.[76]

According to M. Richard's report on the second reading of the National Assembly, the Senate, which had introduced the amendment, had also been influenced by the fact that a number of France's competitors granted a longer period of protection than 50 years.[77] A proposal by the National Assembly to extend the term of protection of all literary and artistic works was rejected by the Senate.[78]

Statutory Exceptions to Protection

As already mentioned above,[79] the 1957 Law had imposed certain **6–034** statutory limitations on the rights of authors in what Tournier described as "certain concessions in the public interest".[80] Seen as respecting the right of the public to information and culture,[81] these limitations were laid down originally in Article 41 (L.122–5) of the 1957 Law and are summarised above. The 1985 Law modified the provisions of Article 41 of the 1957 Law in only two respects. First, it extended the exception allowing broadcasting of public speeches so as

---

[76] A. Kerever, "One Aspect of the Law of July 3, 1985: Modernisation of the Law of March 11, 1957", [1986] 127 R.I.D.A. 22.

[77] Report of A. Richard in the name of the *Commission des lois constitutionelles, de la législation et de l'administration générale de la République* on the bill as modified by the Senate, Document No.2682 of the *Assemblée nationale* (Annex to the minutes of the session of May 15, 1985), [1986] 127 R.I.D.A. 255. See also speech of C. Jolibois in the Journal *officiel*, Senate session of April 3, 1985, p.104.

[78] Jolibois report, *op. cit.*, p.282.

[79] See above, paras 6–029 and 6–030.

[80] A. Tournier, *op. cit.*, n.63, above, p.95. See also A. Françon, "Intérêt public et droit d'auteur en France", in E. Derieux and P. Trudel, "L'intérêt public, principe du droit de la communication", (Victoires Editions, 1996), p.77 *et seq.*.

[81] E. Derieux, "Bases de données et droit du public à l'information", *Les Petites Affiches*, 1998, no.21, p.13; A. and H.-J. Lucas, *op. cit.*, no.28.

to cover any means of telediffusion.[82] Secondly, and of major importance, the exception permitting the making of copies for the private use of the copier[83] was restricted in that the authors and performers of works fixed on phonograms or videograms and the producers of such phonograms or videograms were given the right to receive remuneration for the reproduction of works for private use.[84] Thus, it remained legal for an individual to make a copy for his own use but in consideration therefore the right owners were entitled to be remunerated for the making of the copy. As M. Richard pointed out in his report of the Committee of the National Assembly on the Bill,[85] it was necessary to provide such a system of remuneration because: "the private copying of works had the result not only of reducing the remuneration due individually to each author or auxiliary of creation, but also of reducing the activity of the cultural and artistic professions and hence the level of employment". For this reason, also, the law requires that 25 per cent of the amounts derived from the remuneration for private copying should be used for activities aimed at promoting creativity, live entertainment and the training of performers.[86] The right to remuneration may be exercised only through collecting societies.[87] In July 2001, the law was amended to extend the right to remuneration expressly to private copying on digital recording media. The types of recording media, the rates of remuneration and the conditions of payment of such remuneration are determined by a Committee chaired by a representative of the State and composed of representatives of the beneficiaries and other interested parties, such as the manufacturers and importers of recording media and consumers (Article L.311–5).[88]

---

[82] Art.11 of the Law of July 3, 1985.

[83] Art.41(2) of the Law of March 11, 1957.

[84] Arts 31–37 of the Law of July 3, 1985. *cf* Arts L.311–1–311–8 of the Intellectual Property Code, 1992.

[85] See above n.73, *op. cit.*, p.181.

[86] Art.38 of the Law of July 3, 1985 (*cf* Art.L.321–9 Intellectual Property Code, 1992).

[87] Art.L.311–6 Intellectual Property Code, 1992 and see Title II of the Code on Royalty Collection and Distribution Societies.

[88] The decisions of the Committee are published in the *Journal officiel de la République française*, see decision of June 30, 1986 (JO August 23) and decision of January 4, 2001, concerning remuneration payable with respect to digital media such as CDs, CD ROMs, DVDs and mini-discs (JO, January 7, 2001, p.336). Law No.2001–624 of July 17, 2001, Art.15, amending *inter alia* Art.L 311–1 of the Intellectual Property Code,

Recent Developments

Since the 1985 Law was adopted, there have been a number of leg-   **6–035**
islative developments.[89]

Intellectual Property Code, 1992

An important development was the codification into one legislative   **6–036**
text, the Intellectual Property Code of July 1, 1992,[90] of the laws on
industrial property and those on literary and artistic property. The
new Code groups together in one text all previous laws in the field of
intellectual property, a term used for the first time in French legislation, although, of course, well known in the literature and in international and comparative law. The aim of the legislator in adopting
the Code was to assist the user and to promote legal certainty, by
gathering together the various laws on intellectual property and
restating the law in a systematic, orderly and codified form. Part One
deals with literary and artistic property and brings both authors' rights
and related rights together under this heading.[91] The architect of the
Code, the chairman of the Commission for the codification of laws,
described the aim of the Code as being to "group the texts which
concern, on the one hand, "literary and artistic property" and, on the
other hand, "industrial property": thus, the law concerning works of
the mind—authors' rights, patents, designs and models, trademarks,

---

1992. A proposal in January 2001 by the Minister of Culture, Mme. Catherine Tasca, to
impose levies also on computer equipment such as hard discs, digital decoders and MP3
recording machines was strongly criticised by other members of the Government and
appears to have been dropped.

[89] For contemporary commentaries on the French law, see *inter alia*: A. Bertrand, *Le
droit d'auteur et les droits voisins*, 2nd ed. (Paris, Masson, 1999); C. Colombet, *Propriété
littéraire et artistique*, (Paris, Dalloz, 8th ed., 2001); B. Edelman, *Droits d'auteur, droits
voisins. Droit d'auteur et marché*, (Paris, Dalloz, 1993); A. Françon, *Cours de propriété
littéraire, artistique et industrielle*, Paris, Les Cours de droit 1996–1997 (updated 1999); P.-
Y. Gautier, *Propriété littéraire et artistique*, 4th ed., (Paris, PUF, 2001), coll. Droit fondamental; A. and H.-J. Lucas, *Traité de la propriété littéraire et artistique*, (Paris, Litec, 2nd
ed. 2001); A. Lucas, *Droit d'auteur et numérique*, (Paris, Litec 1998); R. Plaisant, *Propriété
littéraire et artistique*, (Paris, Delmas, 1985); P. Sirinelli, *Propriété littéraire et artistique et droits
voisins*, (Paris, Dalloz, 1992), coll. Mementos.

[90] Law No.92.597 of July 1, 1992, on the Intellectual Property Code (Legislative
Part), Official Journal of July 3, 1992, replacing the Laws of March 11, 1957 and July 3,
1985. The Code has been amended on a number of occasions in the meantime.

[91] In this connection, see A. Lucas, *op. cit.*, paras 1, 3 and 13.

computer programs—will be the subject of a single, coherent text".[92]

The Code has been generally welcomed by the interested circles; the legitimacy of the law of intellectual property is considered to have been reaffirmed and strengthened.[93]

Subsequent amendments to the intellectual property code

6–037 The Code has been frequently amended in the meantime, so far as both authors' rights and related rights are concerned, both to keep up with technical developments and, as in the United Kingdom and Germany, to comply with the European Community Directives on copyright and related rights.

First, increased protection against infringement of all intellectual property, including authors' and related rights, was introduced in 1994.[94] New maximum penalties were imposed of up to two years imprisonment and a fine of up to FFR1 million and the sale, exportation and importation of infringing works were made subject to the same penalties.

The first new law to implement European Union legislation in the field of authors' and related rights was also adopted in 1994. This concerned amending the Code to comply with the EC Directive on the legal protection of computer programs.[95] Meanwhile, the EC Directives on satellite broadcasting and cable retransmission,[96] the

---

[92] G. Braibant, Chairman of the *Commission supérieure de la codification*, speech on November 7, 1989.

[93] For a critical analysis of the Code, see V.-L. Benabou and V. Varet, *La Codification de la propriété intellectuelle*, (IRPI, La Documentation française, Paris, 1998). The Code with annotations is published and regularly updated by both Dalloz and Litec, Paris.

[94] Law No.94–102 of February 5, 1994 (*cf.* Arts 335–2 and L.335–4 Intellectual Property Code).

[95] Law No.94–361 of May 10, 1994 implementing EC Directive No.91/250 EEC of May 14, 1991 on the Legal Protection of Computer Programs. See also Decree No.96–103 of February 2, 1996, in application of Law No.94–361 of May 10, 1994 concerning the Legal Protection of Computer Programs and Amending the Intellectual Property Code, 1992.

[96] Law No.97–283 of March 27, 1997, transposing into the Intellectual Property Code EC Council Directives Nos 93/83 of September 27, 1993 on Coordination of Certain Rules concerning Copyright and Rights Related to Copyright applicable to Satellite Broadcasting and Cable Retransmission and 93/98 of October 29, 1993 harmonising the Term of Protection of Copyright and Certain Related Rights. See also F. Olivier and E. Barbry, "Aperçu rapide relatif à la loi n°97–283 du 27 mars 1997—Quelles dispositions pour la diffusion des oeuvres par cable et satellites?", in *JCP* 1977, éd. G. n°22, *Actualités*; F. Pollaud-Dulian, "Brèves Réflexions sur la loi n°97–283 du 27 mars 1997", *JCP* 1997, éd. G. *Chronique*, 4024, p.233; and A. Françon, "Propriété littéraire et artistique", in *Chroniques de législation et de jurisprudence française*, *RTD com.*, April–June 1997, 50, p.252.

term of protection of copyright and related rights[97] and that on the protection of databases have all been implemented,[98] the former in 1997 and the latter in 1998. However, the EC Directive on rental and lending rights has not been implemented to date[99] and, while the Intellectual Property Code is in conformity with most of the provisions of the Directive, the main outstanding issue is the public lending right. At present, library lending of books is free.[1]

The period of protection for the exploitation rights of authors has been extended fron 50 years to 70 years p.m.a. calculated from the end of the year of the authors' death; however, the moral rights of authors and performers remain perpetual. In the absence of any harmonising provision on the subject of moral rights in the EC Directive, the Member States are free to follow their own traditions and preferences in this regard. The term of protection for the exploitation rights of the beneficiaries of related rights remains unchanged at 50 years. **6–038**

The extension of the duration of the economic rights of authors by means of upwards harmonisation in the European Union has been generally welcomed in France[2]; the justification put forward by the European Directive for the extension, the increase in life expectancy and the desire to give a right to two generations of heirs was not contested, contrary to opinion in the United Kingdom and that of other commentators. Likewise, the freedom for France to continue its policy of protection in perpetuity for moral rights was also welcomed.

---

[97] Law n°.97–283 of March 27, 1997, cf. n.96, above. See also F. Pollaud-Dulian, "The Duration of Copyright", [1999] 176 R.I.D.A. 83 and R. Plaisant, "La Durée du droit pécuniaire de l'auteur et son évolution", (Mélanges A. Françon, Dalloz, 1995), p.351.

[98] Law No.98–536 of July 1, 1998, transposing into the Intellectual Property Code EC Council Directive No.96/9/EC of March 11, 1996 on the legal protection of databases. See also: L. Costes, "Le nouveau régime de la protection juridique des bases de données", in Cahiers Lamy Informatique 1998, no.107 (Part I) and 108 (Part 2), p.1; P. Gaudrat, "Loi de transposition de la directive 96/9 du 11 mars 1996 sur les bases de données: dispositions relatives au droit d'auteur", RTD com. 51(3), July–Sept. 1998, p.598; B. Edelman, "Les bases de données ou le triomphe des droits voisins", D. 2000, p.89; E. Dérieux, "Bases de données et droit à l'information", Les Petites Affiches, 1998, n°21, p.11.

[99] Directive No.92/100 EEC of November 19, 1992 on Rental Right and Lending Right and on certain Rights Related to Copyright in the Field of Intellectual Property.

[1] The Minister of Culture at the time made a proposal for a system where payments to authors would be made not by the users but out of public funds (from the State, public authorities and libraries) but this is still under discussion. Proposal of Mme. Catherine Tasca of December 19, 2000.

[2] See F. Pollaud-Dulian, nn.96 and 97, above; A. Françon, n.96 above.

Implementation of the Directive has necessitated an amendment to the law concerning the term of protection of audiovisual works: the starting point for the term of protection for such works is the death of the last surviving co-author, but to comply with the Directive and in relation to the term of protection only the following are considered to be co-authors: the director, the author of the screenplay, the author of the dialogue and the composer. France has also been able to maintain its opposition to treating the producer of the film as a co-author, the authorship of cinematographic and audiovisual works being left by the Directive to national legislation.[3]

Two new statutory exceptions to protection have resulted from this new legislation. First, in 1997, the Government took the opportunity to overturn a decision of the *Cour de Cassation*,[4] which had held that the complete reproduction of a work, regardless of its format, may not be considered to be a short quotation within the meaning of Article L.122–5(3)(a). In the case in question, reproductions of certain works of Utrillo had been published in miniature in a catalogue of a sale by public auction and the question had arisen whether it was necessary to obtain the consent of the authors' successors in title for such reproduction, a question answered in the affirmative by the *Cour de Cassation*. The new exception (Article L.122–5(d)) permits the complete or partial reproduction of works of graphic or three-dimensional art intended to appear in the catalogue of a sale by public auction held in France by a public or ministerial officer.[5] The second exception concerns databases and permits acts necessary to obtain access to the contents of electronic databases for the purpose of and within the limits of use foreseen by contract (Article L.122–5(5)).[6]

6–039   Traditionalists, such as Pollaud-Dulian,[7] criticised the exception for art auction catalogues as being a typical result of lobbying, giving satisfaction to one particular interest group. In fact, it seems more to reflect a welcome tendency towards a greater recognition by the legislator and the courts of the need to take account of the rights of the public to information in the copyright context.

The implementation of the satellite and cable directive has also led to a limitation on the exclusive rights of authors. The right to

---

[3] Duration Directive, *cf.* n.96, above, Art.2.
[4] *Cass. ass. plén.*, November 5, 1993; [1994] 159 R.I.D.A. 320.
[5] Law n°97–283 of March 27, 1997, Art.17.
[6] Law n°91–536 of July 1, 1998, Art.3.
[7] F. Pollaud-Dulian, n.96, above, at p.236.

authorise the simultaneous, complete and unchanged cable retransmission of a broadcast work may only be exercised through a collecting society approved for the purpose by the Minister for Culture (Article L.132–20–1). As noted by Françon, these provisions show a trend away from the traditional French approach of the individual exercise of rights and fully independent collecting societies.[8]

In 1995, the Intellectual Property Code (Regulatory Part) was adopted by Decree[9] and the Code was further amended to provide for compulsory collective administration of rights with respect to reprographic reproduction of works.[10] Only paper copies made for non-commercial use are covered by the new arrangements. It also dealt with the distribution of royalties payable to foreign authors from private copying of their work on blank audio and video tapes.

New limitations on rights

Limitations on rights in France have taken on a new dimension in recent years. As discussed above, in the past, exceptions to rights were few and, such as they were, tended to be interpreted restrictively by the courts. New restraints on the exclusive rights of authors imposed by recent legislation include the fact that even the exercise of moral rights has been limited in some respects.

6–040

For example, the new Intellectual Property Code provides for legal measures in the event of manifest abuse in the exercise of the moral right of disclosure as well as of other rights of exploitation by a deceased authors' representatives.[11] The concept of manifest abuse in the field of authors' moral rights was introduced by the 1957 Law; although that law and the Intellectual Property Code concern primarily manifest abuse by a deceased authors' representative, it is also

---

[8] A. Françon, n.96, above, at p.254.

[9] Decree No.95–385 of April 10, 1995, Concerning the Regulatory Part of the Intellectual Property Code (subsequently amended by Decree No.97–1316 of December 23, 1997).

[10] Law No.95–4 of January 3, 1995 (*cf.* Arts L.122–10 to L.122–13 of the Code); see also Decree No.95–406 of April 14, 1995, implementing Arts L.122–10 to L.122–12 of the Intellectual Property Code 1992 with respect to the right of reprographic reproduction (Arts R.322–1 to R.322–4 of the Code).

[11] See Arts L.111–3, 121–3 and 122–9, Intellectual Property Code. On the subject of abuse of rights and copyright, see C. Caron, "Abuse of Rights and Authors' Rights", [1998] 176 R.I.D.A. 3; F. Pollaud-Dulian, "Abus de droit et droit moral", *D.* 1993, Chronique, p.97; R. Hauert, "Control and limits of the moral right of the artist", [1959] XXIII R.I.D.A. 50.

argued that the principle of abuse of rights applies to the exercise of moral rights by authors themselves.[12] The right to reconsider and of withdrawal has been held to be used in an abusive manner in circumstances where the author relied on a complaint of insufficient remuneration.[13] From the 1957 Law dates also the rule that moral rights may only be exercised in respect of completed audiovisual works, once the final version has been agreed, and not in relation to previous versions[14] and there are also new limitations on their exercise in relation to software (Article L.124–7). Thus, as Vivant has acknowledged "the introduction by the French law itself of limitations on this moral right (in the audiovisual and information fields, in particular), and the sensible adaptation thereof, that is making it more flexible through case law. .., show once more that it is difficult to maintain a dogmatic position".[15]

Another limitation on the exclusivity of certain rights, those of remuneration for private copying, cable distribution and reprography, lies in the fact that, as seen above, they may only be exercised through collecting societies.

The short quotation exception

6–041   The interpretation by the courts of the exceptions to protection and, in particular, that of short quotation is also of interest, raising as it does issues concerning the rights of the public to information.[16] The recently introduced exception for art auction catalogues settled a much disputed issue. In a series of cases, miniature reproductions of artistic works in literary works had been held over the years to be legitimate quotations. Starting with a 1920s decision of the *Cour de Cassation*, which found that tiny, full reproductions in an art book of works by Rodin could be considered to be short quotations,[17] other courts had taken the same line, including the Court of Versailles in a

---

[12] On this subject see *inter alia*: C. Colombet, *op. cit.*, n.89, above, n°34; A. Françon, Obs. sur l'arrêt Chiavarino, *RTD com.* 1991, p.592; P.-Y. Gautier, *op. cit.*, n.89, above, n°96; R. Plaisant, *Propriété littéraire et artistique*, *op. cit.*, n.89, above, para.140.

[13] *Raymond Chiavarino v Sté. SPE*, [1992] 151 R.I.D.A. 272.

[14] Art.L.124–5 and 6.

[15] M. Vivant, "Pour une épure de la propriété intellectuelle", in *Mélanges A. Françon*, (Paris, Dalloz, 1995), p.415, at 424.

[16] On this subject see *inter alia*: Y. Gaubiac, "Freedom to Quote from an Intellectual Work", [1997] 171 R.I.D.A. 2; C. Geiger, *Droit d'auteur et droit du public à l'information, approche de droit comparé* (Mémoire de DEA, Université de Montpellier, ERCIM, 1998).

[17] Cass. crim. March 19, 1926: D.P. 1927, 1, note Nast.

case relating to the reproduction in miniature of three works by Utrillo in an art auction catalogue. The court justified the reproduction as permissible quotation on the ground that the catalogue provided useful information to the public.[18] Other decisions interpreted the short quotation exception as permitting the reproduction of artistic works in audiovisual works, again on the basis of the need to respond to the requirements of information or of the right of the public to information.[19] These decisions were, however, criticised in the literature. Desbois took the view that an artistic work could not be quoted at all: if the complete work was reproduced, it could not be considered a "short" quotation; if a detail of the work was reproduced then the moral right of the artist to respect for his work would be infringed.[20] This approach was shared, for example, by Françon: "quotation is difficult to conceive of for musical works or a work of the plastic arts and, moreover, in these areas, its legality would be questionable".[21] This was the line adopted by the *Cour de Cassation* in the art auction catalogue case referred to above and since overturned by legislation. However, recent commentators[22] have criticised the traditionalist view arguing that the reproduction of a detail of a painting is no more "mutilating" than a literary quotation and that there is a need to interpret the short quotation exception more liberally.[23]

The public's right to information

This trend has been followed by the *Cour de Cassation* in relation to   **6–042**

---

[18] *Affaire Fabris v Loudmer*, CA Versailles, November 20, 1991, *D.* 1992, p.402; "Il s'agit [le catalogue] d'une production intellectuelle cohérente dotée d'originalité, constituant une oeuvre visant à fournir au public des indications largement utiles à la connaissance actualisée du marché de l'art et à la prise de décision quand à une éventuelle enchère".

[19] *Affaire Van Meegeren v Société Gaumont and ORTF*, TGI Seine, January 4, 1967, LIII R.I.D.A. (1967) p.50; *Christo v Société Sygma, Société Gamma and Madame Adamov*, CA Paris, March 13,1986, *Gaz.Pal.* 1986, 1, p.238.

[20] H. Desbois, *Le droit d'auteur en France, op. cit.*, p.315.

[21] A. Françon, *Cours de propriété littéraire, artistique et industrielle, op. cit.*, p.230.

[22] M. Vivant, "Pour une compréhension nouvelle de la notion de courte citation en droit d'auteur", *JCP* 1989, I, 3372. See also B. Edelman, Note re CA Versailles, Ch. réun. November 20, 1991, *D.* 1992, p.408. T. Foyard, note re Cass. AP, November 5, 1993, *D.* 1994, p.483.

[23] *cf.* Art.10, European Convention on Human Rights; J.-C. Galloux, "L'exclusivité de télédiffusion des évènements face au droit du public à l'information", *JCP* 1997, ed. G., I, 4046, p.373 *et seq.* at 376.

the exclusive rights to broadcast sporting events in a decision invoking the right of the public to information. It held that journalists must be allowed access to public sporting events in order to be able to film and subsequently broadcast short extracts thereof in news programmes, notwithstanding that exclusive rights to film the event have been granted to one specific organisation.[24] Although the case related to a sporting event, the principle that the public is entitled to information is more general and applies in relation to any public event of general interest.

Of particular interest in this context is recent litigation concerning the question whether the public's right to information embraced access not only to sport but also to art. At first instance, in 1999 the *Tribunal de Grande Instance* of Paris, held that it did.[25] On appeal, however, the decision was overturned.[26] Once again the case concerned works of Utrillo; a short programme was made to be broadcast on the television news about an exhibition of his works. Twelve paintings were seen on television and Utrillo's representative complained that permission had not been requested and no payment made. At first instance, the Court, following the decision of the *Cour de Cassation* in the *Loudmer* case,[27] held that the complete reproduction of paintings in a television news programme cannot be considered a short quotation but, invoking Article 10 of the European Convention on Human Rights, which takes precedence over national law and guarantees the public's right to information, went on to decide that the showing of the paintings in the news programme was permissible. The Court found that the right of the public to infor-

---

[24] Cass. 1ère civ., February 6, 1996, *FOCA v FR3*, *Légipresse* n°133, III, p.87, commentaire Basile Ader. See also J.-C. Galloux, *op. cit.*, p.373.

[25] *Jean Fabris v Sté FRANCE 2*, Trib. de grande instance de Paris, 3rd. ch, February 23, 1999. For commentaries on the case, which was both welcomed and criticised, see, *e.g.*: P. Kamina, "Le droit du public à l'information peut-il justifier une exception au droit d'auteur?" *D*. 1999, Jurisprudence, 580; C. Geiger, "Die Informationsfreiheit als Schranke des Urheberrechts-Anmerkung zur Entscheidung des TGI Paris vom 23. Februar 1999", [2001] 3 *GRUR Int.* 252; B. Edelman, "Du mauvais usage des droits de l'homme (à propos du jugement du TGI de Paris du 23 février 1999", *D*. 2000, Chronique, 455.

[26] Cour d'appel de Paris, 4th. ch., May 30, 2001. For commentaries on the decision of the appeal court, see: V. Varet, "Droit d'auteur et liberté d'expression", [2001] *Légipresse*, 184, 137; C. Caron, "Les droits de l'homme réconciliés avec le droit d'auteur", [2001] *D*., Jurisprudence, 2504; C. Geiger, "Zum zweispältigen Verhältnis von Urheberrecht und Informationsfreiheit-Anmerkung zum Urteil der Cour d'Appel de Paris vom 30. Mai 2001", [2002] 4 *GRUR Int.*, 329.

[27] See n.18, above.

mation included the right to be informed rapidly and in an appropriate manner of newsworthy cultural events and that the programme did not interfere with the normal exploitation of the works. The Court of Appeal, however, decided that according to Article 10(2) the right to information was subject to the protection of the rights of third parties, including copyright, and that permission should have been sought to show the paintings.

By contrast, a new law concerning freedom of communication, provides that major events (*évènements majeurs*) may not be exclusively broadcast in such a way that an important section of the public could be deprived of the possibility of following them live or recorded on a free television service[28]; this is a limitation of the exclusive right to broadcast, specifically introduced in the public interest to guarantee public access to such events. The expression "major event" refers not only to sporting events but to other important and newsworthy events such as national festivals, etc.

In the future, it will be interesting to see whether the situation in France as regards exceptions will be influenced by the Directive on the harmonisation of certain aspects of copyright and related rights in the Information Society. The Directive sets out to establish a harmonised approach to the exceptions to reproduction rights throughout the European Union by providing for an exhaustive list of optional exceptions to protection. However, it may be doubted whether France will adapt its present law appreciably, since the present exceptions are closely related to the copyright culture of the country and those permitted by the Directive, moreover, are optional.[29]

Conclusion

The above analysis has shown that, like in England and the United States of America, concern for the public interest was an important   **6–043**

---

[28] Law N° 2000–719 of August 1, 2000 (Art.21), amending Law N°86–1067 of September 30, 1986 relating to freedom of communication (Art.20–2). See C. Caron, "La loi du ler août 2000 relative à la liberté de communication et la propriété intellectuelle", *CEE* 2000, n°9–10, p.10.

[29] European Parliament and Council Directive no.2001/29/EC of May 22, 2001 on the harmonisation of certain aspects of copyright and related rights in the information society (OJ L.167 22.6.2001, p.10).

consideration in the revolutionary French Decrees of 1791 and 1793, which, while giving recognition to the rights of authors, also laid emphasis on the rights of the public to access to those works and the importance of public education. As discussed above, a number of commentators have drawn attention to the prominence the revolutionary Decrees of 1791 and 1793 accorded to the public interest and to their similarity in this respect to Anglo-American notions of intellectual property. Renouard, writing in 1838, described the system of copyright in France as he saw it at the time, stating that authors were:

> workers and not property owners; if the laws ensure them exclusive exploitation of their works, it is by virtue of a positive grant of civil law and of a tacit contract which, at the moment of publication, intervenes between the public and the author. It is by the establishment of a privilege, created as a legitimate and fair compensation, that the full and free exploitation of a published work is forbidden to all persons composing the public. This is the system of the law of July 19, 1793.[30]

Thus, the revolutionary Decrees had reflected the positivist approach to authors' rights, according to which the law is a creation of the State.

In the course of the next 150 years, the law relating to the rights of authors developed gradually. "Both legal writers and the courts relied on a few lines of these [revolutionary] Decrees to adapt authors' rights to the new techniques of communication and reproduction which entirely transformed social and cultural life".[31] During this gradual process, the theoretical approach to authors' rights in France changed in emphasis, the naturalist approach according to which a work is inseparable from the person who has created it, it being an expression of his personality, gaining in influence. Thus authors' rights came to be considered as personal and inalienable rights, rooted in natural law and belonging to the actual physical person who creates a work. It was advocates of the naturalist approach who attempted to introduce perpetual rights for authors during the nineteenth century. It was also

---

[30] A.-C. Renouard, *Des droits des auteurs sur les produits de leur intelligence*, 1838, p.242, and cited in: J.C. Ginsburg, *op. cit.*, p.169.

[31] S.M. Stewart, *op. cit.*, p.374.

the influence of personalist ideas in copyright theory that led to the development through case law of the concept of moral rights. In the naturalist approach, the rights of authors take precedence over the public interest.

However, the naturalist approach did not completely dominate the work of the various committees which considered proposals for reform during the nineteenth century. These committees continued to take account of the public interest. Thus, the 1825 Rochefoucault Committee's terms of reference, for example, called on it "to reconcile the interests of authors and artists, and equally those of the public and trade". The many, repeated debates on the question of perpetual rights for authors, which lasted until 1866, turned on the need to achieve a balance between the interests of the authors, those of the publishers, the rights of the public to access works and avoiding impediments to trade in books, such as piracy and smuggling.

It is pertinent to note that, in 1937, the public interest was evoked by **6–044** Escarra, Rault and Hepp in their joint work on the French law on authors' rights. They made the following observations on the subject:

> All legislation of this kind must essentially represent a labour of seeking to reconcile equally respectable interests. ... Moreover, one forgets too often that the battle—if battle there is—is not limited to the author on the one hand and the publisher on the other. There is a third interested party, namely, the public. It is a first truth to affirm that the general public must be put in a position to enjoy, in the most favourable possible conditions, the fruits of literary and artistic creation.[32]

By the time that the Law of March 11, 1957 was adopted, in French copyright theory the interests of the author had gained ascendancy over those of the public. The moral rights of the author were given pride of place so as to protect the personality of the author through the work. Desbois described the law as having been based on three guiding principles, which ensured the homogeneity and solidity of its construction; these were: "1. authors' rights arise out of the act of intellectual creation alone; 2. authors' rights come into being in the person or patrimony of the creator; 3. moral rights take priority". He

---

[32] J. Escarra, J. Rault and F. Hepp, *La Doctrine française du droit d'auteur* (Paris, Editions Bernard Grasset, 1937), p.19.

added that these rights resulted from the natural order, and arose independently of the intervention of the legislator.[33]

The public interest at that time seems only to have been taken into account in relation to limitations upon the rights of authors, including the question of duration. It was recognised that the author had a social role and must therefore make certain concessions in the public interest.

By 1985, the public interest had reappeared as an issue in the debate on the reform of the law. As quoted above,[34] the Minister of Culture, Jack Lang, emphasised at the time that the national community had a duty to foster the creation of intellectual works and that it was necessary to establish the economic and financial conditions required to do so. The three principles on which the law was based did not place authors in a pre-eminent position; these were:

— to facilitate concerted action among those participating in the creation of intellectual works;

— to provide them with one of the most advanced systems of legal protection in the world;

— to foster the dissemination of works to the public.

6–045 The copyright philosophy of the government of the day, expressed by M. Lang, would not have been surprising coming from a British or US Minister. It laid emphasis on the promotion of creativity and the dissemination of works in the public interest, concepts which had been absent for many years from copyright debate in France. By contrast, reference may be made to Desbois' 1978 description of the nature of authors' rights in France. Making a distinction between government policy as applied to patents for invention and its policy towards authors' rights, he stated:

[The patent system] is in complete opposition to that of authors' rights, since the emphasis is laid on the public interest as opposed to the private interest of inventors. Under the French law, literary and artistic property rights are not considered as instruments of political policy, inspired by considerations of expediency or by concern to

---

[33] H. Desbois, "La loi française du 11 mars 1957", *op. cit.* n.65, above, p.185.

[34] J. Lang, see n.70, above.

stimulate intellectual creativity; they represent the expression of the respect which is due to works of the mind and their creators.[35]

While there is no doubt that the 1985 Law fully respects the rights of authors, it is also clear that the government of the day also once again gave recognition to the positive role that copyright law plays in the public interest, by furthering creativity and promoting access by the public to copyright works. As Kerever has observed: "The social usefulness of copyright consists in providing an economic basis for creation. This usefulness is still there at the end of the 20th century."[36]

This conclusion is confirmed by A. and H.-J. Lucas, writing on the historical rationale for authors' rights in France. They emphasise the preeminence traditionally afforded to the author; these rights are centered on the person of the author, which explains the references in the literature to natural rights and provides the justification for moral rights. However, they acknowledge that other justifications have also played their part. Authors' economic rights have a dual basis, the reward for labour and respect for human personality. The principle of reward for labour naturally leads to authors' rights being regarded as an encouragement to creativity, a function which both the revolutionary legislator and the legislator of 1985 had in mind.[37] They further draw attention to the need for a balance to be struck between the interests of authors and the public. "The French personalist conception of course implies a hierarchy of interests in principle favourable to the author, which is not found in the copyright tradition. But the public interest is nonetheless taken into account."[38]

This study has shown that the original aims and objectives of the French revolutionary laws on copyright did not differ as extensively as has been suggested by most commentators from the Anglo-American approach. As no less an authority than Kerever has recognised: "Far from being personalist in nature, authors' rights as they emerged from the French revolution were inspired above all by legal and economic considerations. ... Thus the French revolution's *droit d'auteur* was perfectly in line with the corresponding English and American *copyrights*".[39]

---

[35] H. Desbois, *Le droit d'auteur en France, op. cit.*, n.43, above, p.7.

[36] A. Kerever, "Is Copyright an Anacronism?", [1983] *Copyright* 374.

[37] A. Lucas, *op. cit.* para.28, p.35.

[38] A. Lucas, *ibid.*

[39] See A. Kerever, "The French Revolution and Authors' Rights", *op. cit.*, n.32, above. p.10.

6–046   Ginsburg's examination of the French revolutionary sources provides powerful evidence that:

> the differences between the U.S. and French copyright systems are in fact neither as extensive nor as venerable as typically described. In particular, despite the conventional portrayal, the French revolutionary laws did not articulate or implement a conception of copyright substantially divergent from that of the régimes across the Channel and across the Atlantic. The French revolutionary sources themselves cast doubt upon the assumed author-centrism of the initial French copyright legislation. The speeches in the revolutionary assemblies, the texts of the laws, and the court decisions construing the laws, all indicate at least a strong instrumentalist undercurrent to the French Decrees of 1791 and 1793.[40]

She concluded that: "The first framers of copyright laws, both in France and in the US sought primarily to encourage the creation of and investment in the production of works furthering national, social goals".[41]

At the outset, the French law of copyright protected the rights of authors of works regardless of the aesthetic merit of the work. Article 1 of the 1793 law referred to "writings of any kind". As Laligant has shown, this "implied that the law sought to protect any piece of writing if its production had required an intellectual effort on the author's part. . . . In view of the expression's general nature, the courts affirmed and reaffirmed that compilations of all sorts enjoyed the protection afforded by the law", including dictionaries, guidebooks, catalogues, almanacs, directories, tariffs and abridgments and all those other works described in the nineteenth century as "even the most paltry productions".[42] In this broad interpretation, the revolutionary laws and the French courts did not differ from the English and American approach.

Laligant points out that it was not until the second half of the

---

[40] J.C. Ginsburg, "A Tale of Two Copyrights: Literary Property in Revolutionary France and America", *op. cit.*, n.25, above, p.125 at 131.

[41] *ibid.*, p.133.

[42] O. Laligant, "The French Revolution and Authors' Rights or Perenniality of the Subject Matter for Protection", [1991] 147 R.I.D.A. 36.

nineteenth century that emphasis began to be placed on the aesthetic character of works in France:

> It was actually around 1860—... when an unprecedented importance began at last to be attached to art ...—that legal literature started to refer less to the law on infringements or the rights of authors and more to literary and artistic property and to affirm more and more frequently that the natural and original calling of the literary and artistic property right was to protect works of the *belles-lettres* and the *beaux-arts*, that is to say works of an aesthetic nature.[43]

Thus, the concept that to be deemed a work of authorship protectable **6–047** by literary and artistic property, a creation had to be aesthetic in nature, was a development of the late nineteenth century. This subsequently had a profound influence on copyright theory in France and became an article of faith for many distinguished commentators, including Plaisant, in whose opinion: "in the field of authors' rights, it is considered that the requisite originality must be aesthetic in nature, even if Article 2 of the Law of March 11, 1957 protects works regardless of their kind, form of expression, *merit* or purpose"[44] (Emphasis added).

Taken together with the personalist conception of authors' rights, which, as we have seen, had gained ascendancy in France by the turn of this century, and according to which only physical persons could be considered authors, the idea that to be protected a work must have an intrinsic aesthetic or artistic value is a further basic reason for the divergences which developed between the French and Anglo-American copyright systems during the first half of the twentieth century. The latter had fewer difficulties in extending copyright to new forms of "writings", such as designs and models, films, phonograms, computer programs and so on. French jurists were slower to afford these protection not only because they were often the work of more than one individual but also, in part, because their artistic value, as opposed to their commercial interest, was in doubt.

Laligant asserts that the aesthetic criterion rests on what he describes as:

---

[43] *ibid.*, p.50.
[44] R. Plaisant, "La protection du logiciel par le droit d'auteur", [1983] *G.P.* 2.348.

a historical misinterpretation. Indeed, what authors' rights were always meant to protect is any expression of thought embodied in a form, and not certain expressions of thought only: namely those testifying to aesthetic concerns. Moreover, the irrelevance of the aesthetic character of the subject matter of authors' rights stems less from the impossibility of finding an objective criterion for this aesthetic element than from the concern of the legislature and the courts open to the protection offered by authors' rights as widely as possible.[45]

There is no doubt that historical examination of the sources of the French revolutionary copyright laws demonstrates conclusively that the popular conception that the French and Anglo-American copyright laws are based on totally different approaches is not valid. As Ginsburg concluded from her study of the matter:

> Appreciation of the similarities between the initial French and U.S. literary property régimes may hold significance for modern copyright systems if only because it undermines "historical" assertions of the inherent and original incompatibility of the French and Anglo-American approaches to copyright.[46]

6–048   At the turn of the twenty-first century, it may be asserted without fear of contradiction that the absolutist theories espoused by such leading commentators as Desbois and Plaisant, according to which authors' rights centre on the person of the author to the exclusion of the interests of the public, are put in question by many working in the field today. As Caron has suggested:

> the public's interest exists discreetly in copyright law. It is a controversial subject. Thus, while Balzac exclaimed "a terrible word looms up here: the public's interest", Victor Hugo considered that "literary property belongs, more than any other, to the general interest". The fact nevertheless remains that the history of authors' rights testifies to a variable consideration of the general interest in literary and artistic property law—which proves that the rights of

---

[45] O. Laligant, *op. cit.*, n.42, above, p.62.
[46] J.C. Ginsburg, *op. cit.*, n.40, above, p.201.

the author and those of the public are indissociable in nature, a fact which was perceived right from the revolutionary period.[47]

In his view, recent developments within the discipline of authors' rights mark a revival of the public interest and a retreat of the personalist dimension of authors' rights.[48]

As we have seen, the public interest in access to information has been recognised by the courts in relation to the reporting of current affairs and events of major importance, and as taking precedence in some respects over exclusive rights.[49] Moral rights have been reined in in certain areas. The recognition and development of related rights in the French law and the implementation of the various EC Directives in the field of authors' rights and related rights, including those on the protection of computer programs and databases, have given rise to a new tendency to protection of the investor in addition to, rather than as opposed to the author, and brings the French law in this area closer to the laws of countries of the copyright tradition. In practice, although starting from different points of departure, the *droit d'auteur* and copyright often arrive at very similar solutions.[50]

Like the rationale for copyright, it is recognised that the protection of intellectual property rights benefits not only right owners but also the public, since such rights by providing rewards to their owners promote creation and production and contribute to guaranteeing the public's right to information.

---

[47] C. Caron, "Abuse of Rights and Authors' Rights", *op. cit.*, n.11, above, p.54.

[48] *ibid.*, p.56.

[49] *cf.* ns 24 and 25, above.

[50] On this subject, see P. Sirinelli, "Le Droit d'auteur à l'aube du 3ème Millénaire", *JCP* 2000, ed. G. n°1–2, p.13; G. Davies, "The Convergence of Copyright and Authors' Rights — Reality or Chimera?", [1995] *IIC* 964.

Chapter 7

Germany

Origins of the Law

The antecedents of copyright in Germany,[1] as in the other major **7–001** European countries, are to be found in the system of privileges granted to printers and publishers from the early sixteenth century onwards. Like in other European countries these privileges served to protect printers and afforded no recognition or protection for authors' rights. Progression towards a real copyright system evolved more slowly than in England and France, where in both cases revolution, by overthrowing privileges derived from the crown, gave an impetus to the recognition of authors' rights.

Privileges were originally granted by the Emperor with effect throughout the territory of the Holy Roman Empire as well as by the Heads of the various German *Länder* for their individual territories. Until the Peace of Westphalia in 1648 bringing the Thirty Years War to a close, the imperial privileges, which had the advantage of applying throughout the Empire, dominated the book trade. Thereafter, the privileges granted by the various *Länder* began to take precedence over the imperial privileges, which declined in importance along with Frankfurt as the book trade's commercial centre. Thus, from the mid-seventeenth century until the Vienna Congress of 1815, when the Federation of German States undertook to protect writers and publishers against piracy, the system of privileges and, subse-

---

[1] In this study Germany means historical Germany up to 1949, thereafter the Federal Republic of Germany and, from 1990, reunited Germany. Copyright developments in the German Democratic Republic during the post-war period until the reunification of Germany in 1990 are not covered.

quently, the rights of publishers and authors, were primarily matters for legislation in various *Länder*. Privileges as such lived on until the late nineteenth century and were specifically abolished only by the North German Federation Law on Copyright in Writings, Designs and Models, Musical Compositions and Dramatic Works of June 11, 1870. This subsequently became part of the law of the "*Reich*" in 1871.

The changeover from privileges to copyright was a slow process, hampered by the fact that the publishers and authors in the many German states had little contact with each other and so were disorganised. First to obtain specific protection in legislation against unauthorised reproduction were the publishers in a Prussian Law of 1794. While this Law was primarily for the benefit of the publisher, the interest of the author was recognised. Although the author was not directly protected, the publisher had to obtain his consent for publication and that consent was only valid for the first edition. Privileges subsisted alongside the publishers' rights. Both privileges and publishers' rights were effective only in the state which granted them. They provided for penal sanctions against pirates, but these flourished in Germany in the seventeenth and eighteenth centuries due to the division of the country into so many small states.

Copyright theories as they evolved were based on the concepts and philosophy underlying the German legal system, namely Roman Law and natural law (*Naturrecht*).[2] "Towards the end of the seventeenth century, the first attempts were made to base the right of the publisher who publishes with the consent of the author on the natural law."[3]

7–002 However, in the early eighteenth century the author was still not regarded as having rights in the product of his labour. "Writing was considered a mere vehicle of received ideas which were already in the public domain, and, as such a vehicle, it too, by extension or by

---

[2] The following definition of natural law is quoted by D.M. Walker in the *Oxford Companion to Law* (Oxford, 1980): "In general, it denotes belief in a system of right or justice common to all men prescribed by the supreme controlling force in the universe and distinct from positive law, law laid down by any particular state or other human organization. The starting points of all natural law thinking have been 'reason' and 'the nature of man'."

[3] S.M. Stewart, *International Copyright and Neighbouring Rights*, 2nd. ed., Vol. I, (London, etc., Butterworths 1989), para. 2.06. See also M. Vogel, "Geschichte des Urheberrechts" in G. Schricker, *Urheberrecht*, Kommentar, 2nd. ed. Introduction, IV, para. 50 *et seq.*, (Munich, C.H. Beck'sche Verlagsbuchhandlung, 1999), at para.60 *et seq.*

analogy, was considered part of the public domain."[4] Recognition of authors' rights as such was not achieved until the nineteenth century. From the mid-eighteenth century onwards, publishers began to offer "honoraria" to authors whose works they printed; these were not real payments, but more in the nature of tokens of esteem or gifts at the discretion of the publisher whose relationship to the author at this period was similar to that of a patron.[5] On receipt of a flat sum, the work became the property of the publisher.

In the last quarter of the century, a debate took place on the nature of the book and the property rights of publishers and authors.[6] Fichte, in an essay arguing against the practice of book piracy, distinguished between three distinct properties in the book. When the book is sold, ownership of the physical object passes to the buyer to do with as he pleases. The material aspect, the thoughts and ideas it presents, also pass to the purchaser. However, "the form of these ideas, the way in which, the combination in which, the phrasing and wording in which they are presented" remain the property of the author for ever.[7] Here, barring the idea of perpetuity expressed by "for ever", we can recognise the modern concept of copyright. Nevertheless, as already noted, the Prussian Law of 1794 did not recognise any rights of authors but reflected the common practice of the time for publishers to obtain the specific consent of authors.

In the early nineteenth century, the idea was conceived that piracy was an attack on the right of personality of the author as opposed to the property right of the publisher. This led in due course of time to the distinction between the so-called moral rights of the author and his economic, property rights in his published works. As the nineteenth century progressed, the concept of intellectual property was advanced in particular by the ideas and writings of leading philosophers like Kant, Hegel and Schopenhauer. Kant defended copyright by considering an author's works not as objects the benefit of which should accrue to the author, but rather as extensions of the personality of the author and subject to protection as such.

---

[4] M. Woodmansee "The Genius and the Copyright: Economic and Legal Conditions of the Emergence of the Author", [1984] 17 Eighteenth Century Studies 425 at 434.

[5] *ibid.* at 435.

[6] *ibid.*, 440 *et seq.*

[7] J.-G. Fichte, "Beweis der Unrechtmäßigkeit des Büchernachdrucks", in *Berlinische Monatsschrift*, (1793) Vol. 21, 443 at 451.

It was not until the last quarter of the nineteenth century that Germany was finally to do away with privileges, to recognise the rights of the author and to find a solution for the whole territory. As elsewhere, the moving force was the book trade. At the Vienna Congress of 1815, a Committee of the German book trade obtained a commitment in the instrument establishing the Federation of German States to safeguard the rights of authors and publishers against piracy. Legislation to implement the declaration remained, however, largely the responsibility of the *Länder*. The Federation intervened to establish some principles. First, in 1832, the *Länder* were obliged to extend the protection of their antipiracy laws to the citizens of the other *Länder*; this resulted in a system of reciprocal protection based on bilateral agreements between the various *Länder*. Some bilaterals were agreed also with non-German States such as, for example, that between Prussia and Great Britain signed in 1848. In 1835, the Federation called for piracy to be prohibited and similar standards of protection for writers to be established throughout the territory of the Federation. In 1837, it provided for authors and their successors in title to have the right to control reproduction of their literary works by mechanical means for a period of 10 years.[8]

7–003 The first modern copyright law based on the rights of the author was the Prussian Law of 1837 for the protection of works of science and art.[9] A major debate took place about the term of protection. Privileges had been granted for longer and longer periods and the publishers' Registry in Leipzig campaigned for protection in perpetuity. Moreover, it was argued that intellectual property should be perpetual like the right to any other property. The legislator, however, according to Ulmer, took account of the interest of the general public[10] and looked to the example of the copyright laws of England and France where duration was limited. Duration was fixed, as a result, at 30 years p.m.a. Other *Länder* followed the example of Prussia and 30 years became the normal period of protection throughout Germany. This period was maintained in the Copyright Act of 1870 and not increased until 1934 when, against substantial opposition, it

---

[8] M. Vogel, *op. cit.*, n.3, above, para. 66, *et seq.*

[9] See Appendix 4 of this study for the original text.

[10] E. Ulmer, *Urheber-und Verlagsrecht*, 3rd. ed., (Berlin, Heidelberg, New York, Springer Verlag 1980), p. 54.

was increased to 50 years to conform with the Berne Convention.[11]

The influences on the origin of German copyright law were therefore many and various:

> It did not grow directly out of the idea of intellectual property but is based on many diverse legal trends. This was reflected in the Acts of 1901 and 1907; the specific rights of the author were enumerated in detail and specific limitations were imposed having regard to conflicting interests.[12]

In this development of the law, the public interest does not appear from the sources to have been a live issue in the arguments in favour of protecting authors' rights. It may be assumed that it was considered to be in the public interest to protect the book trade against piracy but, as they evolved, authors' rights were conceived as natural rights or rights of personality. The property of the author in his work was not derived from the legislator but followed from his intellectual property "which merely found recognition and expression through positive law".[13] Thus, the public interest was not invoked in a positive sense in relation to authors' protection as it was in England, the United States of America and France. It was not suggested that authors needed rights so as to stimulate creativity or to ensure a supply of books to the general public. The public interest was, however,

---

[11] It is ironical that Germany, which for so long opposed any increase in the term of protection on grounds of the public interest should have been the driving force 60 years later behind the increase in term to 70 years p.m.a. throughout the European Union, and possibly as a direct result in the future, in the Berne Convention and the United States of America.

[12] E. Ulmer, *op. cit.*, n. 10, above, p. 55. On the history of German copyright law see especially E. Ulmer, "Vom deutschen Urheberrecht und seiner Entwicklung", [1957] 23 U.F.I.T.A. p. 257 *et seq*; M. Vogel, "Geschichte des Urheberrechts" in G. Schricker, *Urheberrecht, Kommentar, op. cit.*, Introduction, IV, para.50 *et seq.*; M. Vogel, *Deutsche Urheber und Verlagsrechtsgeschichte zwischen 1450 und 1850* (Frankfurt a. M., Buchhändlervereinigung, 1978); M. Vogel "Die Geschichte des Urheberrechts im Kaiserreich", [1987] 12 G.R.U.R. 873; M. Vogel, *Urheberrecht in Deutschland zwischen Aufklärung und Vormärz*, in Buchhandelsgeschichte [1989], 1 Beilage zum Bbl. Nr. 77, p.96; M. Vogel, "Urheberpersönlichkeitsrecht und Verlagsrecht im letzten Drittel des 19. Jahrhunderts", [1994] 8/9 G.R.U.R. 587; G. Schricker, "Hundert Jahre Urheberrechtsentwicklung", in *Festschrift zum hundertjährigen Bestehen der Deutschen Vereinigung für gewerblichen Rechtschutz und Urheberrecht und ihrer Zeitschrift*, (Weinheim, VCH, 1991) Part 4, 1095.

[13] Decision of the German Federal Supreme Court, May 18, 1955, Grundig, 17 B.G.H.Z., 266 at 278.

taken into account in the 1837 Prussian Law in a negative sense when the decision to limit the duration of authors' rights was taken.

The history of copyright theory, case law and legislation in Germany since 1901 has been a steady progression towards an ever-higher level of protection for authors and strengthening of the concept of authors' rights as having their roots in natural law. Its development has also been much influenced by that of the Berne Convention and by the international development of the concept of moral rights, incorporated expressly into German legislation for the first time in an all-embracing way in 1965, as well as by the need to keep pace with technical developments. In the course of the twentieth century, however, both the legislator and the courts have been increasingly concerned with the need to balance the interests of right owners with those of the public interest in the setting of limitations on copyright, its duration and statutory exceptions thereto.

7–004   It remains true that the **primary** justification for copyright today in Germany is natural law. It is regarded as an individual, intellectual property right of the author in his work which, in turn, is considered to be an expression of his personality. Schricker points out that, in this respect, the justification for copyright law differs from that for patent law: "authors' rights have their justification as individual rights only whereas, in patent law theory, in addition to the individual right aspect, the interests of society in technical progress are also stressed".[14] However, as this study shows, the social and cultural dimensions of copyright have also played an increasing part: "Society needs cultural attainments in order to facilitate cultural progress" and copyright law has developed in close association with the cultural industries which in turn have depended on developments in technology. In modern times, copyright protection is considered to be of vital importance for the promotion of cultural production and cultural life.[15]

In considering the development of German copyright law in the twentieth century, it is useful to distinguish between the period before the establishment of the Federal Republic of Germany in 1949 and thereafter. Since then, copyright legislation and case law derive from certain fundamental guarantees in the Basic Law of the Constitu-

---

[14] G. Schricker, in G. Schricker, *Urheberrecht*, Komment ar, *op. cit.*, n. 3, above (2nd. ed., 1999), Introduction, para. 11.

[15] A. Wandtke, "Zur kulturellen und sozialen Dimension des Urheberrechts", [1993] 123 U.F.I.T.A. 5.

tion.[16] The rights of authors are property in the sense of Article 14 of the Basic Law; in addition, the personal law component of copyright stands on the constitutional guarantees of human dignity and personal freedom found in Articles 1 and 2(1) of the Basic Law. However, like any absolute right, copyright brings with it social obligations. As Article 14(2) of the Basic Law lays down, property imposes duties and its use should also serve the public interest. Thus, in the interests of the public, certain limitations are placed on the rights of copyright owners. A number of these exceptions also aim to promote freedom of information and cultural policy in conformity with Article 5 of the Basic Law. The approach to copyright in the late nineteenth and early twentieth centuries would appear to have differed somewhat to that of the post-war period.

Legislative Developments: 1870–1901

The Copyright Act 1870 granted the exclusive right to reproduce a writing by mechanical means to the author (section 1). The publisher was assimilated to the author in the case of collective works. The author's right was transmissible by contract or will. He had the right to authorise translation in certain limited circumstances only, although translations themselves were fully protected against infringement.[17] There were no moral rights. **7–005**

Legal entities, being publishers of collective works, were assimilated to authors but enjoyed protection for 30 years from publication as opposed to 30 years p.m.a. (section 13). The same protection was afforded to designs and models in the field of geography, topography, natural sciences, architecture, technical arts and other similar fields (section 43), as well as to musical compositions. Public performance rights were recognised. No further privileges were to be granted; those possessing privileges could either maintain their privilege or claim the protection of the law.

It would appear that the 1870 Act was not adopted without opposition. The arguments of the opponents to the Act were

---

[16] *Grundgesetz* (Basic Law) of the Federal Republic of Germany (FRG) of May 23, 1949, I Federal Law Gazette (*Bundesgesetzblatt*—B.G.Bl. 1), May 23, 1949.
[17] See M. Vogel, "Die Entfaltung des Übersetzungsrechts im deutschen Ürheberrecht des 19. Jahrhunderts", [1991] G.R.U.R. 16 at 21.

described in 1888 as including: that the protection of literary works was "opposed to the education of the people"; represented "an unjust monopoly"; was a "theft against intellectual well-being" and that the term "intellectual property" was inappropriate.[18]

In the 1880s, Germany was very active in the Conferences which preceded the adoption of the Berne Convention for the Protection of Literary and Artistic Works in 1886. In those discussions, Germany strongly argued against an obligatory period of protection of 50 years and, indeed, continued to do so up to and including the 1928 Rome Conference for the revision of the Berne Convention. Germany also defended the need for exceptions for personal and educational use to be written into the Berne Convention and opposed the efforts of the French to limit these exceptions in the Berlin (1908) and the Rome (1928) Conferences for the revision of the Berne Convention.[19]

7–006 In 1876, a Law concerning the right of the author in works of figurative art was adopted. The 1870 Act was replaced in 1901 by the new Act concerning the "Right of the Author in Literary and Musical Works",[20] which was supplemented by a statute relating to publishing law.[21] The 1876 Law on the figurative arts was likewise replaced in 1907 by the "Act on Authors' Rights in Artistic Works and Photography".[22] These two laws reflected the influence of the Berne Convention. The author was defined as the person who had created the work. Legal entities responsible for publishing works, however, were considered to be the author in certain circumstances.

The 1901 Act spelt out the rights granted in detail and the limitations on those rights. Basically, the rights conferred were those of reproduction, translation and public performance. There were many specific exceptions. The author had no right with respect to lending. Reproduction for personal use was permitted provided it was not done for profit. Likewise, public performance of musical works was permitted when the performance was not organised for profit and no admission charge was made.

More far-reaching and in due course controversial were exceptions permitting reproduction of published musical works on disc, plate,

---

[18] Fleischmann, [1888] 10 *Unsere Zeit*, quoted in: [1888] *Le Droit d'Auteur* 113.

[19] 1908 Berlin Act (entry into force September 9, 1910) and 1928 Rome Act (entry into force August 1, 1931).

[20] Of June 19, 1901 (R.G.B.l. 227).

[21] Also of June 19, 1901 (R.G.B.l. 217).

[22] Of January 9, 1907 (R.G.B.l. 7).

cylinders, tapes, etc. for the mechanical reproduction of music; moreover, in the case of public performance of musical works accompanied by text, the consent of the author of the text was not required. Duration of protection remained as in the 1870 Act. Proposals to extend protection to 50 years p.m.a. were rejected on the grounds that the number of works still of interest after 30 years was small and that the public interest in obtaining free access to such works outweighed any prejudice that might be caused to a small number of authors.[23] The 1907 Act extended protection to buildings and works of applied art.

The Twentieth Century

1901–1949

The development of copyright continued to be influenced by the Berne Convention and its new Acts resulting from the revision Conferences of Berlin (1908) and Rome (1928). The Berlin Act took account of sound recordings and films and this was reflected in an amendment to the law in 1910. The Rome Act incorporated moral rights into the Berne Convention for the first time.

7–007

There was to be no further new legislation, however, until 1934, when the period of protection was extended to 50 years in order to conform with the Berne Convention.[24] Meanwhile, German "case law was able to keep pace with the results of the Rome Conference owing to a liberal interpretation of the texts of the Statute".[25] However, work started after the Rome Conference on new legislation. A series of private drafts were put forward at various times throughout the pre-war period. An official draft was published in 1932, representing a joint proposal of the German and Austrian justice

---

[23] *See* explanatory memorandum (*Begründung*) attached to the draft of the Act (Entwurf eines Gesetzes betreffend das Urheberrecht an Weken der Literatur und der Tonkunst) presented to the Reichstag on December 8, 1900, Reichstag doc. No. 97, 10th legislative period, II Session 1900/1901, at 34. See also the Report of the XI Parliamentary Commission on the Report (Bericht der XI Kommission), doc. No. 214, at 61–62.

[24] Act Relating to the Prolongation of the Period of Protection of Authors' Rights, December 13, 1934, *Reichsgesetzblatt II Partie*, No. 61, December 19, 1934, at 1395.

[25] E. Ulmer & H.H. von Rauscher auf Weeg in S.M. Stewart, *op. cit.*, n. 3, above, para. 15.02.

ministries. That draft resulted in the Austrian Act of 1936. Another draft was put forward in a report of the German Academy of Law in 1939,[26] but further work in Germany was held up as a result of the 1939–1945 Second World War. Work recommenced after the Brussels Revision Conference of the Berne Convention in 1948. Further official drafts were published in 1954, 1959 and 1962, but it was not until 1965 that a new Act was promulgated.[27]

The revision of the 1901 Act was, therefore, under discussion for over 30 years, a time of great changes both in the technology affecting authors' rights and in the development of international copyright.

From 1928 to 1955, Professor Hans Otto de Boor, of Frankfurt University, wrote annual "Letters from Germany" published in "*Le Droit d'Auteur*", with only minor interruptions during the war. These provide a fascinating overview of copyright theory and developments in Germany throughout this period. The author has reviewed these accounts to identify the most important developments in case law and to see to what extent the public interest was taken account of as a justification for copyright law, or for its limitation, in copyright theory during that time. After de Boor's death, Professor Eugen Ulmer continued the letters.[28]

7–008 In 1926, the Reich Supreme Court ruled on the question of whether the German Act of 1901 provided protection against unauthorised broadcasting.[29] According to de Boor, in the opinion of the Court, an opinion shared by exponents of copyright doctrine, the German Act recognised no general intellectual property rights but only protected the author in the exercise of the rights expressly granted to him. Thus, the Court could only afford protection against broadcasting if it could be considered an infringement of such a right. The Court resolved the

---

[26] [1939] 4–5 G.R.U.R. 242.

[27] *Referentenentwurf* (Ministerial draft bill) 1954; *Ministerialentwurf* (Departmental bill) 1959; *Regierungsentwurf* (Government bill) 1962; *Urheberrechtsgesetz* (Copyright Act), September 9, 1965.

[28] From 1972 until "*Le Droit d'Auteur*" and its English language version "Copyright" ceased publication in December 1994, the task of writing regular reports on German copyright developments fell to Adolf Dietz. In writing the first edition of this study, the author relied heavily on these accounts of German law and theory. Prior to 1960, *Le Droit d'Auteur* was published in French only. Quotations therefrom, therefore, are the author's translations. Since 1994, Adolf Dietz has published a report on "Copyright Law Developments in Germany from 1993 to Mid–1997" in *R.I.D.A.* (*Revue internationale du droit d'auteur*); see Part I in [1998] 175 *R.I.D.A.* 96 and Part II [1998] 176 *R.I.D.A.* 167. In this edition, additional sources in German have been taken into account.

[29] R.G.Z. 113, 413.

issue by deciding that broadcasting could be considered to be a case of professional distribution rather than one of public recital and thus was subject to the authors' control; the definition of distribution was thus extended to embrace broadcasting. The question was debated at the time whether, in the interest of "public intellectual life", broadcasters should be given a compulsory licence allowing them to broadcast published works, or works already broadcast with consent, without permission but on payment of equitable remuneration.

In 1928, de Boor also reported on the ongoing dispute between protagonists of the maintenance of a 30-year period of protection, who upheld the interests of the public as against those of the authors' heirs, and those who favoured extending the protection period to 50 years. The leading proponent of the *status quo* was Professor Ernst Heymann[30] of Berlin University, whose views on the issue were apparently shared by de Boor.[31] He argued that the period of protection was not envisaged in Germany as a limitation on a presumed perpetual intellectual property right but rather as an additional period prolonging protection after the death of the author out of respect for his personality. Taking the various interests into account, Heymann considered that the interests of the entire German nation should always take priority in matters of copyright. He maintained that the 30-year period had beneficial effects for German intellectual life by promoting wide distribution of works thereafter; in his view, an extension of the term could present grave dangers by withholding works from general use for too long.

Heymann also argued that German law, by contrast with French law, was inspired by social factors; it took account of the interest of the community, to which the interest of the individual should conform and even subordinate itself. In this debate, the public interest was a live issue at the time. Elster also stressed the social function of copyright and the need to find a balance in copyright law between the individual rights of authors and the interests of the public, not only in relation to the term of protection but also as regards other limitations, such as exceptions. In his view, copyright was enhanced and better

---

[30] E. Heymann, *Die Zeitliche Begrenzung des Urheberrechts* (Berlin, Prussian Academy of Sciences, 1927).

[31] See also A. Elster, "Die wettbewerbliche und die immanente Begrenzung des Urheberrechts", [1926] 31 G.R.U.R. 493 *et seq.*

accepted by the public if the limits thereto were reasonable.[32]

By 1930, four draft Acts had been published[33] and reform of the copyright law continued to preoccupy copyright specialists throughout the 1930s. The major issues on which there was disagreement between the proponents were: the protection of photographs; the nature of the protection to be accorded to films; the question whether legal persons could be considered to be authors; the kind of protection to be accorded to performers and, in later years, producers of phonograms; and, finally, the perennial problem of the period of protection.

7–009 Opinion was divided on whether or not legal persons could be authors. This was of particular importance in relation to the question of who should be considered the author of a cinematographic work. In the early 1930s, it was proposed that performers should enjoy an author's right but, as the years went by, opinion hardened in favour of their being granted a related or neighbouring right. The question of duration of copyright continued to be controversial. In the four private drafts referred to above, only one proposed increasing the period of protection to 50 years, the others all supporting the retention of the 30-year period. It is of interest to note that two of the drafts proposed giving the author a right to authorise or prohibit commercial rental of a work. Another issue was the need to incorporate moral rights in German legislation following their inclusion in the Rome Act of the Berne Convention. While moral rights were recognised satisfactorily by German case law, they were not specifically protected by legislation.

The official 1932 Joint Proposal of the German and Austrian Justice Ministers proposed that the division of the German Act between literary and musical copyright, on the one hand, and artistic and photographic copyright on the other, should be abandoned. The draft took account of new methods of exploitation of literary and artistic works such as film, radio broadcasting and phonograms. Performers and legal persons were not recognised as being capable of benefiting from a copyright. The draft attempted to define and regulate moral rights. The Government remained undecided about increasing the

---

[32] A. Elster, "Der Schutz des Geisteswerkes als Ausgleich zwischen Urheber und Allgemeinheit", [1931] 4 U.F.I.T.A. 215.
[33] By Messrs. Goldbaum/Wolf ([1929] 2 U.F.I.T.A. 185), Elster ([1929] 2 U.F.I.T.A. 652), Hoffmann, ([1929] 2 U.F.I.T.A. 659), and Marwitz ([1929] 2 U.F.I.T.A. 668).

period of protection from 30 years p.m.a. In these various discussions concerning the revision of the law, the point of view was put forward by some that the legislator should take account of the interests of the public.

The long discussion in Germany on the subject of the duration of protection was finally settled in 1934 when the Government legislated, as noted above, to extend the period of protection to 50 years p.m.a. in order to conform with the Rome Act of the Berne Convention. As Ulmer noted, "this was mainly due to international legal development, behind which Germany could not permanently remain. It may also be noted that this was a Government sponsored bill. From a parliamentary point of view it may be assumed that . . . the extension could not have been passed at that time".[34]

By the late 1930s the proposal had gained ground that a distinction should be made between copyright or authors' rights in the strict sense and other matters. The 1939 draft put forward by the German Academy of Law proposed that the Act should be divided into two main sections: one on authors' rights and a second on related rights which would cover technical designs, maps, photographs, phonograms, broadcasts, performers, etc. In October 1939, Professor de Boor described this draft as representing the completion of an evolutionary process rather than any break of principle with the past. He described the fundamental idea behind the draft as being that the person to be protected was the individual human creator. He drew attention to the fact that, in its origins, the protection of authors and inventors did not aim to protect the creative person. Although natural law had recognised the concept of intellectual property, German copyright law had replaced the system of privileges in 'the eighteenth century not by providing protection for the author but by protecting the publisher against counterfeiting. The object of protection in the past had been, therefore, the published work. In the nineteenth century, the emphasis had shifted to protection of the author with the intention of affording remuneration for the intellectual work of the author by means of an exclusive right. Subsequently, protection had been extended gradually to various new works including, in the twentieth century, films.

The 1939 draft, by contrast, instead of listing and enumerating the **7–010** various categories of works to be protected included the general

---

[34] E. Ulmer, "Letter from Germany" [1965] *Copyright* 275 at 282.

formula that all "literary and artistic works" should be protected, provided only that they were individual creations. The author was to be protected in his personal connection with his work by means of moral rights. It followed from these concepts that, in this draft, for the first time, the idea that an author's right could be granted in favour of a legal person was rejected. This applied also in the case of cinematographic works where previously the producer had been considered the author. The draft proposed that ownership of copyright in a film should be vested in all those who had made an important artistic contribution to the film. However, the right to distribute the film would belong only to the producer, for practical reasons. As a consequence of this approach, the draft included a separate chapter dealing with related or neighbouring legal domains, establishing protection for other right owners considered to merit the protection of an exclusive right but not an author's right, as such.

While the 1939 draft was not acted upon, an Act of May 12, 1940 extended the protection of photographs from 10 to 25 years.[35]

In 1942, de Boor compared the copyright system in Germany with that in the United States of America which he described as "more formalistic and more industrial" in character. According to him at that time, "for us Europeans the idea of copyright is to protect the creative personality manifested in his work. This idea is not very old. Copyright has developed from the idea of protecting publishers against counterfeiting, that is, from legal notions of an industrial character". However, the German point of view was that "if we wish to protect the creative personality, it is not sufficient to provide him with a financial reward for his work. Rather personal and cultural interests should be put first".

In 1945, de Boor strongly defended the thesis that the film producer should be recognised as the author of the copyright in a film. In his view, it was the only practical solution, without prejudice to moral rights in any pre-existing works.

1949–1965

7–011   After the Second World War, in 1951, de Boor described how the ongoing debate concerning the need to revise the copyright law had

---

[35] Act of May 12, 1940, *Reichsgesetzblatt I*, 758.

been enlivened by new inventions such as microphotography and recording machines. The courts were called on to consider whether the making of microfiches of printed editions was permitted under the exception for personal use provided for by s.15(2) of the 1901 Act. Similar considerations arose in relation to the recording of broadcasts and phonograms and photographic reproductions of scientific journals.

In the early 1950s, the copyright experts were unanimous that such reproduction constituted a breach of copyright and that the authorisation of the author was required. Proposals were put forward for the granting of licences for such reproduction on payment of a royalty. In this connection, de Boor discussed the theory, with which he concurred, that copyright should be limited for social purposes. The theory in his view allowed for the regulation of relations between the rights of individuals and the public by means of limitations on copyright concerning the period of protection, exceptions for quotation, etc. He stressed, however, that the interests of the public or the collectivity should never be permitted to prevent the author from exercising a right given to him by the law and warned against a tendency to assimilate the public interest with that of a particular industry, for example, the establishments providing microphotographic facilities, who had invoked the public interest in their argument with authors. He pointed out that there are three opposed interests: those of the authors, those of commercial intermediaries (such as the publishers, etc.) and, finally, those of the readers and the general public. The essential task of copyright, he suggested, was to establish an equitable balance between those three groups. All three represented the public or a part thereof. He pointed out that damage caused to the author is as dangerous for the public interest as any prejudice which might affect other groups, and gave as an example of such danger the damage that photocopying and microfiches were causing at the time to scientific reviews.

When after the 1939–1945 Second World War, work resumed on the revision of the copyright law, the Ministry of Justice had in mind to bring the 1901 and 1907 laws up to date and to adapt them to new technology and to the Brussels Act of the Berne Convention. However, according to Ulmer,[36] the authors and their societies were not satisfied with a mere modernisation and argued for a considerable

---

[36] E. Ulmer, "Lettre d'Allemagne", [1956] *Le Droit d'Auteur* 180 at 182.

strengthening of their rights. In Ulmer's view, this claim was well-founded since cultural policy was backward compared with social policy and the situation of intellectual workers had not been reformed to the same extent as that of other workers. Moreover, the courts in a number of cases strengthened the position of authors with respect to new uses of their works.

In 1954, the Federal Supreme Court (*Bundesgerichtshof*), recognised the existence of a general right of personality grounded in the Basic Law (*Grundgesetz*) of the Federal Republic of Germany, adopted in 1949.[37] Art. 1 thereof provides for the respect and protection of the dignity of man and Art. 2 for the right of everyone to the free development of his or her personality. The court reasoned that the expression of ideas is an emanation of the personality of the author. This being so, the author has the right to decide if, and in what form, his writings should be distributed to the public. This case was of considerable importance because, previously, only the right of an individual to be named and to authorise use of his own image had been recognised.[38]

7–012 In 1953, the District Court (*Landgericht*) of Frankfurt-am-Main found that the exception for personal use of s.15(2) of the Copyright Act could be applied to photocopying. However, the Court said that that exception should be interpreted in a strict manner and could not be allowed if it would endanger the interests of the author. To the extent that authors' rights were exploited, they should not suffer essential damage and the Court considered that regular reproduction could be contrary to the interests of the author.[39]

In 1955, the Federal Supreme Court (*Bundesgerichtshof*) handed down a landmark decision on a final appeal from the Regional Appeal Court of Frankfurt-am-Main in a case also concerning the interpretation of s.15(2) of the Copyright Act. It decided that the copying of music onto blank, magnetic reel-to-reel tapes was subject to the authorisation of the author and, when sound recordings were copied, also of the producer of phonograms, even where the copy was made for private use. The Court thus rejected the notion that copyright protection necessarily had its limit in private use. The Court based its

---

[37] *Grundgesetz* (Basic Law) of the Federal Republic of Germany (see above, n.15).

[38] Decision of the German Federal Supreme Court, November 26, 1954, 15 B.G.H.Z. 249. For a full account of the case see H.O. de Boor, "Lettre d'Allemagne", [1955] *Le Droit d'auteur* 180.

[39] Decision of June 11, 1953, *cf.* H.O. de Boor, [1954] *Le Droit d'Auteur*, 74.

decision not on the letter of the law but on its spirit and on general principles of copyright, relying on the fundamental idea of intellectual property.[40] It stated that the author's control over his work and his right to remuneration for its use by third parties is not granted by the legislator but follows from the nature of things, namely, from his intellectual property which the law recognises but does not create. It followed that the copyright owner had absolute control over his creation in respect of a new method of private reproduction which "by its very nature, could cause a serious economic prejudice to authors if it was not subject to their exclusive rights".

It is interesting to contrast this decision with that of the Reich Supreme Court in 1927 concerning broadcasting referred to above, where the Court took the view that the German law recognised no general intellectual property right. In the meantime, copyright law in Germany had been strengthened by its foundation in the Basic Law of 1949.

A few weeks later, the Federal Supreme Court (*Bundesgerichtshof*)[41] gave judgment in a case of photographic reproduction of articles from scientific journals by a firm for the use of its technical personnel. The Court considered such reproduction to be an infringement and not to fall within the exception of s.15(2) of the Copyright Act. A firm, being a legal entity, could not make personal use of a copy; its technical personnel were not using the copies for their personal use but for the benefit of their employer.

In the 1950s, two theories were vigorously debated: the authors' **7–013** societies defended the idea, propounded previously in the nineteenth century, that authors' rights, because they represented intellectual property should be perpetual and give rise once copyright had expired to a perpetual public paying domain. Others, including de Boor and Roeber, contended that an author's right should be considered as a right *sui generis* emanating from the person of the author and having the dual function of protecting both personal and economic interests. Moreover, for them it was a right with social links and, thus, must be subject to exceptions and limited in time.[42] Ulmer expressed his view

---

[40] Decision of the German Federal Supreme Court, May 18, 1955, 17 B.G.H.Z. 266.

[41] Decision of the German Federal Supreme Court, June 24, 1955, 18 B.G.H.Z. 44.

[42] H.O. De Boor, "Lettre d'Allemagne", [1954] *Le Droit d'Auteur* 203 *et seq.*; H.O. De Boor, "Lettre d'Allemagne", [1955] *Le Droit d'Auteur*, 154 *et seq.*; G. Roeber, "Urheberrecht oder Geistiges Eigentum", [1956] 21 U.F.I.T.A. 150. H. Hubmann, *Das*

on this debate as follows:

> Copyright/authors' rights derive from the great idea of intellectual
> property which is common to all Europe. Today this idea has its
> importance ... as, being founded on natural law, it draws attention
> to the element of equity which is inherent in copyright. No doubt,
> unlike a material good, a work is not only attributed to the author
> for the purpose of its economic exploitation, but it is also attached
> to him as a child of his spirit. ... I believe, in particular, that the
> constitutional guarantee of property applies to copyright. The
> Basic Law of Bonn guarantees property. In constitutional language,
> that means that intellectual property is also guaranteed—copyright
> in its component parts consisting both of patrimonial and moral
> rights.[43]

The 1965 Act

7–014 The long debate on the revision of the 1901 and 1907 laws finally
bore fruit with the new Act on Authors' Rights and Related Rights of
September 9, 1965.[44] This represented a major and comprehensive
reform, introducing a clear distinction between authors' rights and
related rights[45] (dealt with respectively in two separate sections of the

---

Recht des schöpferischen Geistes, Berlin, Walter de Gruyter & Co., [1954]. E. Ulmer,
"Lettre d'Allemagne", [1957] *Le Droit d'auteur* 14 *et seq.* (author's translation). See also
for another point of view, E.D. Hirsch–Ballin, "Authors' rights compared with those of
the community" [1956], X *R.I.D.A.* 18.

[43] E. Ulmer, "Lettre d'Allemagne", *op cit.* n.42, above, at 16.

[44] Act on Copyright and Related Rights of September 9, 1965 (*Gesetz über Urhe-
berrecht und verwandte Schutzrechte (Urheberrechtsgesetz)*). The Act entered into force on
January 1, 1966. See also O.-F. von Gamm, *Urheberrechtsgesetz*, Kommentar, C. H.
Beck'sche Verlagsbuchhandlung Munich (1968).

[45] Prior to the 1965 Act, the protection of performers and producers of phonograms
was governed by the Act concerning Copyright in Literary and Musical Works, of June
19, 1901, as amended in 1910, and the Act extending the terms of copyright protection
of December 13, 1934. S.2, para.2 of the Act, as amended in 1910, assimilated the
recording of literary and musical works to adaptations of those works. According to E.
Ulmer ("Lettre d'Allemagne" [1961] *Le Droit d'auteur* 14), the intention of the legislator
in including this provision was to protect the record producer against unauthorised
reproduction. The legislator started from the premise that the contribution of the
performer was similar to an adaptation of a work because of its personal character. Thus,
the performer was designated as the beneficiary of the right, the producer being obliged
to acquire any rights of his own contractually from the performer. The right of the
performer was assimilated, therefore, to the right of the author of an adaptation. The
courts subsequently confirmed that, as a result, the performer, and through the per-

law) and extending the period of protection for authors from 50 to 70 years p.m.a. At the same time, the law was supplemented by additional legislation on the administration of copyright and related rights providing for state supervision of collecting societies.[46] It also paved the way for accession, *inter alia*, to the Brussels Act of the Berne Convention and the ratification of the Rome Convention for the Protection of Performers, Producers of Phonograms and Broadcasting Organisations, 1961.

The new Act, unlike the previous laws, recognised "an all-embracing concept of literary and scientific and artistic works".[47] The various categories of works are mentioned only as examples so as to permit new types of works resulting from technical development to be protected in future. However, "the demarcation of unprotected works is determined by the axiom that only personal intellectual creations are works within the meaning of the law".[48] The author is the person who is the creator of the work. Only natural persons are concerned and the law did away with the previous situation where in certain cases legal entities, including film producers, were regarded as authors.[49] Previous drafts had proposed an exception to this rule in favour of film producers but the solution adopted was to provide a legal presumption of cession from the authors to the producers of all

---

former by contract the producer, benefited not only from rights of reproduction and distribution but also of broadcasting and public performance (Federal Supreme Court, May 31, 1960) "Künstlerlizenz bei öffentlicher Wiedergabe von Schallplatten, [1960] 12 G.R.U.R., 619; see also concerning performers' rights the following three decisions of the same date: Rundfunksendung "Figaros Hochzeit"; Künstlerlizenz bei öffentlicher Wiedergabe von Rundfunksendungen"; and "Orchester Graunke", [1960] 12 G.R.U.R. 614, 627 and 630. For commentaries on these decisions see E. Ulmer, *loc. cit.*, and H.H. von Rauscher auf Weeg, *Das Aufführungsrecht der Interpreten und Schallplattenhersteller nach geltendem deutschen Recht*, Cologne, W. Kohlhammer Verlag, 1960.

[46] Law on the Administration of Copyright and Related Rights of September 9, 1965, [1965] B.G.B.l. I, p.1273 (with subsequent amendments).

[47] E. Ulmer, "Letter from Germany", [1965] Copyright 275.

[48] *ibid.*

[49] Under the 1901 Act as amended in 1910, in certain cases legal entities were recognised as authors of works. Over the years, the courts (the *Reichsgericht* and the *Kammergericht*) repeatedly recognised the film producer as the author of a cinematographic work (see in particular 106 R.G.Z. 365 and 1924 J.W. 413). For a discussion of this case law see F.J. Berthold, H. von Hartlieb, *Filmrecht—ein Handbuch*, Munich-Berlin, C.H. Beck'sche Verlagsbuchhandlung (1957). Early drafts of the 1965 Act had proposed continuing to recognise the producer as the author of a film. However, the 1965 Act provided that authors' rights in cinematographic works vested in the intellectual creations of individuals (the co-authors of the film), and granted the film producer a related right in the picture carrier.

rights required for the exploitation of the film. In contrast to many other legislations, in Germany copyright belongs also to employees who create a work in the course of their employment.

The Act divides authors' rights into moral rights, exploitation rights and other rights.

Moral rights are defined so as to protect the author with respect to his intellectual and personal relations to the work. These provisions consolidate the all-embracing protection of the moral rights of the authors developed over the years by case law. Unlike French and Italian moral rights, the moral right in Germany is not a perpetual right and expires at the same time as economic rights.

7–015 The author was also granted a right of disclosure in the sense of first communication, which Ulmer described "as a fundamental right of the author, depending as well from the moral right as from exploitation rights".[50] The provisions concerning rights of exploitation aimed to include all forms of reproducing and communicating a work which technical progress had made or might in the future make possible in original form and in any adaptation thereof. Thus, the author is afforded a comprehensive right to communicate the work to the public in immaterial, that is, unfixed form. Two new rights were introduced: the artists' resale right and a right of the author to equitable remuneration in the case of lending for profit. Non-profit-making libraries, especially public libraries, were exempt.[51]

The limits imposed on the rights of authors and other right owners in the Act, representing the dividing line between the interests of right owners and those of the public and considered justifiable in the public interest, were described as follows by Ulmer:

> Exploitation rights grant to authors the material gain from their works. This granting is subject to certain limitations which are important from the practical standpoint: the needs of cultural life are served by freedom of quotation and borrowing. In the interests of public information, limits are placed on copyright in favour of press, radio and film reporting.[52]

These limits to copyright, being restrictions on the authors'

---

[50] E. Ulmer, "Letter from Germany", *op. cit.* n.47, above, 277.

[51] See also the decision of the Federal Constitutional Court, which upheld this exemption, in [1972] 8 G.R.U.R. 485.

[52] E. Ulmer, "Letter from Germany", *op. cit.* n. 47, above, at 278.

exclusive rights, have the character of exceptions and for that reason are to be interpreted narrowly.[53] Some exceptions have their basis in the rights to freedom of expression and information guaranteed by Art. 5 of the Basic Law.

The 1965 Law[54] provided a detailed list of exceptions to protection in relation to a number of what may be described as either fair uses in the public interest or limitations serving to make information freely available. In the first category fall such exceptions as those permitting use of copyright works in connection with the administration of justice and public safety[55]; the inclusion of limited parts of works in collections for religious, school or instructional use[56]; and the copying of works included in school broadcasts.[57] Other exceptions such as those permitting the reproduction and distribution of public speeches, newspaper articles and broadcast commentaries and the reproduction of works for the purpose of visual and sound reporting on current events,[58] as well as the right of quotation,[59] fall in the category of the public's right to information. The same applies to the reproduction of works which are permanently located in public places.[60]

Other exceptions, all of which are subject to the payment of equitable remuneration, include the public communication of works in certain special circumstances where the communication serves no gainful purpose on the part of the organiser and is free of charge and at religious services. However, no payment is required in respect of events organised by welfare services.[61] The making or causing to be made of single copies of a work for private use is permitted; however, for audio or video copying this was made subject to remuneration being paid to right owners. Copies may also be made for personal, scientific use and for inclusion in personal files and for other similar personal uses.[62] Other exceptions include the making of ephemeral recordings by broadcasting organisations[63]; the incidental use of

7–016

---

[53] Decision of the Federal Supreme Court, of April 3, 1968, B.G.H.Z. 50, 147, Kandinsky I.
[54] *cf.* Chapter VI, "Limitations on Copyright", Copyright Act 1965.
[55] Copyright Act, s.45.
[56] *ibid.*, s.46.
[57] *ibid.*, s.47.
[58] *ibid.*, ss.48, 49 and 50.
[59] *ibid.*, s.51.
[60] *ibid.*, s.59.
[61] *ibid.*, s.52.
[62] *ibid.*, s.53.
[63] *ibid.*, s.55.

works[64]; the reproduction and distribution of works of fine art in catalogues issued for the purpose of exhibitions or auctions[65]; the reproduction of portraits by photography by or on behalf of the commissioner[66]; and, finally, the compulsory licence for the production of sound recordings was maintained.[67] In all the above cases, the moral rights are preserved as no alteration to the work is permitted and the source of the work reproduced must be clearly acknowledged.[68]

The classical right to make quotations from works is of interest in Germany. Three kinds of quotation are distinguished: the "large" quotation, permitting the reproduction, distribution and communication to the public of an entire individual work in a scientific work to illustrate its contents; the "small" quotation of passages from a literary work; and quotation in musical works of passages from other musical works. As regards "large" quotations, this may include, for example, a complete photograph or press article and the courts have interpreted the notion of scientific work broadly, as covering, for example, popular science magazines, in the interest of the public's right to information.[69] The notion of passages of a work has also been interpreted broadly and even fairly extensive quotations are allowed, when justified by the purpose of criticism and review.[70]

The exceptions permitted by the new law in fact drew the line in a much more favourable position for the author than had the previous law. As regards reproduction for personal use, the law implemented case law by providing for royalties to be paid for audio and video private copying and included detailed regulations concerning reprography, although at the time that practice was to remain royalty-free.[71] The previous legal licence in favour of broadcasting was

---

[64] *ibid.*, s.57.

[65] *ibid.*, s.58.

[66] *ibid.*, s.60.

[67] *ibid.*, s.61.

[68] *ibid.*, ss.62 and 63.

[69] For example, see Decision of the LG Berlin, of December 12, 1960 [1962] 4 G.R.U.R. 207; LG Munich, July 27, 1994 [1994] 4 A.F.P. 1994, 326.

[70] LG Berlin May 26, 1977, [1978] 2 G.R.U.R. 108. See also H. Schack, *Urheber- und Urhebervertragsrecht*, 2nd ed., Tübingen, Mohr Siebeck, 2001, para.487 *et seq.* and M. Löffler, "Das Grundrecht auf Informationsfreiheit als Schranke des Urheberrechts", [1980] 5 N.U.W., 201.

[71] In 1978, the Federal Supreme Court decided that the royalty-free production of individual photocopies of copyrighted portions of a published work or of individual articles from newspapers or magazines for one's own use, permitted according to s.54(1) of the law, may in no case exceed 7 copies.

removed and that in favour of the phonographic industry was converted into a compulsory licence; however, this could only be exercised if the so-called mechanical rights of the author (rights to authorise the reproduction of works in sound recordings) were not administered by a collecting society. The 1965 provisions regarding exceptions remain the core of the present amended law; in the meantime some modifications have been made and specific amendments added, as seen below, but the general picture remains the same.

As regards the principal limitation on copyright, the question of duration, the extension of the term of protection to 70 years had not been proposed in the Government Bill. In the past, there had been great resistance to the adoption of a 50-year term, Germany having defended retaining 30 years for nearly 100 years. Opponents of change had upheld the interests of the public against the interests of the authors' heirs. The 1965 decision was taken in the context that the Bill put forward by the Government had proposed a public paying domain (*Urhebernachfolgevergütung*) with the object of caring for the needs of authors and their dependants. That proposal was rejected mainly because the choice of authors meriting assistance could have involved the danger of a state-controlled culture. However, the 70-year protection period was adopted by Parliament as a compromise. The decision was not expected:

> The wider public had not discussed the question. Nor did the plenary meeting of the *Bundestag* discuss either the pros or the cons. After the experience of the twenties this was surprising and showed a marked change in the emphasis on values. The interests of the public, which formerly had found such eloquent defenders, no longer seemed of such weight as to hold the scale against those of heirs of authors.[72]

Related or so-called neighbouring rights were introduced and regulated in detail by the law for the first time. Related rights in Germany concern not only the rights of performers, producers of phonograms and broadcasting organisations but also of film producers and rights in certain editions. The inclusion of related rights and the distinction drawn between the rights of authors and the beneficiaries of related **7–017**

---

[72] E. Ulmer, "Letter from Germany", *op. cit.*, n.47, above, at 283.

rights reflected the fact that: "from the 1920s onwards German case law had been concerned to define with particular clarity the difference between creation and performance, and consequently between copyright and related rights (*Leistungschutzrechte*)".[73]

The legislator took over the distinction and, as Ulmer pointed out, the rights "are of special design and in general ... are inferior to copyright in both content and duration".[74]

The 1965 Act was in its time considered by many to be the most up-to-date in the world. Kreile has described it as having.

> not only confirmed comprehensive moral rights for authors, but also aimed to shape the pecuniary powers of the author to such an extent that if possible every type of use of the work is subject to his or her control. Furthermore, the law aimed to make it clear that authors can make every use of their work subject to the payment of a fee.[75]

The Act was also considered to set new standards in its creation of specific related rights for phonogram and film producers and performing artists (with a period of protection of 25 years). Extension of the period of protection for authors to 70 years also set a new standard. The 1965 Act is still in force, its provisions having stood the test of time and the various challenges posed to the copyright system by technology very well. It has been amended from time to time, as described below, but its basic structure remains intact.

The Public Interest and the Basic Law

7–018 As has already been pointed out, the development of copyright legislation and case law since 1949 has been influenced by the Basic Law of the Federal Republic of Germany adopted in that year. It is important to note that the Basic Law not only guarantees the economic rights of authors under Art.14 and their moral rights under the rules on the protection of the personality (Arts 1 and 2) but it also lays

---

[73] *ibid.* at 285.

[74] *ibid.*

[75] R. Kreile, "The 1989 Amendment to the German Copyright Act", [1990]. 10 Copyright World 24.

down certain rules as regards the public interest. Moreover, Art.5 of the Basic Law concerning freedom of expression and information is also of importance in relation to copyright, since, as mentioned above in relation to the 1965 Law, certain exceptions to copyright protection, including those in favour of the press, radio and television reporting, the right of quotation and others, find their basis in the interest of the public in access to news and information. Thus, there is an interaction between copyright and freedom of information: while copyright itself is protected as property under Art.14, it has to be interpreted in the light of Art.5 and on social grounds a balance has to be found between the interests of authors and those of the public in establishing exceptions to copyright protection.[76] Copyright does not automatically take precedence over the right of the public to information.[77]

Art.14 of the Basic Law, concerning property, right of inheritance and expropriation, reads as follows:

(1) Property and the right of inheritance are guaranteed. Their content and limits shall be determined by the laws.

(2) Property imposes duties. Its use should also serve the public interest.

(3) Expropriation shall be permitted only in the public interest. It may be effected only by or pursuant to a law which shall provide for the nature and extent of the compensation. Such compensation shall be determined by establishing an equitable balance between the public interest and the interests of those affected. In case of dispute regarding the amount of compensation, recourse may be had to the ordinary courts.

Art.5 of the Basic Law, concerning freedom of expression and information, reads as follows:

---

[76] cf. G. Schricker, in G. Schricker, *Urheberrecht*, Kommentar, *op. cit.*, n.3, above, s.51, para.8; Y. Kleinke, *Pressedatenbanken und Urheberrecht*, Köln, etc. Carl Heymans Verlag (1999) p.67 *et seq.*; H. Schack, *op. cit.* n.67 above, para.463 *et seq.*; M. Rehbinder, *Urheberrecht*, 11th. ed., (C. Beck'sche Verlagsbuchhandlung, Munich 2001), para.38.

[77] On this subject, see M. Löffler, *op. cit.*, n.70, above, and J. Bornkamm, "Ungeschriebene Schranken des Urheberrechts?", in W. Erdmann, W. Gloy, R. Herber, *Festschrift for H. Piper*, Munich, Beck (1996), 641; and C. Geiger, "Les exceptions au droit d'auteur à des fins d'enseignement et de recherche en droit allemand", forthcoming in *PI*, October 2002, n.5.

(1) Everyone shall have the right freely to express and disseminate his opinion by speech, writing and pictures and freely to inform himself from generally accessible sources. Freedom of the press and freedom of reporting by means of broadcasts and films are guaranteed. There shall be no censorship.

(2) These rights are limited by the provisions of the general laws, the provisions of law for the protection of youth, and by the right to inviolability of personal honour.

(3) Art and science, research and teaching, shall be free. Freedom of teaching shall not absolve from loyalty to the constitution.

In a series of cases the German Federal Constitutional Court (*Bundesverfassungsgericht*) has clarified the impact of the Basic Law on copyright law and, in particular, the relationship between copyright and the public interest; the issue has arisen with respect to the extent to which the "limitations upon copyright" provided for by the Copyright Act "are justifiable in the public interest". The Court has also defined the role of the legislature under Art.14(1), sentence 2, of the Basic Law with specific reference to copyright.

7–019 The constitutional validity of the 1901 and 1907 Acts could only be contested up to April 1, 1952, pursuant to Art.93 of the Law Establishing the Federal Constitutional Court. All the cases, therefore, in which the Court has examined the relationship between the Basic Law and copyright law postdate the 1965 Copyright Act. Subsequent amendments to that Act, in 1972 and 1985, were due, in large measure, to the need to implement certain decisions of the Court.[78]

Due to the fact that actions contesting the constitutional validity of newly-enacted legislation[79] must be brought within a year, several cases were filed immediately after the adoption of the 1965 Act, with the result that the Court delivered five copyright decisions in July 1971. The cases covered the constitutional validity of the following provisions of the 1965 Act:

Section 27(1) exemption of public libraries from the payment of royalties;

---

[78] Since 1985, amendments to the Act have been mainly prompted by the need to implement the copyright harmonisation Directives adopted by the European Union.
[79] Art.93(2) of the Law Establishing the Federal Constitutional Court.

Section 46   exemption from the payment of remuneration in the case of collections for religious, school and instructional use;

Section 47   no payment of remuneration for the recording of school broadcasts;

Section 53(5) obligation for manufacturers of tape recorders to pay remuneration with respect to private copying of sound recordings;

Section 135   transformation of the formerly recognised copyright of performers in phonograms into a related right with a shorter protection period.[80]

The Court linked its decisions in these cases by express references and laid down its views on the relationship between the Copyright Act and the Basic Law in a detailed discussion in its judgment on the s.46 case, known as the "school book case". In this study, the judgments are not analysed in all their detail but with special regard to the issue of the relationship between copyright and the public interest.

In the school book case,[81] the Court found:

(a)   Copyright as a right of exploitation constitutes "property" within the meaning of Art.14(1), sentence 1, of the Basic Law;

(b)   Art.14(1), sentence 1, of the Basic Law in principle guarantees the attribution of the economic value of a copyrighted work to the author. It does not, however, provide a constitutional safeguard for any and all kinds of exploitation. It is for the legislature to establish, in the course of determining the contents and limits of authors' rights through the substantive regulation of the copyright law, appropriate standards which guarantee an

---

[80] Decisions of the Federal Constitutional Court dated July 7, 1971: [1972] 8 G.R.U.R. 485 "Bibliotheksgroschen"; [1972] 8 G.R.U.R. 481 "Kirchen–und Schulgebrauch"; [1972] 8 G.R.U.R. 487 "Schulfunksendungen"; [1972] 8 G.R.U.R. 488 "Tonbandvervielfältigung"; [1972] 8 G.R.U.R. 491 "Schallplatten". For commentaries in English on these cases on which the author has relied see A. Dietz, "Letter from Germany", [1973] Copyright 93; and W. Rumphorst, [1972] 3 I.I.C. 405. See also F. Fechner, *Geistiges Eigentum und Verfassung*, (Tübingen, Mohr Siebeck 1999) at 165 *et seq.*
[81] See also Federal Constitutional Court' July 7, 1971 "Kirchen- und Schulgebrauch" [1972] 3 I.I.C. 395.

exploitation of these rights that is commensurate with the nature and social significance of copyright (Art. 14(1), sentence 2, of the Basic Law).

(c) The interest of the general public in free access to things of cultural value justifies the incorporation, without the author's consent, of published protected works into collections which are intended for religious, school or instructional use, but not, however, that the author must make his work available free of charge (s.46, Copyright Act).

7–020 In its judgment, the Court identified a number of considerations relevant to the public interest in connection with the definition of the role of the legislator in determining the content and limits of property.

Having confirmed that the economic rights of authors are to be considered property in the sense of Art.14 of the Basic Law, the Court considered the extent to which the legislator could impose limitations on those rights and held:

Since there is no preexisting and absolute definition of property and since the content and function of property are capable and in need of adapting to social and economic situations, the Basic Law has put the legislature in charge of defining the scope and limits of property (Article 14(1), sentence 2, of the Constitution). This applies also for the economic rights of the author, which, just as tangible property rights, need shaping by the legal order. The legislature, however, being bound by the Basic Law may not deal with this at random. In defining the privileges and duties that make up the content of this right, it must preserve the fundamental substance of the property guarantee while at the same time also keeping in line with the other constitutional provisions. Only to this extent is the copyright protected under the Basic Law. . . . This attribution in principle of economic rights to the author for his free disposal does not mean, however, that thereby every conceivable way of exploitation is constitutionally secured. . . . It is for the legislature to establish in detail, in the course of determining the content of copyright . . . adequate standards which guarantee an appropriate exploitation and a utilisation that corresponds to the nature and the social meaning of the right. . . .

In assessing the constitutional validity of a statutory limitation on authors' rights it is necessary to take into account:

that the legislature is not only obliged to secure the interests of the individual; rather, it is also charged with drawing bounds on the individual rights and powers that are necessary in the interest of the general public; it must bring about a just balance between the sphere of the individual and the interests of the public. Thus, the constitutionality of the contested provision ... hinges upon its justification by the public interest.

Applying this principle to the case in question, the Court found that the general public "had a substantial interest in seeing that its young people, in the course of an up-to-date education, become acquainted with intellectual creations. ... The realisation of this social task would not be guaranteed," if the author could prohibit the inclusion of his work into a collection. However, it decided that, while the public interest demanded that the author could not prevent the use of his work in this case, he was entitled to be paid remuneration.

Under the property guarantee the author has in principle the right to be attributed the economic value of his work to the extent that the interests of the general public do not have priority over the author's affairs ... the general public's interest, as such, in an uninhibited access to copyrighted works is not sufficient. In view of the intensity of the limitation on the copyright owner's position, there must be an increased public interest in order to justify such a regulation under the Constitution.

In the s.47 (school broadcasts) case, the Court found that there was a **7–021** public interest in making it possible that school broadcasts can be presented to the intended audiences at the right moment, and, therefore, in allowing schools to record works included in a broadcast. Since authors are remunerated in respect of the original broadcast, an additional remuneration for the recording (which in any case has to be destroyed in due course) is not necessary.

Again, applying the criteria laid down in the school books case, the Court decided, in the s.27 (exemption of public libraries from payment of royalties) case, that the property guarantee of the Basic Law does not force the legislature to secure for the author all the means of economic exploitation imaginable. S.27 granted authors a right to remuneration if copies of a work were lent and the lending was executed for the financial gain of the lender. This meant that public libraries of all kinds were exempt from payment. The Court ruled that the Basic Law did not oblige the legislator to guarantee remuneration to the author in every case of lending and that the differentiation in the law between profit-making libraries and public libraries was permissible. In this case, the public benefit from the limitation on the authors' rights is evident.

In judging the constitutional validity of s.135 (conversion of performers' copyright into a related right), the Court held that Art.14(1) of the Basic Law cannot be "an insurmountable barrier for the legislature when reforms prove necessary". Thus, it is legitimate to reshape individual rights if it is in the public interest and does not constitute an undue burden. However, as regards the reduction of the term of protection for existing phonograms, resulting from a change in the time when the period of protection began, the Court held it could not be reconciled with the property guarantee of Art. 14(1).

These issues were considered once again by the Federal Constitutional Court in the *Church Music* case in 1978[82] when the constitutional validity of s.52 of the Copyright Act, which permitted free and unauthorised use of musical works in churches, was the subject of examination. The Court held that, whereas the provision allowing the performance without authorisation was in accord with the Constitution, the exclusion of remuneration in the case of church events was unconstitutional and incompatible with the guarantee of property in Art.14 of the Basic Law. The Court observed that "this guarantee of the Basic Law gives the author the economic right to use this intellectual property ... The legislature is, in principle, required to attribute the economic control of the creative work to the author and to allow him the freedom to dispose of it at his own responsibility".

7–022 In its judgment, the Court emphasised the concept of the social obligation of intellectual property. It defined this concept by stating that no disproportionate reduction of the rights of individuals can be tolerated. For the public interest to prevail over the interests of the individual, that interest must be sufficiently important to override the right to remuneration. It held, *inter alia*:

> Legislation moreover has the task of taking the interests of the

---

[82] Decision of the Federal Constitutional Court, October 25, 1978, [1979] 84 U.F.I.T.A. 317; see also M. Ruete, "The *Kirchenmusik* Judgment —Constitutional and Intellectual Property Rights", [1980] E.I.P.R. 198.

general public into consideration. Yet the power of legislative provision is not unlimited. Any restrictions on the right of use that are made in the public interest must therefore be supported by legitimate grounds. An excessive restriction that is not dictated by the social demands on copyright cannot be justified by Art.14(2) of the Basic Law. . . . As the right of use belonging to the author . . . is the result of his own personal effort and not of an unearned property right accruing to him, he may not be denied his right to compensation on the basis of any consideration relating to the public good.

Within the framework of Art.14 of the Basic Law, therefore, the question of the public interest arises in a negative sense as the basis for possible restrictions upon the property rights of authors. The basic rule as regards property in the result of intellectual creation is to give exclusive rights to the author. These rights may be reduced to a right to equitable remuneration if there is a social or public interest in restricting the exclusive right and even expropriated altogether if the public interest in free access to the work is considered of overriding importance.

The Court has established a concept of "proportionality" or "balancing of interests" to reconcile the interests of property owners, including right owners and the public. In each case, the question arises whether, taking the principle of proportionality into account, the "intellectual public interest" is more important than the right of the author. If so, it is justified for the payment of remuneration to be excluded altogether.[83]

So far as the relationship between Arts 14 and 5 of the Basic Law is concerned, the Constitutional Court has made it clear that as a general rule Art.5 must be taken account of in interpreting all legislation, and this obviously includes copyright legislation.[84] Thus, two constitutionally protected basic rights have to be balanced against each other and decided in every case on the particular facts. Opinions are somewhat divided in the literature about the extent to which Art.5 should apply in interpreting the Copyright Act. The Federal Supreme Court has held, however, that the press has no special privileges as regards the right of quotation, stating: "The press does not enjoy any

---

[83] See also more recent case law on this topic at paras 7–025, 7–037 and 7–038, below.

[84] Federal Constitutional Court decision, "Lüth", Bverf.G.F. 7, 198 at 206 *et seq.*

special position in relation to copyright but like any private person is obliged to respect the copyright of others. It should be added that no author is under an obligation to make his work freely available to the public, so long as the law itself in the interest of the public has not specifically made an exception to the obligation to obtain permission for the use under certain conditions".[85] It is considered by some commentators that the right of quotation is too narrowly construed and that, therefore, freedom of information is hindered.[86]

Subsequent Amendments to the 1965 Act

The 1972 Amendment

7–023   As mentioned above, the Federal Constitutional Court handed down its decisions in the five landmark cases already discussed in July 1971. These decisions prompted certain provisions of the 1972 Amendment to the 1965 Copyright Act: s.27 (concerning library royalties), s.46 (concerning textbook royalties) and s.135 (period of protection for performers). The share of the artists' claim with respect to the resale right (*droit de suite*) was also increased (s.26).

The Federal Constitutional Court had held that the exemption of public libraries from the so-called library royalty was not contrary to the Basic Law. The Government, however, in its 1972 Amendment, extended the obligation to pay royalties in all cases of rental or lending to "an institution accessible to the public (library, record library, or other collection)", whether public or private. As regards textbooks, the Court had declared that the exemption from paying remuneration to authors in respect of their works included in collections for religious, school and instructional use was unconstitutional. The amendment to s.46 made it clear that the author should be paid an equitable remuneration for the reproduction and distribution of his works in such collections. The amendment to s.135 took account of the Federal Constitutional Court's decision that the provision was unconstitutional to the extent that the shorter term of 25 years

---

[85] Decision of the Federal Supreme Court, "Verkehrskinderlied", October 17, 1958, B.G.H.Z. 28, 234 at 238. See also G. Romatka, "Bild-Zitat und ungenehmigte Übernahme von Lichtbildern", [1971] 1 Af.P. 20.

[86] See M. Löffler, *op. cit.*, n.70, above.

accorded to producers of phonograms and performers under the 1965 Act was retroactive and applied to phonograms made before January 1, 1966. The amendment provided that such phonograms should remain protected for 25 years from January 1, 1966 unless the protection period applying to them would have expired earlier under the old law. In the latter case, the previous protection period applied.

The Amendment Act 1985

A further significant reform took place in 1985 with the adoption of the Act Amending Provisions in the Field of Copyright of June 24, 1985.[87]   **7–024**

As Margret Möller pointed out at the time: "The central feature of the Amendment Act is its provision for the obligation to pay remuneration for the reproduction of copyright works for private and other personal uses".[88]

The amendments related to s.53, which lays down the conditions under which copies may be made without the authors' consent, and s.54, which specifies what is to be paid, and by whom, for such reproduction. Both private copying of sound and audiovisual recordings and reprography are concerned and claims to remuneration may only be asserted by a collecting society.[89] The levy on recording equipment (appliances), first introduced in 1965 and payable by manufacturers and importers[90] thereof, was extended also to blank audio and video recording media.[91] With regard to reprography, the author is entitled to be paid equitable remuneration by the manufacturer or importer of photocopying appliances in the form of a royalty on equipment. In addition, where such appliances are operated in educational and research institutions, public libraries, and businesses offering photocopying facilities (copy shops), the operators of the

---

[87] [1985] B.G.B.l. 1, at 1137; [1985] *Copyright* 368.

[88] M. Möller, "The Reform of the Copyright Law of the Federal Republic of Germany" [1986] *Copyright* 271, at 272.

[89] s.54h Copyright Act.

[90] By virtue of the Law of July 25, 1994 amending the Patent Fee Act and Other Acts, dealers are now jointly liable with manufacturers for paying the royalty if their turnover exceeds a certain amount specified in s.54b Copyright Act.

[91] For an account of the law and practice with respect to remuneration for private copying in Germany see R. Kreile, "Collection and Distribution of the Statutory Remuneration for Private Copying with Respect to Recorders and Blank Cassettes in Germany", [1992] 23 I.I.C. 449.

appliances must also pay.[92] The Federal Constitutional Court in 1996 rejected a complaint filed by copy shops against the operator royalty finding that it was not in breach of constitutional law. It pointed out that the combination of a royalty on equipment and a royalty payable by operators was an appropriate means to secure equitable remuneration to right owners at low administrative cost, on the one hand, and to take account of the high proportion of copying of copyright-protected material that takes place in educational and research institutions, public libararies and copy shops, on the other.[93]

In a recent decision, the Landgericht Stuttgart found that manufacturers and importers of CD burners were also liable to pay royalties with respect to digital private copying by means of CD burners.[94]

7–025 The rates of remuneration payable for private copying and reprography were laid down in an Annex to s.54 of the Act, giving rise to the risk of the amounts being devalued through inflation; and as a matter of fact, to date, the rates have not been changed. For that reason, Parliament (the *Bundestag*), when voting on the 1985 Act, invited the Federal Government to submit a report every three years following its entry into force on "the development of copyright remuneration under s.54 of the Copyright Act taking into particular account whether the proceeds of remuneration are held equitable within the meaning of s.54 of the Copyright Act", together with a report on the "impact of technical developments on copyright and related rights and where necessary to propose suitable measures to safeguard the economic substance of intellectual property".

The *Bundestag* in the same resolution invited the Government to conduct a study on the economic significance of copyright. This was subsequently carried out and the results published in 1989 by the Institute for Economic Research (IFO) in Munich.[95] Dietz remarks that the invitation of the *Bundestag* to study these and other issues of lesser significance bears

witness to the awareness of the *Bundestag* that an up-to-date

---

[92] s.54a(2) Copyright Act.

[93] Federal Constitutional Court decision of October 20, 1996, "Kopierladen II", N.J.W. 1997, 247 *et seq*; [1997] 2 G.R.U.R. 124. See also F. Fechner, *op. cit.* n.80, above, 180.

[94] *GEMA v Hewlett Packard*, Decision of *Landgericht Stuttgart* of November 11, 2000.

[95] M. Hummel, *Die volkswirtschaftliche Bedeutung des Urheberrechts*, Gutachten im Auftrag des Bundesministers der Justiz, No.125 in der Schriftenreihe des IFO-Instituts für Wirtschaftsforschung, (Berlin/Munich, Duncker & Humblot, 1989).

copyright law is in need of continuous improvement and supplementing. ... Only a well-devised ruling, striking an intelligent balance between the interests involved ..., can provide effective protection for authors and for their successors in title, as for the owners of neighbouring rights, not only as regards the legal aspect but also from an economic point of view.[96]

A number of other reforms were introduced in 1985. Protection for computer programs as literary works was introduced confirming a principle already recognised by the Courts (s.2(1)). A general obligation to pay remuneration for public communication of copyright works, even in cases where the communication takes place free of charge, serves no gainful purpose of the organiser and where the performers receive no fee, was introduced as a result of the Federal Constitutional Court's decision in the *Church Music* case. This principle is subject to only a few specified exceptions in respect of events organised by certain welfare services and for school events, on condition that they are only accessible for a specifically limited circle of persons.[97]

In 1988, the Federal Constitutional Court (*Bundesverfassungsgericht*) considered the compatibility of this amendment with the Basic Law in a case involving events connected with prisoner welfare. It found that, in the public interest, it was compatible with the basic law to exclude payment to right owners with respect to the communication to the public of protected musical and literary works by means of radio broadcasts or audio and video recordings in the recreation rooms of penal institutions. The Court found that the Basic Law does not oblige the legislator to give absolute priority to the individual interests of authors over the public interest. The public interest is the ground for and also sets limits to the exceptions to be imposed on the right owner; these should not exceed what the public interest requires and it is the duty of the legislator to balance these conflicting interests. Once a protected work is published, it is no longer the property of its creator alone but falls into the cultural public domain. This social public interest function is the basis for limiting the period of protection of copyright and is reinforced by the particular circumstances

---

[96] A. Dietz, "Letter from the Federal Republic of Germany, The Development of Copyright between 1984 and the beginning of 1989", [1990] Copyright 58 at 59.

[97] s.52(1) Copyright Act; the welfare services listed are: the Youth, Social, Old Persons and Prisoners Welfare Services.

in which prisoners live; this justifies the legislator giving them precedence over authors in the circumstances.[98]

7–026 The term of protection afforded to photographs was modified and a distinction made between three kinds of photographs according to different levels of creativity. "Photographic works" were to enjoy protection for 70 years p.m.a.; "documentary photographs" 50 years from publication or, if unpublished, from making; and "all other photographs" 25 years from publication or making.

Criminal sanctions against piracy were reinforced to tackle what was seen as an increasing problem. The penalty for unlawful exploitation on a commercial basis was increased to imprisonment for up to five years or a fine. Public prosecution in cases of piracy was also provided for as a general rule. Previously, offenders had to be prosecuted by means of a private complaint except in cases where the public prosecutor found public prosecution to be in the public interest. A number of amendments were also introduced to the Copyright Administration Act.

Follow-up to the 1985 Act

7–027 As mentioned above, at the time of the passage of the 1985 Amendment Act, the *Bundestag* instructed the Government to report every three years on developments regarding: (i) the remuneration payable to right owners pursuant to section 54 of the Act; (ii) the effects of technological developments on copyright and related rights; and (iii) to make proposals for suitable measures to protect intellectual property with particular regard to its economic aspects.[99]

The *Bundestag* had also called for studies on the importance of copyright for the national economy and certain other matters.

The planned triennual reports did not materialise. Since 1985, only two reports have actually been published. The first was submitted in 1989 and the second only in the year 2000. The reasons for this are explained in the second report and were due mainly to the heavy workload of the Ministry of Justice and the fact that the Commission

---

[98] Federal Constitutional Court decision of October 11, 1988, "Vollzugsanstalten", [1992] N.J.W. 1307, [1989] 3 G.R.U.R. 193.

[99] In 1998, the *Bundestag* released the Government from the requirement to report regularly on the impact of technical developments (BT-Protokolle 13/238, session of May 28, 1998).

of the European Communities was expected to come up with proposals for European Union legislation on the subject of private copying and reprography.[1]

The 1989 report, which took account of the economic study into the importance of copyright for the national economy which had been completed in the meantime by IFO, was adopted by the *Bundestag* in February 1990.

The IFO study concluded that works qualifying for copyright protection accounted in 1986, directly and indirectly, for about DM54 billion in income (measured in terms of gross value added) and roughly 799,000 jobs (3.1 per cent of the population in gainful employment), and contributed 2.9 per cent to the generation of domestic income. If computer software had been included—following the method of studies in other countries—a contribution of 3.3 per cent to the domestic generation of income would have resulted. The report also concluded that "the development in West German copyright industries has been more dynamic than for the economy as a whole. ... Thus, the economic importance of copyright industries with respect to the generation of income and jobs deserves to receive special attention".

It concluded, further, that "it must be emphasised that a decisive   **7–028** precondition for this is appropriate copyright legislation, also with respect to the approaching single European market".[2]

The Government's 1989 report analysed four topics. Chapter 1 dealt with the development of the fees payable for private copying and reprography under s.54 of the Act[3] and recommended that the collection of the fees should be facilitated by obliging those liable to pay such fees to provide information as to the nature and quantity of appliances and media sold or placed on the market. It was also proposed that the fee per page for reprography be doubled. Chapter 2 discussed the impact of technical developments on copyright and related rights, dealing in particular with the following issues: the impact of digital recording techniques; rental of sound recordings and videos; the term of protection to be afforded to sound recordings and

---

[1] See *Vergütungsbericht* of July 5, 2000, A II, last para., p.7.

[2] M. Hummel, *op cit.*, n.95, above, quoted from the English summary of the report, at 226–7.

[3] The statutory minimum rates laid down in the annex to s.54d, para. 1, Copyright Act, have not been changed to date in spite of continued pressure from the interested parties for an increase.

performers; and, in the light of initiatives of the European Commission, cable distribution of TV broadcasts and the protection of computer programs and databases. Chapters 3 and 4 addressed respectively the question whether sound engineers should enjoy a related right and legislation on copyright contracts. This is not the place for a detailed consideration of all the Government's proposals.[4]

The Legal Affairs Committee of the Parliament in late 1989 called for a draft Act to be prepared incorporating the Government's proposals. Although it was clear that a comprehensive reform of the law could not be achieved during the legislative period, the Committee considered two matters to be so urgent that they should be dealt with straight away. They called for the extension of the term of protection for the related rights of performers from 25 to 50 years and the improvement of the right to information under section 54 of the Copyright Act to facilitate the collection of levies for private copying and reprography. The recommendation in the report for an increase in the royalties paid for reprography was not followed.

These amendments were incorporated into the Law to Reinforce the Protection of Intellectual Property and to Combat the Piracy of Products, which entered into force on July 1, 1990 and is known as the "Product Piracy Act".

7–029 The right to receive information in connection with the collection of remuneration arises now with the claim for payment (instead of as previously with respect only to the previous calendar year). If the person obliged to provide the information fails to do so, the rate of remuneration payable may be doubled.[5] It may also be mentioned here that subsequently, in 1994, traders were made jointly liable with manufacturers and importers for the payment of remuneration.[6]

An array of effective provisions was also introduced in the Act for the pursuit and punishment of infringers of copyright and related rights. Penal sanctions were increased (commercial piracy being made punishable by up to five years' imprisonment or fine), civil and criminal possibilities for destruction and seizure of infringing goods

---

[4] For a brief account in English see R. Kreile, *op. cit.*, n.75, above.

[5] s.54g Copyright Act.

[6] The opportunity was also taken to restructure s.54 of the Copyright Act, which now consists of paras 54a to 54h. The rates of remuneration payable are laid down in the Annex to para. 54d(1). *Gesetz zur Änderung des Patentgebührengesetzes und anderer Gesetze* of July 25, 1994 (B.G.B.L. 1 S.1739) (Law to amend the Law on Patent Fees and other Laws).

extended, discovery procedures improved and, finally, the possibilities for customs authorities to intervene in product piracy cases improved.

A further piece of legislation on copyright of great importance for Germany must be mentioned here. The Treaty of Union of August 31, 1990,[7] which effected the reunification of Germany, included a number of provisions on industrial and intellectual property. As a result, in the case of copyright, the law of the Federal Republic of Germany (*i.e.* the Copyright Act of September 9, 1965, as amended) has applied in the territory of the former German Democratic Republic since unification took effect on October 3, 1990.

The 1990s: Implementation of the EU Directives on Copyright and Related Rights and Other Recent Developments

Implementation of the EU Directives on Copyright and Related Rights

During the 1990s, as in the United Kingdom and France, German legislation on copyright and related rights was dominated by the need to amend German law to comply with the five EC Directives adopted between 1991 and 2000 with the aim of harmonising the laws of Member States of the European Union in the field of copyright and related rights.[8] Three further laws to amend the Copyright Act 1965 (the second, third and fourth amendment laws) were adopted in this context, implementing all five Directives. In this process, there is little scope for a national approach except where the Commission has failed to take any initiative.[9]

7–030

---

[7] [1990] B.G.B.1. Part II, 885 *et seq.*

[8] The five Directives were: Directive 91/250/EEC on the Legal Protection of Computer Programs; Directive 92/100/EEC on Rental Right and Lending Right and on Certain Rights Related to Copyright in the Field of Intellectual Property; Directive 93/83/EEC on Coordination of Certain Rules concerning Copyright and Rights Related to Copyright applicable to Satellite Broadcasting and Cable Retransmission; Directive 93/98/EEC Harmonising the Term of Protection of Copyright and Certain Related Rights; Directive 96/9/EC of the European Parliament and the Council on the Legal Protection of Databases. For an analysis and the texts of these Directives, see K. Garnett, J. Rayner James and G. Davies, *Copinger and Skone James on Copyright*, Ch.25, and Vol.II, Part H, respectively.

[9] For commentaries on contemporary German copyright law developments, see, *inter alia*; K.-F. Fromm and W. Nordemann, *Urheberrecht*, 9th. ed., (L Stuttgart/Berlin,

The second law[10] to amend the Copyright Act 1965, dated June 9, 1993, had the purpose of bringing German law into line with the EC Directive on the legal protection of computer programs of May 14, 1991.[11]

7–031 The provisions of the Directive were incorporated literally into the German law, resulting in one important change to the standard of protection in relation to computer programs. The Directive provides for a lower standard of originality than the previous German law, which required computer programs to be of a level of creativity considerably surpassing the average to qualify for protection as literary works.[12] To conform with the criteria of originality in the Directive, the law now provides that computer programs shall be protected if they constitute original works in the sense that they are the result of their author's own intellectual creation. *No other criteria, particularly of a qualitative or aesthetic nature, shall be applied to determine their eligibility for protection* (emphasis added).

7–032 The Third Law Amending the Copyright Law of June 23, 1995[13] implemented both the 1992 EC Directive on Rental Right and Lending Right and on Certain Rights Related to Copyright in the Field of Intellectual Property and the 1993 Directive Harmonising the Term of Protection of Copyright and Certain Related Rights.[14] To comply with the former, amendments were necessary to adapt the German law as regards the exclusive right of distribution; previously, according to the principle of exhaustion of rights, the power to authorise rental was exhausted after first sale. The Rental Right Directive was therefore implemented by providing that the exclusive nature of the rental right continues to subsist even after the exhaustion of the distribution right. Further amendments were needed to bring the law into conformity with the Directive as regards certain related rights of performers (in particular, a distribution right in fixations of

---

Verlag W. Kohlhammer 1998); P. Möhring and K. Nicolini, *Urheberrechtsgesetz*, Kommentar, 2nd. ed., Munich, Vahlen, 2000; M. Rehbinder, *Urheberrecht op. cit.*, n.76, above; H. Schack, *Urheber- und Urhebervertragsrecht, op. cit.*, n.70, above; G. Schricker, in G. Schricker, *Urheberrecht*, Kommentar, *op. cit.* n.1, above.

[10] [1993] B.G.Bl. Part I, at 910. For an English-language translation of the Amendment Act see [1994] 1 I.I.C. 51.

[11] Council Directive No. 91/250/EEC of May 14, 1991, OJ EC No.L122, at 42.

[12] Federal Supreme Court Decision of May 9, 1985, "Inkassoprogramm", [1985] 12 G.R.U.R. 1041, at 1048.

[13] Entered into force June 24, 1995.

[14] Council Directive No. 93/98/EEC of October 29, 1993, OJ EC No.L290, at 9.

their performances), producers of films and phonograms and broad-casting organisations.[15] Here it is also of interest to note that authors and performers are granted unwaivable rights to receive equitable remuneration for the rental of phonograms and audiovisual works; these may be assigned in advance only to a collecting society and may only be exercised through such a society. Lending rights may also only be exercised through collecting societies.[16]

As regards the term Directive, although the 70-year term of protection for literary and artistic works was already provided for under the German law, amendments were necessary to increase the period of protection for film and phonogram producers and broadcasting organisations from 25 to 50 years after publication or, if unpublished, 50 years after the production, bringing the term of protection for these right owners to the same as that for the related rights of performers. The term of protection of the moral rights of performers was also extended from the previous term of 25 years to 50 years from the performance.[17] The law has also been changed to provide for nationals of, and companies based in, other Member States of the European Union[18] to receive equal treatment under the Copyright Law to bring the law into conformity with the decision of the European Court in the *Phil Collins* case.[19] It has also been made clear that collecting societies have an obligation to administer the rights of interested parties not only when they are German nationals but also when they are nationals of the EU or EAA. The law has further been amended with respect to photographs to bring it into line with the Directive, which provides that photographs are to be considered original in the sense that they are the author's own intellectual creation; no other criteria such as merit or purpose are to be applied to

---

[15] *cf.* Art.6 *et seq.* of the Directive.

[16] s.27 Copyright Act.

[17] The moral right of the performer expires with the death of the performer; however, it expires 50 years after the performance if before that date the performer has died. See s.83 Copyright Act.

[18] And of countries party to the Agreement on the European Economic Area (EEA).

[19] Decision of October 20, 1993 (case C–92/92 and C–326/92 *Phil Collins v Imtrat Handelsgesellschaft mbH and Patricia Im-und Export Verwaltungsgesellschaft mbH, Leif Emanuel Kraul and EMI Electrola GmbH*), in which the Court decided that the ban on discrimination on the basis of nationality provided for by Art.7 of the Treaty of Rome applies to the law on copyright and related rights and means that nationals of other Member States must receive equal treatment to that given to nationals under the Copyright Law in Germany; (and see [1994] 159 *R.I.D.A.* 304).

determine their eligibility for protection.[20] This necessitated a change to the German law, which previously distinguished between photographic works, documentary and other photographs, giving them different terms of protection. Thus, in future, there will be two categories of photographs, photographic works protected for 70 years p.m.a. and all other so-called simple photographs (not being the author's intellectual creation) will be protected for 50 years from publication or production.[21]

7–033 The Database Directive[22] was implemented in the context of new legislation on multi-media, the Law Governing the Framework for Information and Communications Services,[23] a compendium law dealing *inter alia* also with teleservices and digital signatures. The amendments to the Copyright Act required to implement the Database Directive are contained in one article, Art.7. As regards authors' rights in databases, the relevant sections of the Copyright Act are amended by the insertion of various provisions on the object of protection, database authorship, restricted acts and exceptions, and in particular, by extending the existing provision on collections of works to databases (database works). Thus, such database works are considered to constitute personal intellectual creations by virtue of the selection or arrangement of their contents. The *sui generis* right in other databases not considered to be such intellectual creations has been implemented by the addition of a new section to the related rights chapter of the Copyright Act.

7–034 Finally, the Fourth Law Amending the Copyright Act to comply with the Directive on Satellite and Cable Distribution (1993)[24] was adopted on May 8, 1998.[25] The Directive deals with broadcasting and communication to the public rights of authors, performers, phonogram

---

[20] Art.6 of the Directive.

[21] Here, it is of interest to note that in the *Beuys-Fotografien* case (OLG Düsseldorf, Decision of February 13, 1996, [1997] G.R.U.R. 49) the Court stated that the degree of originality required for photographic works should not be set too low given the substantial, 50-year protection which already exists for simple photographs.

[22] Directive 96/9/EC of the European Parliament and of the Council of March 11, 1996 on the Legal Protection of Databases (OJ EC No.L77, at 20).

[23] *Gesetz Zur Regelung der Rahmenbedingungen für Informations- und Kommunikationsdienste*, [1997] BGBl., Part I, 1870. The Database Directive is implemented in Art.7, which came into force on January 1, 1998.

[24] Council Directive 93/83/EEC of September 27, 1993 on the co-ordination of certain rules concerning copyright and rights related to copyright applicable to satellite broadcasting and cable retransmission (OJ L 248, October 6, 1993, 15).

[25] Entered into force on June 1, 1998 (BGBl. 1 p. 902).

producers and broadcasting organisations in respect of satellite transmissions within the EU and EEA, providing that the act of communication to the public takes place solely in the Member State from
which the programme-carrying signals are transmitted, as well as cable
retransmission of programmes from other Member States. Cable
retransmission means the simultaneous, unaltered and unabridged
retransmission of programmes intended for reception by the public. In
accordance with the Directive, these rights (including rights to equitable remuneration (inalienable in the case of authors and performers))
may only be exercised collectively through a collecting society, except
in the case of the rights of broadcasting organisations.[26]

Meanwhile, two further Directives have been adopted: the Directive   **7–035**
on the harmonisation of certain aspects of copyright and related rights
in the information society, adopted in May 2001 and the Directive on
the resale right for the benefit of the author of an original work of art,
adopted in September 2001.[27] To date these Directives have not been
implemented in Germany.[28] As described in Part IV, below, the
Information Society Directive is of particular importance in the
context of the public interest in view of its provisions concerning
limitations and exceptions to authors' rights and related rights. The
Resale Right Directive is not so controversial for Germany since such
rights are already recognised in the law.

---

[26] *cf.* Arts. 9 and 10 of the Directive and s. 20b Copyright Act.

[27] Directive 2001/29/EC of the European Parliament and the Council of May 22,
2001 ([2001] O J L167/10) ("The Information Society Directive); Directive 2001/84/
EC of the European Parliament and of the Council of September 27, 2001 ([2001] O J
L272/32) ("The Resale Right Directive"). For an analysis and the texts of these
Directives see K. Garnett, J. Rayner James and G. Davies, *Copinger and Skone James on
Copyright, op. cit.*, Supplement to the 14th ed., Ch. 25 and Appendices H11 and H12.

[28] On March 18, 2002, the German Government published a bill to revise the
Copyright Act to implement the Information Society Directive as well as the WIPO
Copyright Treaty 1996 (WCT) and the WIPO Performers and Phonograms Treaty
1996 (WPPT) (*cf.* Part IV, below). The bill is available on the website of the German
Ministry of Justice (*www. bundesjustizministerium.de*). For a brief overview of the bill see
F. Kretschmer, "Gesetzentwurf zur Regelung des Urheberrechts in der Informationsgesellschaft," [2002] G.R.U.R. 501. The bill takes a minimal approach, avoiding
taking position on sensitive subjects; in view of the controversial nature of some issues,
such as technical protection measures and their impact on private copying, it may be
some time before the bill, no doubt considerably amended, becomes law.

Other Recent Developments

Government Report to the *Bundestag*, July 2000

7–036   In July 2000, the German Government presented the *Bundestag* with its second report on the development and suitability of the equitable remuneration payable pursuant to s.54 of the Copyright Act for private copying and reprography.[29] It noted that no proposals for harmonisation of the laws of the Member States of the European Union had yet been adopted on this subject. In its conclusions, the Government expressed the view that the rules concerning this remuneration should be harmonised within the European Union, since the differing situations in the Member States affect competition within the single market. However, it concluded that the German law needed to be brought up to date without waiting further for EU action on the subject. It therefore proposed *inter alia* that the following legislative measures be adopted:

the rates of remuneration payable should be increased by a reasonable amount (to date these have not been increased since 1985 even to take account of inflation) and the law should be changed to enable future increases to be implemented by order;

it should be made clear that all new and future recording equipment and blank media, including digital equipment and media, are covered by the present law and subject to the payment of remuneration in order to avoid the need for litigation in future to establish whether particular new appliances and media are so covered[30];

the present exception according to which commercial organisations and governmental authorities are exempted from paying remuneration for reprography should be scrapped since these too copy protected material.[31]

---

[29] *cf.* n. 1, above.

[30] Litigation was necessary to establish that reader-printers (Decision of the Federal Court of Justice of January 28, 1993, "Reader-printer" [1993] 6 G.R.U.R. 553) and telefax machines (Decision of the Federal Court of Justice of January 28, 1999, "Telefaxgeräte" [1999] 10 G.R.U.R. 928) are subject to the royalty on reprographic reproduction equipment under s.54a (1) of the Copyright Act.

[31] Here it is of interest to note that in 1996 the Federal Constitutional Court held that this distinction between the institutions required to pay the operator royalty did not

The report drew attention to the fact that with digital technology there is the possibility of using technical measures to control or prevent private copying in the audio and audiovisual fields but made no proposals on the subject. It remains to be seen whether when the law is changed it will be permissible to use such technical measures to prevent copying. The German law at present specifically gives the public the right to make single copies of a work for private use (s.53(1) of the Copyright Act) in exchange for remuneration in certain cases. If this right is not qualified, it would seem illegal to use technical measures to prevent private copying.

In the digital environment, it may be questioned whether such an approach is justified. Copyright falls within the guarantee of property in Art.14 of the Basic Law. Limitations on copyright which prevent the right owner from exercising his basic right to control reproduction in the digital environment may be seen as undermining the copyright system. Although the German approach has traditionally been to permit restrictions on copyright in exchange for remuneration, it is doubtful whether any royalty system can provide sufficient compensation to right owners for uncontrolled and unlimited copying by digital means in the private sphere. Art.14(3) indeed permits expropriation of property in the public interest, subject to the payment of compensation. However, it is questionable whether to expropriate rights to control digital private copying is really in conformity with the principle of proportionality established by the Federal Constitutional Court. Restrictions on rights should not go further than the public interest requires and the more a statutory limitation impinges on the specific object (essence) of an exclusive right, the more necessary it is for the reasons for the limitation to be justified.[32] The interests of the right owners would be severely damaged by such expropriation since no remuneration scheme based on the present private copying provisions of the law could compensate for the loss of control digital copying implies. As the German Minister of Justice has recognised, "demands for a prohibition of the private copying of CDs are becoming louder. If the matter is considered carefully, the public

---

justify any complaint under constitutional law. The legislator had acted reasonably in making the distinction in view of the limited copying of copyright material by the exempted institutions (Decision of September 19, 1996, Kopierladen I [1997] 2 G.R.U.R. 123).

[32] See para.7–021 *et seq.*, above. and the decision of the Federal Constitutional Court dated October 25, 1978, "Kirchenmusik", [1980] 1 G.R.U.R. 44, at 48.

interest should not stand in the way; on the contrary, cultural diversity is in the self-evident interests of the general public".[33]

For the sake of completeness, it should also be mentioned that a new and controversial "Law to strengthen the contractual position of authors and performers" was enacted in March 2002. The German Government takes the view that the negotiating position of authors and performers is weak *vis-à-vis* producers and publishers and that it is necessary, therefore, to intervene to limit freedom of contract in this area so as to ensure that the former receive adequate financial reward and are not compelled to assign their rights. The law was strongly opposed by producers' and publishers' organisations.[34]

Recent Case Law Relevant to the Public Interest

7–037 The Federal Constitutional Court had occasion once more to consider copyright in relation to the public interest in its decision "DIN Standards" handed down in 1998.[35] The case concerned s.5 of the Copyright Act, which excludes from copyright protection "Acts, regulations, official decrees and notices as well as decisions and officially drafted headnotes of decisions"; the same applies to "other official works published in the official interest for public information". The question had arisen whether building standards adopted and issued by the DIN (*Deutsches Institut für Normung e. V*—the German Standards Institute—and a non-governmental, private organisation) could be freely reproduced by various government authorities. The Court held that s.5 of the Copyright Act pursued a legitimate aim in the public interest in order that works published for official purposes for the general information of the public should attain the widest possible dissemination. When the work of a private author is published as part of an official communication, therefore, it does not enjoy copyright protection. The Court said that this is compatible with Art.14(1), first sentence, of the Basic Law (the guarantee of

---

[33] Speech of Prof. Dr H. Däubler-Gmelin, then German Minister of Justice, "Privater Vervielfältigung unter dem Vorzeichen digitaler Technik" at POPKOMM, Cologne, August 20, 1999 (see website *www.bundesjustizministerium.de*).

[34] Gesetz zur Stärkung der vertraglichen Stellung von Urhebern und ausübenden Künstlern, March 22, 2002, [2002] 6 G.R.U.R. 502. See M. Schippan, "Codification of Contract Rules for Copyright Owners—The Recent Amendment of the German Copyright Act", [2000] E.I.P.R. 171.

[35] Decision of July 29, 1998, "DIN-Normen" [1999] 3 G.R.U.R. 226.

property) provided that the agreement of the private author is requested and that he has the opportunity to negotiate the payment of equitable remuneration. In this context, the Court stated that, in drafting the copyright law, the legislator has to ensure that the right owner can privately exploit his property right and that such exploitation enables him financially to enjoy an independent standard of living. The guiding principle in shaping the content of the law should be the common weal. The individual interests of the right owner cannot take unconditional priority over the interests of the public. However, the public interest is not only the ground for, but also sets limits to, the restrictions imposed on the right owner. Such restrictions should not go further than the public interest requires. In applying the principle of proportionality and in taking into consideration the principle of equality, the legislator must bring both these concerns into a well-balanced relationship.

The need to balance the interests of the public with those of right owners was also considered in recent years by the Federal Court of Justice in connection with s.53 of the Copyright Act in three separate cases. S.53(1) provides that it is permissible to make single copies of a work for private use and that a person may cause such copies to be made by another person, a third party. According to s.53(2)(2), it is also possible to make single copies of a work for inclusion in personal files, if a personal copy of the work is used as the model for reproduction. However, s.53(5) provides that copies may be neither disseminated nor used for public communication.

In the first of these cases, the *CB-Infobank I* case,[36] a bank created an archive compiled from newspaper and periodical articles and offered reproduction of the articles to third parties without the permission of the copyright owners. The Federal Court of Justice held in 1997[37] that the requirements of s.53 are not met if a copy of a work is stored in an archive which is intended for the use of third parties. The Court further ruled that the reproduction of works is not allowed if it is carried out as part of a research service for third parties. The Court stressed that the right to copy for private use under s.53(1) does not apply to collections of data exploited by companies because private

---

[36] *cf.* also the CB-infobank II case, where the Court also decided that the reproduction of works is not permitted under s.53(2)(4a) if it is carried out as part of a research service for third parties (Decision of January 16, 1997, [1997] 6 G.R.U.R. 464).

[37] Decision of January 16, 1997, B.G.H.Z. 134, 250; [1997] 6 G.R.U.R. 459.

use means personal use and as such can apply only to natural persons. The exemption in s.53(2)(2) permitting the making of single copies to be included in personal files did not apply either because, although such copies could be made by a legal entity, the use of the archives was not restricted to purely internal use but was open to third-party clients. Furthermore, the exception in s.53(2)(4)(a) permitting reproduction for personal use in the case of small parts of published works published in newspapers or periodicals did not apply to the case. The service provided, retrieving and supplying the client with copies of articles at its request, fell outside the exception. The Court argued that s.53, as an exception to the exclusive rights of authors, must be interpreted restrictively in the light of the intention of the legislator, which in this regard had been to permit archives for the mere purpose of securing the original works or copies obtained and did not include maintaining archives for the benefit of third parties.

In two further decisions, the Federal Court of Justice has interpreted s.53 in other cases involving archives. In 1998, in the Electronic Press Archive case,[38] the Court considered the following circumstances: the defendant, a service provider, was provided by clients with their own purchased copies of newspapers and periodicals in which articles had been marked up for archiving. The defendant then scanned, saved and indexed the articles according to the instructions of the clients and made them available to the clients in hard copy or on disc. The clients then stored the articles in their own databases where they were available to their employees. The Court considered that the service provided by the defendant was not permitted by s.53(2)(2). The Court again stressed that this provision of the law has to be interpreted restrictively in the light of the intention of the legislator, which it said was to allow, for example, a library to reproduce its stock on microfiche to save space or for security reasons. The Court took the view that, in the case in question, a company electronic archive was created, which was accessible simultaneously to numerous staff members at their desks. The use of the works reproduced was thereby increased substantially, while the authors thereof did not benefit at all from the extended use of their works.

7–038 Finally, in 1999, the Federal Court of Justice in the Copying Service

---

[38] Decision of the Federal Court of Justice of December 10, 1998, "Elektronische Pressearchive" [1999] 4 G.R.U.R. 325.

case[39] handed down a very important decision defining the limits of the exception permitted by s.53(2)(2). In this case, the German Publishers' Association complained that a public library, the Hanover Technical Information Library (TIB) provides a service to third parties, their customers, reproducing articles at their request and sending them out world-wide by fax or mail. The TIB's services are advertised, its catalogue is available on-line and its services are subject to charges. The Court distinguished this case from the two cases referred to above and found that the particular service provided by TIB was permissible under s.53(2). In its opinion, the TIB service was in the nature of mere technical assistance and was permissible provided the customer could rely on one of the privileged uses foreseen in s.53. The Court based its findings on arguments concerning the public interest. It held that the availability of information is essential in a modern society and in this context the legislator had to find a balance between the interests of the authors and those of the public. The preparatory documents leading to the adoption of the Copyright Act 1965 made it clear that the legislator was aware that libraries in Germany and abroad regularly exchanged photocopies and microfilms of journal articles. Moreover, the preparatory documents for the 1985 Amendment of the Act stated clearly that photocopying by public libraries in the context of a copying service did not require the agreement of authors. In the view of the legislator and the Court, because of the public interest in the availability of information, equitable remuneration should provide a sufficient safeguard for the authors in this situation. A modern, technically developed industrial nation such as Germany was dependent on science and research and therefore required a well-developed, rapid and commercially workable information system.

However, the Court went on to hold that, in the light of the increasing use of public archives and the competing role played by photocopies with original publications, s.54a of the Copyright Act (which entitles authors to claim payment of equitable remuneration from the manufacturer of reproduction equipment) provided insufficient compensation to the right owners and that therefore there was a lacuna in the law resulting from technical and industrial developments. The Court said that, in accordance with Art.9(2) of the Berne

---

[39] Decision of February 25, 1999, "Kopierversanddienst" [1999] 8–9 G.R.U.R. 707

Convention, Art.9 and 13 of the TRIPs Agreement and Art.14 of the Basic Law, authors were entitled whenever feasible to benefit from every form of commercially significant exploitation of their works. It ruled therefore that, by analogy with the provisions in the Copyright Act according to which royalties are payable for other uses such as, for example, public lending and rental of works, the lacuna in the law could be remedied by giving the authors an additional claim to payment against copying services to be exercised through collecting societies. On the facts of the specific case, however, the Court found against the plaintiff, the German Publishers' Association, on the ground that, under section 54h of the Copyright Act, claims to remuneration for reprography may only be asserted by a collecting society.[40]

The Courts have also been concerned recently with the interpretation of two other exceptions to protection, the right of quotation and the reproduction of works in public places in the context of the constitutional guarantees of freedom of expression and information under Art.5 of the Basic Law. The Federal Constitutional Court considered the extent to which quotation under s.51 of the Copyright Act may be justified by its purpose in the context of the constitutional guarantee of freedom of artistic expression under Art.5(3) of the Basic Law. The case concerned a dispute about the insertion of texts by Berthold Brecht in a play by the German playwright Heiner Müller. The extracts were substantial and included whole scenes from two plays by Brecht. The Court held that the quotations were permissible and justifiable by their purpose in conformity with s.51 of the Copyright Act and in the light of Art.5(3) of the Basic Law. It stated that "If, as in the present case, an insignificant interference with authors' rights, which poses no danger of any noticeable commercial disadvantage, is opposed to the freedom of artistic expression, the economic rights of the author as compared with the right to utilise in an artistic analysis must take second place".[41]

In a recent decision more favourable to the copyright owner, the

---

[40] For a commentary on these three cases in English, see R. Mann, "New Aspects of the Right of Reproduction and the Use of Archives in Germany", [2000] E.I.P.R. 93.

[41] Federal Constitutional Court decision of June 29, 2000, "Germania 3" [2001] 2 G.R.U.R. 149. See also A. Metzger, "Germania 3, Gespenster am toten Mann oder Welchen Zweck darf ein Zitat gemäss s.51 Nr. 2 UrhG verfolgen", [2000] 11 ZUM 924. P. Garloff, "Copyright and Kunstfreiheit—Zur Zulässigkeit ungenehmigter Zitate in Heiner Müllers letzten Theaterstücks", [2001] 6 G.R.U.R. 476.

Federal Supreme Court considered the question of whether the
unauthorised sale of picture postcards of the "Wrapped Reichstag", a
temporary work of visual art, was permitted under s.59 of the
Copyright Act. According to that section, it is permissible to reproduce *inter alia* by photographic means works which are permanently
located in public places. The Court, upholding decisions of the
District Court and Court of Appeal of Berlin, found that, since the
wrapping of the Reichstag was temporary, even though the building
was a permanent structure the wrapping could not be considered
permanently located in a public place and that, therefore, the commercial exploitation of postcards thereof did not fall under the
exception of s.59.[42]

Conclusion

In German copyright law theory, the rights of authors have tradi-   **7–039**
tionally been considered to derive from natural law. The legislation
merely recognises and develops these rights, which may only be
limited to the extent required by the social obligations of the author to
the general public. It is as a result of this latter concept that it may be
affirmed that the public interest has, throughout the development of
modern copyright law, been taken into account as an important factor
for consideration in setting limits to the exclusive rights of copyright
owners. It has always been a criterion for determining the term of
protection and, indeed, the reason why it took Germany until 1934 to
extend the term to 50 years p.m.a. was because such an extension was
considered to be against the public interest and of only marginal
potential benefit to authors.

As the case law of the Federal Constitutional Court has shown, the
issue of the balance between the interests of right owners and those of
the public has gained in importance in the years since the adoption of
the 1965 Copyright Act. Indeed, as discussed above, the Court has

---

[42] Decision of the Federal Supreme Court (BGH), January 24, 2002 [2002]
G.R.U.R. 7 605; see also decisions of the District Court (Landesgericht), Berlin, May
31, 1996, [1997] 2 G.R.U.R. 129 and of the Berlin Court of Appeal (Kammergericht),
October 27, 1998 (1ZR 102/99 (KG). See also A. Müller-Katzenburg, "Offener
Rechtsstreit um verhüllten Reichstag", [1996] N.J.W. 2341; B.-H. Poppelmann,
"Verhüllter Reichstag", [1996] 4 Z.U.M. 293.

laid much emphasis in its decisions on the public interest aspects of copyright in interpreting the relationship between the constitutional guarantees of property and freedom of expression and information, and the copyright law. The fact that this has led to the introduction of a whole series of compulsory licences, substituting remuneration for the exclusive right of the author has been criticised. For example, Nordemann[43] has called for a return to an unrestricted exclusive right of the author on the ground that compulsory licences have led to an unjustified advancement of users' interests. According to him, under

> the old German copyright law, there were clear lines of demarcation marking the borderline between the interests of the author and those of the public at large. Either the author had an exclusive copyright or third parties had the right to make free use of his work. The single exception, the compulsory licence for phonograms ... did not really spoil the purity of the system.

On the other hand, it is argued that in the developing information society exclusive rights should not be allowed to stand in the way of speedy and trouble-free access to information by the public and that compulsory licences solve the problem of clearing rights through centralised representative collecting societies for use of works in the media and for inclusion, for example, in databanks.[44] Compulsory licences have the advantage of making copyright works freely available to the public and at the same time ensuring payment of an equitable remuneration to right owners.

It is apparent, moreover, that by contrast with the development of copyright law in the UK and the USA, until recently the public interest has not been considered in Germany as a factor to be taken into account in a positive way in relation to copyright. The concept that an effective system of copyright protection is of itself in the public interest because it has social benefits, stimulating creativity by providing a just reward for labour and encouraging people to write, compose, etc., thus benefiting the community, has not in the past been put forward as a justification for copyright. As we have seen, the

---

[43] W. Nordemann, "A Right to Control or Merely to Payment?—Towards a Logical Copyright System", [1980] 1 I.I.C. 49.

[44] Y. Kleinke, *op. cit.*, n. 76, above, p. 169 *et seq.*

primary justification for copyright has traditionally been considered to be natural law.

Lately, however, there are signs that the public interest in having an **7–040** effective copyright system is being increasingly recognised. A few modern commentators have drawn attention to the significance of intellectual property for the general public from the politico-cultural and commercial points of view. Copyright protection is recognised as being more essential than ever to promote the cultural industries and cultural life and is seen as affording protection not only to the interests of the copyright owner but as having the task also of facilitating access by the general public, namely the consumer or user, to the rich variety of cultural works. Thus, the natural law justification for copyright is supported by its cultural and commercial importance.[45] Fechner suggests that intellectual property protects people in their freedom to create so that their individuality is safeguarded and at the same time their work can benefit the general public.[46]

It is apparent that at a political level the *Bundestag* has become aware of the importance of copyright for the national economy and it is significant that the 1989 IFO Study concluded that appropriate copyright legislation is a precondition for a further increase in the weight of copyright industries with regard to more income and jobs. Here the German experience would appear to be moving towards the concept of copyright as a stimulus to creativity.

Moreover, Schricker notes that, taking account of the economic, social and cultural aspects of copyright, it may well be that there will be a demand in the future for the German legislator to take account of the public interest in a positive way.[47]

While emphasising the fundamental importance of copyright for intellectual creativity and for cultural life, he draws attention to its economic impact and to the fact that publishers, film producers and other cultural industries depend on the copyright system. He suggests that legislative policy should take account of the economic function of copyright by providing adequate protection for protected works in the market place so as to provide a sufficient return to authors and

---

[45] A. Wandtke, *op. cit.*, n. 15, above, p. 5; F. Fechner, *op. cit.*, n. 80, above, p. 121 *et seq.*; Y. Kleinke, *op. cit.* n. 76, above, p. 26 *et seq.*

[46] F. Fechner, *op. cit.*, n. 80, above, 134.

[47] G. Schricker, in G. Schicker, *Urheberrecht*, Kommentar, *op. cit.*, n. 3, above, Introduction, ss.3 and 4.

other right owners and to ensure that the copyright system promotes cultural production.[48]

In his view,[49] therefore, the objective of the copyright legislator should be to formulate the law in such a way that it will make a positive contribution to intellectual, cultural and economic progress. He accepts the view that an efficiently organised system of copyright protection providing adequate financial rewards to the author can provide a framework for optimal creative production and encourage the dissemination of works. He suggests that an acceptance of this point of view and taking into account of economic considerations would not necessarily lead to the underlying principle of natural law being disregarded. Rather, copyright law could find an additional justification in the idea that it stimulates creativity. This could strengthen the case for protection beyond the minimum standards guaranteed by the Basic Law. He suggests also that this justification could provide grounds for ensuring that the interests of industries which act as intermediaries between the author and the public are adequately protected. The Federal Constitutional Court has declared it the task of the legislator to determine the social function of the rights guaranteed by the Basic Law. This could be understood not only as requiring the legislator to set limits to those rights but also to stimulate the development of copyright in a way that takes account of the public interest.

7–041 Finally, the Minister of Justice, who holds responsibility for copyright legislation in Germany, in 1999 also recognised the positive functions of the copyright law in promoting creativity and cultural diversity as being in the public interest. In the context of a speech on the issue of how the problem of private copying of digital sound recordings should be tackled in future legislation, she said: "Copyright policy is challenged by the precarious situation facing music, film and literature. What is needed is an up-to-date and reliable law for the protection of authors' rights and related rights, which gives the cultural industries the security required to trade successfully, thereby encouraging culture to flourish".[50]

---

[48] *ibid.*, s.3, para. 10.
[49] *ibid.*, s.4, para. 13.
[50] *cf.* n. 33, above.

PART III

COPYRIGHT AND PUBLIC POLICY

Chapter 8

Introduction

The noblest motive is the public good.

Sir Richard Steele

The introduction to this study was prefaced by a quotation from Lord **8–001** Macaulay, the British nineteenth century author and statesman, which also provides a starting point for the concluding chapters: "The system of copyright has great advantages and great disadvantages, and it is our business to ascertain what these are, and then to make an arrangement under which the advantages may be as far as possible secured, and the disadvantages as far as possible excluded".

The advantages of the copyright system as generally acknowledged may be summarised as follows. The copyright system guarantees the personal interests of the author in his work. It is also what Macaulay described as the "least objectionable" way of remunerating men of letters by providing mechanisms for authors and other right owners to obtain economic rewards for their efforts. By securing such financial rewards, it stimulates creativity, thereby in the words of the Statute of Anne encouraging "learned men to compose and write useful books", and, in the modern world, investment in the creation of works such as films and works of architecture, in addition to providing the economic basis for the film, publishing, broadcasting and record industries. Finally, it answers to the general public interest in facilitating and promoting the widest possible availability of copyright protected material to the public, thereby encouraging both learning and the progress of science.

However, from the inception of the copyright system, there has been a built-in tension between the interests of the author on the one hand and those of the public on the other. It is seen to be in the public interest that authors and other right owners should be encouraged to publish their works so as to permit the widest possible dissemination of works to the public at large. "If the ideas and experiences of creators can be shared by a wide public in a short space of time they contribute to the advance of society."[1]

> Copyright is a monopoly. ... It is good that authors should be remunerated; and the least exceptionable way of remunerating them is by a monopoly. Yet monopoly is an evil. For the sake of the good we must submit to the evil; but the evil ought not to last a day longer than is necessary for the purpose of securing the good.[2]

Thus, while copyright protection is justified by the public interest, the State imposes certain limitations thereto, again in the public interest. Copyright is always of limited duration; thereafter, the works fall into the public domain and may be used freely by all. Some limited uses of protected subject-matter are free, *e.g.* quotations, the use of short excerpts, and even, in many countries, copies made for private use. Copyright works may be subject to compulsory licensing with the result that the copyright owner cannot prevent the use of his work. In some circumstances, exclusive rights may only be exercised collectively through a representative body.

8–002 Striking the balance between individual and collective interests is an extremely complex procedure and cannot be done effectively unless account is taken of the possible repercussions in all sectors of society. That this is so, is borne out by the controversy associated with the legislative process in matters of copyright today, at the national and international level, in view of the many conflicting interests involved. "Broad principles tend to be buried under bitterly contested narrow issues".[3] This is particularly true at present when the legislator is faced with the task of redefining copyright to fit the digital environment. According to the Berne Convention, "The terms 'literary and artistic works' include all productions in the literary, scientific, and artistic domain, whatever the mode or form of expression ...". Copyright laws were designed with analogue technology in mind. Digital

---

[1] S.M. Stewart, *International Copyright and Neighbouring Rights*, 2nd. ed. (London, Butterworths, 1989), para. 1.05.
[2] T. Macaulay, in: *Hansard*, House of Commons, Vol. 56, February 5, 1841, at 347–348.
[3] Z. Chafee, Jr., "Reflexions on the Law of Copyright", (1945) 45 Columbia Law Rev., 503 at 519.

technology means that new combinations of works are resulting in the creation of a new category of multi-media works. It has also led to new methods of exploitation of works. These do not always fall neatly under the present definitions of protected works and exclusive rights in national laws and under the international conventions. Digital technology also compounds the problems of unauthorised reproduction of works because of the ease with which works in digital format can be modified and copied without loss of quality.

In setting limitations to copyright protection and making such decisions as the period of duration, the extent to which free use may be made, limiting exclusive rights in favour of compulsory licensing, etc., the State makes choices in the light of its various policies—not only cultural but also economic and social policies. Some States, in striking the balance between the copyright owners and the public interest, lean in favour of the former, others in favour of the latter. The consequences of these choices may not be as anticipated. The potential of copyright as an instrument of policy in the hands of the State still remains to be recognised by many governments. The cultural identity of a country may be promoted or damaged by the government's decisions as to the categories of creators and works to be protected, the limitations on protection to be permitted, and so on. There is a continual need, therefore, for States to reassess, in the light of existing technical developments and those that may be anticipated, "what measure of protection is needed to bring about the creation and production of new works and other material within the copyright sphere".[4] As we have seen in Part II of this study, the four jurisdictions analysed therein have been grappling with these issues in the past 10 years or so in the effort to adapt their copyright laws to the digital environment. All have done so in the context of the concurrent intergovernmental developments aimed at adapting the international legislative framework to the information society and which led to the adoption of the WIPO Copyright Treaty and the WIPO Performances and Phonograms Treaty (the so-called WIPO Internet Treaties) in 1996.[5] France, Germany and the United Kingdom are also now constrained by the ongoing programme of the European Union for harmonisation of the copyright and related rights laws of its

---

[4] W.R. Cornish, *Intellectual Property: Patents, Copyright, Trade Marks and Allied Rights* 4th. ed. (London, Sweet & Maxwell, 1999), para. 9–46.
[5] Adopted on December 20, 1996, the Treaties entered into force in early 2002. *Cf.* Part IV, Ch.11, para.12–003 *et seq.*, below.

Member States and, in particular, by the 2001 EC Directive on the harmonisation of certain aspects of copyright and related rights in the information society.[6]

The assertion that the State should aim continually to adapt the law to provide an appropriate framework of copyright legislation, begs several questions, however. First, does the protection afforded by copyright legislation adequately serve the purposes for which it is intended and, in particular, does it serve as a stimulus to creativity? The functions of copyright have themselves been called in question. The arguments deployed in favour of doing away with the system and the suggested alternatives thereto are discussed below in Chapter 9. If the premise is accepted that copyright is necessary, how far should these rights be limited in the public interest? How long should they last? The last 10 years have seen a trend towards extending the period of protection of copyright owners. To what extent is this justified? These questions are discussed below in Chapter 10.

8–003 In recent years, the interrelationship of copyright laws with economic policies has become clear as a result of studies carried out since the 1980s into the economic contribution to national economies of industries which are copyright-based in the sense that their commercial success would be gravely affected if copyright protection did not exist. In the late 1980s, Skilbeck calculated an international value for copyright on the basis of an average from the reports in four countries (Netherlands, Sweden, UK and USA). She estimated the international average contribution of the copyright industries at 2.7 per cent of national income in 1988.[7] In the meantime, new national studies on the economic importance of copyright have been published showing a continual, significant increase in this contribution. Thus in the UK, the copyright industries accounted for 3.6 per cent of GDP (Gross Domestic Product) in 1990[8] and over 5 per cent in 2001[9]; in the United States of America, the core US copyright industries' share

---

[6] Directive 2001/29/EC, OJ L 167/10, June 22, 2001 (the **Information Society Directive**). Member States have until December 31, 2002, to implement the Directive (Art. 13).

[7] J. Skilbeck, *The Economic Importance of Copyright* (London, International Publishers' Association, 1988).

[8] T. Price, *The Economic Importance of Copyright*, (Common Law Institute of Intellectual Property, London, 1993).

[9] *Creative Industries Mapping Document 2001*, (Department of Culture, Media and Sport (DCMS), London, 2001).

of GDP was 3.7 per cent in 1993[10] and by the year 2001 had grown to 5.24.[11] A German report published in 1989 on the basis of 1986 figures arrived at a figure of 3.6 per cent of GDP for the copyright industries, including software.[12] Results from the Netherlands are available for three separate years, 1982, 1989 and 1994. The figures showed a substantial increase from 2.4 per cent in 1982 to 4.3 per cent in 1989 and 5.2 per cent in 1994.[13] The European Commission estimated in 2001 that in economic terms the contribution made by copyright-based goods and services to the Community's GDP is a significant and rising 6 per cent.[14]

> Creation can be encouraged or discouraged, depending on the status assigned creators by society. Copyright, whose position has been complicated by the development of new technologies, is a decisive factor. The production policies of commercial distribution of works of the mind are determined primarily, and much more strictly than before by market principles. Accordingly, legal standards are being drafted or revised in order to adjust classical copyright laws to the new economic imperatives.[15]

The economic importance of copyright made the so-called cultural industries a key factor in the international trade negotiations in the context of the Uruguay Round of the GATT Negotiations concluded in December 1993, which led *inter alia* to the adoption of the Agreement on Trade-Related Aspects of Intellectual Property Rights

---

[10] S.E. Siwek and H. Furchtgott-Roth, *Copyright Industries in the US Economy 1977–1993*, (International Intellectual Property Alliance, January 1995).

[11] S.E. Siwek, Economists Incorporated, *Copyright Industries in the U.S. Economy: The 2002 Report*, (prepared for the International Intellectual Property Alliance, Washington, 2002).

[12] M. Hummel, *Die volkswirtschaftliche Bedeutung des Urheberrechts*, (IFO-Institut für Wirtschaftsforschung, Duncker & Humblot, Berlin-Munich, 1989).

[13] A. Silbertson, "The Economic Importance of Copyright", published in *Creativity and intellectual property rights: evolving scenarios and perspectives*, (records of the International Conference, Vienna, July 1998, published by the EC Commission, DG Internal Market), at 43 *et seq.*

[14] Intellectual Property Overview, EC Commission, DG Internal Market website, August 8, 2001.

[15] Unesco, Third Medium-Term Plan (1990–1995), adopted in November 1989, para. 195.

(the TRIPs Agreement).[16] Simon has described the relationship between copyright and trade as follows:

> International trade may sound alien to copyright and other intellectual property holders, but it is not. Trade is merely the exchange of one class of products for another—products of the mind in this instance—travelling across borders. The products of imagination and creativity are increasingly replacing land and natural resources as the basis for productivity, increased economic welfare and wealth. Works and inventions are today very much an integral part of trade. Treating them as an element of trade policy neither diminishes nor corrupts the value of intellectual creativity. Rather it provides a rational extension to the basic laws and policies which nations have established to nurture and promote these activities.[17]

The growing recognition of the importance of the copyright industries to the economies of the Member States of the European Union and the United States of America as well as to those of their trading partners within the World Trade Organisation has led to unprecedented interest in the formulation of copyright policy and legislation in the past few years. Since the first edition of this book was completed in the Autumn of 1993, we have seen the adoption of a series of no less than seven Directives by the European Union setting harmonised standards in the field of copyright and related rights for its Member States,[18] new legislation in the United States of America,[19] as

---

[16] The TRIPs Agreement is Annex IC of the Marrakesh Agreement Establishing the World Trade Organisation, signed in Marrakesh, Morocco, on April 15, 1994. It deals, *inter alia*, with copyright and related rights. It sets standards for the member States of the World Trade Organisation as regards the availability, scope and use of intellectual property rights generally, covering not only copyright and related rights but also trademarks, geographical indications, industrial designs, patents, layout-designs (topographies) of integrated circuits, know-how (undisclosed information) and control of anti-competitive practices in contractual licences. It includes also provisions for the enforcement of intellectual property rights and dispute prevention and settlement measures.

[17] E. Simon, "The Integration of Intellectual Property and Trade Policy", in *Economy and authors' rights in the international conventions*, (ALAI Geneva study session 1994, *Groupe Suisse de l'ALAI et les auteurs*, Berne 1994), at 33.

[18] *cf.* Ch.13, para.13–016 *et seq.*, below, and in n.37.

[19] See Ch. 5, above, and, in particular, for example, the Digital Millenium Copyright Act, Pub. L. 105–304, 112 Stat. 2860 (October 28, 1998).

well as the WIPO Internet Treaties[20] and the TRIPs Agreement.[21] In Part IV, below, the solutions found and policy choices made in these developments are considered in the context of their response to technical developments, the public interest and perspectives for the future of copyright.

---

[20] World Copyright Treaty (WCT) and World Performers and Phonograms Treaty (WPPT), adopted on December 20, 1996. *cf.* n.5, above.
[21] Agreement on Trade-related Aspects of Intellectual Property Rights (the TRIPs Agreement), signed at Marrakesh, April 15, 1994. *cf.* n.16, above.

Chapter 9

The Functions of Copyright Revisited

There is nothing which can better deserve your patronage than the promotion of science and literature. Knowledge is, in every country, the surest basis of public happiness.[1]

George Washington

A former US Librarian of Congress, writing in 1949, asserted that: **9–001**

determination of sound copyright policies raises, alike in the domestic and foreign field, the fundamental issues of our day: preservation of personal initiative with greater equality of opportunity; avoidance of the evils of monopoly with a minimum of state control; freedom and integrity of thought, speech, and communication reconciled to media of mass communication. Copyright properly understood and wisely handled may be at the same time a powerful stimulus to creation and the means of opening the channels of dissemination of thought, information and debate. Misunderstood, and with its true purposes lost sight of, copyright can become a limitation on creation and a barrier to free interchange and expression. Like many other products of man's genius in the realms both of science and of the law, it has a capacity for good or evil depending on his understanding and the use he makes of it. ... The balancing of conflicting interests and the weighing of ... testimony should be done by others with a broader

---

[1] Address to Congress, January 8, 1790, leading to the enactment of the 1790 Copyright Act.

243

perspective and in a spirit which makes the public interest the paramount test.[2]

The functions of copyright must not therefore be lost sight of. As
we have seen, these have to a great extent been taken for granted.

> The general function of copyright seems but rarely to have figured
> as a topic of debate ... all that can generally be gleaned is a few
> introductory statements to the effect that copyright is based on the
> principle of the labourer being worthy of his hire and that copy-
> right has a stimulating effect on cultural activities.[3]

However, some very valuable analyses of these functions have been
published in the last half century or so. In particular, there is a rich
literature on the subject in the United States of America, both in
connection with the long-drawn-out debates on the revision of the
Copyright Act of 1909, which lasted until 1976, and subsequently.

Chafee's Six Ideals of Copyright

9–002 In 1945, Professor Zechariah Chafee in a well-known article
(described by Barbara Ringer as "probably the best single work on
copyright law ever published in English"[4]) posed the question "What
is it that the law of copyright is really trying to accomplish?".[5] He
postulated six ideals of copyright law, each being a desirable end in
itself. Three of his six ideals were affirmative, in that they favoured
protection of the copyright owner. The others he described as
negative, in that they tended to limit the scope of protection.

His *first* ideal was *complete coverage*: "If a person has invented some
new collocation of visible or audible points,—of lines, colours, sounds
or words", the law should protect this new collocation. This ideal

---

[2] L.H. Evans, "Copyright and the Public Interest", (1949) 53 *Bulletin of the New York
Public Library*, 3 at 4. Also published in 1949 II 1 *Bulletin du droit d'auteur* 2, (Unesco,
Paris).

[3] S. Ljungman, "The Function of Copyright in the Present Day Society", 88
R.I.D.A. 51 (1976).

[4] B. Ringer, "The Demonology of Copyright", Bowker Memorial Lecture, US
Publisher's Weekly, November 18, 1974, at 30.

[5] Z. Chafee, Jr., "Reflexions [sic] on the Law of Copyright" (Parts I and II), 45
Colombia Law Rev. 503 and 719 (1945). The following paragraphs summarise Professor Chafee's arguments, including much of his own language.

concerns what is protected, what the author has given to the world. The *second* ideal he described as a *single monopoly*, *i.e.* copyright means the sole right to produce or reproduce the work or any substantial part thereof in any material form whatsoever. The essential principle is the author's right to control all the channels through which his work or any fragments of his work reach the market. The second ideal concerns what is protected against, what an imitator or appropriator must not do. According to the *third* ideal, protection should be *international*. Copyright law should facilitate the free flow of ideas and imaginative creations across national boundaries by giving the same protection to every author, wherever he lives or creates.

These first *three ideals* require States to pursue a policy of regular review of copyright laws to respond to the agenda set by new technical developments and their impact on copyright. Only in this way can it be ensured that national copyright laws and the relevant international conventions are updated and adapted to guarantee further development of creativity and to safeguard investment.

His other three ideals tended to limit protection. The *fourth* ideal was that protection *should not extend substantially beyond the purposes of protection*; he suggested that this ideal requires more attention than any other. Copyright being a monopoly is open to objection; it burdens competitors and the public. It is permitted and encouraged because of its advantages. However, the burdens must not outweigh the benefits. To ensure this result one must examine who is benefited and how much and at whose expense. The *fifth* ideal was that the protection given the copyright owner *should not stifle independent creation by others*. Nobody else should *market* the author's book, but other people should be able to *use* it. The world goes ahead because each of us builds on the work of our predecessors. Progress would be stifled if an author were to be granted a complete monopoly for a long period. Some use of the contents of a work must be permitted in connection with the independent creation of other authors. The very policy which leads the law to encourage the creativity of an author also justifies it in facilitating the creativity of others. The ideas in a book are not protected but the expression is. Quotation must be allowed; plagiarism prohibited. According to the *sixth* ideal, the legal rules governing copyright should be *convenient to handle*. They should be certain, readily understood, not unduly complicated, and as easy as possible to apply in order to facilitate the avoidance of litigation.

Few commentators on copyright would disagree with these principles as ideals to strive for, and as Chafee points out: "The history of **9–003**

245

copyright law shows a somewhat jerky progress towards realization of the six ideals".[6]

It is the *fourth ideal* which begs the question of the functions of copyright. For Chafee:

> The burden which the monopoly imposes on readers and competing publishers should be roughly limited to what will produce the following benefits: (a) for the author, to supply a direct or indirect pecuniary return as an incentive to creation and to confer upon him control over the marketing of his creation; (b) for the surviving family, to give a pecuniary return which will save them from destitution and impel the author to create, without allowing the family to abuse a prolonged monopoly; (c) for the publisher, to give a continued pecuniary return which will indirectly benefit the author and yield to the publisher an equitable return on his investment, but which will not prevent the public from getting easy access to the creation after the author's death.[7]

Chafee put the emphasis on the economic justifications for copyright, namely, that it provides a pecuniary return to the author, his family and his publisher, thus stimulating creativity and promoting the general well-being of society. As we have seen, the economic and public interest rationales are the basic justifications for copyright in the Anglo-American system. Other laws and commentators lay greater emphasis on the moral justifications for copyright, based on the creator's rights in his creation deriving from natural law and on the obligations of society towards him as well as the notion of just reward for labour.

Both the economic and moral justifications for copyright have, however, been exposed to critical analysis in the United Kingdom and the United States of America to a greater degree than elsewhere.[8] A

---

[6] *ibid.* at 519.

[7] *ibid.* at 510.

[8] Report of the British Commission appointed in 1878 for the Investigation of the Subject of Copyright (London). See also: A. Birrell, *Seven Lectures on the Law and History of Copyright in Books* (London, 1899); S. Breyer, "The Uneasy Case for Copyright: A Study of Copyright in Books, Photocopies, and Computer programs", 84 Harv. L. Rev.281 (1970); see also: "Copyright A Rejoinder", 20 U.C.L.A. L. Rev.75 (1972); B. W. Tyerman, "The Economic Rationale for Copyright Protection for Published Books: A Reply to Professor Breyer", 18 U.C.L.A. Law Rev.1100 (1971); A. Plant, "The Economic Aspects of Copyright in Books", 1 *Economica* (n.s.) 167 (1934) and

similar debate has also taken place since World War II in Scandinavia.[9] Let us take a look at the validity of Chafee's ideals in the light of this debate. His three affirmative ideals favouring the protection of the copyright owner can only be realised if there is general acceptance of the moral and economic functions of copyright. In Chapter 10 we shall explore Chafee's negative ideals, which tend to limit the scope of protection.

The Moral Justifications for Copyright Revisited

The arguments against the moral justifications for copyright include   **9–004** the following: the personal interests of an author in his work do not justify giving him exclusive rights. The rationale for an author's work being his property because it is his creation is unsound. "We do not ordinarily create or modify property rights, nor even award compensation, solely on the basis of labor expended."[10] Moreover, literary property is unlike other kinds of property since it is limited in scope. It is limited in time and protects only the expression of the author's idea, not the idea itself. Copyright is not the only means of protecting the moral rights of the author; the author's personal interests in his work could be given statutory recognition outside the copyright framework

---

"The New Commerce in Ideas and Intellectual Property", Stamp Memorial Lecture 1953, (Athlone Press, University of London, 1953); both also published in A. Plant, *Selected Economic Essays and Addresses* (Routledge and Kegan Paul, London & Boston, 1974) at 57 and 87, respectively (references are to this publication); S. N. Light, "Parody, Burlesque and the Economic Rationale for Copyright", 11 Connecticut Law Rev., No. 4, 615 (1979); W.J. Gordon, "Fair Use as Market Failure: A Structural and Economic Analysis of the Betamax Case and its Predecessors", 82 Colum. Law Rev. 1600 (1982 "An Enquiry into the Merits of Copyright: The Challenges of Consistency, Consent, and Encouragement Theory", 41 Stanford L. Rev. 1343 (1989); A. Adelstein and S. Peretz, "The Competition of Technologies in Markets for Ideas: Copyright and Fair Use in Evolutionary Perspective", 5 Int. Rev. of Law and Economics 209 (1985); G. Kaufmann, "Exposing the Suspicious Foundations of Society's Primacy in Copyright Law: Five Accidents", 10 Colum.-VLA Journal of Law and the Arts, 381 (1986); W. M. Landes and R.A. Posner, "An Economic Analysis of Copyright Law", 18 Journal of Legal Studies 325 (1989); T.G. Palmer, "Are Patents and Copyrights Morally Justified? The Philosophy of Property Rights and Ideal Objects?" 13 Harvard Journal of Law and Public Policy 816 (1990). D. Vaver "Intellectual Property Today: of Myths and Paradoxes", LXIX The Canadian Bar Review 98 (1990).

[9] See S. Ljungman, n.3 above; and B. S. Lassen, "Collectivism and Individual Rights in Norwegian Copyright Law", 1963 Scandinavian Studies in Law, p. 79.

[10] S. Breyer, "The Uneasy Case for Copyright", *op. cit.* at 289.

or according to common law rules of tort.

As regards the moral requirement to reward labour, it is suggested that the expectation of financial reward is not the only reason for authors and other artists to create. They are not necessarily motivated primarily by monetary interests; many are impelled to create as part of their personality, creation being in their nature. As Plant observed: "There is ... an important group of authors who desire simply free publication; they may welcome, but they certainly do not live in expectation of, direct monetary reward".[11]

Some authors to this day pay to have their books published, when they cannot find a publisher ready to take the risk. Publishing brings prestige with it and, in the case of academics, may lead to promotion and greater financial reward in the workplace.

> For such writers copyright has few charms. Like public speakers who hope for a good press, they welcome the spread of their ideas. Erasmus went to Basle in 1522, not apparently to expostulate with Frobenius for daring to print his manuscript writings, but to assist the printer in the good work. The wider the circulation, the more universal the recognition the author would receive.[12]

Besides, it is argued, the copyright system does not especially reward creators of great works of lasting social value. It favours instead the commercial, popular work with large sales.

> The amount of the reward is determined solely by the public's willingness to pay for the work. More importantly, there is no self-evident reason why authors deserve compensation fundamentally different from that given to those who perform other kinds of work; yet workers on the whole are not paid with respect to the value of their work to society, but in the amount necessary to persuade them to perform their work, plus any premium resulting from the scarcity of similar workers.[13]

9–005 Other motives for creation include the desire for fame and recognition. Government subsidies could provide creators with basic financial

---

[11] A. Plant, "The Economic Aspects of Copyright in Books", *op. cit.* at 59.
[12] *Loc. cit.*
[13] S.N. Light, *op. cit.*, at 619.

security. Many governments as well as other institutions already do award substantial sums to creators in the form of grants and prizes. Alternatively, authors, publishers and buyers of works could make arrangements among themselves to provide authors with sufficient money to produce them. In ancient times and in the middle ages, it is argued, authors wrote books even though there was no copyright protection. They still contrived to secure a price for their product. Governments could take over the role of the patron and pay for works to be produced. "It is not unfair to finance through taxes the creation of works that benefit not only those who buy them but also many other members of society as well."[14]

Plant suggested that:

> Patronage itself may not be wholly an evil. There seems to be no reason why a person who wants certain things written and published should not be at liberty to offer payment to suitable people to do the necessary work. If the task is uncongenial, some authors will need high remuneration, and others will no doubt decline any terms...[15]

The Economic Justifications for Copyright Revisited

As regards the economic justifications for copyright, the question to be answered is what would happen were copyright protection to be abolished. Plant argued that professional writers in the past secured a price for their product in the absence of copyright, provided a market existed for it. In support of this thesis, he drew attention to the often quoted example of English authors who in the nineteenth century were paid by US publishers in spite of the fact that their works were unprotected there.

9–006

> During the nineteenth century anyone was free in the United States to reprint a foreign publication, and yet American publishers found it profitable to make arrangements with English authors. Evidence before the 1876–8 Commission shows that English authors sometimes received more from the sale of their books by

---

[14] S. Breyer, "The Uneasy Case for Copyright", *op. cit.* at 287.
[15] A. Plant, "The Economic Aspects of Copyright in Books", *op. cit.* at 60.

American publishers, where they had no copyright, than from their royalties in [the UK] . . .. In the first place, there was the advantage, well worth paying for, which a publisher secured by being first in the field with a new book . . . Secondly, there was a tacit understanding among the larger publishers in America that the books published by one should not be published by another.[16]

Plant concluded that the abolition of copyright need not therefore result in the complete abandonment of the business of book production either by publishers or by professional authors. He did concede, however, that "More authors write books because copyright exists, and a greater variety of books is published; but there are fewer copies of the books which people want to read".[17]

Breyer, in a very thorough analysis of this question written in 1970, of which space only permits a very brief overview here, came to not dissimilar conclusions. He examined whether the benefits of copyright protection are sufficiently valuable to justify not only retaining it but also extending its scope. His analysis was based on the book trade, and focused on the rights of authors and their interrelationship with publishers. He started from the premise that copyright restrictions are justified only when necessary to achieve some important social benefit. Abolishing copyright in books would induce competition in the production and sale of high-volume titles, which would lead to lower prices and wider distribution. However, if competitive prices fell too low, author and publisher would be discouraged from producing the book in the first place and the reader would be worse off. The price of text books would fall; this would have particular social value. He argued that the absence of copyright protection would not lead to the abandonment of the business of book production. Several factors would help to maintain the production of many novels and popular works of non-fiction (tradebooks).

Without copyright, a publisher should still have a few weeks of "lead time" to recoup some of his expenses before copiers can reproduce his book and distribute it to local book sellers. Further, copiers may find that it does not pay to copy "low volume" trade books, *i.e.* books that sell only a few thousand copies. Not only is

---

[16] *ibid.* at 62.
[17] *ibid.* at 64 and 80.

the market for each book small, but also the copier must fear that the book's publisher will retaliate by cutting his price to variable cost...[18]

Thus, the best defence against a rival publisher would be a low-price policy. This was the policy the US publishers adopted in relation to English works. As Plant explained:

American editions might cost one-half as much as the English issue; one-quarter or even one-eighth of the English price was very frequent. In such circumstances, the American public enjoyed cheap books, the American publishers found their business profitable, and the English authors received lump sums for their advance sheets and royalties on American sales.[19]

Abolishing copyright would eliminate the administration costs of obtaining permission to reproduce a work. In this connection, Breyer drew attention to the high costs of copyright administration in clearing rights, for example, for radio and television broadcasting. According to his analysis, the case for copyright in books is weak and he suggested that to abolish protection would not produce a very large or harmful decline in most kinds of book production. It would be possible to sustain the publisher's revenue in other ways. For example, buyers of textbooks are few in number and could contract directly with the publisher. Government subsidies could maintain publishers' and authors' revenues. He pointed out that in any case at that time Government subsidised scientific writing by paying for nearly two-thirds of all research and development work done in the United States of America as well as by spending large sums on the dissemination of its results. The disadvantages of substituting Government money for funds raised through the copyright marketplace, however, would be serious. It would be difficult to obtain the necessary appropriations from Congress to support novels and other works not aimed at the educational/scientific market. The risk of censorship would increase.

9–007

He concluded that, "Taken as a whole, the evidence now available suggests that, although we should hesitate to abolish copyright pro-

---

[18] S. Breyer, "Copyright: A Rejoinder", *op. cit.*, at 77.
[19] A. Plant, "The Economic Aspects of Copyright in Books", *op. cit.* at 63.

tection, we should equally hesitate to extend or strengthen it".[20] He suggested that certain questions should be posed in considering whether or not to extend copyright protection:

> One should first ask: What forces are at work to sustain production in the absence of copyright protection? This query leads in turn to a series of other questions: (a) What other forces might inhibit competitors from responding with sufficient speed and ferocity to deprive the initial producer of a profit? (b) Does the Government now, in any event, pay for production through subsidy, and should it do so? (c) In the absence of protection, are buyers likely to find ways to channel sufficient funds to producers to maintain production? Second, one should ask: To what extent may protection prove harmful? (a) Will it, by driving up the cost of copies, seriously diminish circulation? (b) Are the administrative or "transactions" costs involved likely to be high enough to impede the circulation? (c) Can copyright be used to inhibit competition throughout an industry?[21]

The merit of the major articles referred to above was that they renewed discussion of the functions of copyright, and in particular, of the economic rationale therefor, in both the United Kingdom and the United States of America, a debate in which many other distinguished commentators have participated.[22] While Professor Breyer concluded that there was an "uneasy case for copyright", others who studied the economic rationale for copyright came to rather more positive conclusions on the subject.

---

[20] S. Breyer, "The Uneasy Case for Copyright", *op. cit.*, at 284, and see 321–323 and 350–351.

[21] S. Breyer, "Copyright: A Rejoinder", *op. cit.* at 76.

[22] See, *e.g.*, H. Cohen Jehoram, "Critical Reflections on the Economic Importance of Copyright" (1989) 20 I.I.C. 485; D. De Freitas, "Economic Arguments for Protecting Intellectual Property", (1990) 2 Intellectual Property in Business 26; W.J. Gordon, "Fair Use as Market Failure …", *op. cit.*, n.8, above; M. Hummel, "The Economic Importance of Copyright", 12 I.F.O.-Digest, No.4/89, at 32; R.M. Hurt and R.M. Schuchman, "The Economic Rationale of Copyright", (1966) 56 Am. Econ. Rev. 426; J. Kasdan, "The Economics of Copyright with Applications to Licensing", Working Paper, Columbia Law School, October 1966; W. Landes and R. Posner, *op. cit.*, n.8, above; H. Olsson, "Copyright in the National Economy", [1982] Copyright 130; *id.*, (1984) 7 E.I.P.R. 179; E.T. Pratt, "Intellectual Property Role in US Trade Policy", [1988] Rev. of the L.E.S. 159; U. Uchtenhagen, "The Economic Significance of Copyright", [1989] Copyright 280.

One US commentator, for example, writing at about the same time in a study of book publishing, concluded that copyright permits the publisher:

> to profit substantially on some books (where other publishers would otherwise jump in and divide the market) so as to pay for those books that produce losses. That is, the monopoly right permits the publisher to take risks that he would not take if his more successful books were subject to reprinting without permission and without fee. Thus the copyright promotes the public interest by encouraging a great variety of books to be published, many of them economically marginal, in the hope that some will be highly profitable, and it does this without causing significantly higher book prices on account of monopolistic pricing.[23]

Similarly, Ljungman, in his essay on the function of copyright in present day society, concluded that copyright has the function of encouraging investment in the publication of works. **9–008**

> A work of literature should be printed, a drama should be staged or filmed, a musical composition should be recorded and so forth. Without copyright, or at least without a knowledge of and control over utilisations of the same work, one's chances of financing these measures would be sensibly diminished if not eliminated. ... Individual copyright channels investments in accordance with market demand. Supplementary measures by the State are pre-eminently desirable, but neither system would function properly without the protection of copyright.[24]

Ljungman considered that copyright served two other major purposes; first, if copyright did not exist,

> an author would forfeit the chance of any further proceeds from his work as soon as it was published or performed ... remuneration for the initial utilization of a work would have to be made large enough to cover all the author's overheads and provide him with

---

[23] H.S. Bailey, *The Art and Science of Book Publishing* (Ohio University Press, 1970), at 169.
[24] S. Ljungman, "The Function of Copyright in Present Day Society", *op. cit.* at 67.

reasonable sustenance—all in one fell blow. Copyright on the other hand makes it possible to divide the author's remuneration between several users over a long period of time.[25]

Moreover, and here we come once again to the public interest, "Exclusive rights benefit the actual distribution of the fruits of intellectual labour. Copyright makes it possible, without any risk to the author's interests, for new works to be placed at the disposal of interested parties with a view to their possible reproduction, performance etc."[26]

Finally, he pointed out that contractual agreements concerning exclusive rights to the material would not provide protection against publication by third parties.

9–009 Another article by Landes and Posner, written in 1989, discussed the evolution and major doctrines of the law of copyright from an economic standpoint. The authors addressed themselves specifically to the question "to what extent copyright law can be explained as a means for promoting efficient allocation of resources".[27] For them the economic rationale for copyright protection is to prevent free-riding (appropriation without payment) of the author's expression. Starting from the premise that the "distinguishing characteristic of intellectual property is its public good aspect", they suggested that:

> Copyright protection—the right of the copyright owner to prevent others from making copies—trades off the costs of limiting access to a work against the benefits of providing incentives to create the work in the first place. Striking the correct balance between access and incentives is the central problem in copyright law. For copyright law to promote economic efficiency, its principal legal doctrines must, at least approximately, maximise the benefits from creating additional works minus both the losses from limiting access and the costs of administering copyright protection.[28]

In the absence of copyright,

---

[25] *ibid.* at 69.
[26] *Loc. cit.*
[27] W.M. Landes and R.A. Posner, *op. cit.* n.8, above, at 325.
[28] *ibid.* at 326.

anyone can buy a copy of the book when it first appears and make and sell copies of it. The market price of the book will eventually be bid down to the marginal cost of copying, with the unfortunate result that the book will probably not be produced in the first place, because the author and publisher will not be able to recover their costs of creating the work. The problem is magnified by the fact that the author's cost of creating the work, and many publishing costs (for example, editing costs), are incurred before it is known what the demand for the work will be. Uncertainty about demand is a particularly serious problem with respect to artistic works, such as books, plays, movies and recordings. Even with copyright protection, sales may be insufficient to cover the cost of expression and may not even cover the variable cost of making copies. Thus the difference between the price and marginal cost of the successful work must not only cover the cost of expression but also compensate for the risk of failure. If a copier can defer making copies until he knows whether the work is a success, the potential gains from free riding on expression will be even greater, because the difference between the price and marginal cost of the original work will rise to compensate for the uncertainty of demand, thus creating a bigger profit potential for copies. So uncertainty generates an additional disincentive to create works in the absence of copyright protection.[29]

These analyses are particularly helpful in applying Chafee's first *three ideals* of copyright law, that is, in determining the extent to which copyright should be extended to cover new forms of works and the scope of the rights granted in national laws and at the international level by the copyright and related rights conventions. Light points out that, in the context of the United States of America, the phrase "to promote the progress of science and the useful arts" in the copyright clause of the Constitution embodies the economic rationale for copyright, namely, "to enhance the public welfare by encouraging artistic endeavours through the creator's self-interest". Similarly, the constitutional limitation of the term of copyright protection is embodied in the term "by securing for limited times ... the exclusive right to their respective writings ...". Congress may therefore not grant nor the courts enforce copyright protection which would

---

[29] *ibid.* at 328–329.

impede the progress which is the very purpose of copyright. Thus, he suggests that "Where the extension of copyright would appear to be contrary to this constitutional purpose an analysis of the economic justification should be undertaken".[30]

Alternatives to Copyright

9–010 As seen above, the suggestion has also been made that, while some mechanism is needed to ensure that authors are remunerated,

> it does not necessarily follow that the grant of a copyright monopoly is the only such device, nor that it is the most desirable device. If we wish to encourage works which require long periods of research or high costs of creation before they reach the publishing stage, it may be preferable to support authors during the period of production rather than during the moment of potential income protected through the copyright laws. This can be done through private patronage by tax-exempt foundations, universities, and the like, or even by government support for desired literary creation.[31]

A proposal was even put forward in the form of a private member's bill to the Swedish parliament, the *Riksdag*, in 1960, which gained some support, calling for the Government's pending copyright bill to be rejected and replaced by a grant of 20 million kronor "for the support and promotion of works of art and literature" to be distributed by the Government "with due consideration towards creative writers and artists having to contend with financial difficulties".[32] This proposal was no doubt inspired by two pieces of Norwegian legislation, introduced as long ago as 1948 and 1956, which replaced individual rights by Government subsidy, the first of which is still in force. The 1948 law dealt with the resale of works of art but, instead

---

[30] S.N. Light, *op. cit.*, n.8, above, at 622 and 623. Indeed, the question whether the US Congress overstepped its constitutional authority to grant copyrights "for limited times" by extending the term of copyright by an additional 20 years in 1998 is at present (July 2002) *sub judice* in the U.S. Supreme Court in the case of *Eldred v Ashcroft*, U.S. Sup. Ct., No. 01–618 (grant of *certiorari*, February 19, 2002).

[31] R.M. Hurt, and R.M. Schuchman, *op. cit.*, n.22, above, at 426.

[32] S. Ljungman, *op. cit.* n.24, above, at 55.

of introducing a resale right for artists or *droit de suite*, introduced a 3 per cent purchase tax on public sales of all fine art. "The whole of the surcharge is paid into a fund, administered by artists and representatives of the state, for the support of deserving elderly Norwegian artists and promising young ones."[33] The other similar solution was embodied in the King's Fund set up for performers and producers of phonograms in 1956, which provided for remuneration derived from the public performance of phonograms to be distributed collectively between Norwegian performers.[34] More recently, both Norway in 1981 and Sweden in 1982 adopted legislation imposing taxes on the sale of certain recording equipment (audio and video blank tapes and recording equipment in Norway and blank audio tapes and blank and pre-recorded videocassettes in Sweden), but under these schemes the bulk of this revenue benefited the exchequers of these countries. In Norway, approximately 20 per cent of the revenue collected is paid out by the Department of Culture to right owners to be used for collective purposes. In Sweden, of the total collected in 1988 only 2.3 per cent found its way to the copyright and related rights organisations. Meanwhile, this scheme has been replaced by a private copying remuneration scheme in favour of authors, performers, producers of phonograms and other right owners.[35]

These developments in the Nordic countries represented at the time a movement away from individual rights to collectivist solutions controlled by the State.

Copyright may be an inefficient tool for rewarding authors, but the idea that the revenue that authors and other right owners derive from their individual rights could be replaced by private patronage or State support is difficult to support on economic or social grounds.

If it is accepted that a society's culture rests on the freedom of expression of individuals, then it follows that the individual must have a forum for that expression. In the world today, that forum includes the market place, and, as we have seen, one of the functions of **9–011**

[33] *Loc. cit.*

[34] Fund Law of December 14, 1956. The law was amended in the year 2000 to provide for both performers and producers to have the right to receive equitable remuneration for secondary uses of phonograms (Law No.52 of June 23, 2000).

[35] For further details of the tax schemes see G. Davies and M.E. Hung, *Music and Video Private Copying, An International Survey of the Problem and the Law* (London, Sweet & Maxwell, 1993), at 208 and 209. The new Swedish private copying scheme was introduced in 1998 through an amendment to the Copyright Act (Act SFS 1998:1454) which took effect on January 1, 1999.

copyright is to enable the author to sell or otherwise derive revenue from the products of his activities.[36]

Private patronage was the rule prior to the introduction of copyright legislation in the eighteenth century. At that time, however, there was a very restricted reading public. Readers, as pointed out by Lord Mahon in 1842,

> in truth, were then [in the last quarter of the seventeenth century] only of two classes, of the court or the college—either the gay companions of Charles the second ... or the laborious student ... Reading had then in no degree, as now, penetrated and leavened the great mass and body of the people. The inferior authors, therefore, were left to starve or to beg as they could. ... But with the better, or, if you please, the more fortunate authors, the want of purchasers to their books—the want of a public in fact—was supplied by a system of munificent private patronage.[37]

Subsequently, however, "a reading public began to arise, and then it was that copyright became for the first time a question of interest".[38]

Limited private patronage still exists today in the form of prizes for literary, artistic or musical works, in the private commissioning of works and in commercial sponsorship. However, it is not feasible for such private patronage to be sufficiently extensive so as to constitute a valid substitute for the copyright system. While it may provide financial support to the few, it could not provide a sufficient incentive or stimulus to creativity in general. To replace copyright, direct payment of all creators would require huge increases in the amounts available for this purpose at present. Such patronage would also deprive authors of financial and artistic independence, bringing with it the danger that the creator could be obliged to create to order and not at the promptings of his own genius and imagination. As Goldstein has commented: "Patronage supports only those authors whose creative efforts meet the patron's taste. Patronage depresses authorship by shutting the author off from the wider audience that he might hope to

---

[36] Some passages in this section have been adapted from an article written by the author in 1984: "New Technology and Copyright Reform", [1984] 12 E.I.P.R. 335.

[37] Lord Mahon, moving the recommittal of the Copyright Bill 1842 in the House of Commons, *Hansard*, Vol.123, April 6, 1842, at 1349.

[38] *ibid.* at 1350.

reach."[39] In any event, private patronage is far too haphazard a system for a responsible government to use as the basis of its cultural policy in the twenty-first century.

Patronage by the State as a substitute for copyright protection has the **9–012** overriding disadvantage of resulting in state control with the attendant risk of censorship of artistic creativity. Moreover, as Ricketson has pointed out "immense administrative questions would immediately arise, to say nothing of the problems of political influence and nepotism and the age-old question of 'Where's the money coming from'?"[40] The countries which formerly had socialist economies did recognise the social importance of the author and the international copyright system. At the same time, however, the means of publishing and disseminating literary, artistic, musical and dramatic works, films, phonograms and other subject-matter protected by copyright was in the hands of monopolies, such as state publishing houses, film companies, record companies and state-controlled theatres and cinemas. Thus, the selection of the works to be published was made under state control.

Such state control is clearly incompatible with the overriding public interest that artists should be at liberty to create without any limitation on their freedom of expression. In such a system, aesthetic considerations may be subject to political ideology, the whims of government employees acting as self-appointed arbiters of taste, or the need to conform to the standards of a reactionary establishment. "I can conceive of no system more fatal to the integrity and independence of literary men, than one under which they should be taught to look for their daily bread to the favour of ministers and nobles."[41]

State patronage can operate in various ways and at different levels. It can take the form of subsidies or pensions for authors. The collectivist systems referred to above are one way. The grant of tax relief on the earnings of authors has been suggested as another solution but that would only be of any help to those already having an income on which to pay taxes. Moreover, no state could afford to substitute the income derived by creators from copyright by direct state subsidy. On the basis of statistics available to him in 1976, Ljungman made the calculation that, at that time, there were more than 17,000 persons

---

[39] P. Goldstein, "Copyright: The Donald C. Brace Memorial Lecture", in (1991) 38 *Journal of the Copyright Society of the USA*, no.3, at 109.
[40] S. Ricketson, "The Copyright Term", [1992] 23 I.I.C. 753 at 760.
[41] T. Macaulay, in *Hansard, op. cit.*, at 347.

deriving an income in Sweden from literary and artistic activities amounting to approximately 100 million Swedish kronor. Although such a figure was "a negligible item in the national economy",

> Their importance in the field of cultural policy on the other hand would seem to be considerable. In the present day situation, at least, it would certainly not be easy to secure a new annual state grant of the same proportions for the benefit of Swedish authors ... the automatic functioning of copyright protection produces the money in a way which does little to prejudice the planning of the national economy.[42]

At this distance in time, Ljungman's point has been greatly reinforced by the various studies into the economic importance of the copyright sector, referred to in more detail elsewhere,[43] which have shown that the copyright-related industries account for around 6 per cent of GDP in developed countries.

9–013 It is clear that patronage—whether private or state—is inadequate to assure the freedom upon which the cultural life of a modern State should depend. That freedom should extend not only to the creator's expression but also to the public's choice, that is, the test of the market. It may be that state patronage will continue to have a role to play in supporting certain cultural activities which through their minority appeal or disproportionate expense are unable to compete successfully in the market place. But even in such cases, state assistance should be carefully measured to avoid the uneven distribution of financial support leading to minority activities being removed still further from the competition of the market place.

In this connection, it may be noted that there has been a tendency for much of the revenue derived from the collectivist solutions in existence in the Nordic countries and referred to above to be channelled not to the individual right owners whose works have given rise to the revenue but to support various projects considered worthy by the State. The revenue is paid either to funds for the benefit of the young and talented and the old and indigent or to the public exchequer. In the latter case, the money either disappears into public funds or is used for "cultural" purposes determined not by right

---

[42] S. Ljungman, *op. cit.* at 79.
[43] See Ch. 8, above.

owners but by the State.

Over 30 years ago, Stuevold Lassen, discussing what he saw as a general trend in copyright law away from individualism towards collectivisation, pointed out the dangers of the collectivist approach then gaining ground in Norway, whose legislation was the forerunner of collectivism in Europe:

> It is, admittedly, surprising that during the painstaking preparation of a Copyright Act built on exclusive rights for the author, three subsidiary copyright statutes should come out which completely discard the principle of individual copyright, replacing it with strictly collectivist arrangements. Demands for the extension of authors' and artists' rights are met, not with the creation of new prerogatives for the individual but with the introduction of new taxes, and redistribution of the tax money according to principles of social policy. The welfare state has entered the field of copyright law, and has established what has become known as the "Norwegian" system. Utilisers and consumers are—as long as they pay for what they use—free to choose and reject. There is no question of asking anybody's permission; neither the State nor the foundation board nor the artist has a right to prohibit the use. Fees are paid into a fund and redistributed according to rules strongly resembling socialistic principles.
>
> Such a system has obvious disadvantages. It combines the disadvantages of a system of compulsory licensing with the risk that those controlling the disbursements may use their power as a means of censorship. It may also be maintained that collectivisation might deprive the authors of the motive power of their creative activity— the hope of a "just remuneration" for their toil.[44]

Lassen also pointed out that the danger of censorship is inherent in all **9–014** systems which include a substantial degree of state intervention:

> Moreover, the danger seems to be more or less the same, no matter whether the cause of authors being State-paid and the means of communication being State-owned is a general socialisation or merely the State's pursuance of an active policy to stimulate production in the cultural sphere. It is, therefore, hardly contestable

---

[44] B.S. Lassen, *op. cit.* at 82–83 and 88.

that State broadcasting, State-owned theatres, State-subsidised production of films, State-owned publishing houses, State orchestras, etc. may in the long run present a risk of censorship just as dangerous and far more likely to be realised than the direct socialisation of authors' rights.[45]

Collectivisation carries with it other dangers. It has a stultifying effect on creativity:

But it is perhaps no less disturbing a thought that the collective allocation of income payments—mainly according to need—can in the long run undermine the stimulating function of copyright. A successful creative author . . . may in the long run cease to feel the urge to contribute towards the maintenance of less successful colleagues.[46]

It also prejudices the international copyright system. Revenue from State taxes escapes the international copyright system altogether and revenue distributed through a collective system also avoids the international allocation to foreign right owners of their share of incoming revenues. In both cases, payments are made for the use of foreign works but only the domestic government or its nationals benefit from the revenue.

The question of principle, copyright versus patronage, was succinctly argued by Lord Mahon in 1842:

Literary men can never be fairly rewarded by places or pensions. If left to these and these alone, the influence or at least the suspicion, of partiality could never be vanquished. The fairest rule is, to leave them to the patronage of the public, but at the same time to secure to them the full enjoyment of that patronage. The fairest principle is that of rewarding them according to the sale of their works—the fairest test of their merits is the test of time.[47]

---

[45] *ibid.* at 87.
[46] S. Ljungman, *op. cit.* at 85.
[47] Lord Mahon, in *Hansard*, April 6, 1842, *op. cit.* at 1358.

The Need for International Protection

Chafee's third ideal concerns the need for international protection. As **9–015** he points out, art and literature have always been international in spirit thus transcending national borders. He suggests that copyright law should facilitate the free flow of ideas and imaginative creations across national boundaries by giving the same protection to every author, wherever he lives or creates, without discrimination. He saw international copyright protection as of increasing importance because of the growing intercultural interdependence of the world.[48]

The need for international protection of copyright arose, as seen above in Part II, in the very early days of printing when foreign pirate editions of books were quick to take advantage of the market; but such protection was slow to materialise. Until the late nineteenth century, international copyright was regulated to only a limited extent by bilateral treaties between a number of European nations, treaties which developed gradually as the need was recognised to prevent international piracy of copyright works.[49] In 1884 and 1885, at the initiative of the Swiss Government, conferences were held in an attempt to draw up an international copyright treaty. These culminated in the Diplomatic Conference of 1886 and the adoption of the Berne Convention for the Protection of Literary and Artistic Works. Today a series of international treaties sets the norms of international protection of copyright and related rights, of which the most important are the Berne Convention itself and its various revised Acts,[50] the Universal Copyright Convention,[51] the new WIPO Copyright Treaty,[52] the Rome Convention,[53] the WIPO Performances and Phonograms Treaty[54] and not least the TRIPs Agree-

---

[48] Z. Chafee, *op. cit.*, 505.

[49] S. Ricketson, *The Berne Convention for the Protection of literary and artistic works: 1886–1986*, (Centre for Commercial Law Studies, Queen Mary College, Kluwer, 1987) paras. 1.29 *et seq.*

[50] Berne Convention for the Protection of Literary and Artistic Works, 1886, as revised in Paris, 1971. *Cf.* C. Masouyé *Guide to the Berne Convention*, (WIPO, Geneva, 1978).

[51] Universal Copyright Convention 1952, as revised in Paris, 1971.

[52] WIPO Copyright Treaty, December 20, 1996.

[53] International Convention for the Protection of Performers, Producers of Phonograms and Broadcasting Organisations, October 26, 1961. C. Masouyé, *Guide to the Rome Convention and to the Phonograms Convention*, (WIPO, Geneva, 1981).

[54] WIPO Performances and Phonograms Treaty, December 20, 1996.

ment.[55] These treaties have only gradually set increased standards for a broader list of protected subject-matter and for exclusive rights extended to cover new methods of exploitation.[56] International protection needs international consensus and so inevitably lags behind national laws and only belatedly widens its scope.

The rationale of these treaties has remained constant. On its adoption in 1886, the Berne Convention was said to be destined to stimulate the intellectual effort of mankind through the legitimate protection of works, the protection of authors' rights being seen as one of the best means of developing letters and the arts and encouraging national production.[57] At the same time, it was also recognised that limitations on absolute protection were dictated by the public interest.[58] Most recently, the Preamble to the WIPO Copyright Treaty recognises the outstanding significance of copyright protection as an incentive for literary and artistic creation as well as the need to maintain the balance between the rights of authors and the larger public interest.[59]

Recent years have witnessed unprecedented activity in the setting of new international norms in the field of copyright, in the context of the work leading to the adoption of the WIPO Copyright Treaty and the WIPO Performances and Phonograms Treaty in 1996, as well as that which led to the adoption of the TRIPs Agreement in 1994 and the harmonisation programme of the European Union in the field of copyright and related rights. The extent to which these developments have met Chafee's first three ideals, complete coverage, control of all channels of exploitation and international protection are discussed further in Part IV, below.

---

[55] Agreement on the Trade-related Aspects of Intellectual Property Rights, April 15, 1994.

[56] On the subject of the Conventions see *inter alia:* P. Goldstein, *International Copyright, Principles, Law and Practice*, (Oxford, Oxford University Press, 2001; S. Ricketson), *op. cit.* n. 49, above; *Copinger and Skone James on Copyright, op. cit.*, (Ch. 4, n. 9, above), Ch.24; H. Desbois, A. Françon and A. Kerever, *Les Conventions Internationales du droit d'auteur et des droits voisins*, Dalloz, Paris, 1976; J.A.L. Sterling, *World Copyright Law*, Sweet & Maxwell, London, 1999; D. Gervias, *The TRIPS Agreement—Drafting History and Analysis*, Sweet & Maxwell, London, 1998.

[57] N. Droz, President of the Third Conference in Berne 1886, Minutes of the First Meeting, September 6, 1886.

[58] N. Droz, President of the First Conference in Berne 1884, Minutes of the Sixth Meeting, September 18, 1884.

[59] Preamble, paras.4 and 5.

Chapter 10

Limitations on Copyright

All property has its proper limit, extent and bounds.

Mr. Justice Yates

Property has its duties as well as its rights.

Benjamin Disraeli

Let us turn now to Chafee's three negative copyright ideals, all of which concern the public interest. The most important of these is his fourth ideal, namely, that protection should not extend substantially beyond the purposes of protection. In this connection, perhaps the issue that has been most debated in copyright is the question of duration. The fifth ideal that protection should not stifle independent creation by others concerns exceptions to protection, including the Anglo-American concepts of fair dealing and fair use. Finally, limitations on protection are relevant to Chafee's sixth ideal, that the legal rules of copyright should be convenient to handle.

10–001

Duration of Protection

As demonstrated by Part II of this study, the question of how long copyright should last has been a controversial matter from the outset. It has been pointed out that the very first national laws granted rights to authors for limited times on policy grounds, it being considered essential to protect the rights of the public to have access to works. As Ricketson has pointed out:

10–002

This "public interest" viewpoint has continued to pervade all copyright legislation, both nationally and internationally....

Natural rights theories with their focus on the individual (and corresponding absence of attention to the wider interests of the public) have therefore never triumphed in their pristine form and authors' rights, unlike those of other property owners, have remained limited in time.[1]

Nevertheless, partisans of perpetual rights remained vocal for many years and their arguments were met in part by a gradual extension of the term of protection. Following the incorporation of the term of 50 years p.m.a. first as a goal in the Berlin Act 1908 of the Berne Convention and subsequently as the standard of the Berne Convention following the Brussels Conference in 1948, that term came to be considered the norm and to represent a proper balance between the rights of the authors and the public interest. It should be noted in this connection that "the historical development of these norms is also notable for an almost complete absence of debate of the policy and theoretical issues involved".[2]

Recently, however, as discussed in Part II with respect to the copyright laws of France, Germany and the United States of America, there has been a move towards extending the period of protection. In 1992, the European Commission put forward a proposal[3] to extend the period of protection for authors throughout the Community to 70 years p.m.a. This resulted in the adoption in October 1993 of a Directive harmonising the term of protection of copyright and certain related rights.[4] The Directive provided for a uniform period of protection for authors of 70 years p.m.a.,[5] thus harmonising upwards to the longest period of protection in any Member State. This happened in spite of the fact that only three of the then 12[6] Member States previously protected certain works for longer than 50 years p.m.a.,

---

[1] S. Ricketson, "The Copyright Term", (1992) 23 I.I.C. 755.

[2] *ibid.*, at 777.

[3] Proposal for a Council Directive Harmonising the Term of Protection of Copyright and Certain Related Rights, COM (92) final-Syn 395, OJ EC No.C92/6, 23 I.I.C. 806 (1992). For a discussion of the proposal see S. von Lewinski, "EC Proposal for a Council Directive Harmonizing the Term of Protection of Copyright and Certain Related Rights", (1992) 23 I.I.C. 785.

[4] See Directive 93/98: [1993] OJ L290/9 (the **Term Directive**).

[5] The duration of the related rights of performers, producers of phonograms and films and broadcasting organisations were fixed at 50 years from the relevant starting point for the calculation of the term, *i.e.* the respective performance, fixation, transmission, lawful publication, or lawful communication to the public.

[6] On January 1, 1995, Austria, Finland and Sweden joined the European Union.

namely France (70 years for musical works only), Germany (70 years for literary, artistic and musical works) and Spain (60 years also for literary, artistic and musical works). The World Intellectual Property Organisation (WIPO) in 1991 also suggested, in connection with a possible Protocol to the Berne Convention, an extension of the term of protection for authors to 70 years p.m.a.[7]

The Commission justified extending the term of protection as follows in the Preamble to the Term Directive: "The Commission stresses the need to harmonise copyright and neighbouring rights at a high level of protection since these rights are fundamental to intellectual creation and stresses that their protection ensures the maintenance and development of creativity in the interest of authors, cultural industries, consumers and society as a whole".[8]

It should be noted, however, that the principal concern of the **10–003** Commission in this respect was to harmonise the period of protection throughout the Community in view of the completion of the Single Market, which took effect on January 1, 1993, so as "to establish a legal environment conducive to the harmonious development of literary and artistic creation in the community".[9] Harmonisation upwards was simpler to achieve in view of the difficulties inherent in cutting back acquired rights. Other arguments deployed in favour of the extension included longer life expectancy and the desire to protect the interests of the author's direct descendants for two successive generations.

The rationale for WIPO's proposal was similar:

The main reason for envisaging a possible extension of the term of protection was that the 50-year p.m.a. term of protection (which is the minimum provided for by the Berne Convention) had originally been adopted to make reasonably certain that at least the first generation of authors' heirs should normally be able to enjoy the rights protected, but, because of the continuous increase in life expectancy, such certainty no longer existed.[10]

These proposals did not meet with unanimous approval and,

---

[7] Memorandum of the International Bureau of WIPO on Questions concerning a possible Protocol to the Berne Convention, Doc. BCP/CE/I/3, October 1991.

[8] See Term Directive, Recital 10.

[9] *ibid.*, Recital 11.

[10] WIPO Memorandum, *ibid.*, para.159.

indeed, the proposal to extend the term of protection to 70 years in the possible Protocol to the Berne Convention was subsequently dropped.[11]

According to von Lewinski, the European Commission's proposals were countered by doubts being expressed as to whether

> an author's descendant can participate sufficiently, if at all, in the fruits of his creation. Usually, assignment or transfer of copyright goes to an exploiting enterprise for the entire duration of protection. Therefore, an extension of the term of protection lies primarily in the interest of such exploiting enterprises in regaining their investments.[12]

10–004 The extension was also opposed by the Economic and Social Committee of the EU, which favoured harmonisation at 50 years p.m.a.[13]

Following the event, the extension of the period of protection for literary, artistic and musical works under the EU Directive to 70 years in the Member States of the European Union[14] was seen as controversial and strongly criticised. This may well be why the WIPO proposal was dropped. Cornish has argued that

> it cannot be that an extension of the right from fifty to seventy years *post mortem auctoris* is required as an economic incentive to those who create and those who exploit works. They make their decisions by reference to much shorter time scales than these. It is only considerations of moral entitlement which can possibly justify even the present minimum term in the Berne Convention...

He points out that the principal argument put forward that the lifespan of authors has increased is without foundation because "this added longevity is brought into account under the existing system of

---

[11] Extension of the duration of the protection of works under the Berne Convention, other than photographic works, was dropped from the list of topics to be covered by the Committee of Experts on a Possible Protocol to the Berne Convention as from its third session, following a decision of the Assembly of the Berne Union on September 19, 1992.

[12] S. von Lewinski, *op. cit.* at 788–9.

[13] OJ 1992 C287/53.

[14] Directive 93/98 of October 29, 1993. The deadline for implementation of the Directive by the Member States was July 1, 1995. Meanwhile, all the Member States have done so.

measurement. At least the first generation of inheritors is compensated by that, since it is not argued that children are on average being born to older parents". In his view "it is clear that simple, unsubstantiated pressure from the copyright industries for more protection has been the governing factor in getting the Directive onto the books with such alacrity" ... and ... "to say that consumers and society as a whole will benefit is eye-wash".[15]

In the WIPO context, some delegations opposed the proposal for extension, considering that basing an extension of the term on continuous increases in life expectancy was not valid, and asked for further study of the justifications for any extension. It was also suggested that extension of the term of protection would lead to practical difficulties for the access of developing countries to protected works and for the users of works, in general, since the author's heirs were often difficult to find for the purpose of obtaining their authorisation. Others argued that extension of the period of protection was justified not only by the increased life expectancy of authors, but also because a longer term of protection would increase the value of copyright.[16]

As seen in Part II, in 1998, the United States of America enacted **10–005** legislation to extend the term of copyright by twenty years.[17] Ginsburg views this development as "Keeping up with the Joneses in the European Union".[18] In her view, because the public domain is a crucial counterpart to the copyright system,

> Congress should not have revised the 1976 Copyright Act's balance between protected and expired works without compelling reasons for term extension. It is not clear that such reasons have been demonstrated...
>
> In sum, there may be strong international trade reasons to favor US term extension, but, as a matter of copyright law, the extension may have been undesirable ... One may be concerned that term extension will result in an overall *weakening* of copyright protection. This outcome may seem paradoxical, since the idea of term

---

[15] W.R. Cornish, "Intellectual Property", in 13 *Yearbook of European Law* (1994) 485 at 489 *et seq.*

[16] Report of the Committee of Experts on a Possible Protocol to the Berne Convention for the Protection of Literary and Artistic Works, second session, Geneva, February 10–18, 1992, paras 147 to 160.

[17] The Sonny Bono Copyright Term Extension Act, Pub.L.No.105–298, 112 Stat.2827 (1998).

[18] J. Ginsburg, "News from US", *op. cit.*, n.?, above, at 265.

extension is to reinforce copyright protection. In fact, however, one may fear that "user rights" advocates will contend, and courts will agree, that copyright now endures for so long a time, that the subsisting (and excessive) period of exclusivity must be tempered by more vigorous exceptions to copyright protection.

The constitutionality of the 20-year extension of copyright protection has been challenged in the courts and the issue is to be heard by the US Supreme Court.[19] This guarantees a lively debate on the issue once more in the United States of America.

That a serious discussion of the rationale for the term of copyright protection took place internationally during the 1990s, and is still continuing in the United States of America, is in itself positive, particularly since, as Ricketson pointed out in 1992, in previous years there had been relatively little discussion of this question, either at national or international levels.[20] Many commentators start from the premise that any extension of the term of protection necessarily represents progress, and, as Ricketson puts it, those favouring extension of the term have latterly occupied as it were the high moral ground, those opposing extension of the term being put on the defensive to justify the *status quo*. As Ricketson reminds us, in the various debates on the subject of the term of protection leading to the adoption of the term of 50 years p.m.a. as the minimum standard in the Berne Convention, by the Brussels Revision Conference in 1948:

> One is hard pressed to find reasoned justifications for the adoption of longer terms of protection. The 50-year post mortem term was taken as a self-evident "good thing", and the onus was clearly on countries with shorter or restricted terms to justify their deviance from this standard. ... One must conclude that the 50-year post mortem adherents had won the higher moral ground in the argument and therefore had their opponents at a disadvantage.[21]

10–006 Moreover, as we have observed in Part II, the comparatively recent extensions of term adopted in France in 1985 and Germany in 1965, which served as the ground for fixing the period of protection in the

---

[19] *Eldred v Ashcroft*, US SupCt, No.01–618; grant of *certiorari* February 19, 2002.

[20] S. Ricketson, "The Copyright Term", *op. cit.* at 753.

[21] S. Ricketson, "Duration of Term of Protection Under the Berne Convention", [1991] Copyright 88.

EC Term Directive and subsequently the law of the United Kingdom at 70 years, took place without serious debate as to the justification therefore. In France, as already discussed, it was the music publishers who persuaded the French legislators to extend the term of protection of musical compositions to 70 years on the ground that in the field of serious music it was necessary for them to be able to recoup their investments over a longer period than 50 years p.m.a. There was no attempt to justify the extension in the interests of the author or his heirs. The public interest was not even mentioned.

Assuming that there is general agreement with the proposition that authors should be protected during their life time, and for a limited period thereafter,[22] the point in issue here is how long should copyright last after the death of the author? As Macaulay put it: "It can hardly be disputed by any rational man that this is a point which the legislature is free to determine in the way which may appear to be most conducive to the public good".[23]

The legislature, however, should arrive at what it considers a period most conducive to the public good after debating the issue and taking account of the arguments. That such debate has been scarce in recent times, and that the EC Directive providing for a period of protection of 70 years p.m.a. for authors should have been adopted with so little public discussion of the issues, is regrettable. Ricketson in his 1992 article,[24] sought to remedy that deficiency by drawing attention once more to the main arguments, which in former times played such a vital role in the shaping of the modern copyright system, as discussed in Part II. It is not the aim of the author here to rehearse all these arguments anew, nor does space permit. The following summary focuses on the public policy aspects of the debate.

Since the Statute of Anne first introduced a period of protection for copyright works of 14 years from publication, renewable by the

---

[22] The major advantage of a term *post mortem* over a fixed term after publication is that the term ceases at one and the same time with respect to all the works of the author. A fixed term of a period of years calculated from the date of publication was strongly advocated, however, *inter alia*, by E. Pouillet, *op. cit.* Ch.3, n.2, above, para.137. This was, of course, also the system of the USA until January 1, 1978, and remains the system for calculating the term of protection of certain categories of works protected by copyright or related rights such as films and phonograms.

[23] T. Macaulay, in *Hansard*, House of Commons, Vol.56, February 5, 1841, at 365.

[24] S. Ricketson, "The Copyright Term", *op. cit.*, n.1, above; see also on this subject L. Evans, *op. cit.*, Ch.9, n.1, above; C. Masouyé, "Towards a Prolongation of the General Duration of Protection", XXIV R.I.D.A. 93 (1959).

author for a further 14 years, the arguments put forward in favour of either perpetual rights or longer periods of protection based on the life of the author, plus a certain number of years after his death, have become traditional.

10–007   A man ought to have the same property in productions of his mind as in those of his hands. It is in the interests of the public that valuable literature should be encouraged, and the great and good authors will benefit most from long periods of protection because such works have a lasting public. Authors are stimulated to create by the need to provide for their dependants; long periods of protection ensuring the provision of financial support to their descendants even after their death will, therefore, encourage them in their chosen profession. The author has expenses and works without being assured of certain and immediate returns; his heirs should be in a position to recoup his investment. Likewise, publishers need time to recover their investment costs; long terms are necessary because publishers usually offset losses on less popular books by their profits on the more successful. This is especially true of serious works of literature and music in respect of which investments are only recovered on a long-term basis. Long terms of protection strengthen the negotiating position of the copyright owner, thus ensuring him of a higher income while he is still alive.

The author and his descendants should be able "to protect the public from the evil of garbled editions" of his books. "It is to the public advantage that works of literature should be protected from those whose habit is to mutilate or misapply them, and that the authors' representative and one publisher should have power and interest to do so".[25]

Finally, uniformity (which in effect means harmonisation upwards) of terms of protection at the international level provides advantages in facilitating world-wide dissemination of works. As Ricketson points out:

> national differences in term ... will lead to various disadvantages. Rights owners will be uncertain as to the duration of their rights in different countries and it will be expensive to monitor this. Third parties will also be under a similar burden. Furthermore, there may be distinct imbalances created in international trade, where a work

---

[25] C. Morgan, *The House of Macmillan*, (London, Macmillan, 1944), at 174–177.

can be exploited freely in one country but not in another where it is still protected.[26]

This was clearly the main reason for the 1998 20-year extension of the term of protection by the United States of America.[27] Without it, US works would not have enjoyed the full duration of copyright available to domestic works in the European Union.

The arguments against long periods of protection include the fol- **10–008** lowing, most of which were eloquently phrased by Macaulay in the famous debate in the UK House of Commons in 1841, to which reference has already been made. The same arguments obviously gain additional strength in the case against perpetual rights. A strong case against such rights was argued also by Renouard in his treatise published two years previously.[28]

It is doubtful that authors are inspired to create by the possibility of their grandchildren obtaining remuneration for their efforts: "But an advantage that is to be enjoyed more than half a century after we are dead, by somebody unborn, by somebody utterly unconnected with us, is really no motive to action".[29] The descendants of the author may not be his chosen heirs; the author should be free to dispose of his property as he sees fit. Authors thus do not obtain greater motivation from a 60-year period of protection than from a 20-year period. Moreover, long periods of protection benefit not the individual author but his publisher to whom the rights in his works are more than likely to have passed before his death.

Long terms of protection "inflict grievous injury on the public,

---

[26] S. Ricketson, "The Copyright Term", *op. cit.*, n.1 above, at 771. It would seem likely that this argument will be put forward forcefully in the future by the EU Member States to promote a general increase of the term of protection to 70 years p.m.a. As has already been noted above, the USA has been prompted by the EU Directive to increase the term of protection by 20 years. Should this be upheld by the Supreme Court, the combined pressure of the EU and USA for a general increase in the Berne Convention and the TRIPs Agreement (a general review clause requires a review of the latter agreement two years after expiration of the transitional period following the entry into force of the WTO and at regular intervals thereafter (Art.71)) will be difficult to resist.

[27] See n.17, above.

[28] A.-C. Renouard, *op. cit.* Vol.I, at 466 *et seq.*: "Making books more expensive in perpetuity, the complete destruction of any competition, for the present and for the future, would cause a mortal prejudice to social progress by slowing down the circulation of ideas. Not only society would suffer; the glory of the author and of his memory would be diminished; his dearest and most noble desire to see his ideas propagated would be compromised and betrayed."

[29] T. Macaulay, *op. cit.*, n.23, above, at 349.

without conferring any compensating advantage on men of letters".[30] The publisher will not give appreciably more for a copyright of 60 years than for one of 20. Taste and fashion in literature and the arts change and very few books have a life of more than a few years. "Such is the inconstancy of the public taste, that no sensible man will venture to pronounce, with confidence, what the sale of any book published in our days [1841] will be in the years between 1890 and 1900."[31]

As Chafee observed: "The publisher must have always shaped his lump sum offer according to his expectations of sales within the first few years of the copyright. That is when he makes his killing. ... Good publishing accounting writes off all books within three years after publication as no longer an asset".[32]

10–009 Here the US experience of the copyright renewal scheme, in force until the 1976 Act, provides evidence in support of Macaulay's thesis. Evans tells us that, in 1949, only 11 per cent of original copyrights were renewed for a further term after the expiration of the initial term of 28 years, suggesting that this provided pertinent evidence that the longer full-term was not much of an inducement to either original creation or publication.[33] In a more recent study of the same subject undertaken by Barbara Ringer in 1960, she found that on average only 15 per cent of copyright owners saw any need to renew their copyright for a further term.[34]

Long terms are contrary to the public interest in that they enable descendants of the author and indeed publishers to either suppress works altogether or to limit access to and exploitation of works by demanding unreasonable royalties or imposing various restrictive conditions on their publication or performance. Long terms encourage piracy because they represent an unacceptable monopoly, which burdens the user with high prices, and thus leads to disrespect for the law.

Long periods of copyright protection lead to difficulties in identifying the successors in title of the original authors to whom application should be made for permission to reproduce the work, and are thus contrary to Chafee's sixth ideal of convenience. As Ricketson

---

[30] *ibid.* at 344.
[31] *ibid.* at 351.
[32] Z. Chafee, *op. cit.* at 721.
[33] L. Evans, *op. cit.* at 10.
[34] B. Ringer, "Renewal of Copyright", Study No.1 (Vol.1, *Studies in Copyright*, 1963), at 583.

points out, "this is a concern to all users of copyright material, but the problems of educationalists, librarians, historians and performers probably loom largest in this respect".[35]

The problem with the issue of duration as Ricketson suggests is that "There has been little sustained discussion of the economic, social and cultural issues involved, and the steady trend towards longer terms has remained largely unquestioned".[36]

In 1992, Ricketson proposed that national and international studies should be carried out to seek to establish on a factual basis what the appropriate term for copyright protection should be. He called for such studies also to take account of the fact that copyright protection embraces many different subject-matters, and while there may be a case for long periods of protection for certain categories of works, this may not be so for all works. The case of computer programs, to take an example, is one where increasing the term of protection would seem inappropriate in view of the short useful life of such works.

It is regrettable that Ricketson's proposal was disregarded by the European Commission. Requests for a study of the justifications for an increase in the term of protection in the context of the negotiations concerning a possible Protocol to the Berne Convention in the mid-1990s have not been followed up either. This is presumably because the issue was dropped from the agenda leading to the adoption of the WIPO Internet Treaties, so that, for the time being, the issue is not under discussion in the context of the Berne Convention and the said Treaties.

The increase in term in the EU is a *fait accompli*. It remains to be seen if that in the United States of America will be upheld by the Supreme Court. However, before other Member States of the Berne Union, or of the World Trade Organisation as regards any future review of the TRIPs Agreement, adopt a minimum term of 70 years p.m.a. for the protection of literary, musical and artistic works, they would be wise to adopt Ricketson's proposal. The limitation on the duration of protection is imposed in the public interest in order to provide the public with free access to copyright works as soon as possible and to promote the widest possible dissemination of such works for the benefit of the public. To extend the term of protection without having first ascertained the likely benefits and disadvantages

10–010

---

[35] S. Ricketson, "The Copyright Term", *op. cit.*, n.1, above, at 766.
[36] *ibid.* at 783.

to be derived therefrom on the basis of factual evidence and discussion of the public policy issues involved is not in the best interests of the public at large.

On the subject of duration, the last word may be left to Dr. Johnson:

> Were an author's right in his book to be perpetual, no book, however useful, could be universally diffused among mankind, should the proprietor take it into his head to restrain its circulation For the good of the world, therefore, whatever individual work has once been created by an author, and issued out by him, should be understood as no longer in his power, but as belonging to the public; at the same time, the author is entitled to an adequate reward. This he should have by an exclusive right to his work for a considerable number of years.[37]

Exceptions to Protection

10–011   Chafee's fifth ideal was that the protection given the copyright owner should not stifle independent creation by others. Thus, other people should be able to use the work in the sense that there is no monopoly in the ideas or facts contained therein but only in the form in which they are expressed. This ideal is a well-established principle of copyright legislation and, in Chafee's view, of all the six ideals, the one most successfully attained[38]. "The limitations on copyright are necessary to keep the balance between two conflicting public interests: the public interest in rewarding creators and the public interest in the widest dissemination of their works, which is also the interest of the users of such works".[39]

In determining the scope of such exceptions, it is incumbent on the State to strike a fair balance between the interests of the authors on the one hand and those of the public on the other hand. "Limitations on the author's exclusive right may be imposed in order to facilitate the work's contribution to the intellectual and cultural enrichment of the

---

[37] Cited by T. Macaulay, *Hansard*, House of Commons, Vol.127, April 6, 1842, at 1384.

[38] Z. Chafee, *op.cit.*, at 527.

[39] S.M. Stewart, *op. cit.*, Ch.2, n.13, above, para.4.50.

community. However, the limitations must not be such as to dampen the will to create and disseminate new works".[40]

Limited Freedom to Use Works

The international copyright conventions and national laws permit limited free use of protected works in certain special cases in the public interest. As we have seen in Part II, at national level these limitations are generally prescribed by statute but the extent thereof has given rise to abundant case law in France, Germany, the United Kingdom and the United States of America. The exceptions specifically permitted by the Berne Convention include free use of public speeches, lectures and speeches in legal proceedings; use of short excerpts by way of quotation or illustration for teaching[41]; use justified in connection with the reporting of current events; use solely for the purposes of private study and research; and, finally, the Convention contains a catch-all provision, allowing reproduction in certain special cases provided that such reproduction does not conflict with a normal exploitation of the work and does not unreasonably prejudice the legitimate interests of the author.[42]

10–012

These limitations on the author's exclusive right to exploit his work aim at meeting the public's thirst for information.[43]

The limitations sanctioned by the Berne Convention fall into three categories; specific exceptions of limited scope for informational and educational purposes, limitations on the right of reproduction and non-voluntary licensing systems.

---

[40] M. Fabiani, "A Profile of Copyright in Today's Society", [1982] Copyright 154.
[41] In such cases, the use must be compatible with fair practice and justified by the purpose.
[42] Berne Convention, Paris Act 1971, Articles 2bis(1) and (2), 9(2), 10bis(1), (2) and (3).
[43] C. Masouyé, *WIPO Guide to the Berne Convention, op. cit.*, para.10.1.

Exceptions for Informational and Educational Purposes

Rights of Quotation

10–013 The right to make quotations from a published work[44] allows the inclusion of one or more passages from someone else's work in one's own to illustrate a theme or defend some proposition or to describe or criticise the work quoted therefrom. There are three limits on this licence to quote. In the first place, the work from which the extract is taken must have been lawfully made available to the public. Second, the quotation must be "compatible with fair practice", implying an objective appreciation of what is normally considered acceptable. The fairness or otherwise of the quotation is ultimately a matter for the courts to decide. Third, the quotation must only be to the extent justified by the purpose, which again is a matter for the courts.

Use for Teaching Purposes

10–014 This exception aims to meet teaching needs, permitting the utilisation of works by way of illustration in publications, broadcasts or sound or audiovisual recordings for teaching, subject to the same conditions as those governing quotations. The word "teaching" means teaching at all levels, including educational institutions, municipal and state schools and private schools.[45]

The exceptions for quotation and teaching are both subject to the condition that where such use is made the source and name of the author must be mentioned.[46]

Exceptions for the Benefit of the Media

10–015 The reproduction by the press, the broadcasting or the communication to the public by wire of articles published in newspapers or periodicals on current economic, political or religious topics, and of

---

[44] Berne Convention, Art.10(1); *cf* C. Masouyé, *op. cit.*, paras 10.2–10.7.
[45] *ibid.*, paras 10.8–10.10.
[46] Berne Convention, Art.10(3).

broadcast works of the same character may also be permitted by national legislation, an exception of particular value to the news media. The source must always be clearly indicated to protect moral rights and an author has the right to expressly reserve his consent to such use.[47]

Reporting Current Events

Legislation may also lay down the conditions under which, for the purpose of reporting current events by means of photography, cinematography, broadcasting or communication to the public by wire, literary or artistic works seen or heard in the course of the event may, to the extent justified by the informatory purpose, be reproduced and made available to the public. This exception deals with the situation where, during the reporting of current events, protected works are fortuitously seen or heard in the background.[48] The problems which may arise in this context are well illustrated by French and German case law on the subject described in Chapters 6 and 7, above.

10–016

Limitations on the Right of Reproduction

The Three-Step Test of the Berne Convention

The Berne Convention lays down the principle in Article 9(1) that authors have the exclusive right of authorising the reproduction of their works, in any manner or form. All methods of reproduction and processes known or yet to be discovered are envisaged. However, under Article 9(2), exceptions to this principle are permitted in certain special cases, provided that the permitted reproduction does not conflict with a normal exploitation of the work and does not unreasonably prejudice the legitimate interests of the author. Assessing whether any given exception satisfies the criteria laid down in Article 9(2) has come to be known as the "three-step test": first, the reproduction must be for a specific purpose and is allowed only in certain special cases; secondly, the reproduction should not conflict

10–017

---

[47] *ibid.*, Art.10bis(1); cf C. Masouyé, op. cit., paras 10bis.1 to 10.4.
[48] *ibid.*, Art.10bis.(2); *cf* C. Masouyé, *ibid.*, paras 10bis.85–10bis.10.

with a normal exploitation of the work; and thirdly the use must not unreasonably prejudice the legitimate interests of the author. These three rules are cumulative, all three having to be satisfied before reproduction is allowed. Ricketson describes the first criterion thus:

> First, the use must be for a specific, designated purpose: a broadly framed exemption, for example, for private or personal use, generally, would not be justified here. Secondly, there must be something "special" about this purpose, "special" here meaning that the use is justified by some clear reason of public policy or other exceptional circumstance.

However, even where a special case is established, if the contemplated reproduction would be such as to conflict with a normal exploitation of the work, it is not permitted at all under Article 9(2). If there is no such conflict, then the next step is to consider whether there is unreasonable prejudice to the legitimate interests of the author. "In cases where there would be serious loss of profit for the copyright owner, the law should provide him with some compensation", such as, for example, a system of compulsory licensing with equitable remuneration.[49]

The WIPO Copyright Treaty 1996 has extended the scope of Article 9(2) of the Berne Convention to make it applicable to all authors' rights and not merely to the reproduction right.[50] It is also understood that national legislation may carry forward and appropriately extend into the digital environment limitations and exceptions in their national laws, which have been considered acceptable under the Berne Convention. Similarly, new exceptions and limitations may be devised which are appropriate in the digital network environment.[51] The WIPO Performances and Phonograms Treaty 1996 has applied the same principles to the field of related rights, including the extension of existing limitations and exceptions into the digital environment and the devising of new exceptions for that environment.[52] Thus, the same kinds of limitations or exceptions are permitted with regard to the protection of performers and producers of phonograms as are provided for in national legislation, in con-

---

[49] C. Masouyé, *op cit.*, para.9.8.
[50] WCT, Art.10.
[51] WCT: agreed statement concerning Art.10.
[52] WPPT, Art.16 and agreed statement relating thereto.

nection with the protection of copyright in literary and artistic works. However, such limitations or exceptions must be confined to those which meet the three-step test, that is to certain special cases which do not conflict with a normal exploitation of the performance or phonogram and do not unreasonably prejudice the legitimate interests of the performer or of the producer of the phonogram.

These new dispensations are in line with the TRIPs Agreement which provides that, with respect to literary and artistic works, Member States shall confine limitations or exceptions to exclusive rights to certain special cases which do not conflict with a normal exploitation of the work and do not unreasonably prejudice the legitimate interests of the right holder.[53] As regards related rights, the TRIPs Agreement permits Member States to provide for conditions, limitations, exceptions and reservations to the extent permitted by the Rome Convention[54] but qualifies this by applying the three-step test of the Berne Convention also to limitations on related rights.[55]

The three-step test of the Berne Convention has been recognised also **10–018** in the EU Information Society Directive, which aims at regulating limitations and exceptions to the reproduction right as well as to the rights of communication to the public of works and making available to the public of other subject-matter of related rights. The Directive provides for an exhaustive list of permissible but not mandatory exceptions,[56] subject to the proviso that they shall only be applied if they comply with the three-step test.[57] Member States will be free to pick and choose which of the permitted exceptions to allow; far from harmonising the régime of exceptions in the European Union, this leaves a wide discretion to Member States with the result that there will be no Single Market so far as exceptions are concerned, a problem which is likely to cause particular problems as regards the exception for private use.[58]

---

[53] TRIPs Agreement, Art.13.
[54] See Rome Convention, Art.15, which permits exceptions for: private use; use of short excerpts in connection with the reporting of current events; ephemeral recordings by broadcasting organisations; use solely for purposes of teaching or scientific research. Moreover, the same kinds of limitations are permitted as are provided for in respect of literary and artistic works. Compulsory licences are only permitted to the extent they are compatible with the Convention.
[55] TRIPs Agreement, Art.14(6).
[56] Only one mandatory exception is provided for, that in Art.5(1) of the Directive concerning temporary, transient or incidental acts of reproduction.
[57] Directive, Art.5(2), (3) and (5).
[58] See also para.12–008, et seq., below.

Of particular interest in this connection is the application of the three-step test by a World Trade Organisation panel in its report on a complaint brought against the United States of America by the European Union[59] and which would appear to be the first judicial interpretation of the test. The panel found that the term "special cases" in the first condition requires that a limitation or exception in national legislation should be clearly defined and should be narrow in its scope and reach. However, a limitation or exception may be compatible with the first condition even if it pursues a special purpose whose underlying legitimacy in a normative sense cannot be discerned. Thus, the first condition does not imply passing a judgment on the legitimacy of the exceptions in dispute (as had been argued by the European Union).[60] As regards the second condition that an exception should not conflict with the normal exploitation of a work, the panel considered that a conflict arises when the exception or limitation enters into economic competition with the ways that right holders normally extract economic value from that right to the work (*i.e.*, the copyright) and thereby deprive them of significant or tangible commercial gain.[61] The panel finally gave its opinion on the third condition of the three-step test, that the exception or limitation must not unreasonably prejudice the legitimate interests of the right holder, finding that there is unreasonable prejudice where an exception or limitation causes or has the potential to cause an unreasonable loss of income to the copyright holder.[62]

---

[59] Panel Report WT/DS160/R of June 15, 2000: United States—Section 110(5) of the US Copyright Act.

[60] *ibid.*, para.6.112.

[61] *ibid.*, para.6.183

[62] Concerning the Panel Report, see J.C. Ginsburg, "Toward Supranational Copyright Law? The WTO Panel Decision and the "Three-Step Test" for Copyright Exceptions", (2001) 187 R.I.D.A. 3; D.J. Brennan, "The Three-Step Test Frenzy—Why the TRIPs Panel Decision might be considered Per Incuriam", [2002] I.P.Q. 2, 212; Y. Gaubiac, "Les exceptions au droit d'auteur: un nouvel avenir", in [2001] *Communication Commerce électronique*, n.6, 12; B.C. Goldmann, "Victory for Songwriters in WTO Music-Royalties Dispute between U.S. and E.U.—Background of the Conflict Over the Extension of Homestyle Exemption", (2001) 32 *I.I.C.* 412; M. Ficsor, "How much of What? The "Three-Step Test" and its application in two recent WTO dispute settlement cases", (2002) 192 R.I.D.A. 110; and J. Bornkamm, "Copyright and the Public Interest—The Three-Step Test in International Copyright", paper delivered at the Fordham University School of Law 10th. Annual Conference on International Intellectual Property Law and Policy, New York, April 4 and 5, 2002.

Exceptions in National Laws

National legislation generally provides for specific, statutory excep-   **10–019**
tions and limitations to exclusive rights. As seen in Part II, this is true
of all four jurisdictions considered in this study.

However, in the United Kingdom and the United States of
America, in addition to miscellaneous statutory exceptions, the main
defences against infringement are referred to respectively as "fair
dealing" in the United Kingdom and "fair use" in the United States of
America. However, the two defences should be clearly distinguished,
even though both permit minor borrowings from copyright works.
The difference lies in the fact that the fair dealing provisions of the
UK Copyright Act impose statutory limitations permitting minor
borrowings of certain works for specific and limited purposes: research
or private study; criticism or review; and reporting current events.
Other types of dealing will not be permitted, however "fair" they
may be. By contrast, in the United States of America, the concept of
"fair use" is of more general scope, giving a privilege to others than
the owner of a copyright to use the copyrighted material in a reasonable manner without the owner's consent. Thus, as a general rule,
the copyright owner may not object to minor borrowings from his
protected work. The Copyright Act only provides guidelines as to
what may amount to fair use, identifying six exemplary purposes:
criticism, comment, news reporting, teaching (including multiple
copies for classroom use), scholarship or research. It is the courts in
both countries which have to decide whether any particular use has
been fair dealing or fair use or not, in the light of the particular
circumstances, but this is a far more open question in the United
States of America. The case law on these subjects has been described
above.[63]

For the public, specific statutory exceptions may be considered
preferable and to provide greater legal security than the open-ended
fair use defence of the US law. In the United States of America,
however, the fair use defence is seen as very much in the public
interest. As Goldstein puts it:

the object of the fair use defence is to confirm, not contradict,
copyright law's basic goal—to put copyright works to their most

---

[63] See Chs 4 and 5, above.

beneficial use so that "the public good fully coincides ... with the claims of individuals". Congress and the courts have reconciled the public good with the claims of individuals through two, over-lapping, approaches to the fair use defence. One, a private benefit approach, excuses uses that the copyright owner would have licensed but for insurmountable transaction costs. The other, a public benefit approach, will excuse a use, even in the absence of transaction costs, if the social benefit of the use outweighs the loss to the copyright owner.[64]

Non-Voluntary Licensing Systems

10–020 Limitations may also take the form of statutory or compulsory licences, according to which, subject to certain conditions including the payment of equitable remuneration, a work may be used without the authorisation of the author. Such limitations permitted by the Berne Convention include the possibility for national legislation to substitute a system of compulsory licences with respect to the right of broadcasting and the right of cable distribution; this applies to both sound and television broadcasts intended to be received directly by the general public.[65] Compulsory licences are also envisaged for the right of recording musical works, the composers' so-called mechanical rights. Such licences may cover not only the music but also the accompanying words but are only permitted if the author (or authors) have earlier consented to a recording of the work.[66] Under compulsory licensing schemes, the right owner loses control of his work; he cannot prevent its use. In a statutory licence scheme, the amount of the remuneration is laid down by statute. In the case of a compulsory licence, the right owner is entitled to negotiate with the user to fix the terms of the use, including the amount of the equitable remuneration. If the parties do not agree, the amount of remuneration is fixed by government authority, often a special government-appointed body or tribunal. As regards the choice between a statutory licence and a

---

[64] P. Goldstein, *Copyright, op. cit.*, s.10.1.

[65] Berne Convention, Art.11bis(2); see also Appendix for developing countries providing for compulsory licensing of reproduction and translation rights.

[66] *ibid.*, Art.13(1).

compulsory licence, the German Federal Supreme Court has suggested that:

> There should be no limitations on copyright which serve merely the financial interests of individual users of works. One must also ensure that a limitation imposed in the public interest does not lead to the unjustified advancement of private commercial interests of users. In this dilemma, it seems appropriate to control merely the author's power to forbid but to leave him with the right to claim an equitable reward for the use of his work.[67]

The compulsory licence for broadcasting and cable distribution was introduced in the Berne Convention in the interest of the public, but there are restrictions placed on it. Such licences apply only in the country which has provided for them; they may not prejudice the authors' moral rights, and fair remuneration must be paid. The rationale for the compulsory licence concerning the right of recording musical works, the composers' so-called mechanical rights, introduced in the Berne Convention as long ago as the Berlin Act in 1908, was also done in the public interest, the aim being to prevent one powerful record company from acquiring the monopoly of recording most of the successful new music. It aimed at promoting competition in what was at that time a fledgling recording industry.

In the field of related rights, many national legislations, including those of France and Germany, as well as the Rome Convention[68] and the WIPO Performances and Phonograms Treaty,[69] provide for non-voluntary licensing of phonograms and recorded performances for broadcasting and communication to the public, the right owners' rights being limited to a right to equitable remuneration for such use. Indeed, in the field of related rights, there are other examples of rights being reduced to mere rights to remuneration, such as the rental rights of performers and producers of phonograms in certain circumstances.[70]

Compulsory licenses aim to strike a fair balance between the conflicting interests of the public in access to works and those of the authors in securing payment for their use. They represent the most

---

[67] 17 B.G.H.Z. 266–278—*Tonband*.
[68] Rome Convention, Art.16.
[69] W.P.P.T., Art.15.
[70] W.P.P.T., Arts 9 and 13; see also Art.14(4) TRIPs Agreement.

practical means of exercising rights in cases where it is difficult or impossible for the user to negotiate with all the right owners involved, for example, in the case of broadcasting or cable distribution of foreign television programmes or phonograms. In these cases, the transaction costs of clearing exclusive rights (identifying the right owners, negotiating with them and implementing any resulting contract) would be too great, and non-voluntary licences provide solutions that promote the public interest in affording maximum access by the user to copyright material.

10–021 A comparatively new form of limitation imposed by statute on the exclusive rights of authors, again designed to facilitate the exercise of such rights and access by the user, is the grant of rights subject to the condition that such rights be exercised through a representative collecting society. This is the solution, for example, adopted by all national laws providing for remuneration to be paid in respect of private copying to authors, producers of phonograms and performers. It is recognised that in this particular case individual collection would be impossible in practice. EU Directives in the field of copyright and related rights have opted for this solution as regards the rights of authors and holders of related rights to equitable remuneration for rental[71] and generally in the case of cable distribution.[72]

The tendency to impose an increasing number of non-voluntary licensing schemes on right owners has its critics. Such licences prevent right owners objecting to the use of their works, the right to authorise or prohibit the use of their works being reduced to a mere right to remuneration, over the amount of which they also have little control. Strowel describes the impact of non-voluntary licensing as the "socialisation" of copyright. "The subjective right of the author is by these means subordinated to a social objective, that of increasing the access of the public to works, as well as to an economic imperative: that of guaranteeing the exploitation of works."[73]

It should also be noted that this socialisation of copyright through non-voluntary licensing in some cases goes so far as to allocate some of the equitable remuneration paid to social purposes. This is the case with remuneration paid for private copying, for example, even in France and Belgium, where a substantial proportion of the proceeds

---

[71] Art.4(3) and (4) of the Rental Right Directive, see paras 13–016 *et seq.*, below.
[72] Art.9 of the Cable and Satellite Directive, see *ibid.*
[73] A. Strowel, "Licences non volontaires et socialisation du droit d'auteur: un danger ou une nécessité?", [1991] *Cahiers de propriété intellectuelle*, at 161.

from the private copying royalty is paid to social funds for the promotion of new talent and live entertainment. That these two countries, bastions of the continental authors' rights approach to copyright, should have taken this direction is surprising. The socialisation of copyright is often seen as a betrayal of the theory that intellectual property rights are based on natural rights as opposed to the public good.[74]

It may be that in the future one of the main arguments for non-voluntary licensing, the transaction costs of clearing exclusive rights with individual right owners, will be countered by technical developments in the digital environment which will facilitate automatic logging and payment for use of works protected by copyright and related rights and, thereby, voluntary licensing. In the 1980s it was possible for Barbara Ringer to assert that "We have reached the point where any new right under the copyright law apparently cannot be exclusive rights. If a new technological development makes new forms of exploitation possible, compulsory licensing seems to offer the only solution."[75] Technological developments, as discussed in more detail below, now show the promise of returning to the right owner the possibility of exercising his exclusive rights personally. Nevertheless, it is evident that, at the international level, non-voluntary licences have become a widely-used device to solve the problem of finding compromises between the interests of right owners and those of the public.

The Private Use Exception and Modern Technology

Traditionally, as we have seen above, most copyright laws have **10–022** permitted reproduction of works for limited and defined purposes, including reproduction for private and educational use. Modern technical developments, the speed and sophistication of which have accelerated continuously over the past 30 years, have put these generally recognised exceptions under strain. When such exceptions were first introduced in national legislation, they were very limited in

---

[74] A. Kerever, "Le Droit d'auteur est-il anachronique?", [1983] *Le Droit d'auteur*, 369. G. Kauffman, "Exposing the Suspicious Foundation of Society's Primacy in Copyright Law: Five Accidents", *op. cit.*, Ch.9, n.7, above, at 417.
[75] B. Ringer, "Copyright in the 1980's", [1976] *Bulletin of the Copyright Society of the USA*, 299.

scope. What the legislator envisaged was the painstaking copying by hand of books, manuscripts and music. The exceptions were justified originally by the fact that there was no technology permitting the duplication of works. Private copying was therefore regarded as a *de minimis* use and as causing no harm to right owners. In the digital environment, the general public now has the means to make perfect copies of works cheaply and easily for private and educational use. As discussed above, under Art.9(2) of the Berne Convention, exceptions to the right to authorise or prohibit the reproduction of works are only permitted in national legislation, "in certain special cases, provided that such reproduction does not conflict with a normal exploitation of the work and does not unreasonably prejudice the legitimate interests of the author".

The exceptions permitted by the Berne Convention and reproduced in many legislations were framed either before the advent of modern reproduction techniques or, at the least, before the use of offset printing, the photocopier and audio and video recording machines became widespread. Over the past 30 years, the availability of these new machines led to two major new uses of works, known respectively as "reprography", as regards the copying of printed matter and "private copying" or "home taping" as regards recording of sound recordings, film and video. These practices are both consequences of technical progress and pose closely related, although not identical, legal problems.[76] The main difference is that private copying is the copying of copyright material for personal use by a private individual in the home, whereas the bulk of photocopying is done by institutions and offices and much of what is copied is non-copyright material. Moreover, while vast numbers of private individuals have audio and video reproduction equipment at home, they still do not yet generally possess photocopying machines for personal use. Thus, while private copying is a problem caused in the main by private individuals, reprography is a problem caused by institutions, and especially educational institutions and public libraries.

In the digital environment these problems are compounded. Text, music and images are reduced to digital data which can be transmitted in digital form at high speed throughout the world to everybody with

---

[76] For more information on these subjects see G. Davies and M.E. Hung, *op. cit.*, on private copying; and T. Neumann, *Urheberrecht und Schulgebrauch*, (Nomos, Baden-Baden, 1994), on reprography and audiovisual copying in schools.

a connection to the internet and can be copied off-line.

In the 1980s and 1990s, it became generally recognised that copying of this kind made possible by modern technology cannot be considered a special case under Art.9(2) of the Berne Convention. Moreover, it does not represent a normal exploitation of the work and does unreasonably prejudice the interests of the author. As a result, copyright laws began slowly to adapt to the new realities by intro-ducing legislation to provide for exceptions to the reproduction right permitting audiovisual private copying and reprography for the per-sonal use of the copier as a corollary to remuneration being paid to right owners with respect to these new uses of their works. These exceptions were introduced in the context of analogue technology and were a response to the impossibility of controlling private copying at the time.

However, digital technology and the world of the internet has put all this in question. The exceptions permitted by national legislation and the Berne Convention are still predicated on national, analogue and mono-media environments. In the circumstances prevailing at the time, the legislator tolerated copying for personal use, partly because it was impossible to prevent but also because it was thought that pro-viding for remuneration to be paid on blank reproduction media and copying equipment would provide sufficient compensation to right owners. **10–023**

Since the early 1990s, the digital revolution has compounded these problems and the world has entered a new communications era, that of the Information Society,[77] made possible by the Global Informa-tion Infrastructure, combining computer, telephone, satellite and cable technologies, which has made the internet world available to all with a computer and a modem. All kinds of works, including multi-media works,[78] recorded in digital form and therefore capable of

---

[77] The House of Lords Select Committee on Science and Technology in its report, *Information Society: Agenda for Action in the UK* has defined the "Information Super-highway" as meaning "a publicly accessible network capable of transferring large amounts of information at high speed between users". The principle feature distin-guishing a superhighway from existing telecommunications networks is that it should be capable of handling the two-way delivery of text, pictures, sound and video (*i.e.* multi-media). HL Paper 77, Session 1995–96, 5th Report, July 1996, para.1.1.

[78] Multi-media works have been defined by the EU as being "combinations of data, text, sound, graphics, animation, still and moving images, stored in digital form and interactively accessible". See Council Decision of May 20, 1996 adopting a multiannual Community programme to stimulate the development of a European multi-media content in the emerging information society (INFO 2000), Art.1.

perfect-quality reproduction, are now distributed on a world-wide scale over the internet.[79]

> As computers plug into the global net and so-called cyberspace, the physical containers in which we are used to seeing information bottled up—like floppy discs and CD Roms—may become obsolete. Once that happens, all products of the information age, from books to films to computer programs, will exist as speeding electrons darting around the world on the computer net. Where do we put the copyright turnstile on the global computer network in order to charge users and copiers?[80]

In recent years, Governments and right owners have been struggling to seek ways to keep pace with these developments and to ensure that the use of copyright works over the internet and other such information systems is monitored and controlled.

In this context, exceptions to copyright protection permitting free copying for private use need to be reassessed and the copyright system needs to evolve to secure adequate reward to right owners for use of their works in these new information systems.

10–024 Indeed, in the digital environment, it may be questioned whether private copying exceptions are any longer valid. As we have discussed, when these exceptions were first introduced, the harm done to right owners was *de minimis* and later on as the phenomenon of home taping of sound and audiovisual recordings grew during the 1970s and 1980s there was also a public policy reluctance on the part of governments to enforce exclusive rights in the private sphere. The home taping exceptions introduced in national legislations in the context of analogue technology as a corollary to royalties being paid on blank

---

[79] "The Internet is a global network of computers linked mainly via the telephone system and the academic, research and commercial computing networks. The Internet is a fledgling superhighway network which is limited by the rate at which the network components can transmit and handle data. The Internet is not a genuine superhighway because it does not offer the basic capability of two-way real-time video transmission and interactivity. It is, however, widely available and highly functional as an information exchange and electronic mail service. The Internet also provides a useful prototype from which a full information superhighway might evolve. Part of that evolution has been the development of a user-friendly interface in the form of the World Wide Web (WWW). The WWW allows access to a global network of computers by millions of people with no formal training in computer technology". *ibid.*, paras 1.8 and 1.9.

[80] J.T. McCarthy, "Intellectual Property—America's Overlooked Export", 28 Intellectual Property L.Rev. (1996) 315.

tape and/or recording equipment in some countries were seen as the only feasible and equitable solution to private copying since the practice could not be controlled. The existing remuneration schemes providing some compensation for right owners remain the only means of tackling analogue home taping but no levy system, however sophisticated, and even assuming such a system were universally in place, could remunerate right owners adequately for digital copying in the world of digital broadcasting and the internet. While electronic distribution systems have opened up new ways of doing business, giving right owners and consumers access to new on-line markets, the new digital media environment has caused the problem of private copying as well as piracy of protected works to escalate in an unprecedented manner.

It is in this context that the music and film industries have been developing copy-protection systems to control the use of their works in the new digital media environment. Technology such as encryption can protect works in this environment and enable them to be delivered safely and conveniently to the consumer.

The new digital world-wide media environment makes it imperative both to encourage e-commerce and to protect rightholders and it can no longer be argued that private copying is a commercially unimportant use of works. Effective technical devices, combined with adequate and uniform protection of technological measures under the copyright law, could in the future provide a solution to the problem of private copying. At present, the technical measures required to achieve this goal are not generally in place and, in Europe, national legislation protecting such measures are only now being put in place in implementation of the relevant provisions of the Information Society Directive.[81] In the future, technical measures could enable right owners to control access to and copying of their works and the proper world-wide implementation of the obligations imposed on Contracting Parties by the WIPO Internet Treaties concerning technical measures and copyright management information should provide a legal framework to enable right owners to exercise that control. These provisions are discussed further in Part III, below.

Nevertheless, many take the view that there is no satisfactory

---

[81] Directive 2001/29/EC of the European Parliament and the Council of May 22, 2001, on the harmonisation of certain aspects of copyright and related rights in the information society, OJ L167/10, June 22, 2001 (**Information Society Directive**).

justification for private copying exceptions in the digital environment. As Ginsburg and Gaubiac have maintained:

> Even in the analogue world, many countries recognised that home taping strained the *de minimis* justification ... The nature of digital copying further undermines that justification. Digital copies are uniquely replicable: not only can one copy be fruitful and multiply, but its quality, copy after copy, remains as good as the original. This feature illustrates the potential anomaly of recognising a private copying exception in the digital world: individual copies can no longer be considered *de minimis*. Private copying in perfect copies does substitute for sales of the work. As such, it runs afoul of international copyright norms...[82]

10–025   Such exceptions also do not promote what they describe as the principle of freedom of creation and expression, that is, Chafee's fifth ideal of promoting independent creation by others. "Private copying for the purpose of consuming the copies, rather than working from them to create a new work, does not share this justification."[83] It can be argued, therefore, that now that new technology can prevent digital home taping, the home taping exceptions introduced at a time when effective enforcement of rights was not possible are no longer appropriate. A return to the principle of the exclusive reproduction right is therefore justified. The copyright system foresees no inherent and inalienable right of the public to make copies for private use.[84] Logically, if and when technical measures become widely used and succeed in preventing private copying, the existing remuneration schemes would become redundant and would be phased out.[85]

Other traditional exceptions, such as those relating to use for educational purposes, also involve conflicts of interest between private interests as represented by right owners, on the one hand, and public interests represented by the State on the other. Again, the State is

---

[82] J. Ginsburg and Y. Gaubiac, "Private Copying in the Digital Environment", in *Intellectual Property and Information Law*, Essays in Honour of Herman Cohen Jehoram, (Kluwer Law International, The Hague, London, Boston, 1998), 149.

[83] *ibid.*, at 150.

[84] U. von Diemar, "Kein Recht auf Privatkopien-Zur Rechtsnatur der gesetzlichen Lizenz zu Gunsten de Privatverfielfältigung", (2002) 7 G.R.U.R. 587.

[85] J. Ginsburg and Y. Gaubiac, "L'avenir de la copie privée numérique en Europe", (2000) *Communication Commerce éléctronique*, Chron.No.1, p.9. See also A. Lucas, Droit d'auteur et numérique, Paris, Litec, 1998, paras 383 *et seq.*

called on to strike a balance between the interests of the copyright owners and those of the public and, in so doing, in the modern world, the State should have regard to technical developments and should not lightly set aside the individual rights of creators.

The new means of reproduction and communication made possible by new technology have given rise to claims—supported by consumer groups—that the general public should be entitled to take full advantage thereof, regardless of the rules of copyright. Kerever has described this argument as follows:

> New communication techniques make it possible for programs to be distributed instantaneously anywhere, and for recorded programs to be appropriated by individuals. The public has the right to benefit fully from these techniques, especially since they are used for the dissemination of information and culture. The legitimate demands of the public—in other words the general interest—are not done justice if each of the many uses of one and the same work is subject to the authorisation of a holder of rights. What makes the obstacle all the more formidable is that the right asserted is exclusive, monopolistic and discretionary, and that each program is made up of several protected works to which a complex web of intertwined rights is applicable....[86]

This is the political challenge facing the law-maker who seeks to maintain the balance between the interests of creators and the disseminators of their works, on the one hand, and the interest of the public in access thereto, on the other. As Stewart points out:

> Even under the Berne Convention, each member country has to decide what the legitimate interests of the author are, whether the prejudice of these interests, which is inevitable, is reasonable or unreasonable, and what amounts to a normal exploitation of the work, which must be safeguarded. Fair dealing must always be a matter of degree.[87]

---

[86] A. Kerever, "Reflections on the Future Development of Copyright", [1983] Copyright 373.
[87] S.M. Stewart, *op. cit.* at 80.

The Exercise of Rights

10–026   Chafee's sixth ideal of copyright is that the legal rules thereof should be convenient to handle. He remarked: "The rules should be certain, readily understood, not unduly complicated, as easy as possible to apply", to facilitate *inter alia* the avoidance of litigation.

> The lawyers who advise authors, publishers, and other business men in drafting contracts and other transactions should be able to ascertain the rights of the parties and protect those rights with assurance. To require officials, judges, and lawyers to work with a statute which is intricate and leaves many important points unsettled is like asking an engineer to do his calculations with a warped and illegible slide-rule.[88]

In some respects, the rules of copyright meet this ideal. According to the Berne Convention, copyright protection is automatic and arises free from all formalities as soon as the work is created. As a matter of domestic law, a country is free to subordinate the existence or exercise of rights to formalities, such as deposit of copies with national libraries, registration, etc., but outside the country of origin the author is fully protected by the Berne Convention.[89] This is obviously of great benefit not only to the right owner but also to the public, since to determine anywhere in the world whether a work is protected is a comparatively simple task.

Some of the exceptions and limitations on exclusive rights referred to above have been adopted by governments in response to the needs, interests and the convenience of the public. It would be clearly burdensome for the writer of an essay to have to clear the copyright in every quotation used. The difficulty of clearing the rights of authors long dead with their successors in title is one practical restraint on increasing terms of protection. Systems of non-voluntary licensing have also been introduced for the sake of convenience in order to facilitate the exercise of rights.

Another extremely important aspect of the administration of copyright, which meets Chafee's ideal of convenience, is the role of

---

[88] Z. Chafee, *op. cit.* at 514.
[89] C. Masouyé, *op. cit.* at 33.

the collecting societies. In fact, regardless of whether non-voluntary licensing systems exist or not, the need to negotiate with the various categories of right owners does not normally present problems to the user because of the existence of representative collecting societies which are well placed to represent their members in negotiations with all potential users of their works.[90]

Collective administration through such societies operates world-wide. **10–027** Although the precise nature, representation and practices of collective licensing bodies vary from country to country, collective administration of copyrights by licensing bodies is standard practice. Such collecting societies are generally recognised as being the best means of protecting the right owners' interests, on the one hand, while facilitating the ease of access of copyright protected works to the consumer, on the other hand. Indeed, given the emergence of secondary mass usage by means of new uses such as reprography, private copying of sound and audiovisual recordings, satellite broadcasting, cable distribution, rental of phonograms and videograms, storage of protected works in databases, and the use of computer technology to digitise and store works in combination with the new distribution and communication technologies mentioned above, the need for collective licensing bodies has become even more acute. It would be idealistic and impracticable to expect owners of exclusive rights to be able to control such exploitation on an individual basis and likewise to force users to negotiate with individual right owners.

Collective administration of copyrights serves two principal purposes:

(i) to enable right owners to enforce and administer their copyrights effectively and cheaply; and

(ii) to provide a service to users by facilitating access to copyright works and making it possible for users to comply with their obligations under the law to obtain licences for the use of copyright works.

There is a general consensus today that such collective administration bodies provide the best available mechanism for licensing and administering copyrights. The convenience offered by such bodies

---

[90] See also G. Davies, "The Public Interest in Collective Administration of Rights", [1989] Copyright 82.

both to the owner and the user of copyright cannot be matched by any other means and, in their absence, in a totally free market, individual users and copyright owners would be at a serious disadvantage in negotiating and subsequently enforcing their rights. Thus, such bodies benefit right owners and users alike and operate in the public interest.

As seen above,[91] the exercise of certain exclusive rights such as rental rights and cable distribution rights, as well as certain rights to remuneration, have been made subject to the condition that they be exercised through a representative collecting society, due to the difficulty or impossibility of exercising them individually. This trend can be seen as a compromise imposed by government in the public interest to promote access to works. Users and other creators, such as, for example, producers of multi-media works and of newspaper databases, have the advantage of being able to address themselves to one entity in order to clear rights. The compromise is less at odds with the principles of copyright than compulsory licences because the exclusive rights are preserved and the collecting society has the possibility to prohibit use, if they are not satisfied by the conditions and remuneration offered.[92] Thus, they have the upper hand in negotiations and can impose conditions as well as secure higher levels of remuneration than they would be likely to get under a compulsory licence where the user has the right to use the work subject to paying equitable remuneration and the right owner is put in a correspondingly weak negotiating position.

10–028 However, collecting societies are currently facing perhaps the greatest test of their history in facing the challenge of monitoring and securing reward for the use of their members' works on the Information Superhighways. Digital technology has the potential to facilitate the administration of rights. It offers scope for identifying, controlling access to, tracing, monitoring and rewarding all uses of works. It provides right owners for the first time with tools to control uses such as private copying. For the collecting societies, "the challenge is both to secure reward for use and also to ensure that securing that reward is

---

[91] See para.10–021, above.

[92] *cf.* P. Noguier, "Le Pillage de l'écrit, photocopies, télécopies et copies différées; la gestion collective obligatoire, une solution juridique", [1994] Légicom No.3, 69; and Y. Kleinke, *Pressedatenbanken und Urheberrecht; Zur urheberrechtlichen Bewertung der Nutzung von Zeitungsartikeln in Pressedatenbanken*, (Cologne, Berlin, Bonn, Munich, Carl Heymanns Verlag, 1998), Ch.6, at 169.

for the users as fast, simple and painless as possible".[93] To that end, the organisations and collecting societies representing the various copyright owners are establishing systems, which take advantage of digital technology to provide for digital identification of all works. Such digital identification is the first step in building an electronic system which will enable the use of copyright materials to be tracked, the users to be identified, recorded and charged in order for appropriate payment to be made for the use made. "The Answer to the Machine is in the Machine."[94]

As the 1995 US NII Report stated, such identification will be critical to the efficient operation and success of the NII.

> Copyright management information will serve as a kind of license plate for a work on the information superhighway, from which a user may obtain important information about the work. The accuracy of such information will be crucial to the ability of consumers to find and make authorised uses of works on the NII. Reliable information will also facilitate efficient licensing and reduce transaction costs for licensable uses of copyright works (both fee-based and royalty-free).[95]

The Report recommended that to provide legislative back-up for such systems, the following should give rise to criminal offences and penalties: the circumvention of copyright protection systems, the providing of false copyright management information, and the removal or alteration of copyright management information.[96]

Meanwhile, an international consensus developed on the need for legislative back-up of the kind recommended by the US NII Report. WIPO took up the challenge of providing a legal framework of **10–029** protection for copyright in the global environment of the internet and the protection of technical devices at a comparatively early stage. The WIPO Copyright Treaty (WCT) and the WIPO Performers and Phonograms Treaty (WPPT) adopted in 1996 (known as *the WIPO*

---

[93] C. Clark, "The Copyright Environment for the Publisher in the Digital World", (International Publishers' Association, March 1996). See also T.C. Vinje, "A Brave New World of Technical Protection Systems: Will there Still be Room for Copyright?" [1996] 8 E.I.P.R. 431.

[94] C. Clark, *op. cit.*, at 20.

[95] N.I.I. Report, see Ch.5, n.33 above, at 235.

[96] *ibid.*, App.1—Proposed Legislation, s.4, paras 1201 and 1202.

Internet Treaties)[97], recognise the importance of the use of technical anti-copying devices and rights management systems.

The Treaties lay down that Contracting Parties should provide adequate legal protection and effective legal remedies against the circumvention of effective technological measures used by right owners to prevent unauthorised use of their works. They also include certain further obligations with respect to the protection of electronic rights management information. For the copy-protection and rights management systems to be effective in the long run in safeguarding the interests of copyright and related right owners, it is to be hoped that the WIPO Internet Treaties will be widely ratified and translated into national laws.[98] In what has become a global media marketplace, only universal legal structures will protect right owners in the future.

The WIPO Treaties are the inspiration for the chapter on the protection of technological measures and rights management information contained in the recently adopted EC Directive on Copyright and Related Rights in the Information Society[99] and also for the Digital Millenium Copyright Act adopted in the United States of America as long ago as 1998.[1]

The digital revolution and the unprecedented scope for new means of distribution underway in the information society has once more altered the balance between copyright owners and users. This is a clear case where the legislator is required to intervene to re-establish the balance and to take proper account in the law of the current technology. In doing so, however, the public interest in the dissemination of and access to works should not be lost sight of. As Vinje reminds us:

> So far, the debate on anti-circumvention legislation ... has occurred in a relative atmosphere of specialists who have special interests. Policy-makers, who no doubt seek a balanced and fair approach, would be wise to reach out and involve a broader circle of those representing the public interest in the current debate ... Even if representatives of the public interest are more difficult to

---

[97] The WIPO Internet Treaties (the WCT and the WPPT) were adopted in December 1996 (for details of the relevant provisions, see below, Part III and the Appendices).

[98] The WCT entered into force on March 6, 2002, and the WPPT on May 20, 2002, following the deposit of 30 instruments of ratification respectively of the Treaties.

[99] See n.81, above.

[1] See Ch.5, n.66, above.

find in the corridors of power in Brussels, Washington and Geneva than those advocating current anti-circumvention proposals, policy-makers have a duty to seek them out and listen to them carefully. In the end, perhaps legislators can devise a law that achieves the laudable purposes behind the existing proposals without threatening the public interest.[2]

The setting of limits to the rights afforded by copyright must be seen as a balancing process between the conflicting interests of the copyright owners and the users, a process which requires adjustment from time to time by the legislature and the courts in the light of new circumstances and methods of exploitation. In making such adjustments the law-maker should have regard to the public interest in seeking solutions which will: "safeguard, in a concern for equity and justice, the interests both of the intellectual creators and those that make lawful use of the works and thus render a fundamental service to both the author and the community at large".[3] **10–030**

In Part IV, we shall take a look *inter alia* at the WIPO Internet Treaties, the EC Information Society Directive and the DMCA to determine how successful the legislators have been in meeting these challenges.

---

[2] T.C. Vinje, *op. cit.*, at 432 and 440.
[3] M. Fabiani, *op. cit.* at 156.

PART IV

THE FUTURE OF COPYRIGHT—OBSTACLES AND PERSPECTIVES

Chapter 11

Introduction

Change is inevitable. In a progressive country change is constant.
Benjamin Disraeli

The purpose of this study is to explore and evaluate the general **11–001**
principles which underlie the subject of copyright. In this Part, let us
discuss the impact that digital technology and recent international
developments are likely to have on the future of copyright and do
some crystal ball gazing to see the direction copyright may be
expected to take in the next few years. To what extent are the six
ideals of Chafee likely to be realised and the public interest in the
copyright system respected?

As seen above, Chafee's first three ideals require States to pursue a
policy of regular review of copyright laws to respond to the agenda set
by new technical developments and their impact on copyright.
National copyright laws and the relevant international conventions
must be periodically updated and adapted to guarantee the further
promotion of creativity and to safeguard investment. In the past, the
Berne Convention was revised at regular intervals of 20 years or so.
Political difficulties foreseen in reaching a consensus on revision have
precluded any further revision since the adoption of the Paris Act of
the Berne Convention in 1971[1]; similar difficulties stand in the way of
a revision of the 1961 Rome Convention on related rights.[2] This
paralysis of political will has been particularly damaging because the

---

[1] According to Art.27, Berne Convention, unanimity is required for a revision of the
Convention.
[2] Under Art.29, Rome Convention, a two-thirds majority of the States attending a
revision Conference is required, providing this majority includes two-thirds of the
States at the time party to the Rome Convention.

25-year period between the adoption of the Paris Act of the Berne Convention in 1971 and the adoption of the WIPO Internet Treaties in 1996 saw an unprecedented increase in the economic importance of copyright and a proliferation of technological developments affecting it. The 1996 WIPO Internet Treaties, as well as the TRIPs Agreement, have filled the gap, introducing new international rules and clarifying the interpretation of certain existing rules. The WIPO Internet Treaties are mainly concerned with the problems of the digital environment but also, like the TRIPs Agreement, set new standards on issues such as the right of distribution, the rental right, the right of communication to the public and enforcement of rights. Some outstanding issues are clarified: the protection of computer programs as literary works under the Berne Convention is confirmed, as is protection for those databases which, by reason of the selection or arrangement of their contents, constitute intellectual creations.

Chafee's three ideals which tend to limit protection and which are discussed in Chapter 10 must also be respected in new legislation. As we have seen, according to these ideals, protection should not extend substantially beyond the purposes of protection; copyright should not stifle independent creation by others; and the legal rules governing copyright should be convenient to handle. The WIPO Internet Treaties address these issues by providing for limitations and exceptions to the rights granted by the Treaties and the Berne Convention, subject to the three-step test of the Berne Convention, and by imposing on Contracting States certain obligations concerning rights management information.

These matters are discussed in Chapter 12 in relation to the impact of digital technology on copyright and the solutions found to date to the problems posed. We will also consider in Chapter 13 the extent to which global solutions are being found to meet Chafee's third ideal of international protection by the adoption of harmonised international standards to strengthen copyright for the benefit of right owners and the public.

Chapter 12

The Impact of Digital Technology on Copyright

What is remarkable in the history of copyright is its resilience ...
There seems no insuperable difficulty in using the constructs of
copyright to protect material which is created and stored in digital
form.[1]

William R. Cornish

Legal Frameworks Required for Protection

Digital technology has transformed the marketplace for copyright-
protected works. It has opened up new ways of doing business and
given right owners and consumers access to new on-line markets via
digital networks. Text, music and images are reduced to digital data
which can be transmitted in digital form at high speed throughout the
world to everybody with a connection to the internet. This is posing
new challenges in relation to enforcement of rights, since the internet
also increases the ease with which intellectual property rights in works
in digital form can be infringed.[2] This means that two perennial
problems for right owners, commercial piracy and copying for private
use, have become ever more difficult to control. At the same time,

12–001

---

[1] W.R. Cornish, *Intellectual Property*, 4th. ed., (Sweet and Maxwell, London, 1999),
paras 13–61 and 13–62.
[2] On this subject generally, see T. Dreier, "Copyright Law and Digital Exploitation
of Works—The Current Copyright Landscape in the Age of the Internet and Multi-
media", 1997, available online at *www.ipauie.org/copyright/copyright_pub/dreier.html*
(English translation of original German text: *Urheberrecht im Zeitalter von Internet und
Multi-media*, Friedrich-Ebert-Stiftung, Bonn 1997.)

digital technology offers the promise of enabling right owners to control the use of their protected material and access thereto by technical means.

The internet is already a major and growing conduit for the retail trade in traditional copyright products.[3] On-line music services offering music for downloading to personal computer hard discs have proliferated in the past five years, most of them being unauthorised. The best known is the notorious Napster service which was shut down following litigation in the United States of America[4] and is now planning a legitimate on-line music service, having been taken over by Bertelsmann. The major labels of the music and film industries are all grappling with the market potential of the internet, engaging in making content available on-line and trying to solve problems of controlling access to music and film in digital form and to find mechanisms for getting paid for it. Sales of digital content, such as e-books, music and film, for downloading from the internet are forecast to grow sharply.[5] Much of the material being published and traded on the internet relies very strongly on copyright.

Intellectual property rights apply on the internet but the difficulty is to make them enforceable. Digital technology has the potential to greatly facilitate enforcement. However, effective enforcement pre-supposes that right owners are given the legal framework necessary to enable them to control these new markets. But it has been widely recognised that rights alone will not solve the enforcement difficulties associated with controlling rights in cyberspace. The second requirement for successfully controlling such rights is for right owners to manage their product by means of secure technical protection measures to control access to their works, combined with digital rights management systems (DRM systems) to provide for remuneration when copying is permitted.[6]

---

[3] See M. Symonds, "The dot.com imperative", *The World in 2000*, (The Economist Group, London, 1999), p.104.

[4] *A and M Records v Napster Inc.*, 239 F.3d 1004 (9th Cir. 2001).

[5] The on-line music market alone is forecast to grow to US$5.5 billion by 2006, up from US$900 million in 2001. (Jupiter Research Report "Music Forecast 2001", *www.jmm.com*).

[6] J. Reinbothe, "Digital Rights Management: The Legal Framework", (paper delivered at the Fordham University School of Law 10th Annual Conference on International Intellectual Property Law and Policy, New York, April 4 & 5, 2002). See also B. Bechthold, "From Copyright to Information Law—Implications of Digital Rights Management", in *Security and privacy in digital rights management*, (T. Sander, ed.), (Berlin, Heidelberg, Springer), p.213.

What is needed is secure systems such as encryption and water-marking which will enable right owners to keep control over access to their works and to track use thereof. In this area, much work is being done in developing systems to identify works by providing them with a kind of digital identity card, providing data concerning the content of the work, the right owners, permitted uses, conditions of use, etc. Alternatively, the data may connect the user automatically to a central registry run by, for example, a collecting society representing the right owners. Such identification data, embodied in the original digital version of the work, provide the right owner new opportunities to deliver digital files of copyright subject-matter over the internet, to trace and monitor uses thereof and to receive payment for that delivery and to protect the file from any unauthorised distribution. The availability of such systems also benefits users, for whom legit-imate access to the works is facilitated; moreover, it also permits individual licensing of protected material, based on actual use. So far, however, progress seems patchy and unco-ordinated.[7]

---

[7] On the development of such systems, see *inter alia*. C. Clark, "The Answer to the Machine is in the Machine", in *The Future of Copyright in a Digital Environment*, (B. Hugenholtz, ed.) (The Hague, Kluwer, 1996), p.139; Proceedings of the ALAI Study Days, *Copyright in Cyberspace*, (M. Dellebeke, ed.), (Otto Cramwinckel, Amsterdam, 1997); A. Strowel and S. Dusollier, "La protection légale des systèmes techniques", in *WIPO Workshop on Implementation Issues of the WIPO Copyright Treaty (WCI) and the WIPO Performances and Phonograms Treaty (WPPT)*, WIPO doc.WCT-WPPT/IMP/2; A. Strowel and J.-P. Triaille, *Le droit d'auteur, du logiciel au multimédia*, (Bruylant, Brussels, 1997), para.588 *et seq.*; S. Dusollier, "Electrifying the Fence: The Legal Pro-tection of Technological Measures for Protecting Copyright", [1999] E.I.P.R. 285; A. Thomas, "DVD Encryption-DeCSS", [2000] ENT.L.R. 135; "MP3 Wars: The Battle for Copyright in Cyberspace", [2000] ENT.L.R. 165; G. Davies:"Technical Devices as a Solution to Private Copying", in I.A. Stamatoudi and P.L.C. Torremans, *Copyright in the New Digital Environment*, (Sweet and Maxwell, London, 2000), p.163; G. Davies, "Copyright in the Information Society-Technical Devices to Control Private Copy-ing", in P. Ganea, C. Heath and G. Schricker (eds) Urheberrecht-Gestern-Heute-Morgen, *Festschrift für Adolf Dietzzum 65. Geburtstag*, (Verlag C.H. Beck, Munich, 2001), p.307; D.S. Marks & B.H. Turnbull, "Technical Protection Measures: The Intersection of Technology, Law and Commercial Licences", [2000] E.I.P.R., 198; S. Lai, "Digital Copyright and Watermarking", [1999] E.I.P.R., 171. Imprimatur Report on "Watermarking Technology for Copyright Protection: General Requirements and Interoperability, IMP/14062/A, May 18, 1998; P. Wand, "Technische Identifizier-ungs- und Schutzsysteme—Urheber- und Wettbewerbsrecht", in *Internet- und Multi-mediarecht* (Cyberlaw), (M. Lehmann, ed.), (Schöpfer-Poeschel Verlag, Stuttgart, 1997); A. Lucas, *Droit d'auteur et numérique*, (Paris, Litec, 1998), para.510; A. Latreille, "La protection des dispositifs techniques, Entre suspicion et sacralisation", in (2002) 2 *Propriétés intellectuelles* 35. R. Owens, "Digital Rights Management (DRM)—A Look Ahead", (paper delivered at Fordham University School of Law Ninth Annual Con-ference on International Intellectual Property Law and Policy, April 19–20, 2001).

12–002 The situation is constantly changing with new encryption techniques being developed, tried out, and then implemented or abandoned, if too easily hacked. The search is on for secure, universally applicable and compatible systems for application to all kinds of copyright subject-matter and which can become international standards under the auspices of the International Standards Organisation (ISO).

However, such technical measures are vulnerable to circumvention or removal (so-called "hacking") and it is clear that without harmonised legislation in place to encourage and back up the use of such systems and to enforce them by preventing their circumvention, it will be extremely difficult to implement such systems successfully. This means that without adequate protection it will be impossible to normally exploit works in the new media and the legitimate interests of right owners will be unreasonably prejudiced.[8]

At the same time, the use of technical protection measures also raises questions in the copyright context. What price the public interest, if copyright works cannot be copied in any circumstances so that the usual exceptions and limitations of the copyright law cannot be made use of? Moreover, works in the public domain could be protected indefinitely by such means. Secure technical protection measures could give copyright owners complete control of the market for their works, regardless of the law on limitations of copyright and duration. Strowel has suggested that such systems would become a means of controlling access and obtaining payment for use not so much of the embodiment of the expression of the work, as is the case with copyright, but of the information and ideas contained therein. Thus information would be unavailable to those unwilling to accept the conditions of access to the work, contrary to the public interest and the important rationale of copyright to encourage publication so as to make learning and information available to the public.[9]

In response, it may be argued that technical protection measures will only apply in the digital environment, and, in particular, to works made available in digital form on-line over the internet. The public will still be able to have access to works on paper, to make analogue copies of sound and audiovisual recordings and so on. Limitations on protection aim at securing the public interest in making information available to the public but do not guarantee the public the possibility

---

[8] *cf.* Art.9(2), Berne Convention.
[9] A. Strowel and J.P. Triaille, *op. cit.*, para.592

of making private copies of the highest possible quality. As discussed in Chapter 5, above, the U.S. Court of Appeals recently upheld the copyright owner's right to use encryption codes to bar access to copyrighted materials and found that fair use does not guarantee access to such materials in order to copy it by the optimum method or in the identical format.[10] Moreover, it must be stressed that the rights in question are for the most part exclusive rights to authorise or prohibit use and right owners are entitled to keep digital marketing of such rights fully under their control and to license them on their own terms.

The Solutions Found—the New Right of Access

The WIPO Internet Treaties 1996

As we have seen, the WIPO Internet Treaties sought solutions to these problems at a comparatively early stage and were designed to encourage the development of technical protection devices and rights management systems. Adopted in 1996, they entered into force in early 2002.[11] According to the Preambles to both Treaties, they address the need to introduce new international rules and clarify the interpretation of certain existing rules in order to provide adequate solutions to the questions raised by new economic, social, cultural and technological developments. The Preambles of both Treaties also recognise the need to maintain a balance between the rights of copyright and related rights owners and the larger public interest, referring, in particular, to education, research and access to informa-

12–003

---

[10] *Universal Studios, Inc., v Corley*, 273 F.3d 429 (2d. Cir. 2001). See Ch.5, para.5–034 and n.20, above.

[11] The WCT entered into force on March 6, 2002 and the WPPT on May 20, 2002, following ratification respectively by the required 30 Member States. *Cf.* Appendices 5 and 6, below. Commentaries on the Treaties include: J. Reinbothe and S. von Lewinski, *The WIPO Treaties 1996*, (Butterworths, London, 2002); T. C. Vinje, "The New WIPO Copyright Treaty: A Happy Result in Geneva", [1997] E.I.P.R., 230; M. Fabiani, "The Geneva Diplomatic Conference on Copyright and the Rights of Performers and Phonogram Producers", [1997] ENT.L.R. 98; V.A. Espinel, "Harmony on the Internet: The WIPO Performances and Phonograms Treaty and United Kingdom Copyright Law", [1998] ENT.L.R. 21; J.-L. Goutal, "The WIPO Treaty of 20 December 1996 and the French Conception of Author's Rights", 187 R.I.D.A. 66 (2001); M. Ficsor, *The Law of Copyright and the Internet*, (Oxford University Press, Oxford, 2002).

tion. As regards the WCT, it is important to note that it is a special agreement within the meaning of Art.20 of the Berne Convention and Contracting Parties must comply with all the substantive law provisions of that Convention,[12] moral rights included. For its part, the WPPT does not derogate from existing obligations under the Rome Convention.[13]

The provisions of these Treaties of particular relevance to the digital environment are those relating to the right to control communication to the public of copyright works and other subject-matter, as well as the obligations concerning technical protection measures and rights management systems. It should also be noted that, while the WCT has no specific provision concerning the reproduction right (merely referring back to the Berne Convention), the Agreed Statement concerning Art.1(4) of the Treaty lays down that the reproduction right, as set out in Art.9 of the Berne Convention, and the exceptions permitted thereunder, fully apply in the digital environment, in particular to the use of works in digital form. It also specifies that the storage of a protected work in digital form in an electronic medium constitutes a reproduction within the meaning of Art.9 of the Berne Convention. A similar clarification is made with respect to performances and phonograms in digital form in an agreed statement on the WPPT, which also guarantees the reproduction rights of performers and producers.[14]

The right of communication guaranteed to authors under the WCT includes the right to make their works available to the public in such a way that members of the public may access these works from a place and at a time individually chosen by them.[15] This right, dubbed the "access right", gives authors the exclusive right to control the user's access to their works in the context of interactive on-line systems, including pay-TV systems and the internet. Equivalent rights are

---

[12] WCT, Art.(1) and (4); the substantive provisions of the Berne Convention are contained in Arts 1–21 and the Appendix.

[13] WPPT, Art.1(1).

[14] Agreed Statement concerning Art.1(4) WCT; Agreed Statement concerning Arts 7,11 (reproduction rights of performers and producers) and 16 (limitations and exceptions), WPPT. It should be noted that unanimous agreement could not be reached on the issues dealt with in the Agreed Statements on various articles of the two Treaties. For this reason, the provisions do not appear in the Treaties themselves and are not binding on the Contracting Parties, being only of interpretative value, representing as they do the majority view, as opposed to a unanimous view.

[15] Art.8 WCT.

granted under the WPPT to performers in respect of their fixed performances[16] and producers of phonograms in respect of their phonograms.[17] The access right is generally considered to have been implicit in the reproduction, communication on the public and distribution rights under copyright, so that these provisions may be regarded as clarifying the existing situation.[18]

These provisions of the WIPO Internet Treaties, once implemented **12–004** in national legislation, should provide copyright owners with the legal framework to control access to their works on the internet by means of encryption technology linked to click-on contractual licensing of copyright material. The copyright industries have continued to seek technical means of protecting their interests by way of access controls, anti-copying devices and the development of electronic rights management information systems.

The WIPO Internet Treaties have encouraged these developments since they provide international recognition of the right to use such technical devices. The Contracting Parties undertake to provide adequate legal protection and effective legal remedies against the circumvention of effective technical measures used by right owners to prevent unauthorised use of their works.[19] As regards electronic rights management information, the Contracting Parties must provide adequate and effective legal remedies against the following: acts which may induce, enable, facilitate or conceal an infringement of any right protected under the Treaties or the Berne Convention, both exclusive rights and rights of remuneration, and including such acts as the removal or alteration of electronic rights management information without authority; the distribution, importation for distribution, broadcast or communication to the public, without authority, of works or copies of works knowing that electronic rights management information has been removed or altered without authority.[20]

Limitations and exceptions under the WIPO Internet Treaties

As far as limitations and exceptions are concerned, the WCT and **12–005**

---

[16] Art.10 WPPT.
[17] Art.14 WPPT.
[18] See, however, T. Heide, "Copyright in the E.U. and United States: What 'Access Right'?" [2001] E.I.P.R., 469.
[19] WIPO Copyright Treaty, Art.11; WIPO Performances and Phonograms Treaty, Art.18.
[20] *ibid.*, Arts 12 and 20, respectively.

WPPT permit the same limitations and exceptions as those permitted by the Berne and Rome Conventions, but specifically makes all these, not only the exceptions to the reproduction right, subject to the three-step test of the Berne Convention.[21] As already noted, the preambles to both Conventions refer to the need to maintain a balance between rights holders and the larger public interest.[22] Agreed Statements on these provisions of the WCT and WPPT make it clear that Contracting Parties may carry forward and appropriately extend into the digital environment limitations and exceptions in their national laws under the Berne and Rome Conventions. Similarly, these provisions should be understood to permit Contracting Parties to devise new exceptions and limitations that are appropriate in the digital network environment.[23] Both Treaties are silent on the specific subject of private use. As noted above, reconciling the use of technical measures to control access to works in the digital environment with the full application of present limitations and exceptions as well as devising new ones appropriate to the digital environment may prove difficult and conflict with the aim of providing right owners with the right to control reproduction and communication to the public in the digital environment. There is a real ambiguity and conflict here which is reflected in the EU Information Society Directive.[24]

For the copy-protection and rights management systems to be effective in the long run in safeguarding the interests of copyright and related right owners, it is to be hoped that the WIPO Internet Treaties will be widely ratified and translated into well-thought-through national laws. In what has become a global media marketplace, only universal legal structures will protect right owners in the future.

In September 1999, WIPO put forward a Digital Agenda addressing abuses of intellectual property rights on the internet and specifically calling on its Member States to examine the feasibility of creating agreed procedures and forms for world-wide licensing of intellectual property rights in digital form. It is seen to be in the interests of both right owners and users seeking convenient access to digital works that a world-wide electronic rights clearance system be established. WIPO also urged further coordination and implementa-

---

[21] WCT, Art.10; WPPT, Art.16.; see Ch.10, above.
[22] WCT, Preamble, para.5; WPPT, Preamble, para.4.
[23] Agreed Statement Concerning Art.10 of the WCT; Agreed Statement Concerning Art.16 of the WPPT.
[24] See below.

tion of global systems promoting the interoperability and inter-connection of electronic copyright management systems and the online administration of intellectual property disputes.[25]

EC Directive on Copyright and Related Rights in the Information Society 2001

The provisions of the WIPO Internet Treaties described above are the inspiration for the parallel provisions contained in the Information Society Directive adopted by the EU in 2001.[26] As far as the repro-duction right is concerned, the Directive goes further, specifically providing for an exclusive right to authorise or prohibit direct or indirect, temporary or permanent reproduction by any means and in any form, in whole or in part, for the various beneficiaries of their protected works and other subject-matter. Other provisions include the access right provided for authors and other right owners, (also defined as the right of making available to the public in such a way that members of the public may access them from a place and at a time individually chosen by them,[27]) and the chapters on the protection of technological measures and rights management information.[28] According to the latter, Member States are to be obliged to provide adequate legal protection against the circumvention without authority of any effective technological measures designed to protect any copyright or any rights related to copyright, which the person con-cerned carries out in the knowledge, or with reasonable grounds to know, that he or she pursues that objective.[29] Adequate legal pro-tection is also to be provided against any activities, including the manufacture, import, distribution, sale, rental, advertisement for sale or rental, or possession for commercial purposes of devices, products or components or the provision of services, which are promoted, advertised or marketed for the purpose of circumvention of, or have only a limited commercially significant purpose or use other than to circumvent, or are primarily designed, produced, adapted or per-

12–006

---

[25] WIPO Magazine, September 1999, p.4.
[26] Directive 2001/29/EC of the European Parliament and of the Council of May 22, 2001 on the harmonisation of certain aspects of copyright and related rights in the information society, OJ L167/10, 22.6.2001. *Cf.* Appendix 7, below.
[27] Directive, Art.3.
[28] Directive, Ch.III, Arts 6 and 7.
[29] Directive, Art.6(1).

formed for the purpose of enabling or facilitating the circumvention of, any effective technological measures designed to protect any copyright or related right.[30]

Technological measures are defined as meaning any technology, device or component that, in the normal course of its operation, is designed to prevent or restrict acts, in respect of works of other subject-matter, which are not authorised by the rightholder of any copyright or any right related to copyright as provided for by law. Such measures are to be deemed "effective" where the use of a protected work or other subject-matter is controlled by the right holders through application of an access control or protection process, such as encryption, scrambling or other transformation of the work or other subject-matter or a copy control mechanism, which achieves the protection objective.[31]

As regards rights-management information, Member States are obliged to provide for adequate legal protection against any person knowingly performing without authority any of the following acts: the removal or alteration of any electronic rights-management information; the distribution, importation for distribution, broadcasting, communication or making available to the public of works or other protected subject-matter from which electronic rights-management information has been removed or altered without authority, if such person knows or has reasonable grounds to know, that by so doing he is inducing, enabling, facilitating or concealing an infringement of any copyright or any rights related to copyright as provided by law.[32] The expression "rights-management information" is defined as meaning any information provided by right holders which identifies the work or other protected subject-matter, the author or other right holder, or information about the terms and conditions of use of the work or other subject-matter, and any numbers or codes that represent such information.[33]

These provisions are to be backed up by Member States with sanctions and remedies in respect of the rights and obligations set out in the Directive. The sanctions are to be effective, proportionate and dissuasive.[34] Among the remedies to be provided must be an action

---

[30] *ibid.*, Art.6(2).
[31] *ibid.*, Art.6(3)
[32] *ibid.*, Art.7(1).
[33] *ibid.*, Art.7(2).
[34] *ibid.*, Art.8(1).

for damages, the possibility to apply for an injunction and, where appropriate, the seizure of infringing material as well as of circumvention devices, products or components.[35]

Member States are obliged to introduce the legislation necessary to comply with the proposed Directive by December 22, 2002.[36] It is likely that this time table will slip somewhat in view of the complexity of the required national legislation.[37]

12–007

These provisions of the Directive, backed by the corresponding provisions of the WIPO Internet Treaties already referred to, give the right owners every incentive to develop technical measures for the protection of their works. Such measures could enable right owners to monitor the use of their works and ensure that remuneration is paid for all the new forms of exploitation made possible for the communication to the public of works and other protected subject-matter in the new global information system. They have also the potential advantage of bringing the problem of private copying under control.

The question remains whether the interested parties are ready and able to take advantage of the new legal framework being put at their disposal.

As discussed above,[38] work is underway on the development of a number of copyright protection systems and digital rights management systems in different industries and in various parts of the world. No universally applicable, general system of the kind called for by WIPO either of technical copyright protection or of rights management appears to be under discussion. A number of copyright protection schemes are already operational and many more are being developed. The various industries involved, principally the music and film industries, are also working on rights management systems.

Limitations and exceptions under the Information Society Directive

There is one area, however, in which the Information Society **12–008**

---

[35] *ibid.*, Art.8(2).

[36] *ibid.*, Art.13(1).

[37] For example, by June 30, 2002, the UK Patent Office had not commenced public consultation on the subject (see *www.patentgov.uk*, "Update on UK Implementation", June 7, 2002). A Consultation Paper on UK Implementation of the EC Directive on the harmonisation of certain aspects of copyright and related rights in the information society was published by the UK Patent Office on August 7, 2002, with a request for observations by October 31, 2002 (see Notice "The Copyright Directive (2001/29/EC)—UK Implementation" dated August 7, 2002.)

[38] See para.12–001 and n.7, above.

Directive would appear to have fallen short of Chafee's ideals. It permits so many exceptions, including private use, that it does not respect Chafee's first two ideals, complete coverage and single monopoly, or his ideas tending towards limitations on protection. It does not permit either full control of the exploitation of works or establish clear rules as regards exceptions to protection.

The exceptions and limitations to the reproduction right and the communication to the public right, including interactive making available to the public, aim at harmonisation in the light of the new electronic and digital environment. According to the Recitals to the Directive, these provisions are required to avoid divergent interpretations in Member States and the risk of obstacles to trade within the Community, as well as to safeguard a fair balance of rights between right holders themselves and between right holders and users of protected subject-matter.[39] The aim is also to promote learning and culture by protecting works and other subject-matter, while permitting exceptions or limitations in the public interest for the purpose of education and teaching.[40] However, the result so far as exceptions are concerned neither achieves its aim of harmonisation nor produces any legal certainty; nor is the public interest well served. It establishes only one mandatory exception but permits no less than 20 optional exceptions, thus failing to achieve any degree of harmonisation. Hugenholtz greeted the provisions of the Directive on this point with the strongest criticism:

> What makes the Directive a total failure, in terms of harmonisation, is that the exemptions allowed under Article 5 are optional, not mandatory [with one exception]. Member States are not obliged to implement the entire list, but may pick and choose at will. It is expected that most Member States will prefer to keep intact their national laws as much as possible. At best, some countries will add one or two exemptions from the list, now bearing the EC's seal of approval. So much for approximation!
>
> Of course, the whole idea of drawing up a finite set of limitations was ill-conceived in the first place. The last thing the information industry needs in these dynamic times is rigid rules that are cast in concrete for the years to come. How can a legis-

---

[39] Recital 31.
[40] Recital 14.

lature in its right mind even contemplate an exhaustive list of limitations, many of which are drafted in inflexible technology-specific language, when the internet produces new business models and novel uses almost each day?[41]

The Directive contains, first, a mandatory exception with respect to temporary acts of reproduction, which are transient or incidental and an integral and essential part of a technological process and whose sole purpose is to enable a transmission in a network between third parties by an intermediary or a lawful use of a work which has no economic significance.[42] This exception includes acts which enable browsing as well as acts of caching.[43] Secondly, the Directive provides for an exhaustive, closed list of permitted exceptions and limitations to the reproduction right and the right of communication to the public. These exceptions are optional and Member States will be free to keep or introduce them at national level or not to do so; however, no further exceptions will be permitted, except in certain cases of minor importance limited to existing national exceptions and analogue uses.[44] Thus, if a need for a new exception arises, the Directive will have to be revised. It is questionable whether this last limitation is compatible with the Agreed Statements concerning the WIPO Internet Treaties. These specifically provide, as seen above, that Contracting Parties are permitted to devise new exceptions and limitations that are appropriate in the digital networked environment.[45]

All the exceptions of the Directive are subject to the three-step test of the Berne Convention. The list of exceptions represents, in practice, all the specific exceptions presently to be found in the copyright laws of the Member States and also those of the international copyright and related rights conventions. These include standard exceptions concerning, for example, use for teaching or scientific research, use by persons with disabilities and the use of quotations for the

---

[41] B. Hugenholtz, "Why the Copyright Directive is Unimportant, and Possibly Invalid", [2000] E.I.P.R. 499. See also T.C. Vinje, "Should we Begin Digging Copyright's Grave", [2000] E.I.P.R. 551; G. P. Cornish, "Libraries and the Harmonisation of Copyright", [1998] E.I.P.R. 241.

[42] Directive, Art.5(1).

[43] Recital 33.

[44] Directive, Art.5(3)(o).

[45] See para.12–005, above.

purpose of criticism or review etc.[46] The exceptions include some common to many national laws, such as, for example, religious use, incidental use and use for the purpose of caricature, parody or pastiche, as well as some more unusual exceptions, peculiar to particular Member States.[47] These include, for example, use of works, such as works of architecture or sculpture, made to be located permanently in public places[48] and use for the purpose of advertising the public exhibition or sale of artistic works.[49]

12–009 Member States may also provide for exceptions or limitations as regards reprography[50] and copying for private use, provided that fair compensation is paid to the right owners.[51] These latter exceptions are again not mandatory. However, the Directive does not impose harmonisation of remuneration schemes. As regards reprography, the existing remuneration schemes, where they exist, are not considered to create major barriers to the internal market, and are permitted to continue. As regards private copying, the Directive makes no distinction between analogue and digital technology. However, fair compensation is to be paid for private copying when it is permitted and Member States are free to introduce or continue national remuneration schemes to compensate for the prejudice to right holders. A Recital acknowledges that differences between those remuneration schemes affect the functioning of the internal market but asserts that, with regard to analogue private reproduction, those differences should not have a significant impact on the development of the information society. By contrast, digital private copying is recognised in the Recital as likely to be more widespread and to have a greater economic impact. Fair compensation paid for private copying is to take account of the application or non-application of technological protection measures. In certain cases where the prejudice to the right holder would be minimal, no obligation for payment may arise.[52] These latter provisions are presumably aimed at encouraging the phase-out of remuneration schemes when and if technical protection means become available to bring private copying

---

[46] *Directive*, Art.5(3)(a), (b), (d).

[47] *ibid.*, Art.5(3)(g), (i), (k).

[48] *ibid.*, Art.5(3)(h), *cf.* s.59, German Copyright Act 1965 (as amended to 1998).

[49] *ibid.*, Art.5(3)(j); *cf.* French Code on Intellectual Property, Art.L122–5(3) (d).

[50] Except in the case of sheet music, the paper reproduction of which remains prohibited, Directive, Art.5(2)(a).

[51] *ibid.*, Art.5(2)(b).

[52] Recital 35.

under control, but do not amount to a specific requirement to do so.[53]

More ambiguous provisions follow. Notwithstanding the legal protection of technological measures apparently guaranteed by the Directive, the normal operation of electronic equipment and its technological development is not to be prevented.[54] Moreover, the legal protection of such measures is to apply without prejudice to public policy, as reflected by the provisions of the Directive concerning exceptions and limitations. Thus, it is provided that, in the absence of voluntary measures taken by rightholders, including agreements between rightholders and other parties concerned, Member States **shall** take appropriate measures to ensure that rightholders make available to beneficiaries of certain exceptions or limitations the means of benefiting from that exception or limitation, either by "modifying an implemented technical measure or by other means". This applies *inter alia* to reprography, non-commercial reproduction by libraries, the making of ephemeral recordings by broadcasting organisations and non-commercial reproductions of broadcasts in hospitals and prisons. In this respect, an obligation is imposed on Member States to take such measures.[55]

In the case of private copying, the Directive is more cautious. Voluntary measures to facilitate such copying are to be promoted by Member States but, in their absence, Member States **may** take measures to enable beneficiaries of a private use exception to take advantage thereof but they are not obliged to do so. At the same time, it is also stipulated that rightholders are not to be prevented from using technological measures in order to control the number of reproductions made.[56] *A contrario* this presumably means that they cannot use such measures to prevent copying altogether.

Finally, it is recognised that the protection of technological measures should ensure a secure environment for the provision of interactive on-demand services. Thus, it is made clear that the provisions

---

[53] The European Commission has indicated that it considers proper use of DRMs would lead to phasing down or out of levies for private copying in the context of a proper application of the framework laid down by the Directive; *cf.* J. Samnadda, "Technical Measures, Private Copying and Levies: Perspectives on Implementation", (paper delivered at the Fordham University School of Law 10th Annual Conference on International Intellectual Property Law and Policy, New York, April 4 and 5, 2002).

[54] Recital 48.

[55] Art.6(4), para.1 and Recital 51.

[56] *ibid.*, para.2 and Recital 52.

enabling Member States to take measures to give beneficiaries of exceptions access to works do not apply to works or other subject-matter made available to the public in the on-line context on agreed contractual terms in such a way that members of the public may access them from a place and at a time individually chosen by them.[57]

12–010　The apparent guarantee in the Directive that exceptions permitting private copying should not inhibit the use of technological measures or their enforcement against circumvention is welcome.[58] However, it is open to doubt whether the legal protection of technological measures prevails over the exceptions permitted under the proposed Directive or not. Moreover, Member States are to be free to set their own rules on this issue; this will inevitably lead to the various industries involved being obliged to adapt their protection systems to comply with various national exceptions and differing definitions of what private copying is and how much should be allowed. The Directive is disappointing in this respect and has not provided any solution, thus giving rise to considerable criticism. It is also surprising in view of the fact that the Directives concerning computer programs and databases have both taken a stronger line. Private copying of computer programs is not allowed except to make a single back-up copy and such copying is not allowed at all in respect of electronic databases, private copying being restricted to non-electronic databases.[59] As Lucas has pointed out, it is paradoxical to treat, for example, musical and audiovisual works less favourably than databases.[60]

The provisions of the Directive seeking to reconcile the interests of right owners and their use of technical protection measures with the interests of users wishing to benefit from exceptions are ambiguous and confusing. What voluntary measures are envisaged? It is hard to see how technical measures could be adapted to allow copying in certain circumstances and not in others. "How will a rights management system know when a copy (whatever that term means electronically) is required for "fair" purposes and when not? On the other hand, to permit the circumventing of systems to achieve "fair"

---

[57] *ibid.*, para.5.

[58] *ibid.*, Recital 39, last sentence: "Such exceptions or limitations should not inhibit the use of technological measures or their enforcement against circumvention".

[59] Computer Programs Directive, Art.5.2 and Databases Directive, Arts 6(2) (a) and 9(a).

[60] A. Lucas, *Droit d'auteur et numérique, op. cit.*, n.7, above, para.391.

purposes will mean that such mechanisms will also be available for "unfair" purposes".[61] Or as Hugenholtz suggests "are Member States effectively obliged to prohibit the use of technological protection schemes if public access to works is impaired on a serious scale?"

One is left with the feeling that it would have been preferable to leave the matter of exceptions to the Berne Convention and national legislation. As Vinje points out:

> In short, it is unfortunate that the E.U. institutions have not made a more ambitious attempt to ensure the harmonised adoption by Member States of at least certain core copyright exceptions. Ensuring the existence of appropriate limits and exceptions to copyright is vital not only to achieving a Single Market in copyright-protected materials, it is essential to ensuring an appropriate balance in the law. Setting copyright limits and exceptions is crucial not only to ensure public access to information and freedom of expression and debate, but also to enable and encourage future creativity. Even the greatest of authors stand on the shoulders of those who have gone before them, and authorship will suffer if copyright control is extended too far.[62]

The US Approach

The United States of America led the field in its support for technical **12–011** solutions to copyright problems in the digital environment. As seen above in Chapter 5, in 1992, the Audio Home Recording Act[63] was enacted to introduce a degree of protection for right owners with respect to audio private copying by means of digital technology. The Act only applies to audio private copying, leaving aside the problem of video private copying, and to digital technology. It did not tackle analogue private copying. The Act combines a royalty payment system with the obligation to incorporate a technical control mechanism to prevent unauthorised serial copying of protected works in digital audio recording and interface devices.

---

[61] G. P. Cornish, "Libraries and the Harmonisation of Copyright", *op. cit.*, n.40, above, at 243.

[62] T.C. Vinje, "Should we Begin Digging Copyright's Grave?", *op. cit.*, n.40, above, at 552.

[63] Public Law 102–53, October 28, 1992 (incorporated in US Code, Title 17, as Chapter 10—Digital Audio Recording Devices and Media).

Further support for technical solutions to copyright problems generally was forthcoming from the United States of America when in October 1998 the Digital Millenium Copyright Act (DMCA) was enacted.[64] The DMCA was intended primarily to implement the requirements of the WIPO Internet Treaties[65] but also addresses a number of other copyright-related issues. In particular, as described in detail in Chapter 5, above, the DMCA creates two new prohibitions in Title 17 of the US Code, one on circumvention of technological measures used by copyright owners to protect their works and one on tampering with copyright management information; the prohibitions are backed up by civil and criminal penalties for their violation.

S.1201 of the DMCA prohibits the act of circumvention of a technological measure that effectively controls *access* to a protected work[66] as well as making or selling devices or services used to circumvent those measures. Measures that prevent unauthorised *copying* of a protected work[67] are also protected in that making or selling devices or services used to circumvent them is prohibited although, since in some circumstances *copying* of a work may be a fair use, the actual act of circumventing a technological measure that prevents *copying* is not prohibited. The fair use doctrine, however, is not a defence to the act of gaining unauthorised *access* to a work, which is why the act of circumventing a technological measure in order to gain *access* is prohibited. The prohibition on circumvention of measures that prevent unauthorised *access* to works did not take effect for two years from enactment[68] and was subject to review by the Copyright

---

[64] Digital Millenium Copyright Act, Pub.L.105–304, 112 Stat.2860 (October 28, 1998). See US Copyright Office Summary, December 1998 (*http://lcweb.loc.gov/copyright*). See also S. Begue and L. Cohen-Tanugi, "Droit d'auteur et copyright face aux technologies numériques: comparaisons transatlantiques", (2001) 178 *Légipresse* 1; P. Wand, *Technische Schutzmaßnahmen und Urheberrecht—Ein Vergleich des international, europäischen, deutschen und US—amerikanischen Rechts*, (Beck, Munich, 2001); H.M. Gladney, "Digital Intellectual Property: Controversial and International Aspects", [2000] 24 Colum—VLA J.L. and Arts, p.47.

[65] DCMA, Title 1, is headed "WIPO Treaties Implementation".

[66] DCMA, Ch.12, s.1201(a)(1)(A). See also J. Ginsburg, "From Having Copies to Experiencing Works: The Development of an Access Right in US Copyright Law", in *US Intellectual Property Law and Policy* (H. Hanson, ed., 2001), p.3.

[67] *ibid.*, s.1201(b). By "copying" is meant the exercise of any of the exclusive rights of an author under s.106 of the Copyright Act.

[68] *ibid.*, s.1201(a)(1)(A) and (B). Furthermore, the prohibition is not to apply to persons who are users of a copyrighted work which is in any particular class of works, if such persons are, or are likely to be in the succeeding three-year period, adversely affected by virtue of such prohibition in their ability to make non-infringing uses of that

Office. It has now entered into force.

Subject to this, the DMCA is subject to the fair use doctrine of US law, like the provisions of the Copyright Act. Thus, it is left principally to the courts to determine the extent of limitations on rights in the digital environment and to adapt the case law on fair use to the new means of exploitation. The challenges of on-line digital exploitation of works have led to a number of confrontations between copyright owners and internet intrepreneurs in the courts. On the whole, these have been favourable to right owners but the fair use doctrine compels respect for the public interest. As Ginsburg concludes:

> The tools the DMCA and copyright caselaw give copyright owners to confront copyright use on the Internet should be employed to promote broad distribution of works of authorship at reasonable, and variable, prices. If copyright owners instead wield these tools to enhance control without facilitating dissemination, we can expect to see courts expand the zones of excused uses, whether or not the excuses are doctrinally persuasive. Copyright owners cannot, and should not, control every Internet use, but neither should every use prompt an excuse, lest we undermine the ability of copyright owners, and especially of individual creators, to make a living from their creativity".[69]

The DMCA also deals with the protection of copyright management **12–012** information systems, prohibiting the knowing provision or distribution or import for distribution of false electronic rights management information, if done with the intent to induce, enable, facilitate or conceal infringement. The intentional removal or alteration of rights management information without authority, as well as the dissemination of such information or copies of works, knowing that the information has been removed or altered without authority is also barred. Liability in this last respect requires that the act be done with

---

particular class of works. During the two-year period, and in each succeeding three-year period, the DCMA directs the Librarian of Congress, upon the recommendation of the Register of Copyrights, to assess the impact of the circumvention ban on users adversely affected by the prohibition in their ability to make non-infringing uses of a particular class of copyright works, *i.e.* on traditional fair use practices.

[69] J. Ginsburg, "Copyright Use and Excuse on the Internet", [2000] 24 Colum—VLA J.L. and Arts, p.1 at 45.

knowledge or, with respect to civil remedies, with reasonable grounds to know that it will induce, enable, facilitate or conceal an infringement.

Remedies under the DMCA are similar to those available under the Copyright Act and comprise a range of equitable and monetary remedies, including statutory damages and it is a criminal offence to infringe the provisions described above wilfully and for purposes of commercial advantage or private financial gain.[70]

The Promise of Technical Solutions

12–013 The US legislative example and experience would appear to show that effective technical devices, combined with adequate protection under the copyright law, may in the future provide the means of giving right owners control over access to works in the digital environment. They will recreate direct links between right owners and users and improved contractual mechanisms governing conditions of access to works. Thus, exclusive rights will regain their integrity via technical means and even make it easier to enforce moral rights by means of electronic signatures. Licensing will be facilitated thus reducing transaction costs and furthering Chafee's sixth ideal of convenience in handling the rules of copyright.

At present, the technical measures required to achieve these goals are not generally in place either in the United States of America or in Europe. Moreover, to date, in Europe, pending the implementation of the Information Society Directive by the Member States of the European Union, neither is the necessary legislation. The technical measures being developed promise to enable right owners to control access to and copying of their works and the implementation of the obligations imposed on Member States by the WIPO Internet Treaties and the EU Information Society Directive concerning technical measures and copyright management information will it is hoped provide a legal framework that will enable right owners to exercise that control. The danger with respect to downloading works from the internet is that the notion that making copies for private use is a fair use or fair dealing to which the public has a right, and that

---

[70] DCMA, ss.1203 and 1204.

therefore technical measures which actually allow right owners to exercise their rights to block access to works and prevent such copying should not be permitted, is likely to be argued fiercely by users and consumers. This is a real dilemma and, as seen above in the context of the limitations and exceptions permitted by the Information Society Directive it is difficult to envisage technical measures which are sufficiently robust to prevent piracy but at the same time flexible enough to allow limitations and exceptions to be enforced. In this context, the question may be posed whether it would not be opportune to revoke exceptions such as that permitting private use of sound and audiovisual recordings subject to remuneration; such exceptions were introduced in circumstances where it was impossible to control copying and are no longer relevant in circumstances where technical development gives right owners the possibility to exercise control over copying. In principle, the rights are, after all, exclusive rights.[71]

Although the development of technical measures and rights management information and systems appears at present to be somewhat disorganised and haphazard, much research and development activity is under way, which is likely to lead to the adoption of effective technical protection measures in the future. Furthermore, there has been an unprecedented level of negotiation between right owners and representatives of the consumer electronics industries, all directed at finding ways to deliver digital music and audiovisual programming to consumers which offer both security for the right owners and creative community and ease of use for consumers. In the United States of America these developments have been promoted by the DMCA and there is no reason to doubt that the adoption of similar legislation on technical measures by the Member States of the EU will have the same effect and encourage the European counterparts of the US industries to new co-operative ventures. Solutions to these problems can only benefit both right owners, the electronics industries and the general public.

Pitfalls for technical solutions

There are a number of pitfalls for technical solutions to copyright protection and rights management schemes generally.   **12–014**

---

[71] A. Lucas, "Le droit d'auteur et protections techniques", in *Copyright in Cyberspace, op. cit.*, p.343 *et seq.*

First, while technology can provide protection, it can also be used to crack copyright protection systems. In August 1999, Microsoft launched its own internet music software featuring a digital rights management system. Within days hackers had managed to crack its security features.[72] Similarly, the encryption system CSS used to protect DVD-formatted movies from being copied was cracked as soon as it was launched.[73] More recently Sony Music's "Key2Audio", CD disc copy-protection technology, billed as copy-proof, was defeated by scribbling around the disc rim with a felt-tip pen.[74]

Increasingly sophisticated protection systems will be ever more difficult to hack but there will always be people who will do their best to get around them. However, assuming copyright owners are provided with the legal framework, encryption technology linked in the case of the internet to click-on contractual licensing of copyright material will provide a high level of control to right owners and, although there will always be some people or groups determined to get around the encryption, these would not be enough to break the system.

The need for a global approach

12–015   As already mentioned, for the copy-protection and rights management systems described to be effective, it is essential not only that the EC Directive be implemented responsibly by the Member States but also that the major trading partners of the European Union and the United States of America put similar legislation in place and ratify the WIPO Treaties referred to above. Only if there is an international system of legal protection in force can technical measures in the long run provide a solution to the problems of enforcement of rights in the global media marketplace.

---

[72] Newsbytes News Network, November 10, 1999.

[73] Washington Post, November 4, 1999. On January 20, 2000, a New York Federal Court ruled that three websites posting the program were in violation of the 1998 Digital Millenium Copyright Act (DMCA) and granted the film industry a preliminary injunction.

[74] Factiva Dow Jones and Reuters, Press Release, May 20, 2002.

Chapter 13

International Protection—Towards More Harmonisation of Copyright?

The notion of two diverging cultures of copyright has made for unnecessary obstacles in international transactions.[1]

Paul Goldstein

Achieving the Ideal of International Protection

Chafee's third ideal, concerning the need to find global solutions to strengthen copyright for the benefit of the public, is more important than ever in the global marketplace of the early twenty-first century. Chafee himself noted that the intellectual difficulties of finding agreement on copyright issues are vastly increased by its international aspects and that his third ideal of international protection has been realised only painfully and imperfectly.[2] The reasons for this are several. Even where governments and the relevant intergovernmental agencies are convinced, in principle, of the need to address Chafee's first two ideals and to bring national and international copyright legislation up-to-date to address new subject-matter worthy of protection and to provide protection against new means of exploitation of such subject-matter, the obstacles to progress are formidable. First, the competing interests of the various copyright and related rights owners among themselves must be addressed. Secondly, new rights of control

13–001

---

[1] P. Goldstein, *Copyright's Highway—The Law and Lore of Copyright from Gutenberg to the Celestial Jukebox*, (Hill and Wang, New York, 1994), p.170.

[2] Z. Chafee, *op. cit.*, at 523.

or remuneration are sure to be opposed by users, such as for example, broadcasting organisations and libraries, providers of internet services and the general public. It is difficult enough to reconcile these incompatible interests and to find a balance in the public-interest at the national level, let alone at the international level. The developments discussed above in Chapter 12 provide ample evidence of these difficulties.

A further real obstacle is the differing principles governing copyright protection in common law countries and those governing authors' rights in countries of civil law tradition. The distinctions between the two systems—what Goldstein has called "the two cultures of copyright"[3]—have always seriously complicated the determination of the rights to be guaranteed under the international conventions. The negotiations leading to the adoption of the TRIPs Agreement and the WIPO Internet Treaties in the 1990s drew attention to the difficulties of reconciling differing approaches to the protection of the various categories of right owners protected by copyright and authors' rights respectively, while endeavouring to provide adequate solutions to the questions raised by new economic, social, cultural and technological developments. The same difficulties continually complicate the harmonisation programme of the European Commission in the field of copyright and related rights.

13–002   For all these reasons there has been steady pressure to further bridge the gap between the common law and civil law approaches to authorship, that is, copyright and authors' rights.

To attain the needed level of protection internationally, ways to span differences between the continental *droit d'auteur* and neighbouring rights systems and the Anglo-American copyright systems must be developed.[4]

In the following discussion, we explore the nature and extent of the gap and the degree to which the gap is narrowing, or not, as the case may be.[5]

---

[3] P. Goldstein, "The Two Cultures of Copyright", ch.25 in *Copyright's Highway, op. cit.*, n.1, above.

[4] *Report of the Working Group on Intellectual Property Rights, Information Infrastructure Task Force*, chairman, B.A. Lehman, September 1995, p.155.

[5] The following comparison of the copyright and authors' rights systems draws on and updates an article by the author, "The Convergence of Copyright and Authors' Rights—Reality or Chimera?", (1995) 26 I.I.C. 964 *et seq*. On this subject, see also D. Gervais, *La notion d'oeuvre dans la Convention de Berne et en droit comparé*, (Librairie Droz, Geneva, 1998), Ch.3, p.100 *et seq.*; A. Strowel, *Droit d'auteur et copyright—Divergences et*

The Obstacles to Universal Solutions—Copyright or *Droit d'Auteur*

Standards of Protection

All copyright laws in both civil law and common law systems require **13–003** that a work be "original" in order for it to be protected and that it be connected to its author. In both systems, originality has nothing to do with merit or any qualitative standard and copyright subject-matter need not be novel. However, the meaning of the word "original" varies under national laws and, in principle, the degree of creativity required to satisfy the criterion of "originality" in civil law countries has traditionally been higher than in common law countries.

In common law countries, the meaning of "original" **has traditionally been that the work should originate from the author; it must not be copied from another source.** It does not mean that the work must be the expression of original or inventive thought; the originality required relates to the expression of the thought. The standard of originality is low and has to be determined taking into account whether the author has expended sufficient independent **skill, labour and judgment to justify copyright protection for the result**. According to Sterlng, "The word skill has an extensive import, and covers creative endeavour. So a United Kingdom judgement should have no difficulty applying the test of skill as requiring intellectual creation".[6] In the United States of America, the expenditure of "sweat of the brow" was until recently the test for originality. However, in 1991, the Supreme Court held in the *Feist* case that to qualify for copyright protection, a work must display some minimal

---

convergences, (Bruylant, Bruxelles, 1993); A. Strowel, "Droit d'auteur and Copyright: Between History and Nature", in B. Sherman and A. Strowel, *Of Authors and Origins*, (Oxford, 1994), p.10; A. Strowel, "Convergences entre droit d'auteur et copyright dans la société de l'information", in Intergu (ed), *Schutz von Kultur und geistigem Eigentum in der Informationsgesellschaft, Baden-Baden,* (Nomos Verlag, 1998), p.59; J.A.L. Sterling, "Creator's right and the bridge between author's right and copyright", in Intergu (ed), *ibid.*, p.77; A. Dietz, "Brückenschlag zwischen Droit d'auteur und Copyright in der Informationgellschaft", *op. cit.*, p.83; A. Françon, "Le Droit d'auteur au-delà des frontières: une comparaison des conceptions civiliste et de common law", [1991] 149 R.I.D.A. 2; M. Vivant, "Entre droit d'auteur et Copyright—L'Europe au carrefour des logiques", [1997] *10 Cahiers de Propriété intellectuelle*, p.41; and P. Goldstein, *Copyright's Highway, op. cit. n.1, above.*

[6] See J.A.L. Sterling, *op. cit.*, n.4, above, at 79.

creativity, finding that telephone directory white pages do not pass the originality test.[7]

In civil law countries, however, originality has always meant more than that the work originates from the author and is not copied. Toil and effort are not enough. There must be a degree of creativity, reflecting the individuality of the author's personality. As Dreier has said, "it is the personality of the author which is protected in the work. It is this which may be determined as the essential characteristic of *droit d'auteur*".[8]

These differing standards of originality have had in the past an important impact on the concept of authorship and categories of works protected in the two systems. However, as discussed below, these differences are slowly fading and in recent years there has been a movement towards a unified threshold of originality.[9]

Formalities

13–004   Originally, copyright in the common law countries depended upon compliance with certain formalities, such as, *e.g.* registration or printing the proper copyright notice on the work, and were regarded as a feature of the common law system with its origins in the Statute of Anne. In civil law countries, no formalities are required and this principle was embodied in the Berne Convention by the Berlin Act of 1908. Thus, Art.5(2) of the Convention provides: "The enjoyment and exercise of these rights shall not be subject to any formality ...". Common law countries which were members of the Berne Convention therefore did away with formalities as a condition of protection long ago, led by the United Kingdom which abolished them in the 1911 Copyright Act. The major exception to this was the United States of America, where, until it amended its law on joining the Berne Convention in 1989, copyright was obtained by publication with the required copyright notice.

Thus, formalities can no longer be regarded as a divisive issue between the civil law and common law traditions.

---

[7] *Feist Publications, Inc. v Rural Telephone Service Co.*, 111 S.Ct.1282 (1991).

[8] T. Dreier, "Authorship and New Technologies from the Viewpoint of Civil Law Traditions", (paper presented at the WIPO World-wide Symposium on the Future of Copyright and Neighbouring Rights, Paris, June, 1994), p.3.

[9] D. Gervais, *op. cit.*, n.5, above, p.209.

Ownership and Assignability of Rights

In the civil law authors' rights system, it follows from the fact that it is **13–005** considered to be the personality of the author which is protected in the work that the author can only be a natural person. Legal entities may not be regarded as authors. There are exceptions to this rule as, for example, in the case of collective works in France.[10] Authorship being confined to physical persons means, for example, that it is the individuals who have contributed to the making of a film who are considered the co-authors (namely, the authors of the script, adaptation, dialogue, music and the director of the film). Nevertheless, most civil laws provide for a *cessio legis* or presumption of assignment of rights to the film producer in order to facilitate the effficient exploitation of the rights in the film.

In common law countries, in many cases the author will also be a physical individual, initial ownership of copyright vesting in the author or authors of a work. However, legal entities are considered to be copyright owners in certain cases, for example, film producers, producers of sound recordings, broadcasters.

Legal entities may also be owners of copyright in the context of employer/employee relations. In the common law countries, if a work is made by an employee in the course of his employment, his employer is the first owner of any copyright in the work, subject to any agreement to the contrary. In the United States of America, an employer or other person for whom a "work made for hire" is prepared is considered the "author" of the work.

In most civil law countries the principle that copyright vests in the individual who creates the work extends even to works created by an author in the course of his employment.

There are differences of approach also with respect to transfer of **13–006** rights. In common law countries there are no restrictions on transfer of rights, whereas this is not the case in civil law countries. For example, in some countries, moral rights are inalienable.

These differences of approach are derived from the different philosophies underlying copyright and authors' rights. It is as well to remember, however, that the emphasis on the personal link between an individual author and a work is of comparatively recent origin. Thus, in France, legal entities have long been regarded as authors in

---

[10] Code on Intellectual Property, Art.L.113–2, para.3, 113–5.

the case of collective works. Moreover, prior to the 1957 Law on Artistic and Literary Property, case law had recognised the film producer as the author of a cinematographic work[11] and, indeed, that the producer of a sound recording was entitled to protection with respect to his original recordings, which had to be assimilated in all respects to original literary and artistic works.[12] Similarly, legal entities were regarded in certain circumstances as authors under the German laws of 1870 and 1901, as amended in 1910. This was the case for collective works and over the years the courts (the *Reichsgericht* and the *Kammergericht*) repeatedly recognised the film producer as the author of a cinematographic work.[13] In Germany, the question whether legal persons should be considered as authors was hotly debated, particularly in relation to films, during the long-drawn out move to reform the law. The question was not finally settled until the adoption of the 1965 Act, which vested authors' rights in films in the individual creative contributors thereto and gave the film producer a neighbouring or related right in the picture carrier.

Thus, the present-day opposed approaches of the civil law and common law traditions on the question of corporate ownership of rights are of comparatively recent date and not rooted in the origins of the two systems.

Moral Rights

13–007 Perhaps the most important historical divergence between the civil law and common law traditions is the respective attitudes to moral rights. The personalist emphasis laid by such rights on the inseparability of the work from the person who has created it represents a major difference of approach between the two systems. Although as we have seen, most common law countries have always provided a degree of protection for moral rights and, for example, the United Kingdom and the United States of America have now legislated to

---

[11] In 1905, it was held that a cinematographic film was an artistic work protected under the 1793 Law (Civil Court of the Seine, February 10, 1905) and that the property in the work belonged to the film maker. See also E. Pouillet, *Traité théorique et pratique de la propriété littéraire et artistique*, (Paris, Marchal et Billard, 3rd. ed., 1908), at 140.
[12] March 13, 1957, Civil Court of Paris. XVII R.I.D.A. 162 (1957).
[13] See in particular 106 R.G.Z. 365 and 1924 J.W. 413.

provide specific protection for certain of such rights,[14] it is evident that the common law system lays greater emphasis on the economic rights of authors while the civil law countries, and particularly France and Germany, give pre-eminence to moral rights.

Related Rights

A striking difference between the common law and civil law systems **13–008** is and has long been their conflicting attitudes to the protection of the categories of right owners protected by the Rome Convention. Until comparatively recently, these categories were left without specific protection under the laws of the civil law countries except by case law and the law of unfair competition. Producers of sound recordings and broadcasting organisations, normally legal entities, did not fit the civil law concept of authorship. Broadcasts and sound recordings tended to be regarded as uncreative, industrial productions, lacking the originality required for authors' rights protection. Performers were regarded as auxiliaries of creators, in second place to authors, but not worthy of the same degree of protection. Thus, specific protection for these categories was introduced for the first time in Germany in 1965 and in France in 1985. The nature of that protection was that provided for by the Rome Convention and known as neighbouring or related rights.

The approach of the common law countries was different. The British Copyright Act of 1911, subsequently extended throughout the world through the imperial copyright scheme, gave copyright protection to sound recordings, the ownership of which vested in the maker thereof. The right comprised not only a reproduction right but also the right to authorise public performance and broadcasting of sound recordings.[15] The Copyright Act 1956 provided copyright protection for broadcasting organisations in respect of both sound and television broadcasts and performers were provided with protection by way of penal sanctions against certain unauthorised uses of their live performances by the Performers Protection Acts 1958–1972. Copyright in films was vested by the Copyright Act 1956 also in the maker, defined as the person by whom the necessary arrangements for

---

[14] UK:Copyright, Designs and Patents Act 1988, Ch.IV; USA: Visual-Artists Rights Act 1990, Public Law 101–650, 104 Stat.5089 (December 1, 1990), S.106A.
[15] Copyright Act 1911, s.19(1), as interpreted by the *Gramophone Co Ltd v Stephen Cawardine and Co* [1934] Ch.450.

making of the film are undertaken.[16] In the UK 1988 Act, sound recordings and broadcasts are categorised as copyright works. The author in relation to a sound recording is stated to be the producer thereof, defined as the person by whom the arrangements for making it are undertaken. For broadcasts the author is the creator, defined as the maker.[17]

The introduction of federal legislation concerning these rights in the United States of America is comparatively recent. There was no protection for sound recordings until 1971, when a limited copyright in favour of producers of phonograms—a right to authorise or prohibit reproduction—was introduced.[18] Under the 1976 revision Act sound recordings (along with films—motion pictures and other audiovisual works) became one of the seven categories of works of authorship protected by copyright; the authors of a sound recording include those who make a creative contribution to the recorded sound, namely the performer(s) and the producers.[19] Broadcasts as such are not protected by specific rights unless the programmes transmitted are "fixed" or recorded before or simultaneously with the broadcast, when they are protected as films or sound recordings, as the case may be, the producer being the author thereof. Broadcasts licensed by the Federal Communications Commission are protected against rebroadcasting and unauthorised reception, interception and rebroadcasting of signals under the Federal Communications Act of 1934.

This brief and incomplete summary of the development of these rights in the civil law and common law systems illustrates the impact that the basic differences of approach to copyright/authors' rights have had on the legislative solutions applied to them.

---

[16] Copyright Act, 1956, s.13. The courts had earlier provided protection for films by holding in 1912 that each photograph in a film was protected as an artistic work (*Barker v Hutton*, 28 T.L.R. 496).

[17] C.D.P.A. 1998, ss.9(2)(aa) and 9(2)(b).

[18] Public Law, 92–140 (92nd, Congress s.646) of October 15, 1971.

[19] Copyright Act 1976, Title 17 US Code, s.301.

The Converging Impact of International Harmonisation to Date

Having considered the extent of the divergences between the systems, **13–009** the question now to be answered is whether the gap between the two systems is being bridged as a result of increased intergovernmental attention to the subject, over the past 15 years or so. These divergences have dominated negotiations within the Berne Union and in the context of the Rome Convention in the course of the work leading to the adoption of the TRIPs Agreement in 1993 and the WIPO Internet Treaties in 1996, as well as in connection with the harmonisation programme of the European Union. And, if so, to what extent?

The Converging Influence of the Berne Convention

Historically, since its adoption in 1886, the Berne Convention and its **13–010** successive revision conferences served as a forum in which the differences of approach of the civil law and common law systems could generally be accommodated. The successive Acts of the Convention[20] were framed in such a way as to obtain the adherence of countries of both civil law and common law traditions. The Convention was influenced by national law developments, adding new subject-matter of protection as time went by,[21] and became a harmonising influence on national laws. For example, in the case of the term of protection, increased at Berlin in 1908 to 50 years p.m.a., many countries including Britain and Germany had to amend their laws so as to conform with the Convention. As regards the authorship of films, the Berne Convention provided a compromise according to which the determination of the ownership of copyright in a film was left to national legislation in the country where protection is claimed, thus embracing both the civil law approach of considering the individual

---

[20] See K. Garnett, J. Rayner James and G. Davies, "The Berne Convention and its Revisions", in *Copinger and Skone James on Copyright, op. cit.*, Ch.24(2).

[21] For example, cinematographic works were added to the list of works in Art.2(1) of the Berne Convention at Brussels in 1948. The Berne Convention had in fact accorded protection to certain kinds of cinematographic production since the Berlin Act 1908 (Art.14(2) and (3)). See S. Ricketson, *The Berne Convention for the Protection of Literary and Artistic Works: 1886–1986, op. cit.*, Ch.10.

creators to be co-authors and the common law approach whereby the producer was recognised as the author.[22]

Moral rights were not dealt with by the Convention until 1928, when Art.6*bis* was introduced in the Rome Act of the Convention. This was a compromise draft that was acceptable to the common law countries since it refrained from requiring national copyright laws to contain express moral rights provisions, but also tacitly acknowledged that the protection then offered at common law and equity by the common law countries was adequate for the purposes of the new provision.

The influence of the moral rights provision of the Berne Convention has gradually had an impact on the major common law jurisdictions. The United Kingdom introduced specific protection for moral rights in the 1988 Copyright Act.[23] When the United States of America joined the Berne Union in 1989, it declared that the existing protection afforded authors under a great many common law precedents, state statutes and federal laws satisfied its obligations under Berne, and the moral rights doctrine was not incorporated expressly in US law. Moreover, in 1990, Congress enacted the Visual Artists' Rights Act, which affords limited rights of attribution and integrity to a narrowly defined class of visual artists with respect to certain artistic works and photographs.[24]

The United States also brought its legislation into line with the Berne Convention by abolishing the formalities previously required for the subsistence of copyright and by providing for a term of protection based on the life of the author and 50 years thereafter.

The Diverging Influence of the Rome Convention

13–011   Following the adoption of the Rome Convention in 1961, many civil law countries revised their legislation to conform to the classification of rights exemplified by the Convention. Thus, countries which had previously incorporated the protection of sound recordings in their authors' rights legislation, often by extension of the existing law to the new category of works by legislation or case law (see, for example, the

---

[22] *cf.* Berne Convention, Art.14bis(2)(a)
[23] C.D.P.A. 1988, Ch.4, ss.77–89.
[24] Visual Arts Rights Act, Title VI of Pub.Law 101–650 of December 1, 1990.

cases of Spain[25] and Germany[26]) when revising their legislation distinguished clearly between literary and artistic works on the one hand and neighbouring or related rights on the other. Meanwhile, the common law countries continued to protect sound recordings under their copyright laws.[27] This difference of approach remains a thorny issue, particularly as concerns sound recordings, and was the subject of dispute during the negotiations on the TRIPs Agreement and those concerning a possible Protocol to the Berne Convention, which preceded the adoption of the WIPO Internet Treaties.

There has therefore developed a so-called international classification of rights as reflected in the international conventions—particularly the Berne and Rome Conventions. As WIP0 noted in connection with the preparation of a Model Law on Copyright in 1990:

> According to that classification, only the protection of literary and artistic works can be regarded as copyright protection; the protection of any productions not qualifying as literary and artistic works can either be called by their own name, *e.g.* the protection of performances, phonograms or broadcasts, or be referred to by the said general term—used for the sake of brevity—that is, the protection of neighbouring rights.[28]

This classification argument overlooks the fact that it is for national legislation to determine what may or may not be considered to be a literary or artistic work under the Berne Convention. The definition of such works in Art.2(1) is non-limitative and by merely listing

---

[25] Decree of July 10, 1942 conferring on phonographic works the character of works protected by the Law of Intellectual Property, 1879.

[26] Prior to the 1965 Act, the protection of performers and producers of phonograms was governed by the Act Concerning Copyright in Literary and Musical Works, of June 19, 1901, as amended in 1910, and the Act extending the term of copyright protection of December 13, 1934. S.2(2) of the Act, as amended in 1910, assimilated recordings of literary and musical works to adaptations of those works. The performer was the beneficiary of the right, the producer acquiring rights of his own by contract. According to E. Ulmer, 1961 *Le Droit d'auteur* 14, the intention of the legislature was to protect the record producer against unauthorised reproduction.

[27] The major exception to this rule was the United States of America, which did not introduce specific federal protection under the copyright law for sound recordings until 1971 (Pub.Law 92–140 (92d Congress s.646) of October 15, 1971).

[28] Committee of Experts on Model Provisions for Legislation in the Field of Copyright, Third Session, Geneva, July 2–13, 1990, para.42.

examples allows member countries to go further and treat other productions in the literary, scientific and artistic domains as protected works.

However, on the positive side, although the Rome Convention owes its origins to differences in the civil law and common law traditions, in the long run it has exercised a profound influence on the development of national legislation in the field of copyright/authors' rights and related rights. Since at the time the Convention was adopted, there were very few countries whose legislation was in conformity with it in respect of all three of its beneficiaries, it has often been referred to as a pioneering Convention. Yet today there is hardly a new law passed in this area which does not provide protection for the beneficiaries of the Convention, whether by copyright or related rights. The scope of the protection given has tended also in recent years towards a standard similar to that afforded to copyright works proper and is substantially higher than the minimum standards laid down over 40 years ago in the Rome Convention.

The Impact of the TRIPs Agreement

13–012 The Agreement on Trade-Related Aspects of Intellectual Property Rights (the TRIPs Agreement), adopted in April 1994 in Marrakesh, as part of the successful outcome of the Uruguay Round of the GATT trade negotiations, contains in s.1 of Pt.II, entitled "Standards Concerning the Availability, Scope and Use of Intellectual Property Rights", new international rules for the protection of "copyright and related rights". The negotiations leading to the adoption of the TRIPs Agreement were hotly contested; thus, its impact on the convergence between the common law and civil law approaches to copyright and related rights is of particular interest.

There is little in the TRIPs Agreement to illustrate a narrowing of the gap between the copyright and authors' rights approaches. As Correa pointed out, "the negotiations in the copyright area were characterised by a North-North confrontation on a number of issues"[29] including the concept of the author as applied to various

---

[29] C.M. Correa, "TRIPs Agreement: Copyright and Related Rights", 25 I.I.C. 543 (1994).

works and on the scope of protection accorded to them. The negotiations drew attention, in particular, to copyright policy differences between the United States of America on the one hand and other Berne Union members, including those of the European Union, on the other. The USA proposed a "Berne Plus" package, including eight issues not covered by the Berne Convention:

(1) the right to control public distribution of copies of works, including parallel imports;

(2) rental rights for computer programs and sound recordings;

(3) a definition of the term "public", in relation to public performance rights;

(4) affirmation of the entitlement of a Member State of the Berne Convention to treat legal entities as authors in domestic legislation;

(5) copyright protection for sound recordings;

(6) an international "fair use" standard;

(7) express incorporation into the Berne Convention of computer programs (as literary works) and databases (as works that would qualify under the Convention as collections or compilations);

(8) detailed enforcement obligations for the suppression of piracy.[30]

Of these, only items (2), (6), (7) and (8) were expressly achieved. The **13–013** right to control parallel importation, corporate authorship and copyright for sound recordings were rejected, although **related** rights to authorise or prohibit reproduction and commercial rental of sound recordings were recognised. In relation to corporate authorship, the US position was accommodated to the extent that Art.12 of the TRIPs Agreement provides that, where the term of copyright protection of a work is calculated on a basis other than the life of a natural person, the term should be not less than 50 years. The United States of America succeeded, however, in its aim of excluding the moral rights provisions of the Berne Convention from the Agreement, so that to this extent it may be described as a "Berne-Minus" text. The pro-

---

[30] For a description of the US negotiating position, see R. Oman, "Berne Revision: the Continuing Drama", (1993) 7 *World Intellectual Property Report* 160.

ponents of the authors' rights approach ensured that databases would only merit protection as copyright works if they constituted intellectual creations and that sound recordings remained protected by means of related rights and not as works.

The rights of performers and producers of sound recordings have undoubtedly been strengthened as a result of the TRIPs Agreement in that it will be applicable to a very considerably larger number of States than the Rome Convention, which at present has 69 Member States.[31] They will also benefit from a 50-year term of protection.

The TRIPs Agreement would appear to have achieved the extremely important objective of establishing minimum international standards for the protection of intellectual property, including copyright and authors' rights and certain related rights. It has not, however, established a bridge between the different legal approaches to these latter rights. On the contrary, the negotiations would appear to have provided yet another forum for dogmatic defence of doctrinal differences. Indeed, the negotiations were characterised by what seems to have become a regular feature of intergovernmental discussions on these issues in recent years, namely what Cornish has described as "mutual incomprehension ... and much sterile argument ... over the comparative virtues of different national approaches"[32] and the increasing entrenchment of the proponents of the various approaches in their divergent views.

The Influence of the WIPO Legislative Programme Pre-1996

Draft model law on copyright

13–014 The difficulties of reaching agreement on bridging the gap between the copyright and authors' rights approaches were thrown into sharp relief in the context of the work of WIPO in this area over the past 20 years or so. During the 1980s, WIPO held a series of meetings to discuss the copyright problems affecting various categories of works in

---

[31] As of June 30, 2002; 24 States have adhered to the Rome Convention since the TRIPs Agreement was adopted in 1994. For many years membership of the Convention was limited but the TRIPs Agreement and the WIPO Internet Treaties would appear to have breathed new life into it.

[32] W.R. Cornish, "The Notions of Work, Originality and Neighbouring Rights from the Viewpoint of Common Law Traditions", in *WIPO World-wide Symposium on the Future of Copyright and Neighbouring Rights*, WIPO, Geneva 1994, p.81 at 82.

the light of new technology. These meetings were followed in 1989 and 1990 by three meetings of a Committee of Experts for the purpose of drafting a Model Law on Copyright. Difficulties arose from the outset. As the preparatory document for the last meeting noted:

> The main dividing line seemed to be between delegations from countries with "continental" (or "Roman") legal traditions and delegations from countries with "common law" (or "Anglo-Saxon") traditions.

On a number of issues, the advocates of the "continental" approach insisted that the Model Law should be based exclusively on that approach, arguing that only such provisions corresponded to the spirit and letter of the Berne Convention. Partisans of both approaches exacerbated the situation by describing the controversy in terms of battles and religious wars[33]: "The battle between the *droit d'auteur* and copyright is planetary and smells of a religious war".[34]

An important issue in this respect was sound recordings. As already discussed, many common law countries protect these as copyright works and indeed there are also countries which protect them specifically as literary and artistic works. There were, therefore, calls for sound recordings to be covered by the model law. WIPO considered them to fall within the category of related or so-called neighbouring rights, however, and described the problem thus:

> The protection of the so-called neighbouring rights is one of the points where the "common law" and the "continental" copyright approaches differ from each other, although the difference seems, in general, more of a terminological nature than of a really substantive one. The notion of "copyright" is used in a wider meaning in countries with "common law" traditions than the one in which this word is used in respect of the Berne Convention ... In the face of the differing meanings of the notions of "copyright" and "neighbouring rights", the draft model law followed the international classification of the various productions involved as reflected

---

[33] N. Turkewitz, "Authors' Rights are Dead", in (1990) 38 *Journal of the Copyright Society of the USA* 45. See the reply by A. Dietz, "Copyright in the Modern technological World: a Mere Industrial Property Right?", in (1991) 39 *Journal of the Copyright Society of the USA* 83.

[34] M. Vivant, *op. cit.*, n.5, above, p.44.

in the international conventions—particularly the Berne Convention and the Rome Convention—administered by WIPO. According to that classification, only the protection of literary and artistic works can be regarded as copyright protection; ... The Model Law ... therefore ... should only cover the protection of literary and artistic works and should not extend to the so-called neighbouring rights.

This approach was endorsed by the continental law countries, while the common law countries argued forcefully but in vain for sound recordings to be included, the United States stressing "that the future of the Berne Convention depended, to a large extent, on the constructive coexistence and cooperation between the 'continental' and 'common law' approaches".[35]

Proposed New Protocol to the Berne Convention

13–015 The work on the Model Law set the scene for continuing disagreement on these issues in WIPO's subsequent work. Positions had become polarised by the time work began on the proposed new Protocol to the Berne Convention in 1991. It had become apparent by 1990 that there was a need for a new international instrument to update the Berne Convention in order to deal with the technical developments which had emerged since the adoption of the Paris Act 1971 and to remedy shortcomings in the standards of protection set thereby. Thus, the purpose of the proposed Protocol, according to WIPO's programme, was to clarify the existing or establish new international standards where, under the present text of the Berne Convention, doubts existed as to the extent to which the Convention applied to certain subject-matters of protection and certain rights. The desirability of covering the rights of producers of sound recordings in the protocol was also to be examined ... After the first two meetings, the terms of reference of the Committee of Experts responsible for the Protocol were modified, mainly because it had not been possible to reach agreement on the inclusion of the protection of producers of sound recordings in the possible Protocol. The outcome of the discussion on this issue was described in the following terms by a US representative.

---

[35] Report adopted by the Committee, [1990] Copyright 282, para.26.

To the United States, the Protocol was not only an instrument that would advance the norms of the Berne Convention. It would also act as a "bridge" convention between countries that favour neighbouring rights protection for sound recordings, and those that favour copyright. ... We wanted to reconcile differences between how Europe protects record producers and performers and how we protect authors of sound recordings—in short, a bridge between the principles, of authorship, subject matter and ownership which the US brings to Berne and others have brought to the Rome Convention. It went down in flames...[36]

As a result, a separate Committee of Experts on a Possible Instrument for the Protection of the Rights of Performers and Producers of Phonograms was established to discuss all questions concerning the effective international protection of the rights of performers and producers of sound recordings. This led in due course to the adoption of the WIPO Performances and Phonograms Treaty (WPPT) in parallel to the WIPO Copyright Treaty (WCT).

All this served only to emphasise and deepen differences of approach and to confirm the international classification of rights according to the continental law system, with a sharp divide between authors' rights and related rights.

Harmonisation Within the European Union

By contrast, the past 20 years have seen considerable progress in the harmonisation of the national laws of the present Member States of the European Union in the field of copyright/authors' rights and related rights.   **13–016**

Quite apart from any measures taken by the Commission, the individual Member States of the Community have been faced with the need to modernise their laws in the area of copyright/authors' rights and related rights in the light of technical developments and of the new categories, and new uses, of works requiring protection. Thus, since the mid-1980s, all 15 of the current Member States of the European Union have undertaken major reforms of their legislation in this area, as well as adapting their laws to implement the seven EU

---

[36] R. Oman, "Berne Revision: The Continuing Drama", *op. cit.*, n.30, above, at 162.

Directives on copyright and related rights.[37] Within the present Union, there are of course representatives of both the common law and continental law approaches to copyright/authors' rights and the influence of the Commission's harmonisation programme on bridging the gap between the two is discussed below. What is noticeable, however, is the extent to which in the last 20 years the differences in approach to the protection of related rights have narrowed, both under the influence of the Rome Convention and as a result of the phenomenon of piracy of sound recordings; this first became a serious problem in the 1970s and drew attention to the need for adequate protection for producers of sound recordings and performers in this context. Twenty years ago, in 1982, of the then nine Member States of the European Union, only six provided any specific protection by means of copyright or related rights for one or more of the beneficiaries of the Rome Convention, namely Denmark, the Federal Republic of Germany, Ireland, Italy, Spain and the United Kingdom. Of these, only Ireland and the United Kingdom provided any such protection for as much as 50 years. In the meantime, all the present 15 EU Member States have legislated to provide a level of protection for all the beneficiaries of the Rome Convention, which is generally higher than the minimum provided for therein, and to conform with the EC Directive on rental, lending and other rights in the copyright field, which prescribes certain minimum rights for the beneficiaries of related rights. In addition, all have brought their legislation into line with the Term Directive by extending the period of protection afforded to these categories of right owners to 50 years.

In this respect, therefore, there has been a considerable bridging of the gap between the countries of common and civil law traditions within the European Union, even though producers of sound recordings and broadcasters benefit from copyright protection and are

---

[37] Directive 91/250/EEC on the legal protection of computer programs; Directive 92/100/EEC on the rental right and lending right and on certain rights related to copyright in the field of intellectual property; Directive 93/83/EEC on the co-ordination of certain rules concerning copyright and rights related to copyright applicable to satellite broadcasting and cable transmission; Directive 93/98/EEC harmonising the term of protection of copyright and certain related rights; Directive 96/9/EC on the legal protection of databases; Directive 2001/29/EC of the European Parliament and of the Council on the harmonisation of certain aspects of copyright and related rights in the information society; Directive 2001/84/EC of the European Council and of the Council on the resale right for the benefit of the author of an original work of art (*droit de suite*).

recognised as authors in Ireland and the UK, while in the other Member States they are protected by virtue of related rights. Thus, while a difference of philosophy remains and is reflected in the different classifications of the rights, in practice, the level of protection afforded to authors and holders of related rights respectively, in terms of rights, duration and remedies, has been steadily converging.

This process has been accelerated by the implementation of the EU copyright and related rights Directives already referred to and as a result of decisions of the European Court.[38] Moreover, a bridging of the gap is beginning to be perceived in relation to copyright and authors' rights proper.

The first area in which an approximation of the common law and civil **13–017** law systems can be observed is in the treatment of the issue of originality in Community legislation. Within the Member States, there were as many as three approaches:

(i) the common law approach of the UK and Ireland requiring the expenditure of skill, labour and judgment and that the work must originate from the author;

(ii) the generally recognised civil law approach according to which the work must be an expression of the personality of the author;

(iii) finally, the very high standard set in Germany where a personal intellectual creation has traditionally been required. There, in interpreting this requirement, the courts in the past applied qualitative tests concerning the level of skill used, in relation in particular to computer programs.[39]

In reconciling these standards, the Computer Program Directive defines original as "original in the sense that it is the authors' own intellectual creation" and makes it clear that no other criteria are to be

---

[38] In the absence of a unitary system of intellectual property rights, it fell to the Court of Justice to resolve conflicts between the national intellectual property rights and the aims of the Community, giving rise to decisions conflicting with national legislation. See *Copinger and Skone James on Copyright, op. cit.*, Ch.25.

[39] Copyright Act 1965, s.2(2); and see Federal Supreme Court, Case No.IZR 52/83—Inkasso-Programm, 17 I.I.C. 681 (1986); according to that decision, computer programs had to be of a level of creativity considerably surpassing the average to qualify for protection as literary works. The law was changed to bring it into conformity with the EC Directive on the legal protection of computer programs in 1993 (see Ch.7, n.109, above).

applied to determine the eligibility of a computer program for protection. This steers a middle course, ruling out the high standard formerly set by Germany for computer programs—a level of creativity considerably surpassing the average—but requiring a higher standard than that of the common law test for originality in that the creation has to be *intellectual*. The same definition of originality has also been used by the Commission in other Directives, in relation to photographs in the Directive on Duration and to Databases in the Directive on Databases.[40]

The issue of the authorship of legal entities (corporate authorship) has also arisen in relation to the authorship of films, computer programs and databases. In the UK and Ireland, the film producer was until recently considered the author of the film, whereas in the civil law countries of the Community various creative contributors to the making of the film have been considered to be co-authors, subject to presumptions of assignments of their economic rights to the producers. The Community compromised by providing that "the principal director of a cinematographic or audiovisual work shall be considered as its author or one of its authors. Member States may provide for others to be considered as one of its co-authors".[41] This definition has been repeated in the Satellite Directive[42] and in the Term Directive.[43] This compromise has permitted the UK and Ireland to continue to treat the producer as author of a film but has forced them to change their laws in order to provide that the principal director of a film is also to be considered a co-author.[44] The Computer Program Directive also provides that the beneficiaries of protection shall be "all natural or legal persons eligible under national copyright legislations as applied to literary works".[45] The Database Directive similarly provides that, "where collective works are recognised by the legislation of a Member State, the economic rights in a database shall be owned by the person owning the copyright", who again may well be a legal entity. In this connection, it may be recalled that in spite of the personalist approach of the French copyright law, in the case of

---

[40] Term Directive, Art.6; Directive on Databases, Art.3(1).

[41] Rental Directive, Art.2(2).

[42] Satellite Directive, Art.1(5).

[43] Term Directive, Art.2(1).

[44] C.D.P.A. 1988, s.9(2)(ab); Copyright and Related Rights Act 2000 (C.R.R.A.), No.28 of 2000, s.21(b). It is also significant that the term "Related Rights" has been introduced into the title of the Irish Copyright Act.

[45] Computer Programs Directive, Art.3.

collective works, the author's rights vest in the natural **or legal person** under whose name it has been disclosed.[46]

Finally, compromise has also been reached in relation to works made in the course of employment. In the UK and Ireland (in this case joined by the Netherlands), where a work is made in the course of employment, the employer is deemed to be the copyright owner in the absence of any agreement to the contrary; whereas, in the continental countries' copyright vests in the author of the work in the first place. The Computer Program Directive follows the common law approach so far as economic rights are concerned, providing that: "Where a computer program is created by an employee in the execution of his duties or following the instructions given by his employer, the employer exclusively shall be entitled to exercise all economic rights in the program so created unless otherwise provided by contract".[47]

Here the compromise lies in the fact that the moral rights remain with **13–018** the employee author, although in the case of computer programs this seems a questionable proposition, especially in the light of the fact that the duration of protection for computer programs has been set at 70 years p.m.a.

However, the dividing line between authors' rights and related rights has been emphasised in the Term Directive. The Directive provides for a uniform period of protection of 70 years p.m a. for authors, while as regards related rights, the period of protection is set at 50 years from publication or communication to the public. This posed a problem for Ireland and the United Kingdom, which both protect producers of sound recordings and makers of broadcasts as authors of copyright works.[48] The Directive precludes them from granting these right owners protection for 70 years as that would defeat the object of harmonisation. The result has been to introduce a new distinction between various categories of authors under the national laws of these countries.

While the various compromises on matters of principle referred to may not appear very daring, they nevertheless will lead to harmonisation on topics of great importance where the common law and civil law approaches were previously opposed. Standards of originality,

---

[46] French Intellectual Property Code, Art.L.113–5; see also M. Vivant, *op. cit.*, n.5, above, p.51.
[47] Art.2(3).
[48] C.D.P.A. 1988, s.9(2)(aa) and (b); C.R.R.A. 2000, s.21(c).

corporate authorship and employed authorship are key issues in copyright law. They also go further than any other international harmonisation initiatives to date in bridging the gap between the two approaches. The impact of these developments on the international copyright scene is likely to be important. As Loewenheim has observed: "Even if this process may have direct effects only in the Member States, one should not forget that meanwhile the European Union represents a powerful economic and political factor which is likely to have considerable influence on the future development of copyright in the world".[49] The dominant role of the European Union in this respect has also been noted by Oman, who commented in 1993 on the "forceful emergence of the Commission of the European Communities as the copyright arbiter of western Europe and the shaper of every copyright law from Dublin to Vladivostok".[50]

As described above, the WIPO Internet Treaties have given further formal recognition to the continental approach and divide between the authors' rights system and the copyright system. The collapse of efforts to include the protection of sound recordings in a protocol to the Berne Convention in the early 1990s would appear to have cast in stone the division between authors' rights and related rights so far as the international classification of rights is concerned.

Perspectives for the Harmonisation to Come

13–019   As this study has demonstrated, in the analyses of the national laws in Part II, divergences in the common law and civil law copyright systems are not rooted in the origins of these laws.

> The two cultures of copyright have much in common. The similarities lie not only in the practicalities of the market place but in the laws' underlying premises ... The historical foundations of French copyright law are remarkably similar to those of American copyright.[51]

---

[49] U. Löwenheim, "Copyright in Civil Law and Common Law Countries: A Narrowing Gap", (paper presented at the Conference on the Economics of Intellectual Property Rights, University of Venice, October 1994).

[50] See R. Oman, *op. cit.* n.30, above, at 160.

[51] P. Goldstein, *Copyright's Highway*, *op. cit.*, n.1, above, at 170.

Both systems were founded on a shared, common approach and the differences in copyright theory and practice as may now exist should not be regarded as precluding future convergence of the two systems. In relation to authors' rights, for over 100 years, the Berne Convention evolved in such a way as to provide a bridge between the two approaches in many respects. As noted by several commentators in recent years, differences in relation to such matters as the requirement of originality, formalities, ownership of rights and moral rights appear to be diminishing so far as authors' rights are concerned.[52]

Neither authors' rights nor copyright have emerged unscathed from the harmonisation process. While those in the copyright camp consider that the *droit d'auteur* has made inroads into copyright, partisans of the *droit d'auteur* are convinced that copyright has taken the upper hand. For example, many copyright commentators regret the failure of the negotiations for a Protocol to the Berne Convention and the consequent need to establish the WCT and WPPT and see this development as a victory for the *droit d'auteur*. Others see the WCT as being closer to copyright than it is to *droit d'auteur* and as "marking in certain respects the decline of the *droit d'auteur* conception existing in France and the civil law world by consecrating an approach and concepts that are inspired by the copyright conception of our friends in the common law countries".[53]

If everybody is dissatisfied, it probably means that real progress is being made towards convergence. However, as Strowel has demonstrated, the differences in the field of copyright proper are not so significant as has often been suggested and elements of the copyright approach are present in *droit d'auteur* just as there are elements of *droit d'auteur* in copyright.[54] While the TRIPs Agreement does not appear to have contributed to furthering the convergence of the two systems, it is clear that, as regards authors' rights, both the WIPO legislative programme and the harmonisation programme of the European Union have done so.

It is in the area of related rights and, in particular, the protection of **13–020** sound recordings, that the differing approaches of the two groups have not only failed to converge but rather to have hardened in recent

[52] See n.5, above.

[53] J-L. Goutal, "The WIPO Treaty of 20 December 1996 and the French Conception of Authors' Rights", (2001) 187 R.I.D.A. 66 at 72.

[54] A. Strowel, *Droit d'auteur et copyright. Divergences et Convergences, op. cit.*, n.5, above, para 9

years. This is, however, more a difference of philosophy than a practical one. There is general agreement on the part of all concerned that the subject-matter of related rights deserves to benefit from a high level of protection; the dispute lies in the nature of the rights to be bestowed on the beneficiaries.

While theoretical and even ideological differences have undoubtedly developed over the years as regards the objects of protection under authors' rights and copyright legal systems, and as regards the scope of that protection, the modern legislation in this field of the countries discussed in this study shows a remarkable harmony with respect to the categories of works protected and to the beneficiaries of such protection, whether such protection be by means of copyright, *droit d'auteur* or related rights. In practical terms, there has been a considerable convergence in the scope of the protection afforded under the common law and civil law systems. To this extent, convergence is a reality.

The present period of increasingly rapid technological change is bringing new opportunities for the production and marketing of new creative products and there is a corresponding need for modern, national legislation on copyright and related rights to evolve flexibly in order to provide adequate protection for them. The Global Information Infrastructure with its digital distribution systems and multi-media works dictates pragmatic solutions and reconsideration of the nineteenth century concepts on which legislation in this area has hitherto been based.

In this context, common solutions to new problems are required within the framework of the international copyright conventions and it is incumbent on the law-maker to bear in mind Ginsburg's conclusion that: "There is in fact a rich tradition of copyright congruity upon which modern advocates of international copyright harmonization may draw to formulate mutually acceptable principles for the protection of works of authorship".[55]

13–021 It should be a priority, therefore, for all concerned to steer clear of theological debates about the respective merits of various national approaches and to seek solutions and an international framework which can accomodate both the common law and civil law approaches, thus building further bridges between the systems as traditionally

---

[55] J. C. Ginsburg, "A Tale of Two Copyrights: Literary Property in Revolutionary France and America", [1981] 147 R.I.D.A., p.131, 133.

the Berne Convention has done in the past. As Goodenough has suggested:

> Copyright and *droit d'auteur* suffer from the constraints of historical aesthetic theory and from over-particularisation. Such pointillist jurisprudence has gone on long enough. We need to step back, view the canvas as a whole, and identify the broader social principles which draw the picture together.[56]

To aim for complete convergence or assimilation between the respective philosophies of the common law and civil law systems would appear for the time being to remain a chimera. The best way forward, therefore, would seem to be to set objectives for the standard of protection to be achieved for various categories of works and other subject-matter, and to leave it to the individual governments to implement such protection in accordance with their own national approach.

In such a way forward, Goldstein's prediction that "the two great systems for protecting the authorial enterprise—authors' right and copyright—will continue on their converging paths and at some early but undetected point will simply assimilate each others' identity", has its best hope of being realised.[57]

---

[56] O.L. Goodenough, "Pointillism, Copyright and the Droit d'auteur: Time to See a Bigger Picture", [1994] 2 ENT.L.R.35.

[57] P. Goldstein, "Copyright and Authors' Right in the XXIst Century", (paper delivered at the WIPO World-wide Symposium on the Future of Copyright and Neighbouring Rights, Paris, June 1994).

Chapter 14

Conclusions

Consider what you think justice requires and decide accordingly
Lord Mansfield

In the course of this study, attention has been directed to the public **14–001**
interest in the copyright system. An objective definition of the public
interest in relation to copyright was suggested in 1981 by Barbara
Ringer:

> Given the political and cultural framework of a particular society
> and the economic resources at its disposal, the public interest is the
> aggregate of the fundamental goals that the society seeks to achieve
> for *all* of its members—not for a majority of its members or for any
> large and powerful group, but for all of the people within the
> society. Considered separately, a society's goals are often in conflict
> with one another, and in that case there must be a balancing. The
> art of government consists of achieving a harmonious rather than a
> destructive balance among conflicting goals.[1]

As we have seen, copyright provides the framework required to
induce authors, artists and other creators, to create and to reward them
for their work. It acts as an incentive for others to invest in the
dissemination and exploitation of works for the ultimate benefit of the
public. At its inception, copyright had as its purpose to provide a
reward and stimulus to creators, and to encourage and improve
learning and the progress of the arts and sciences. This study has

---

[1] B. Ringer, "Authors' Rights in the Electronic Age: Beyond the Copyright Act of
1976", 1 Loyola Entertainment Law Journal 1 (1981).

shown that this was the common purpose of the first laws on the subject in the United Kingdom, United States of America and France. As Ginsburg concluded in her study of the origins of the copyright laws in France and the USA, "the first framers of copyright laws ... sought primarily to encourage the creation of and investment in the production of works furthering national, social goals".[2]

Copyright also serves the public interest in freedom of expression. By enabling the creator to derive a financial reward from his work, his artistic independence and right to create and publish according to his own wish and conscience is assured. Alternative methods of rewarding creators, such as patronage, whether by the State or by individuals, carry the risk of control or censorship.

From the outset, it has also been seen to be in the public interest that copyright law should balance the interest of the copyright owner, on the one hand, and the interest of the public, in the sense of the user or consumer, on the other, in obtaining access as cheaply and easily as possible to information of all kinds. Although there is an apparent conflict between these two latter interests, the reality seems to be that any conflict is more imaginary than real. Protection of the rights of the creator of new works, in the form of a limited monopoly, and the possibility for the creator to derive profit from the exercise of those rights, has been shown to favour creativity, and ultimately, therefore, to be of more benefit to the consuming public than if there were no rewards based on copyright.

14–002 The temptation to think in terms of making desirable goods and services free to those who need them is deeply rooted in our culture, and may be seen already in the proposal that all loans should be made free of interest, as is suggested in Exodus XXII, 25. It is still advocated at the present time in some Islamic countries. The problem is to find lenders in any such society. The situation is no different when it comes to deciding whether or not to protect works through copyright.

In 1989, the Organisation for Economic Cooperation and Development (OECD), in a research paper setting out the case for the effective international protection of intellectual property rights, concluded that the existence of such rights is a way to (a) encourage and safeguard intellectual and artistic creation; (b) disseminate new ideas

---

[2] See J.C. Ginsburg, "A Tale of Two Copyrights: Literary Property in Revolutionary France and America", 147 R.I.D.A. 125 at 131, 133 (1991).

and technologies as quickly as possible; (c) promote investment; (d) provide consumers with the fruits of creation and invention; and (e) distribute these positive effects across all countries in a manner commensurate with their level of economic, industrial and technological development. The study also found that the existence of such rights has a positive economic effect. It encourages international trade; it supports the innovation process; it encourages investment and improves competition and, finally, has a positive effect on national creativity.[3]

These conclusions remain valid today. In January 2002, the Director General of WIPO issued a statement to similar effect:

> In this 21st Century, intellectual property (IP) is a powerful driver of economic growth. When linked to the development of human capital, it results in educated, skilled and motivated individuals and becomes a dynamic combination in terms of stimulating creativity and innovation, generating revenue, promoting investment, enhancing culture, preventing "brain drain", and nurturing overall economic health.[4]

Reference has already been made to the national studies carried out into the economic importance of copyright in the United Kingdom, United States of America, Germany and elsewhere, which have shown that the copyright industries comprise one of the fastest-growing sectors of the economy, and make significant contributions to domestic job and revenue growth as well as to international trade. Both in developed and developing countries, these studies have generally reported contributions to GDP in the 3 per cent to 6 per cent range of their total national economies. In the United States of America and the Member States of the European Union, the average contribution of the copyright industries today are estimated at over 5 per cent to 6 per cent of national income.[5] The various national

---

[3] Economic Arguments for Protecting Intellectual Property Rights, (Paris, Organisation for Economic Cooperation and Development, Trade Division, 1989). For a summary of the results of the study, see 2 Intellectual Property in Business, Issue 6, at 26 (1990).

[4] Message of K. Idris, January 2002.

[5] J. Skilbeck, *The Economic Importance of Copyright* (London, International Publishers Association, 1988). See also the recent reports cited in Ch.8, nn 7 to 14; and A. Silbertson, "The Economic Importance of Copyright", in *Creativity and Intellectual Property Rights: Evolving Scenarios and Perspectives*, (EU International Conference, Vienna, July 1998, European Commission DG Internal Market), pp 43–62.

studies undertaken around the world have also shown the level of copyright-related employment to be up to 3.5 per cent of the workforce.[6] These studies further demonstrated that the development of the copyright-related industries during the 1980s and 1990s was more dynamic than for the economy as a whole and that this trend is continuing.[7] The sector is growing faster than the rest of the economy, and new jobs are being created, whereas in other sectors of the economy jobs are being lost. Thus, the economic importance of copyright in all the economies studied has been amply illustrated, as well as the dynamic nature of the copyright industries. As Marlies Hummel pointed out in a comparative analysis of the results of the various national economic studies available in 1990: "Thus, the economic importance of copyright industries with respect to the generation of income and jobs deserves to receive special attention".[8]

14–003 The economic importance of copyright at a national level, allied to the vast increase in international trade involving intellectual property rights, has led to concern for greater respect for these rights at an international level. The US Government estimated in 1990 that the proportion of total world trade in goods protected by intellectual property had doubled since the Second World War.[9] In the same year, the International Chamber of Commerce, however, calculated that up to 6 per cent of *total* world trade was in products which *infringed* intellectual property rights.[10]

This being so, in the early 1990s, issues relating to intellectual property came to be regarded as new trade barriers.

> In terms of international trade and GATT, the absence of adequate protection, or the existence of excessive protection, amount to trade barriers often having similar effects to quantitative restrictions

---

[6] M. Hummel, "The Economic Importance of Copyright", UNESCO Copyright Bulletin, Vol. XXIV, No.2, at 14 (1990).

[7] Recent reports confirm the trend. Over the last 24 years (1977–2001), for example, the US copyright industries' share of the GDP grew more than twice as fast as the remainder of the US economy, 7% as against 3%; (see S.E. Siwek, *Copyright in the US Economy, 2002 Report*, International Intellectual Property Alliance, Washington 2002). In the UK, the copyright industries output grew by 16% in 1997–1998, compared with under 6% for the economy as a whole; (see Creative Industries Mapping document, 2000, UK Department of Media, Culture and Sport (DCMS) 2001.

[8] M. Hummel, *ibid.* at 21.

[9] J. Slaughter, "TRIPs: The GATT Intellectual Property Negotiations Approach their Conclusion", 11 E.I.P.R. 418 (1990).

[10] J. Slaughter, *ibid.*

or distortion of competition within a country ... [And] upon addressing technical barriers to trade mainly in the Uruguay Round, issues relating to intellectual property were increasingly felt as a third generation of trade barriers. Insufficient protection not only frustrated and nullified advantages and market access in the country concerned. It also distorted competition in third markets.[11]

It is in this context that international measures to control trade in counterfeit goods were incorporated in the Agreement on Trade Related Aspects of Intellectual Property Rights, 1994 (the TRIPs Agreement),[12] in order to counter increasing problems of counterfeiting and piracy originating, in particular, in newly industrialised countries throughout the world.

Works protected by copyright represent a significant proportion of international trade in addition to their economic importance at national level. Since the adoption of the TRIPs Agreement, the proportion of world trade in copyright infringing products has not diminished. The Organisation for Economic Co-operation and Development (OECD) in 1998 put a figure of more than 5 per cent on such trade. Meanwhile, violations of intellectual property as a whole are estimated to have grown to as much as 9 per cent of world trade.[13] It is crucial therefore for governments to recognise that they have an obligation to foster the creation of intellectual works and that a basic precondition for the continued success of creators and the copyright-related industries is appropriate and up-to-date copyright legislation.

Copyright exists to encourage and protect creativity. In an economic sense, too few resources will be devoted to the production of creative "works" if the creator is subsequently unable to exploit this creativity, by earning a sufficient return on the effort and investment expended in producing the work.[14]

---

[11] T. Cottier, "The value and effects of protecting intellectual property rights within the World Trade Organisation", in *ALAI Geneva study session 1994*, (Groupe suisse de l'ALAI et les auteurs, Berne 1994), p.16.

[12] Signed at Marrakesh on April 15, 1994.

[13] H. Vithlani, *The Economic Impact of Counterfeiting*, (OECD Paris, 1998), p.4; see also *Financial Times*, March 11, 2002, p.18.

[14] T Price, *op. cit.*, Ch.8, below n.8.

14–004 Governments, therefore, should have a positive "copyright policy", the aims of which should be to keep their copyright laws continually under review, so as to adapt them quickly to the changing environment and the challenges posed by rapid technological change, and to maintain a balance between the interests of creators, on the one hand, and those of the public, on the other, thus ensuring the protection of both individual and collective interests. European Commissioner, Mario Monti, well expressed the task of the legislator in this respect in the Single Market in a speech in 1998. Noting that intellectual property protection significantly contributes to fostering investment, job creation and growth, he said:

> At national and at international level, copyright legislation has always emerged from, and has to a large extent been dependant on new technology and new markets. In this respect, intellectual property rights have been during all times "the currency" of access to markets and of the market place itself. Continuous adaptation is needed as new scenarios and perspectives are constantly evolving. A particular challenge for any copyright legislative action is the specific characteristic of copyright law which must not only take into account legal, but also economic, social and cultural aspects and concerns.[15]

There would be wisdom in keeping in mind Chafee's six ideals when contemplating such a copyright policy. Chafee suggested that:

> The law should seek to attain, so far as practicable, the six ideals I have described: complete coverage for all intellectual and artistic creations ...; a monopoly against all forms of reproduction; international protection; absence of excessive protection for the monopoly; refusal to stifle independent creation; and legal rules convenient to handle."[16]

Chafee admitted that the mere formulation of general principles would not solve all problems. Nevertheless, he added: "Yet general principles will help a good deal. We can keep aiming at them. If we

---

[15] M. Monti, Opening Speech, International Conference on Intellectual Property Rights, Vienna, July 1998 (see European Commission DG Internal Market website: *www.europa.eu.int*).

[16] Z. Chafee, *op. cit.*, Ch.1, n.16 above, at 515.

fall short of them, it is worth while to know that fact and then ask whether the failure is permanently necessary or is merely preservation of the inadequate work of past legislators."[17]

Chafee's principles were propounded in 1945, but, as David Ladd has reminded us:

> Copyright principles are eternal—or should be to those who care at all about human progress and freedom—but the precise rules by which we achieve copyright's objectives must vary and may need substantial changes to meet substantially changed circumstances.[18]

From the beginning, the law of copyright has developed in response to significant changes in technology. Indeed, as we have seen, it was first introduced as a consequence of the invention of printing. The greatest challenge to the copyright system of the past 50 years has been to keep pace with the proliferation of new categories of creative works made possible by new technology and of the new uses of works resulting from the new communication media. Experience has demonstrated the need for copyright legislation to be adapted swiftly to new technology, and new uses of works. If government fails in this task, users and consumers come to believe that they have a right to free use of works. Subsequently, the entrenched interests they represent make the task of the law-maker in redressing the balance between the interests of the copyright owners and the public at large much more difficult.

14–005

> As habits of free use proliferate, the prospects for dislodging them diminish. Ideal, balanced laws that might have been possible within a year or two of a new technology's arrival in the marketplace can, five years later, be politically impossible.[19]

It is the law-maker who has the duty to evaluate the issues and the conflicting interests of the various, often warring factions within the interested parties, to consider what justice requires and to take the necessary hard decisions in the general public interest of society as a

---

[17] Z. Chafee, *ibid.* at 519.
[18] D. Ladd, "To Cope with the World Upheaval in Copyright", [1983] *Copyright* 289 at 294.
[19] P. Goldstein, *Copyright's Highway, The Law and Lore of Copyright from Gutenberg to the Celestial Jukebox*, (Hill and Wang, New York, 1994), at 134.

whole. This remains the principal challenge that the law-maker faces today in the field of copyright.

At the turn of the twenty-first century, this challenge is compounded by the risk that the legislative process will be overtaken by events in the light of the accelerating pace of technological innovation. Over the past 10 years, as governments have been commissioning reports on the impact of the transmission of works in digital form over the information superhighways[20] and discussing in the various international fora concerned how to address the copyright issues involved,[21] the internet has been developing apace (the number of people with internet access from home world-wide is nearing 500 million[22]) and governments have been putting into place the telecommunications networks for the Global Information Infrastructure. International cooperation and rules are of course essential for copyright interests to be adequately protected in the global marketplace but such cooperation by its nature takes time.

In order for modern copyright legislation to meet Chafee's three positive ideals, first *complete coverage* of new forms of works, secondly *the single monopoly*, *i.e.* the sole right to control all the channels through which a work or a fragment of a work reach the market, and thirdly *international protection*, existing legislation and the international

---

[20] See, for example, in addition to the US N.I.I. Report, *cf.* Ch.5, n.33 below: "Europe's Way to the Information Society, An Action Plan", Communication of the Commission to the Council and the European Parliament, (COM (94) 347 final) July 1994; European Commission "Green Paper on Copyright and Related Rights in the Information Society", (COM (95) 382 final) July 1995; *The Challenge of the Information Highway*, (Final Report of the Information Highway Advisory Council, Canada, 1995). *Industrie Culturelle et Nouvelle Technique*, (Sirinelli report, Ministère de la Culture et de la Francophonie, Paris, 1994); *Information Society: Agenda for Action in the UK*, Report of the House of Lords Select Committee on Science and Technology, HL Paper 77, Session 1995–96, 5th. Report, July 1996.

[21] In parallel with the discussions which led to the adoption of the WCT and WPPT in 1996, WIPO also held a series of Conferences (the WIPO World-wide Symposium on the Impact of Digital Technology on Copyright and Neighbouring Rights, Harvard University, 1993; the WIPO World-wide Symposium on the Future of Copyright and Neighbouring Rights, Paris, 1994; WIPO World-wide Symposium on Copyright in the Global Information Infrastructure, Mexico City, 1995).

[22] The Fourth Quarter 2001 Global internet Trends report on internet access and penetration found that 498 million people now have internet access from home. One-third of households have internet access in Europe, the Middle East and Africa, compared to more than half in the USA. It is estimated that by 2004 there will be 165.5 million US internet users, accounting for 23% of the global total. In 1998, there were a mere 60 million net users world-wide, (Nielsen/NetRatings report March 6, 2002, and eMarketer report July 14, 1998, ITN Media Group, *www.internetnews.com*.)

conventions need regular fine tuning. As the Preamble to the Information Society Directive states:

> Technological development has multiplied and diversified the vectors for creation, production and exploitation. While no new concepts for the protection of intellectual property are needed, the current law on copyright and related rights should be supplemented to respond adequately to economic realities such as new forms of exploitation.[23]

The ideal of securing complete coverage of new forms of works under **14–006** copyright legislation has not always been swiftly accomplished. Edison invented the art of recording sound in 1877, for example, but sound recordings were given specific protection against unauthorised commercial reproduction by copyright or related rights law only in 1976 in the United States of America and 1985 in France. International protection of related rights under the Rome Convention remains limited by the relatively small number of member States, 69 as of June 30, 2002, as compared with the 150 of the Berne Convention at the same date. Another example is the case of computer programs, which have been generally accepted for the past 25 years as being capable of protection as literary works under national legislation and the Berne Convention. Specific protection to that effect under the law, however, has only gradually found its way into national laws (although the 1991 EC Directive[24] on the subject has hastened the process for the Member States of the European Union). Likewise, the question of the international protection of computer programs as literary works was only settled with the adoption of the WIPO Copyright Treaty 1996.

The intervals at which states have legislated in the past to bring copyright legislation up to date have arguably been too long. In the past century, taking as examples the four countries covered by this study, the United Kingdom has undertaken major revisions of its legislation on only three occasions (1911, 1956 and 1988), the United States of America on two occasions, 1909 and 1976, France on two occasions, 1957 and 1985 and Germany also on two occasions, 1901 and 1965. Technical and international developments in the meantime

---

[23] Information Society Directive, Recital 5.
[24] Council Directive 91/250/EEC of May 14,1991, on the legal protection of computer programs (OJ EC No.L122/42).

have made regular and ever more frequent adaptation and revision of the most recent laws necessary, as has been seen above in Part II.

In adapting copyright legislation to technical and marketplace developments, as the US N.I.I. report stated:

> Certain issues merely require an explanation of the application of the current law, and clearly are appropriately covered. Others present rights or limitations that clearly fit within the spirit of the law but the letter of the law is in need of clarification to avoid uncertainty and unnecessary litigation. Still others need new solutions.[25]

Issues which have required explanation in the context of the Global Information Infrastructure include the question of multi-media works and, as discussed above, the impact of digitisation of works. A consensus has developed that multi-media works are not a new category of work but may be considered to be compilations or collections of works, and, as such, protected under national laws and the Berne Convention.[26] Digital technology can record, store and communicate throughout the world electronic marketplace virtually simultaneously, all existing works, whether originally expressed as the written word or as films, sound recordings, pictures, photographs and so on. However, the process of digitisation of works does not create a new category of work; it merely constitutes the expression of copyright subject-matter in a different format, the ease of distribution of which is unprecedented. By contrast, examples of issues which have had to be addressed include the various matters dealt with in the WIPO Internet Treaties and the EU Information Society Directive and discussed above in Chapter 11, including the access right and the protection of technical devices and rights management systems.[27] The balance of

---

[25] US N.I.I. report, *op. cit.* at 211.

[26] Art.2(5) of the Berne Convention provides: "Collections of literary or artistic works such as encyclopaedias and anthologies which, by reason of the selection and arrangement of their contents, constitute intellectual creations shall be protected as such, without prejudice to the copyright in each of the works forming part of such collections."

[27] On the impact of digital technology on copyright and related rights, see, in addition to the references given in previous chs of Part III of this study, *inter alia*: *Records of the WIPO World-wide Symposium on the Impact of Digital Technology on Copyright and Neighbouring Rights*, (Harvard University, 1993, WIPO Publication No.723 1993); *WIPO International Forum on the Exercise and Management of Copyright and Neighbouring Rights in the Face of the Challenges of Digital Technology*, (Seville, 1997, WIPO Publication

interests between right owners and the general public has also required review. The Information Society Directive "should seek to promote learning and culture by protecting works and other subject-matter while permitting exceptions or limitations in the public interest for the purpose of education and teaching".[28]

As discussed above, achieving a satisfying balance of interests is the most controversial and difficult aspect of copyright law. **14–007**

The draftsman of copyright legislation, moreover, is faced with a dilemma. Chafee described the dilemma as the "Problem of wide range", pointing out that:

> if legislation is tuned to the modes of artistic expression and the methods of infringement which are already well-known, the danger is that within a few years the progress of invention will produce new devices which will fall outside the statute. Consequently the author will be denied the protection which he deserves. On the other hand, if the draftsman inserts broad clauses for the purpose of including all conceivable new relevant devices, it may easily happen that a court will be obliged to apply a statutory remedy which gives too much protection to the author...
>
> Whichever way the draftsman decides, it is always possible when a defect appears for Congress to remedy it by an amendment. Yet this often takes many years, and meanwhile injustice may be widespread.

A major disadvantage of the narrow approach, limiting protection

---

No.756). A. Christie, "Reconceptualising Copyright in the Digital Era", [1995] 11 E.I.P.R. 522; M. Davison, "Geographical Restraints on the Distribution of Copyright Material in a Digital Age: Are they Justified?" [1996] 9 E.I.P.R. 477; A.N. Dixon, and L.C. Self, "Copyright Protection for the Information Superhighway", [1994] 11 E.I.P.R. 465; T. Dreier, "Copyright Law and Digital Exploitation of Works", originally published in German under the title "Urheberrecht und digitale Werkverwertung: die aktuelle Lage des Urheberrechts im Zeitalter von Internet und Multi-media", (1997, Friedrich Ebert Foundation, Bonn); P.E. Geller, "The Universal Electronic Archive: Issues in International Copyright", 25 I.I.C. 54 (1994); Y. Gendreau, "Digital Technology and Copyright: Can Moral Rights Survive the Disappearance of the Hard Copy?", [1995] 6 ENT. L.R. 214. S. Olswang, "Accessright: An Evolutionary Path for Copyright into the Digital Era?" [1995] 5 E.I.P.R. 215; P. Samuelson, "Digital Media and the Changing Face of Intellectual Property Law", 16 Rutgers Computer and Technology Law Journal 323 (1990).

[28] Information Society Directive, Recital 14.

to known works and methods of exploitation, is that copyright laws are always out of date and the situation worsens as the pace of technological change quickens. When new technologies arise, such as we have seen with reprography, private copying and most recently digital copying from the internet, the public gets used to unrestricted access to and use of works free of charge and vehemently opposes changes in the copyright law to regulate the situation; this puts governments in the unenviable situation of legislating to bring entrenched consumer habits under control. Sometimes, like the United Kingdom and the United States of America faced with the problem of private copying a government completely fails to resolve the issue. Moreover, experience in all four jurisdictions discussed in this study has shown also that where legislation is limited and specific the courts are reluctant to extend the law to new situations.[29]

Goldstein puts the problem succinctly:

> In the two centuries since it passed the first American copyright act, it [Congress] has been playing catch-up with new technologies—first photographs, then phonograph records, motion pictures, radio, broadcast television, and cable television—usually about twenty years behind the new technologies. As new copying technologies—audiotape and videotape machines, personal computers—spread through America today, the idea of subjecting them to copyright control has become politically unpalatable.[30]

14–008 On the other hand, wide-ranging and technologically neutral copyright laws which would protect right owners against all conceivable new technologies are difficult to justify in view of the public interest in preserving the balance between the interests of copyright owners and those of the public.

In any case, legislative proposals for change should meet certain

---

[29] See, *e.g.* UK: *Amstrad Consumer Electronics plc v British Phonographic Industry* [1986] F.S.R. 159 concerning private copying of sound recordings; USA: *Williams and Wilkins Co. v the USA*, 172 U.S.P.Q. 670 (Ct.Cl. 1972) concerning the library photocopying of medical journals; *Sony Corp of Am. v. Universal City Studios, Inc.*, 220 U.S. P.Q. 665 (1984) concerning home videotaping.

[30] P. Goldstein, *Copyright's Highway*, *op. cit.*, n.19, above, at 33.

general standards. In 1985 Kastenmeier and Remington[31] put forward a political test for intellectual property legislation in the United States of America, which holds good today and is relevant to law-makers in all jurisdictions. They suggested that legislation should respond to specific problems and "at the outset the proponents of change should have the burden of showing that a meritorious public purpose is served by the proposed Congressional action". The change should be necessary, fair and practical. To discharge that burden, the proposed legislation would have to satisfy a four-fold political test.

First, the proponent of a new interest ought to show that the interest can fit harmoniously within the existing legal framework without violating existing principles or basic concepts. The proponent must further indicate whether fundamental aspects of current law, such as the term of protection and exclusive rights are compatible with the protection sought for the new interest...

Second, the proponent of a new intellectual property interest must be able to commit the new expression to a reasonably clear and satisfactory definition...

Third, the proponent of change should present an honest analysis of all the costs and benefits of the proposed legislation. The proponent must show the difference between the status quo and the future contemplated by the legislation...

Fourth, any advocate of a new protectable interest should show in the record how giving protection to that interest will enrich or enhance the aggregate public domain. The aggregate public benefit should outweigh the proprietary gains which result from protection...[32]

Congress will attempt to recognise and balance the legitimate rights of producers, creators or copyright holders and the interests of the public. The legislator must attend to the voices of less powerful

---

[31] R.W. Kastenmeier, and M. J. Remington, "The Semiconductor Chip Protection Act of 1984: A Swamp or Firm Ground?" 70 Minnesota L. Rev. 417 (1985). Mr. Kastenmeier was at the time the Chairman of the House Committee on the Judiciary Subcommittee on Courts, Civil Liberties and the Administration of Justice; Mr. Remington was Chief Counsel to the Committee. See also *Kastenmeier, R.W.*, The 1989 Horace S. Manges Lecture—"Copyright in an Era of Technological Change: A Political Perspective", 14 Colum.-VLA J.L. & Arts, 1 (1989).

[32] R.W. Kastenmeier and M.J. Remington, *op. cit.*, at 440–441.

interests in order to achieve sound public policy.[33] They suggest that Congress can safely move forward if the cost to the public of the monopoly is deemed to be less than the value to the public of the total benefits caused by the law.[34]

14–009   In 2002, Chafee's third ideal, according to which protection should be *international*, takes on far greater significance than when he first propounded it in 1945. The world has become a much smaller place in the meantime. The international copyright system has grown dramatically: in 1945, the Berne Convention numbered 35 Member States, as of June 30, 2002, it had 150. The influence of the harmonisation programme of the European Union cannot be overlooked either by its Member States or their trading partners. The TRIPs Agreement has highlighted the essential need for adequate protection of intellectual property in all countries which take part in the international trading system of the World Trade Organisation. Governments can therefore no longer pursue national copyright policies and consider legislation only as regards its domestic impact; they must take account also of the consequences of their domestic policies on other countries, on their bilateral and multilateral partners and on trade.

It is submitted, therefore, that the economic and cultural policies of states as expressed through copyright legislation should ensure that an adequate framework exists to provide "a proper balance based upon equity, fair competition and fair access and the public interest",[35] and to ensure the level of investment required to take full advantage, for the benefit both of right owners and the public, of new means of communication and distribution of copyright works made possible by new technology. Such policies should keep uppermost the principle that, as this study has shown, the interests of the public in general are ultimately best served by safeguarding the interests of creators and giving them a level of protection sufficient to encourage them to continue to create.

> Providing high levels of legal and technical protection of creative content will be one of the essential conditions to ensure the necessary climate for the investment needed for the development of the information society. Thus, there is a need for internationally

---

[33] R.W. Kastenmeier, *op. cit.*, at 6.

[34] R.W. Kastenmeier and M.J. Remington, *op. cit.*, at 442.

[35] G. Dworkin & R.D. Taylor, *Blackstone's Guide to the Copyright, Designs and Patents Act 1988*, (London, Blackstone Press Ltd., 1989).

recognised protection for the creators and providers of materials that will be disseminated over the Global Information Infrastructure.[36]

---

[36] Conclusions of the G7 Ministerial Conference on the Global Information Society, (Round-table meeting of business leaders, Brussels, February 1995).

APPENDICES

APPENDICES

Appendix 1

United Kingdom

Statute of Anne 1709

Cap XIX

An Act for the Encouragement of Learning, by vesting the Copies of printed Books in the Authors or Purchasers of such Copies, during the Times therein mentioned.

S.I. Whereas Printers, Booksellers and other Persons have of late frequently taken the Liberty of printing, reprinting and publishing, or causing to be printed, reprinted and published, Books and other Writings, without the Consent of the Authors or Proprietors of such Books and Writings, to their very great Detriment, and too often to the Ruin of them and their Families: For preventing therefore such Practices for the future, and for the Encouragement of learned Men to compose and write useful Books; May it please your Majesty, that it may be enacted, and be it enacted by the Queen's most Excellent Majesty, by and with the Advice and Consent of the Lords Spiritual and Temporal, and Commons, in this present Parliament assembled, and by the Authority of the same, That from and after the tenth Day of April, one thousand seven hundred and ten, the Author of any Book or Books already printed, who hath not transferred to any other the Copy or Copies of such Book or Books, Share or Shares thereof, or the Bookseller or Booksellers, Printer or Printers, or other Person or Persons, who hath or have purchased or acquired the Copy or Copies of any Book or Books, in order to print or reprint the same, shall have the sole Right and Liberty of printing such Book and Books for the Term of one and twenty years, to commence from the said tenth Day of April, and no longer; and that the Author of any Book or

Books already composed, and not printed and published, or that shall hereafter be composed, and his Assignee or Assigns, shall have the sole Liberty of printing and reprinting such Book and Books for the Term of fourteen Years, to commence from the Day of the first publishing the same, and no longer; and that if any other Bookseller, Printer or other Person whatsoever, from and after the tenth Day of April, one thousand seven hundred and ten, within the Times granted and limited by this Act, as aforesaid, shall print, reprint, or import, or cause to be printed, reprinted, or imported, any such Book or Books, without the Consent of the Proprietor or Proprietors thereof first had and obtained in Writing, signed in the Presence of two or more credible Witnesses; or knowing the same to be so printed or reprinted, without the Consent of the Proprietors, shall sell, publish, or expose to Sale, or cause to be sold, published or exposed to Sale, any such Book or Books, without such Consent first had and obtained, as aforesaid; Then such Offender or Offenders shall forfeit such Book or Books, and all and every Sheet or Sheets, being Part of such Book or Books, to the Proprietor or Proprietors of the Copy thereof, who shall forthwith Damask and make Waste Paper of them; and further, That every such Offender or Offenders shall forfeit one Penny for every Sheet which shall be found in his, her, or their Custody, either printed or printing, published or exposed to Sale, contrary to the true Intent and Meaning of this Act; the one Moiety thereof to the Queen's most excellent Majesty, her Heirs and Successors, and the other Moiety thereof to any Person or Persons that shall sue for the same, to be recovered in any of her Majesty's Courts of Record at Westminster, by Action of Debt, Bill, Plaint, or Information, in which no Wager of Law, Essoin, Privilege, or Protection, or more than one Imparlance shall be allowed.

S.II. And whereas many Persons may through Ignorance offend against this Act, unless some Provision be made, whereby the Property in every such Book, as is intended by this Act to be secured to the proprietor or Proprietors thereof, may be ascertained, as likewise the Consent of such Proprietor or Proprietors for the printing or reprinting of such Book or Books may from time to time be known; Be it therefore further enacted by the Authority aforesaid, That nothing in this Act contained shall be construed to extend to subject any Bookseller, Printer, or other Person whatsoever, to the Forfeitures or Penalties therein mentioned, for or by Reason of the printing or reprinting of any Book or Books without such Consent, as aforesaid, unless the Title to the Copy of such Book or Books hereafter published shall, before such Publication, be entred in the Register Book of the Company of Stationers, in such Manner as hath been usual, which Register Book shall at all Times be kept at the Hall of the said Company, and unless such Consent of the Proprietor or Proprietors be in like Manner entred as aforesaid, for every of which several Entries six Pence shall be paid, and no more; which said Register Book may, at all seasonable and convenient times, be resorted to, and inspected by any Bookseller, Printer or other Person, for the Purposes before-mentioned, without any Fee or Reward; and the Clerk of the said Company of Stationers shall, when and as often as thereunto required, give a Certificate under his hand of such Entry or Entries, and for every such Certificate may take a Fee not exceeding six Pence.

S. III. Provided nevertheless, That if the Clerk of the said Company of Stationers for the Time being, shall refuse or neglect to register, or make such Entry or Entries, or to give such Certificate, being thereunto required by the Author or Proprietor of such Copy or Copies, in the Presence of two or more credible Witnesses, That then such Person and Persons so refusing, Notice being first duly given of such Refusal, by an Advertisement in the Gazette, shall have the like Benefit, as if such Entry or Entries, Certificate or Certificates had been duly made and given, and that the Clerks so refusing, shall, for any such Offence, forfeit to the Proprietor of such Copy or Copies the Sum of twenty Pounds, to be recovered in any of her Majesty's Courts of Record at Westminster, by Action of Debt, Bill, Plaint, or Information, in which no Wager of Law, Essoin, Privilege or Protection, or more than one Imparlance shall be allowed.

S.IV. Provided nevertheless, and it is hereby further enacted by the Authority aforesaid, That if any Bookseller or Booksellers, Printer or Printers, shall, after the said five and twentieth Day of March one thousand seven hundred and ten, set a Price upon, or sell, or expose to Sale, any Book or Books at such a Price or Rate as shall be conceived by any Person or Persons to be too high and unreasonable; it shall and may be lawful for any Person or Persons, to make Complaint thereof to the Lord Archbishop of Canterbury for the time being, the Lord Chancellor, or Lord Keeper of the Great Seal of Great Britain for the time being, the Lord Bishop of London for the time being, the Lord Chief Justice of the Court of Queen's Bench, the Lord Chief Justice of the Court of Common Pleas, the Lord Chief Baron of the Court of Exchequer for the time being, the Vice Chancellors of the two Universities for the time being, in that Part of Great Britain called England; the Lord President of the Sessions for the time being, the

Lord Chief Justice General for the time being, the Lord Chief Baron of the Exchequer for the time being, the Rector of the College of Edinburgh for the time being, in that Part of Great Britain called Scotland; who, or any one of them, shall and have hereby full Power and Authority, from time to time, to send for, summon, or call before him or them such Bookseller or Booksellers, Printer or Printers, and to examine and enquire of the Reason of the Dearness and Inhauncement of the Price or Value of such Book or Books by him or them so sold or exposed to Sale; and if upon such Enquiry and Examination it shall be found, that the Price of such Book or Books is inhaunced, or any wise too high or unreasonable, then and in such case the said Archbishop of Canterbury, Lord Chancellor or Lord Keeper, Bishop of London, two Chief Justices, Chief Baron, Vice Chancellors of the Universities, in that Part of Great Britain called England, and the said Lord President of the Sessions, Lord Justice General, Lord Chief Baron, and Rector of the College of Edinburgh, in that Part of Great Britain called Scotland, or any one or more of them, so enquiring and examining, have hereby full Power and Authority to reform and redress the same, and to limit and settle the Price of every such printed Book and Books, from Time to Time, according to the best of their Judgments, and as to them shall seem just and reasonable; and in case of Alteration of the Rate or Price from what was set or demanded by such Bookseller or Booksellers, Printer or Printers, to award and order such Bookseller and Booksellers, Printer and Printers, to pay all the Costs and Charges that the Person or Persons so complaining shall be put unto, by Reason of such Complaint, and of the causing such Rate or Price to be so limited and settled; all which shall be done by the said Archbishop of Canterbury, Lord Chancellor or Lord Keeper, Bishop of London, two Chief Justices, Chief Baron, Vice Chancellors of the two Universities, in that Part of Great Britain called England, and the said Lord President of the Sessions, Lord Justice General, Lord Chief Baron, and Rector of the College of Edinburgh, in that Part of Great Britain called Scotland, or any one of them, by Writing under their Hands and Seals, and thereof publick Notice shall be forthwith given by the said Bookseller or Booksellers, Printer or Printers, by an Advertisement in the Gazette; and if any Bookseller or Booksellers, Printer or Printers, shall after such Settlement made of the said Rate and Price, sell, or expose to Sale, any Book or Books, at a higher or greater Price, than what shall have been so limited and settled, as aforesaid, then, and in every such Case such Bookseller and Booksellers, Printer and Printers,

374

shall forfeit the Sum of five Pounds for every such Book so by him, her, or them sold or exposed to Sale; one Moiety thereof to the Queen's most excellent Majesty, her Heirs and Successors, and the other Moiety to any Person or Persons that shall sue for the same, to be recovered, with Costs of Suit, in any of her Majesty's Courts of Record at Westminster, by Action of Debt, Bill, Plaint or Information, in which no Wager of Law, Essoin, Privilege, or Protection, or more than one Imparlance shall be allowed.

S.V. Provided always, and it is hereby enacted, That nine Copies of each Book or Books, upon the best Paper, that from and after the said tenth Day of April, one thousand seven hundred and ten, shall be printed and published, as aforesaid, or reprinted and published with Additions, shall, by the Printer and Printers thereof, be delivered to the Warehouse keeper of the said Company of Stationers for the Time being, at the Hall of the said Company, before such Publication made, for the use of the Royal Library, the Libraries of the Universities of Oxford and Cambridge, the Libraries of the four Universities in Scotland, the Library of Sion College in London, and the Library commonly called the Library belonging to the Faculty of Advocates at Edinburgh respectively; which said Warehouse keeper is hereby required within ten Days after Demand by the Keepers of the respective Libraries, or any Person or Persons by them or any of them authorized to demand the said Copy, to deliver the same, for the Use of the aforesaid Libraries; and if any Proprietor, Bookseller, or Printer, or the Warehouse keeper of the said Company of Stationers, shall not observe the Direction of this Act therein, that then he and they so making Default in not delivering the said printed Copies, as aforesaid, shall forfeit, besides the Value of the said printed Copies, the Sum of five Pounds for every Copy not so delivered, as also the Value of the said printed Copy not so delivered; the same to be recovered by the Queen's Majesty, her Heirs and Successors, and by the Chancellor, Masters, and Scholars of any of the said Universities, and by the President and Fellows of Sion College, and the said Faculty of Advocates at Edinburgh, with their full Costs respectively.

S.VI. Provided always, and be it further enacted, That if any Person or Persons incur the Penalties contained in this Act, in that Part of Great Britain called Scotland, they shall be recoverable by any Action before the Court of Session there.

S.VII. Provided, That nothing in this Act contained do extend, or shall be construed to extend to prohibit the Importation, Vending or Selling of any Books in Greek, Latin, or any other foreign Language printed beyond the Seas; any thing in this Act contained to the contrary notwithstanding.

S.VIII. And be it further enacted by the Authority aforesaid, That if any Action or Suit shall be commenced or brought against any Person or Persons whatsoever, for doing or causing to be done any Thing in pursuance of this Act, the Defendant in such Action may plead the General Issue, and give the special Matter in Evidence; and if upon such Action a Verdict be given for the Defendant, or the Plantiff become nonsuited or discontinue his Action, then the Defendant shall have and recover his full Costs, for which he shall have the same Remedy as a Defendant in any Case by Law hath.

S.IX. Provided, That nothing in this Act contained shall extend, or be construed to extend, either to prejudice or confirm any Right that the said Universities or any of them, or any Person or Persons have, or claim to have, to the printing or reprinting of any Book or Copy already printed, or hereafter to be printed.

S.X. Provided nevertheless, That all Actions, Suits, Bills, Indictments or Informations for any Offence that shall be committed against this Act, shall be brought, sued, and commenced within three Months next after such offence committed, or else the same shall be void and of none Effect.

S.XI. Provided always, That after the Expiration of the said Term of fourteen Years, the sole Right of printing or disposing of Copies shall return to the Authors thereof, if they are then living, for another Term of fourteen years.

Appendix 2

USA

Copyright Act 1790

Chap. XV.

An Act for the encouragement of learning, by securing the copies of maps, charts, and books, to the authors and proprietors of such copies, during the times therein mentioned.

S.1. Be it enacted by the Senate and House of Representatives of the United States of America in Congress assembled, That from and after the passing of this act, the author and authors of any map, chart, book or books already printed within these United States, being a citizen or citizens thereof, or resident within the same, his or their executors, administrators or assigns, who hath or have not transferred to any other person the copyright of such map, chart, book or books, share or shares thereof; and any other person or persons, being a citizen or citizens of these United States, or residents therein, his or their executors, administrators or assigns, who hath or have purchased or legally acquired the copyright of any such map, chart, book or books, in order to print, reprint, publish or vend the same, shall have the sole right and liberty of printing, reprinting, publishing and vending such map, chart, book or books, for the term of fourteen years from the recording the title thereof in the clerk's office, as is herein after directed: And that the author and authors of any map, chart, book or books already made and composed, and not printed or published, or that shall hereafter be made and composed, being a citizen or citizens of these United States, or resident therein, and his or their executors, administrators or assigns, shall have the sole right and liberty of printing, reprinting, publishing and vending such map, chart, book or books, for the like term of fourteen years from the time of recording the title thereof in the clerk's office as aforesaid. And if, at the expiration of the said term, the author or authors, or any of them, be living, and a citizen or citizens of these United States, or resident therein, the same exclusive right shall be continued to him or them, his or their executors, administrators or assigns, for the further term of fourteen years: Provided, he or they shall cause the title thereof to be a second time recorded and published in the same manner as is herein after directed, and that within six months before the expiration of the first term of fourteen years aforesaid.

S.2. And be it further enacted, That if any other person or persons, from and after the recording the title of any map, chart, book or books, and publishing the same as aforesaid, and within the times limited and granted by this act, shall print, reprint, publish, or import, or cause to be printed, reprinted, published, or imported from any foreign kingdom or state, any copy or copies of such map, chart, book or books, without the consent of the author or proprietor thereof, first had and obtained in writing, signed in the presence of two or more credible witnesses; or knowing the same to be so printed, reprinted, or imported, shall publish, sell, or expose to sale, or cause to be published, sold, or exposed to sale, any copy of such map, chart, book or books, without such consent first had and obtained in writing as aforesaid, then such offender or offenders shall forfeit all and every copy and copies of such map, chart, book or books, and all and every sheet and sheets, being part of the same, or either of them, to the author or proprietor of such map, chart, book or books, who shall forthwith destroy the same: And every such offender and offenders shall also forfeit and pay the sum of fifty cents for every sheet which shall be found in his or their possession, either printed or printing, published, imported or exposed to sale, contrary to the true intent and meaning of this act, the one moiety thereof to the author or proprietor of such map, chart, book or books who shall sue for the same, and the other moiety thereof to and for the use of the United States, to be recovered by action of debt in any court of record in the United States, wherein the same is cognizable. Provided always, That such action be commenced within one year after the cause of action shall arise, and not afterwards.

S.3. And be it further enacted, That no person shall be entitled to the benefit of this act, in cases where any map, chart, book or books, hath or have been already printed and published, unless he shall first deposit, and in all other cases, unless he shall before publication deposit a printed copy of the title of such map, chart, book or books, in the clerk's office of the district court where the author or proprietor shall reside: And the clerk of such court is hereby directed and required to record the same forthwith, in a book to be kept by him for that purpose, in the words following, (giving a copy thereof to the said author or proprietor, under the seal of the court, if he shall require the same.) "District of ... to wit: Be it remembered, That on the ... day of ... in the ... year of the independence of the United States of America, A.B. of the said district, hath deposited in this office the title of a map, chart, book or books, (as the case may be) the right whereof he claims as author or proprietor, (as the case may be) in the words following, to wit: [here insert the title] in conformity to the act of the Congress of the United States, intituled 'An act for the encourage-ment of learning, by securing the copies of maps, charts, and books, to the authors and proprietors of such copies, during the times therein mentioned.' C. D. clerk of the district of—." For which the said clerk shall be entitled to receive sixty cents from the said author or pro-prietor, and sixty cents for every copy under seal actually given to such author or proprietor as aforesaid. And such author or proprietor shall, within two months from the date thereof, cause a copy of the said record to be published in one or more of the newspapers printed in the United States, for the space of four weeks.

S.4. And be it further enacted, That the author or proprietor of any such map, chart, book or books, shall, within six months after the publishing thereof, deliver, or cause to be delivered to the Secretary of State a copy of the same, to be preserved in his office.

S.5. And be it further enacted, That nothing in this act shall be construed to extend to prohibit the importation or vending, repri-nting or publishing within the United States, of any map, chart, book or books, written, printed, or published by any person not a citizen of the United States, in foreign parts or places without the jurisdiction of the United States.

S.6. And be it further enacted, That any person or persons who shall print or publish any manuscript, without the consent and approbation of the author or proprietor thereof, first had and obtained as aforesaid, (if such author or proprietor be a citizen of or resident in these United States) shall be liable to suffer and pay to the said author or proprietor all damages occasioned by such injury, to be recovered by a special action on the case founded upon this act, in any court having cognizance thereof.

S.7. And be it further enacted, That if any person or persons shall be sued or prosecuted for any matter, act or thing done under or by virtue of this act, he or they may plead the general issue, and give the special matter in evidence.

APPROVED, May 31, 1790.

Appendix 3

France

Le Décret des 13–19 Janvier 1791

Relatif aux Spectacles

L'Assemblée nationale, ouï le rapport de son comité de constitution décrète ce qui suit:

Article premier: Tout citoyen pourra élever un théâtre public et y faire représenter des pièces de tous les genres, en faisant préalablement à l'établissement de son théâtre sa déclaration à la municipalité des lieux.

Article 2: Les ouvrages des auteurs morts depuis cinq ans et plus sont une propriété publique et peuvent nonobstant tous anciens privilèges qui sont abolis, être représentés sur tous les théâtres indistinctement.

Article 3: Les ouvrages des auteurs vivants ne pourront être représentés sur aucun théâtre public, dans toute l'étendue de la France, sans le consentement formel et par écrit des auteurs sous peine de confiscation du produit total des représentations au profit des auteurs.

Article 4: La disposition de l'article 3 s'applique aux ouvrages déjà représentés, quels que soient les anciens règlements.

Article 5: Les héritiers, ou les cessionnaires des auteurs seront propriétaires de leurs ouvrages durant l'espace de cinq années après la mort de l'auteur.

Le Décret des 19–24 Juillet 1793

La Convention nationale après avoir entendu son comité d'instruction publique, décrète ce qui suit:

Article premier: Les auteurs d'écrits en tous genres, les compositeurs de musique, les peintres et dessinateurs qui feront graver des tableaux ou desseins, jouiront leur vie entière, du droit exclusif de vendre, faire vendre, distribuer leurs ouvrages dans le territoire de la République et d'en céder la propriété en tout ou en partie.

Article 2: Leurs héritiers ou cessionnaires jouiront du même droit durant l'espace de dix ans après la mort des auteurs.

Article 3: Les officiers de paix seront tenus de faire confisquer à la réquisition et au profit des auteurs, compositeurs, peintres ou dessinateurs ou autres, leurs héritiers ou cessionnaires, tous les exemplaires des éditions imprimées ou gravées sans la permission formelle et par écrit des auteurs.

Article 4: Tout contrefacteur sera tenu de payer au véritable propriétaire une somme équivalente au prix de trois mille (3.000) exemplaires de l'édition originale.

Article 5: Tout débitant d'édition contrefaite, si'il n'est pas reconnu contrefacteur, sera tenu de payer au véritable propriétaire une somme équivalente au prix de cinq cents exemplaires de l'édition originale.

Article 6: Tout citoyen, qui mettra au jour un ouvrage soit de littérature ou de gravure, dans quelque genre que ce soit, sera obligé d'en déposer deux exemplaires à la Bibliothèque Nationale ou au Cabinet des Estampes de la République dont il recevra un reçu signé par le bibliothécaire; faute de quoi, il ne pourra être admis en justice pour la poursuite des contrefacteurs.

Article 7: Les héritiers de l'auteur d'un ouvrage de littérature ou de gravure ou de toute autre production de l'esprit ou du génie qui appartient aux Beaux-Arts en auront la propriété exclusive pendant dix années.

Appendix 4

Germany

Preußisches Gesetz zum Schutze des Eigenthums an Werken der Wissenschaft und Kunst gegen Nachdruck und Nachbildung vom 11. Juni 1837

Wir Friedrich Wilhelm von Gottes Gnaden, König von Preußen...

Damit dem Eigenthum an den Werken der Wissenschaften und Kunst der erforderliche Schutz gegen Nachdruck und Nachbildung gesichert werde, haben Wir Uns bewogen gefunden, die darüber bestehenden Gesetze einer Abänderung und Ergänzung zu unterwerfen, und verordnen demnach auf den Antrag Unseres Staats= Ministeriums und nach erfordertem Gutachten Unseres Staats=Raths, für den ganzen Umfang Unserer Monarchie, was folgt.

s.1.

1) Schriften

a. Ausschließendes Recht der Schriftsteller

Das Recht, eine bereits herausgegebene Schrift, ganz oder theilweise, von neuem abdrucken oder auf irgend einem mechanischen Wege vervielfältigen zu lassen, steht nur dem Autor derselben oder denjenigen zu, welche ihre Befugniß dazu von ihm herleiten.

s.2

b. Verbot des Nachdruckes

Jede solche neue Vervielfältigung, wenn sie ohne Genehmigung des dazu ausschließlich Berechtigten (s.1.) geschieht, heißt Nachdruck, und ist verboten.

s.3

c. Was dem Nachdruck Gleich zu Achten

Dem Nachdruck wird gleich geachtet, und ist daher ebenfalls verboten, der ohne Genehmigung des Autors oder seiner Rechtsnachfolger bewirkte Abdruck

a.   von Manuscripten aller Art;

b.   von nachgeschriebenen Predigten und mündlichen Lehrvorträgen, gleichviel, ob dieselben unter dem wahren Namen des Autors herausgegeben werden oder nicht.

Dieser Genehmigung bedarf auch der rechtmäßige Besitzer eines Manuscripts oder einer Abschrift desselben (litt. a.), imgleichen nachgeschriebener Predigten oder Lehrvorträge (litt. b.).

s.4

d. Was Nicht als Nachdruck Anzusehen

Als Nachdruck ist nicht anzusehen

1)   das wörtliche Anführen einzelner Stellen eines bereits gedruckten Werkes;

2)   die Aufnahme einzelner Aufsätze, Gedichte u.s.w. in kritische und literar=historische Werke und in Sammlungen zum Schulgebrauche;

384

3) die Herausgabe von Uebersetzungen bereits gedruckter Werke.

Ausnahmen

Ausnahmsweise sind jedoch Uebersetzungen in folgenden Fällen dem Nachdruck gleich zu achten:

a. Wenn von einem Werke, welches der Verfasser in einer todten Sprache bekannt gemacht hat, ohne seine Genehmigung eine Deutsche Uebersetzung herausgegeben wird.

b. Wenn der Verfasser eines Buches solches gleichzeitig in verschiedenen lebenden Sprachen hat erscheinen lassen, und ohne seine Genehmigung eine neue Uebersetzung des Werkes in eine der Sprachen veranstaltet wird, in welchen es ursprünglich erschienen ist. Hat der Verfasser auf dem Titelblatte der ersten Ausgabe bekannt gemacht, daß er eine Uebersetzung, und in welcher Sprache, herausgeben wolle, so soll diese Uebersetzung, wenn sie innerhalb zweier Jahre nach dem Erscheinen des Originals erfolgt, als mit dem Original gleichzeitig erschienen behandelt werden.

s.5

e. Dauer des Ausschließlichen Rechts

Der Schutz des gegenwärtigen Gesetzes gegen Nachdruck und diesem gleichgestellte Handlungen (ss.2. und 3.) soll dem Autor einer Schrift, Predigt oder Vorlesung während seines Lebens zukommen.

s.6

Auch die Erben des Autors sollen denselben Schutz noch dreißig Jahre lang nach dem Tode ihres Erblassers genießen, ohne Unterschied, ob während seines Lebens ein Abdruck bereits erschienen ist oder nicht. Nach Ablauf dieser dreißig Jahre hört der Schutz dieses Gesetzes auf.

s.7

In so fern von dem eigentlichen Nachdrucke die Rede ist (ss.1. und 2.), setzt die in den ss.5. und 6. vorgeschriebene Dauer des Schutzes voraus, daß der wahre Name des Verfassers auf dem Titelblatte oder unter der Zueignung oder Vorrede angegeben ist. Eine Schrift, die entweder unter einem andern, als dem wahren Namen des Verfassers erschienen, oder bei welcher gar kein Verfasser genannt ist, soll funfzehn Jahre lang, von der ersten Herausgabe derselben an gerechnet, gegen den Nachdruck geschützt sein, und zur Wahrnehmung des Rechts auf diesen Schutz der Verleger an die Stelle des unbekannten Verfassers treten. Wird innerhalb dieser funfzehn Jahre der wahre Name des Verfassers von ihm selbst oder von seinen Erben, vermittelst eines neuen Abdruckes oder eines neuen Titelblattes für die vorräthigen Exemplare, bekannt gemacht, so wird dadurch dem Werke der Anspruch auf die in den s.5. und 6. bestimmte Dauer des Schutzes erworben.

s.8

Akademien, Universitäten, öffentliche Unterrichts=Anstalten, gelehrte und andere erlaubte Gesellschaften genießen das ausschließende Recht zur neuen Herausgabe ihrer Werke dreißig Jahre lang.
Diese Frist ist

a. bei Werken, die in einem oder mehreren Bänden eine einzige Aufgabe behandeln, und mithin als in sich zusammenhängend betrachtet werden können, zu denen namentlich auch die lexikalischen zu zählen sind, von dem Zeitpunkt ihrer Vollendung an,

b. bei Werken aber, die nur als fortlaufende Sammlungen von Aufsätzen und Abhandlungen über verschiedene Gegenstände der gelehrten Forschung anzusehen sind, von dem Erscheinen eines jeden Bandes an zu rechnen.

Veranstalten jedoch die Verfasser besondere Ausgaben solcher Aufsätze und Abhandlungen, so kommen ihnen die Bestimmungen der ss.5. und 6. zu statten.

s.9

f. Abtretung Desselben

Das ausschließende Recht zur Veröffentlichung und Verbreitung von Schriften, welches dem Autor und dessen Erben zusteht, kann von diesen ganz oder theilweise durch eine hierauf gerichtete Vereinbarung auf Andere übertragen werden.

s.10

g. Strafen des Nachdrucks

Wer das, den Autoren, ihren Erben oder Rechtsnachfolgern zustehende, ausschließende Recht dadurch beeinträchtigt, daß er ohne deren Genehmigung von demselben Gebrauch macht, ist den Beeinträchtigten vollständig zu entschädigen verpflichtet und hat, außer der Confiscation der noch vorräthigen Exemplare, eine Geldbuße von funfzig bis tausend Thalern verwirkt.

s.11

War das Werk von dem Berechtigten bereits herausgegeben, so ist der Betrag der Entschädigung nach Beschaffenheit der Umstände auf eine dem Verkaufswerthe von funfzig bis tausend Exemplaren der rechtmäßigen Ausgabe gleichkommende Summe richterlich zu bestimmen, in so fern der Berechtigte nicht einen höheren Schaden nachzuweisen vermag.

s.12

Die confiscirten Exemplare der unrechtmäßigen Ausgabe sollen vernichtet oder dem Beschädigten auf sein Verlangen überlassen werden. Im letzten Falle muß sich jedoch der Beschädigte die von dem Verurtheilten auf diese Exemplare verwendeten Auslagen auf die Entschädigung anrechnen lassen.

s.13

Wer widerrechtlich vervielfältigte Werke wissentlich zum Verkauf hält, ist dem Beeinträchtigten, mit dem unbefugten Vervielfältiger solidarisch, zur Entschädigung verpflichtet, und hat, außer der Confiscation, eine nach Vorschrift des s.10. zu bestimmende Geldbuße verwirkt.

s.14

Das Vergehen des Nachdrucks ist vollendet, wenn Exemplare eines Buches vorgefunden werden, welche den gegenwärtigen Vorschriften zuwider angefertigt worden sind.

s.15

h. Untersuchungs=Verfahren

Die gerichtliche Untersuchung der in den ss.2.3.4. bezeichneten Vergehen ist nicht von Amtswegen, sondern nur auf den Antrag der Verletzten einzuleiten.

Will der Verleger der Schrift den Antrag nicht machen, so kann dieses von dem Autor oder dessen Erben geschehen, in so fern dieselben noch ein von dem Verleger unabhängiges Interesse haben.

s.16

Nach einmal erfolgter Einleitung der Untersuchung kann die Zurücknahme des Antrags zwar in Beziehung auf die Entschädigung stattfinden, nicht aber in Beziehung auf die Confiscation und Geldbuße.

s.17

Scheint es dem Richter zweifelhaft, ob eine Druckschrift als Nachdruck oder unerlaubter Abdruck zu betrachten ist, oder wird der Betrag der Entschädigung bestritten, so hat der Richter das Gutachten eines aus Sachverständigen gebildeten Vereins einzuholen.

Die Bildung eines oder mehrerer solcher Vereine, die vorzüglich aus geachteten Schriftstellern und Buchhändlern bestehen sollen, bleibt einer besonderen, von Unserem Staats=Ministerium zu erlassenden Instruction vorbehalten.

s.18

2) Geographische, Topographische, Naturwissenschaftliche, Architektonische und ähnliche Zeichnungen

Was vorstehend in den ss.1.2.5 bis 17. über das ausschließende Recht zur Vervielfältigung von Schriften verordnet ist, findet auch Anwendung auf geographische, topographische, naturwissenschaftliche, architektonische und ähnliche Zeichnungen und Abbildungen, welche nach ihrem Hauptzwecke nicht als Kunstwerke (s.21.) zu betrachten sind.

s.19

3) Musikalische Compositionen

Dieselben Vorschriften gelten hinsichtlich der ausschließenden Befugniß zur Vervielfältigung musikalischer Compositionen.

s.20

Einem verbotenen Nachdruck ist gleich zu achten, wenn Jemand von musikalischen Compositionen Auszüge, Arrangements für einzelne Instrumente, oder sonstige Bearbeitungen, die nicht als eigenthümliche Compositionen betrachtet werden können, ohne Genehmigung des Verfassers herausgiebt.

s.21

4) Kunstwerke und Bildliche Darstellungen

Die Vervielfältigung von Zeichnungen oder Gemälden durch Kupferstich, Stahlstich, Holzschnitt, Lithographie, Farbendruck, Uebertragung u.s.w. ist verboten, wenn sie ohne Genehmigung des Urhebers des Original=Kunstwerks oder seiner Rechtsnachfolger bewirkt wird.

s.22

Unter gleicher Bedingung ist die Vervielfältigung von Sculpturen aller Art durch Abgüsse, Abformungen u.s.w. verboten.

s.23

Hinsichtlich dieser Verbote, ss.21. und 22., macht es keinen Unterschied, ob die Nachbildung in einer andern Größe, als das nachgebildete Werk, oder auch mit andern Abweichungen von demselben vorgenommen worden ist; es seien denn die Veränderungen so überwiegend, daß die Arbeit nicht als eine bloße Nachbildung, sondern als ein eigenthümliches Kunstwerk betrachtet werden könnte.

s.24

Als eine verbotene Nachbildung ist es nicht zu betrachten, wenn ein Kunstwerk, das durch die Malerei oder eine der zeichnenden Künste hervorgebracht worden ist, mittelst der plastischen Kunst, oder umgekehrt, dargestellt wird.

s.25

Die Benutzung von Kunstwerken als Muster zu den Erzeugnissen der Manufakturen, Fabriken und Handwerke ist erlaubt.

s.26

Dauer des Ausschließenden Rechts der Künstler,
a. bei unveräußertem Original

Der Urheber eines Kunstwerkes und seine Erben genießen die ihnen in den ss.21 u. f. zugesicherten, ausschließenden Rechte, so lange das Original in ihrem Eigenthum bleibt.

s.27

Wollen sie in dieser Lage von dem ihnen ausschließend zustehenden Rechte der Vervielfältigung Gebrauch machen und sich gegen die Eingriffe Anderer sichern, so haben sie von ihrem Unternehmen, ehe noch die erste Kopie an einen Andern abgelassen wird, zugleich mit der Erklärung, daß sie eine Vervielfältigung durch Andere, welche nicht die besondere Erlaubniß von ihnen erhalten haben, nicht zulassen wollen, dem obersten Curatorium der Künste (Ministerium der geistlichen, Unterrichts= und Medizinal=Angelegenheiten) Anzeige zu machen. Ist diese Anzeige und Erklärung erfolgt, so soll dem Künstler und seinen Erben das ausschließende Recht zur Vervielfältigung des Kunstwerkes für die Dauer von zehn Jahren zustehen. Wenn daher ein Anderer das von dem Urheber oder dessen Erben bereits vervielfältigte Kunstwerk mittelst irgend eines Kunstverfahrens nachbilden und das Nachbild verbreiten will, so hat er zuvor eine amtliche Aeußerung des obersten Curatoriums der Künste darüber einzuholen, ob eine Anzeige und Erklärung der obgedachten Art bei demselben abgegeben worden sei. Ist eine solche Anzeige und Erklärung unterblieben oder seit ihrer Abgebung ein Zeitraum von zehn Jahren abgelaufen, so ist die Nachbildung erlaubt.

s.28

b. nach Veräußerung des Originals

Begeben sich der Urheber oder seine Erben des Eigenthums des Kunstwerkes, ehe mit dessen Vervielfältigung ein Anfang gemacht worden ist, so geht, falls eine ausdrückliche Verabredung darüber nicht Statt gefunden hat, das ausschließende Recht dazu gänzlich verloren. Es kann aber auf die Dauer von zehn Jahren fortbestehen, entweder zu Gunsten des Urhebers oder seiner Erben, indem sie sich solches vorbehalten, oder zu Gunsten des Erwerbers, indem sie ihm solches übertragen, in so fern nur in beiden Fällen gleichzeitig mit der Veräußerung eine Verabredung in glaubhafter Form darüber getroffen und davon dem obersten Curatorium der Künste die obgedachte Anzeige gemacht wird.

s.29

Abbildungen von Original=Kunstwerken

Die Abbildung eines Kunstwerkes, welche durch ein anderes, als bei dem Original angewendetes Kunstverfahren, z. B. durch Kupferstich, Stahlstich, Holzschnitt u. s. w. (s.21.), oder durch Abgüsse, Abformungen u.s.w. (s.22.) rechtmäßig angefertigt worden, darf nicht ohne Genehmigung des Abbildners oder seiner Rechtsnachfolger, durch ein rein mechanisches Verfahren vervielfältigt werden, so lange die Platten, Formen und Modelle, mittelst welcher die Abbildung dargestellt wird, noch nutzbar sind. Auch hierbei kommt die Bestimmung des s.23. zur Anwendung.

s.30

Strafen und Untersuchungs=Verfahren

Die Vorschriften der ss.10 bis 16. sollen auch in Beziehung auf Kunstwerke und bildliche Darstellungen aller Art in Anwendung kommen.

Die im s.10. vorgeschriebene Confiscation ist auch auf die zur Nachbildung der Kunstwerke gemachten Vorrichtungen, als der Platten, Formen, Steine u. s. w. auszudehnen.

s.31

Der Richter hat, wenn Zweifel entsteht, ob eine Abbildung unter die
Fälle des s.18. oder unter die des s.21. gehöre, ob im Falle des s.20. ein
Musikstück als eigenthümliche Composition oder als Nachdruck, in
den Fällen der ss.21. bis 29. eine Nachbildung, als unerlaubt zu
betrachten, oder wie hoch der Betrag der dem Verletzten zustehenden
Entschädigung zu bestimmen sei, und ob die im s.29. als Bedingung
gestellte Nutzbarkeit der Platten, Formen und Modelle noch Statt
finde, in gleicher Weise, wie s.17. verordnet ist, das Gutachten eines
aus Sachverständigen gebildeten Vereins zu erfordern. Die Bildung
solcher Vereine, welche vorzugsweise aus Kunstverständigen und
geachteten Künstlern bestehen sollen, bleibt ebenfalls der im s.17.
erwähnten Instruction vorbehalten.

s.32

5) Oeffentliche Aufführung dramatischer und musikalischer Werke

Die öffentliche Aufführung eines dramatischen oder musikalischen
Werkes im Ganzen oder mit unwesentlichen Abkürzungen darf nur
mit Erlaubniß des Autors, seiner Erben oder Rechtsnachfolger Statt
finden, so lange das Werk nicht durch den Druck veröffentlicht
worden ist. Das ausschließende Recht, diese Erlaubniß zu ertheilen,
steht dem Autor lebenslänglich und seinen Erben oder Rechtsnachfolgern noch zehn Jahre nach seinem Tode zu.

s.33

Hat der Autor jedoch irgend einer Bühne gestattet, das Werk ohne
Nennung seines Namens aufzuführen, so findet auch gegen andere
Bühnen kein ausschließendes Recht Statt.

s.34

Wer dem ausschließenden Rechte des Autors oder seiner Rechtsnachfolger zuwider, ein noch nicht durch den Druck veröffentlichtes dramatisches oder musikalisches Werk öffentlich aufführt, hat eine Geldbuße von zehn bis hundert Thalern verwirkt.

Findet die unbefugte Aufführung eines dramatischen Werkes auf einer stehenden Bühne Statt, so ist der ganze Betrag der Einnahme von jeder Aufführung, ohne Abzug der auf dieselbe verwendeten Kosten, und ohne Unterschied, ob das Stück allein, oder verbunden mit einem andern, den Gegenstand der Aufführung ausgemacht hat, zur Strafe zu entrichten.

Von den vorstehenden Geldbußen fallen zwei Drittheile dem Autor oder seinen Erben, und ein Drittheil der Armen=Casse des Orts zu.

s.35

6) Allgemeine Bestimmungen

Das gegenwärtige Gesetz soll auch zu Gunsten alter bereits gedruckten Schriften, geographischen, topographischen und ähnlichen Zeichnungen, musikalischen Compositionen und vorhandenen Kunstwerke in Anwendung kommen.

s.36

Dem Inhaber eines vor Publikation des gegenwärtigen Gesetzes ertheilten Privilegiums steht es frei, ob er von diesem Gebrauch machen, oder den Schutz des Gesetzes anrufen will.

s.37

All diesem Gesetze entgegenstehende oder von ihm abweichende frühere Vorschriften treten außer Kraft.

s.38

Auf die in einem fremden Staate erschienenen Werke soll dieses Gesetz in dem Maaße Anwendung finden, als die in demselben festgestellten Rechte den in Unseren Landen erschienenen Werken durch die Gesetze dieses Staates ebenfalls gewährt werden. Urkundlich unter Unserer Höchsteigenhändigen Unterschrift und beigedrucktem Königlichen Insiegel.

Gegeben Berlin, den 11ten Juni 1837.

(gez.) Friedrich Wilhelm.

Carl, Herzog von Mecklenburg.

Frhr. v. Altenstein. v. Kamptz. Mühler.

Beglaubigt:

Für den Staats=Secretair Düesberg.

Gesetz zum Schutze des Eigenthums an Werken der Wissenschaft und Kunst gegen Nachdruck und Nachbildung.

Appendix 5

WIPO Copyright Treaty

Geneva, December 20, 1996

Contents

Preamble

The Contracting Parties,

Desiring to develop and maintain the protection of the rights of authors in their literary and artistic works in a manner as effective and uniform as possible,

Recognizing the need to introduce new international rules and clarify the interpretation of certain existing rules in order to provide adequate solutions to the questions raised by new economic, social, cultural and technological developments,

Recognizing the profound impact of the development and convergence of information and communication technologies on the creation and use of literary and artistic works,

Emphasizing the outstanding significance of copyright protection as an incentive for literary and artistic creation,

Recognizing the need to maintain a balance between the rights of authors and the larger public interest, particularly education, research and access to information, as reflected in the Berne Convention,

Have agreed as follows:

Article 1

Relation to the Berne Convention

(1) This Treaty is a special agreement within the meaning of Article 20 of the Berne Convention for the Protection of Literary and Artistic Works, as regards Contracting Parties that are countries of the Union established by that Convention. This Treaty shall not have any connection with treaties other than the Berne Convention, nor shall it prejudice any rights and obligations under any other treaties.

(2) Nothing in this Treaty shall derogate from existing obligations that Contracting Parties have to each other under the Berne Convention for the Protection of Literary and Artistic Works.

(3) Hereinafter, "Berne Convention" shall refer to the Paris Act of July 24, 1971 of the Berne Convention for the Protection of Literary and Artistic Works.

(4) Contracting Parties shall comply with Articles 1 to 21 and the Appendix of the Berne Convention.

Article 2

Scope of Copyright Protection

Copyright protection extends to expressions and not to ideas, procedures, methods of operation or mathematical concepts as such.

Article 3

Application of Articles 2 to 6 of the Berne Convention

Contracting Parties shall apply *mutatis mutandis* the provisions of Articles 2 to 6 of the Berne Convention in respect of the protection provided for in this Treaty.

Article 4

Computer Programs

Computer programs are protected as literary works within the meaning of Article 2 of the Berne Convention. Such protection applies to computer programs, whatever may be the mode or form of their expression.

Article 5

Compilations of Data (Databases)

Compilations of data or other material, in any form, which by reason of the selection or arrangement of their contents constitute intellectual creations, are protected as such. This protection does not extend to the data or the material itself and is without prejudice to any copyright subsisting in the data or material contained in the compilation.

Article 6

Right of Distribution

(1) Authors of literary and artistic works shall enjoy the exclusive right of authorizing the making available to the public of the original and copies of their works through sale or other transfer of ownership.

(2) Nothing in this Treaty shall affect the freedom of Contracting Parties to determine the conditions, if any, under which the exhaustion of the right in paragraph (1) applies after the first sale or other transfer of ownership of the original or a copy of the work with the authorization of the author.

Article 7

Right of Rental

(1) Authors of

(i) computer programs;

(ii) cinematographic works; and

(iii) works embodied in phonograms, as determined in the national law of Contracting Parties,

shall enjoy the exclusive right of authorizing commercial rental to the public of the originals or copies of their works.

(2) Paragraph (1) shall not apply

(i) in the case of computer programs, where the program itself is not the essential object of the rental; and

(ii) in the case of cinematographic works, unless such commercial rental has led to widespread copying of such works materially impairing the exclusive right of reproduction.

(3) Notwithstanding the provisions of paragraph (1), a Contracting Party that, on April 15, 1994, had and continues to have in force a system of equitable remuneration of authors for the rental of copies of their works embodied in phonograms may maintain that system provided that the commercial rental of works embodied in phonograms is not giving rise to the material impairment of the exclusive right of reproduction of authors.

Article 8

Right of Communication to the Public

Without prejudice to the provisions of Articles 11(1)(ii), 11bis(1)(i) and (ii), 11ter(1)(ii), 14(1)(ii) and 14bis(1) of the Berne Convention, authors of literary and artistic works shall enjoy the exclusive right of authorizing any communication to the public of their works, by wire or wireless means, including the making available to the public of their works in such a way that members of the public may access these works from a place and at a time individually chosen by them.

Article 9

Duration of the Protection of Photographic Works

In respect of photographic works, the Contracting Parties shall not apply the provisions of Article 7(4) of the Berne Convention.

Article 10

Limitations and Exceptions

(1) Contracting Parties may, in their national legislation, provide for limitations of or exceptions to the rights granted to authors of literary and artistic works under this Treaty in certain special cases that do not conflict with a normal exploitation of the work and do not unreasonably prejudice the legitimate interests of the author.

(2) Contracting Parties shall, when applying the Berne Convention, confine any limitations of or exceptions to rights provided for therein to certain special cases that do not conflict with a normal exploitation of the work and do not unreasonably prejudice the legitimate interests of the author.

Article 11

Obligations concerning Technological Measures

Contracting Parties shall provide adequate legal protection and effective legal remedies against the circumvention of effective technological measures that are used by authors in connection with the exercise of their rights under this Treaty or the Berne Convention and that restrict acts, in respect of their works, which are not authorized by the authors concerned or permitted by law.

Article 12

Obligations concerning Rights Management Information

(1) Contracting Parties shall provide adequate and effective legal remedies against any person knowingly performing any of the following acts knowing, or with respect to civil remedies having reasonable grounds to know, that it will induce, enable, facilitate or conceal an infringement of any right covered by this Treaty or the Berne Convention:

(i) to remove or alter any electronic rights management information without authority;

(ii) to distribute, import for distribution, broadcast or communicate to the public, without authority, works or copies of works knowing that electronic rights management information has been removed or altered without authority.

(2) As used in this Article, "rights management information" means information which identifies the work, the author of the work, the owner of any right in the work, or information about the terms and conditions of use of the work, and any numbers or codes that represent such information, when any of these items of information is attached to a copy of a work or appears in connection with the communication of a work to the public.

Article 13

Application in Time

Contracting Parties shall apply the provisions of Article 18 of the Berne Convention to all protection provided for in this Treaty.

Article 14

Provisions on Enforcement of Rights

(1) Contracting Parties undertake to adopt, in accordance with their legal systems, the measures necessary to ensure the application of this Treaty.

(2) Contracting Parties shall ensure that enforcement procedures are available under their law so as to permit effective action against any act of infringement of rights covered by this Treaty, including expeditious remedies to prevent infringements and remedies which constitute a deterrent to further infringements.

Article 15

Assembly

(1) (a) The Contracting Parties shall have an Assembly.

(b) Each Contracting Party shall be represented by one delegate who may be assisted by alternate delegates, advisors and experts.

(c) The expenses of each delegation shall be borne by the Contracting Party that has appointed the delegation. The Assembly may ask the World Intellectual Property Organization (hereinafter referred to as "WIPO") to grant financial assistance to facilitate the participation of delegations of Contracting Parties that are regarded as developing countries in conformity with the established practice of the General Assembly of the United Nations or that are countries in transition to a market economy.

(2) (a) The Assembly shall deal with matters concerning the maintenance and development of this Treaty and the application and operation of this Treaty.

(b) The Assembly shall perform the function allocated to it under Article 17(2) in respect of the admission of certain intergovernmental organizations to become party to this Treaty.

(c) The Assembly shall decide the convocation of any diplomatic conference for the revision of this Treaty and give the necessary instructions to the Director General of WIPO for the preparation of such diplomatic conference.

(3) (a) Each Contracting Party that is a State shall have one vote and shall vote only in its own name.

(b) Any Contracting Party that is an intergovernmental organization may participate in the vote, in place of its Member States, with a number of votes equal to the number of its Member States which are party to this Treaty. No such intergovernmental organization shall participate in the vote if any one of its Member States exercises its right to vote and *vice versa*

(4) The Assembly shall meet in ordinary session once every two years upon convocation by the Director General of WIPO.

(5) The Assembly shall establish its own rules of procedure, including the convocation of extraordinary sessions, the requirements of a quorum and, subject to the provisions of this Treaty, the required majority for various kinds of decisions.

Article 16

International Bureau

The International Bureau of WIPO shall perform the administrative tasks concerning the Treaty.

Article 17

Eligibility for Becoming Party to the Treaty

(1) Any Member State of WIPO may become party to this Treaty.

(2) The Assembly may decide to admit any intergovernmental organization to become party to this Treaty which declares that it is competent in respect of, and has its own legislation binding on all its Member States on, matters covered by this Treaty and that it has been

duly authorized, in accordance with its internal procedures, to become party to this Treaty.

(3) The European Community, having made the declaration referred to in the preceding paragraph in the Diplomatic Conference that has adopted this Treaty, may become party to this Treaty.

Article 18

Rights and Obligations under the Treaty

Subject to any specific provisions to the contrary in this Treaty, each Contracting Party shall enjoy all of the rights and assume all of the obligations under this Treaty.

Article 19

Signature of the Treaty

This Treaty shall be open for signature until December 31, 1997, by any Member State of WIPO and by the European Community.

Article 20

Entry into Force of the Treaty

This Treaty shall enter into force three months after 30 instruments of ratification or accession by States have been deposited with the Director General of WIPO.

Article 21

Effective Date of Becoming Party to the Treaty

This Treaty shall bind

(i) the 30 States referred to in Article 20, from the date on which this Treaty has entered into force;

(ii) each other State from the expiration of three months from the date on which the State has deposited its instrument with the Director General of WIPO;

(iii) the European Community, from the expiration of three months after the deposit of its instrument of ratification or accession if such instrument has been deposited after the entry into force of this Treaty according to Article 20, or, three months after the entry into force of this Treaty if such instrument has been deposited before the entry into force of this Treaty;

(iv) any other intergovernmental organization that is admitted to become party to this Treaty, from the expiration of three months after the deposit of its instrument of accession.

Article 22

No Reservations to the Treaty

No reservation to this Treaty shall be admitted.

Article 23

Denunciation of the Treaty

This Treaty may be denounced by any Contracting Party by notification addressed to the Director General of WIPO. Any denunciation shall take effect one year from the date on which the Director General of WIPO received the notification.

Article 24

Languages of the Treaty

(1) This Treaty is signed in a single original in English, Arabic, Chinese, French, Russian and Spanish languages, the versions in all these languages being equally authentic.

(2) An official text in any language other than those referred to in paragraph (1) shall be established by the Director General of WIPO on the request of an interested party, after consultation with all the interested parties. For the purposes of this paragraph, "interested party" means any Member State of WIPO whose official language, or one of whose official languages, is involved and the European Community, and any other intergovernmental organization that may become party to this Treaty, if one of its official languages is involved.

Article 25

Depositary

The Director General of WIPO is the depositary of this Treaty.

Agreed Statements Concerning the WIPO Copyright Treaty

GENEVA, DECEMBER 20, 1996

Concerning Article 1(4)

The reproduction right, as set out in Article 9 of the Berne Convention, and the exceptions permitted thereunder, fully apply in the digital environment, in particular to the use of works in digital form. It is understood that the storage of a protected work in digital form in an electronic medium constitutes a reproduction within the meaning of Article 9 of the Berne Convention.

Concerning Article 3

It is understood that in applying Article 3 of this Treaty, the expression "country of the Union" in Articles 2 to 6 of the Berne Convention will be read as if it were a reference to a Contracting Party to this Treaty, in the application of those Berne Articles in respect of protection provided for in this Treaty. It is also understood that the expression "country outside the Union" in those Articles in the Berne Convention will, in the same circumstances, be read as if it were a reference to a country that is not a Contracting Party to this

Treaty, and that "this Convention" in Articles 2(8), 2*bis*(2), 3, 4 and 5 of the Berne Convention will be read as if it were a reference to the Berne Convention and this Treaty. Finally, it is understood that a reference in Articles 3 to 6 of the Berne Convention to a "national of one of the countries of the Union" will, when these Articles are applied to this Treaty, mean, in regard to an intergovernmental organization that is a Contracting Party to this Treaty, a national of one of the countries that is member of that organization.

Concerning Article 4

The scope of protection for computer programs under Article 4 of this Treaty, read with Article 2, is consistent with Article 2 of the Berne Convention and on a par with the relevant provisions of the TRIPS Agreement.

Concerning Article 5

The scope of protection for compilations of data (databases) under Article 5 of this Treaty, read with Article 2, is consistent with Article 2 of the Berne Convention and on a par with the relevant provisions of the TRIPS Agreement.

Concerning Articles 6 and 7

As used in these Articles, the expressions "copies" and "original and copies," being subject to the right of distribution and the right of rental under the said Articles, refer exclusively to fixed copies that can be put into circulation as tangible objects.

Concerning Article 7

It is understood that the obligation under Article 7(1) does not require a Contracting Party to provide an exclusive right of commercial rental to authors who, under that Contracting Party's law, are not granted rights in respect of phonograms. It is understood that this obligation is consistent with Article 14(4) of the TRIPS Agreement.

Concerning Article 8

It is understood that the mere provision of physical facilities for enabling or making a communication does not in itself amount to communication within the meaning of this Treaty or the Berne

Convention. It is further understood that nothing in Article 8 precludes a Contracting Party from applying Article 11*bis*(2).

Concerning Article 10

It is understood that the provisions of Article 10 permit Contracting Parties to carry forward and appropriately extend into the digital environment limitations and exceptions in their national laws which have been considered acceptable under the Berne Convention. Similarly, these provisions should be understood to permit Contracting Parties to devise new exceptions and limitations that are appropriate in the digital network environment.

It is also understood that Article 10(2) neither reduces nor extends the scope of applicability of the limitations and exceptions permitted by the Berne Convention.

Concerning Article 12

It is understood that the reference to "infringement of any right covered by this Treaty or the Berne Convention" includes both exclusive rights and rights of remuneration.

It is further understood that Contracting Parties will not rely on this Article to devise or implement rights management systems that would have the effect of imposing formalities which are not permitted under the Berne Convention or this Treaty, prohibiting the free movement of goods or impeding the enjoyment of rights under this Treaty.

Appendix 6

WIPO Performances and Phonograms Treaty

Geneva, December 20, 1996

Contents

CHAPTER III

RIGHTS OF PRODUCERS OF PHONOGRAMS

Article 11: Right of Reproduction
Article 12: Right of Distribution
Article 13: Right of Rental
Article 14: Right of Making Available of Phonograms

CHAPTER IV

COMMON PROVISIONS

Article 15: Right to Remuneration for Broadcasting and Communication to the Public
Article 16: Limitations and Exceptions
Article 17: Term of Protection
Article 18: Obligations concerning Technological Measures
Article 19: Obligations concerning Rights Management Information
Article 20: Formalities
Article 21: Reservations
Article 22: Application in Time
Article 23: Provisions on Enforcement of Rights

CHAPTER V

ADMINISTRATIVE AND FINAL CLAUSES

Article 24: Assembly
Article 25: International Bureau
Article 26: Eligibility for Becoming Party to the Treaty
Article 27: Rights and Obligations under the Treaty
Article 28: Signature of the Treaty
Article 29: Entry into Force of the Treaty
Article 30: Effective Date of Becoming Party to the Treaty
Article 31: Denunciation of the Treaty
Article 32: Languages of the Treaty
Article 33: Depositary

Preamble

The Contracting Parties,

Desiring to develop and maintain the protection of the rights of performers and producers of phonograms in a manner as effective and uniform as possible,

Recognizing the need to introduce new international rules in order to provide adequate solutions to the questions raised by economic, social, cultural and technological developments,

Recognizing the profound impact of the development and convergence of information and communication technologies on the production and use of performances and phonograms,

Recognizing the need to maintain a balance between the rights of performers and producers of phonograms and the larger public interest, particularly education, research and access to information,

Have agreed as follows:

CHAPTER I

GENERAL PROVISIONS

Article 1

Relation to Other Conventions

(1) Nothing in this Treaty shall derogate from existing obligations that Contracting Parties have to each other under the International Convention for the Protection of Performers, Producers of Phonograms and Broadcasting Organizations done in Rome, October 26, 1961 (hereinafter the "Rome Convention").

(2) Protection granted under this Treaty shall leave intact and shall in no way affect the protection of copyright in literary and artistic works. Consequently, no provision of this Treaty may be interpreted as prejudicing such protection.

(3) This Treaty shall not have any connection with, or shall it prejudice any rights and obligations under, any other treaties.

Article 2

Definitions

For the purposes of this Treaty:

(a) "performers" are actors, singers, musicians, dancers, and other persons who act, sing, deliver, declaim, play in, interpret, or otherwise perform literary or artistic works (or expressions of folklore);

(b) "phonogram" means the fixation of the sounds of a performance or of other sounds, or of a representation of sounds, other than in the form of a fixation incorporated in a cinematographic or other audiovisual work;

(c) "fixation" means the embodiment of sounds, or of the representations thereof, from which they can be perceived, reproduced or communicated through a device;

(d) "producer of a phonogram" means the person, or the legal entity, who or which takes the initiative and has the responsibility for the first fixation of the sounds of a performance or other sounds, or the representations of sounds;

(e) "publication" of a fixed performance or a phonogram means the offering of copies of the fixed performance or the phonogram to the public, with the consent of the rightholder, and provided that copies are offered to the public in reasonable quantity;

(f) "broadcasting" means the transmission by wireless means for public reception of sounds or of images and sounds or of the representations thereof; such transmission by satellite is also "broadcasting"; transmission of encrypted signals is "broadcasting" where the means for decrypting are provided to the public by the broadcasting organization or with its consent;

(g) "communication to the public" of a performance or a phonogram means the transmission to the public by any medium, otherwise than by broadcasting, of sounds of a performance or the sounds or the representations of sounds fixed in a phonogram. For the purposes of Article 15, "communication to the public" includes making the sounds or representations of sounds fixed in a phonogram audible to the public.

Article 3

Beneficiaries of Protection under this Treaty

(1) Contracting Parties shall accord the protection provided under this Treaty to the performers and producers of phonograms who are nationals of other Contracting Parties.

(2) The nationals of other Contracting Parties shall be understood to be those performers or producers of phonograms who would meet the criteria for eligibility for protection provided under the Rome Convention, were all the Contracting Parties to this Treaty Contracting States of that Convention. In respect of these criteria of eligibility, Contracting Parties shall apply the relevant definitions in Article 2 of this Treaty.

(3) Any Contracting Party availing itself of the possibilities provided in Article 5(3) of the Rome Convention or, for the purposes of Article 5 of the same Convention, Article 17 thereof shall make a notification as foreseen in those provisions to the Director General of the World Intellectual Property Organization (WIPO).

Article 4

National Treatment

(1) Each Contracting Party shall accord to nationals of other Contracting Parties, as defined in Article 3(2), the treatment it accords to its own nationals with regard to the exclusive rights specifically granted in this Treaty, and to the right to equitable remuneration provided for in Article 15 of this Treaty.

(2) The obligation provided for in paragraph (1) does not apply to the extent that another Contracting Party makes use of the reservations permitted by Article 15(3) of this Treaty.

Chapter II

Rights of Performers

Article 5

Moral Rights of Performers

(1) Independently of a performer's economic rights, and even after the transfer of those rights, the performer shall, as regards his live aural performances or performances fixed in phonograms, have the right to claim to be identified as the performer of his performances, except where omission is dictated by the manner of the use of the performance, and to object to any distortion, mutilation or other modification of his performances that would be prejudicial to his reputation.

(2) The rights granted to a performer in accordance with paragraph (1) shall, after his death, be maintained, at least until the expiry of the economic rights, and shall be exercisable by the persons or institutions authorized by the legislation of the Contracting Party where protection is claimed. However, those Contracting Parties whose legislation, at the moment of their ratification of or accession to this Treaty, does not provide for protection after the death of the performer of all rights set out in the preceding paragraph may provide that some of these rights will, after his death, cease to be maintained.

(3) The means of redress for safeguarding the rights granted under this Article shall be governed by the legislation of the Contracting Party where protection is claimed.

Article 6

Economic Rights of Performers in their Unfixed Performances

Performers shall enjoy the exclusive right of authorizing, as regards their performances:

(i) the broadcasting and communication to the public of their unfixed performances except where the performance is already a broadcast performance; and

(ii) the fixation of their unfixed performances.

Article 7

Right of Reproduction

Performers shall enjoy the exclusive right of authorizing the direct or indirect reproduction of their performances fixed in phonograms, in any manner or form.

Article 8

Right of Distribution

(1) Performers shall enjoy the exclusive right of authorizing the making available to the public of the original and copies of their performances fixed in phonograms through sale or other transfer of ownership.

(2) Nothing in this Treaty shall affect the freedom of Contracting Parties to determine the conditions, if any, under which the exhaustion of the right in paragraph (1) applies after the first sale or other transfer of ownership of the original or a copy of the fixed performance with the authorization of the performer.

Article 9

Right of Rental

(1) Performers shall enjoy the exclusive right of authorizing the commercial rental to the public of the original and copies of their performances fixed in phonograms as determined in the national law of Contracting Parties, even after distribution of them by, or pursuant to, authorization by the performer.

(2) Notwithstanding the provisions of paragraph (1), a Contracting

Party that, on April 15, 1994, had and continues to have in force a system of equitable remuneration of performers for the rental of copies of their performances fixed in phonograms, may maintain that system provided that the commercial rental of phonograms is not giving rise to the material impairment of the exclusive right of reproduction of performers.

Article 10

Right of Making Available of Fixed Performances

Performers shall enjoy the exclusive right of authorizing the making available to the public of their performances fixed in phonograms, by wire or wireless means, in such a way that members of the public may access them from a place and at a time individually chosen by them.

CHAPTER III

RIGHTS OF PRODUCERS OF PHONOGRAMS

Article 11

Right of Reproduction

Producers of phonograms shall enjoy the exclusive right of authorizing the direct or indirect reproduction of their phonograms, in any manner or form.

Article 12

Right of Distribution

(1) Producers of phonograms shall enjoy the exclusive right of authorizing the making available to the public of the original and copies of their phonograms through sale or other transfer of ownership.

(2) Nothing in this Treaty shall affect the freedom of Contracting Parties to determine the conditions, if any, under which the

exhaustion of the right in paragraph (1) applies after the first sale or other transfer of ownership of the original or a copy of the phonogram with the authorization of the producer of the phonogram.

Article 13

Right of Rental

(1) Producers of phonograms shall enjoy the exclusive right of authorizing the commercial rental to the public of the original and copies of their phonograms, even after distribution of them by or pursuant to authorization by the producer.

(2) Notwithstanding the provisions of paragraph (1), a Contracting Party that, on April 15, 1994, had and continues to have in force a system of equitable remuneration of producers of phonograms for the rental of copies of their phonograms, may maintain that system provided that the commercial rental of phonograms is not giving rise to the material impairment of the exclusive rights of reproduction of producers of phonograms.

Article 14

Right of Making Available of Phonograms

Producers of phonograms shall enjoy the exclusive right of authorizing the making available to the public of their phonograms, by wire or wireless means, in such a way that members of the public may access them from a place and at a time individually chosen by them.

CHAPTER **IV**

COMMON PROVISIONS

Article 15

Right to Remuneration for Broadcasting and Communication to the Public

(1) Performers and producers of phonograms shall enjoy the right to a single equitable remuneration for the direct or indirect use of phonograms published for commercial purposes for broadcasting or for any communication to the public.

(2) Contracting Parties may establish in their national legislation that the single equitable remuneration shall be claimed from the user by the performer or by the producer of a phonogram or by both. Contracting Parties may enact national legislation that, in the absence of an agreement between the performer and the producer of a phonogram, sets the terms according to which performers and producers of phonograms shall share the single equitable remuneration.

(3) Any Contracting Party may in a notification deposited with the Director General of WIPO, declare that it will apply the provisions of paragraph (1) only in respect of certain uses, or that it will limit their application in some other way, or that it will not apply these provisions at all.

(4) For the purposes of this Article, phonograms made available to the public by wire or wireless means in such a way that members of the public may access them from a place and at a time individually chosen by them shall be considered as if they had been published for commercial purposes.

Article 16

Limitations and Exceptions

(1) Contracting Parties may, in their national legislation, provide for the same kinds of limitations or exceptions with regard to the protection of performers and producers of phonograms as they pro-

vide for, in their national legislation, in connection with the protection of copyright in literary and artistic works.

(2) Contracting Parties shall confine any limitations of or exceptions to rights provided for in this Treaty to certain special cases which do not conflict with a normal exploitation of the performance or phonogram and do not unreasonably prejudice the legitimate interests of the performer or of the producer of the phonogram.

Article 17

Term of Protection

(1) The term of protection to be granted to performers under this Treaty shall last, at least, until the end of a period of 50 years computed from the end of the year in which the performance was fixed in a phonogram.

(2) The term of protection to be granted to producers of phonograms under this Treaty shall last, at least, until the end of a period of 50 years computed from the end of the year in which the phonogram was published, or failing such publication within 50 years from fixation of the phonogram, 50 years from the end of the year in which the fixation was made.

Article 18

Obligations concerning Technological Measures

Contracting Parties shall provide adequate legal protection and effective legal remedies against the circumvention of effective technological measures that are used by performers or producers of phonograms in connection with the exercise of their rights under this Treaty and that restrict acts, in respect of their performances or phonograms, which are not authorized by the performers or the producers of phonograms concerned or permitted by law.

Article 19

Obligations Concerning Rights Management Information

(1) Contracting Parties shall provide adequate and effective legal remedies against any person knowingly performing any of the following acts knowing, or with respect to civil remedies having reasonable grounds to know, that it will induce, enable, facilitate or conceal an infringement of any right covered by this Treaty:

    (i) to remove or alter any electronic rights management information without authority;

    (ii) to distribute, import for distribution, broadcast, communicate or make available to the public, without authority, performances, copies of fixed performances or phonograms knowing that electronic rights management information has been removed or altered without authority.

(2) As used in this Article, "rights management information" means information which identifies the performer, the performance of the performer, the producer of the phonogram, the phonogram, the owner of any right in the performance or phonogram, or information about the terms and conditions of use of the performance or phonogram, and any numbers or codes that represent such information, when any of these items of information is attached to a copy of a fixed performance or a phonogram or appears in connection with the communication or making available of a fixed performance or a phonogram to the public.

Article 20

Formalities

The enjoyment and exercise of the rights provided for in this Treaty shall not be subject to any formality.

Article 21

Reservations

Subject to the provisions of Article 15(3), no reservations to this Treaty shall be permitted.

Article 22

Application in Time

(1) Contracting Parties shall apply the provisions of Article 18 of the Berne Convention, *mutatis mutandis*, to the rights of performers and producers of phonograms provided for in this Treaty.

(2) Notwithstanding paragraph (1), a Contracting Party may limit the application of Article 5 of this Treaty to performances which occurred after the entry into force of this Treaty for that Party.

Article 23

Provisions on Enforcement of Rights

(1) Contracting Parties undertake to adopt, in accordance with their legal systems, the measures necessary to ensure the application of this Treaty.

(2) Contracting Parties shall ensure that enforcement procedures are available under their law so as to permit effective action against any act of infringement of rights covered by this Treaty, including expeditious remedies to prevent infringements and remedies which constitute a deterrent to further infringements.

CHAPTER V

ADMINISTRATIVE AND FINAL CLAUSES

Article 24

Assembly

(1) (a) The Contracting Parties shall have an Assembly.

(b) Each Contracting Party shall be represented by one delegate who may be assisted by alternate delegates, advisors and experts.

(c) The expenses of each delegation shall be borne by the Contracting Party that has appointed the delegation. The Assembly may ask WIPO to grant financial assistance to facilitate the participation of delegations of Contracting Parties that are regarded as developing countries in conformity with the established practice of the General Assembly of the United Nations or that are countries in transition to a market economy.

(2) (a) The Assembly shall deal with matters concerning the maintenance and development of this Treaty and the application and operation of this Treaty.

(b) The Assembly shall perform the function allocated to it under Article 26(2) in respect of the admission of certain intergovernmental organizations to become party to this Treaty.

(c) The Assembly shall decide the convocation of any diplomatic conference for the revision of this Treaty and give the necessary instructions to the Director General of WIPO for the preparation of such diplomatic conference.

(3) (a) Each Contracting Party that is a State shall have one vote and shall vote only in its own name.

(b) Any Contracting Party that is an intergovernmental organization may participate in the vote, in place of its Member States, with a number of votes equal to the number of its Member States which are party to this Treaty. No such intergovernmental organization shall participate in the vote if any one of its Member States exercises its right to vote and vice versa.

(4) The Assembly shall meet in ordinary session once every two years upon convocation by the Director General of WIPO.

(5) The Assembly shall establish its own rules of procedure, including the convocation of extraordinary sessions, the requirements of a quorum and, subject to the provisions of this Treaty, the required majority for various kinds of decisions.

Article 25

International Bureau

The International Bureau of WIPO shall perform the administrative tasks concerning the Treaty.

Article 26

Eligibility for Becoming Party to the Treaty

(1) Any Member State of WIPO may become party to this Treaty.

(2) The Assembly may decide to admit any intergovernmental organization to become party to this Treaty which declares that it is competent in respect of, and has its own legislation binding on all its Member States on, matters covered by this Treaty and that it has been duly authorized, in accordance with its internal procedures, to become party to this Treaty.

(3) The European Community, having made the declaration referred to in the preceding paragraph in the Diplomatic Conference that has adopted this Treaty, may become party to this Treaty.

Article 27

Rights and Obligations under the Treaty

Subject to any specific provisions to the contrary in this Treaty, each Contracting Party shall enjoy all of the rights and assume all of the obligations under this Treaty.

Article 28

Signature of the Treaty

This Treaty shall be open for signature until December 31, 1997, by any Member State of WIPO and by the European Community.

Article 29

Entry into Force of the Treaty

This Treaty shall enter into force three months after 30 instruments of ratification or accession by States have been deposited with the Director General of WIPO.

Article 30

Effective Date of Becoming Party to the Treaty

This Treaty shall bind

(i) the 30 States referred to in Article 29, from the date on which this Treaty has entered into force;

(ii) each other State from the expiration of three months from the date on which the State has deposited its instrument with the Director General of WIPO;

(iii) the European Community, from the expiration of three months after the deposit of its instrument of ratification or accession if such instrument has been deposited after the entry into force of this Treaty according to Article 29, or, three months after the entry into force of this Treaty if such instrument has been deposited before the entry into force of this Treaty;

(iv) any other intergovernmental organization that is admitted to become party to this Treaty, from the expiration of three months after the deposit of its instrument of accession.

Article 31

Denunciation of the Treaty

This Treaty may be denounced by any Contracting Party by notification addressed to the Director General of WIPO. Any denunciation shall take effect one year from the date on which the Director General of WIPO received the notification.

Article 32

Languages of the Treaty

(1) This Treaty is signed in a single original in English, Arabic, Chinese, French, Russian and Spanish languages, the versions in all these languages being equally authentic.

(2) An official text in any language other than those referred to in paragraph (1) shall be established by the Director General of WIPO on the request of an interested party, after consultation with all the interested parties. For the purposes of this paragraph, "interested party" means any Member State of WIPO whose official language, or one of whose official languages, is involved and the European Community, and any other intergovernmental organization that may become party to this Treaty, if one of its official languages is involved.

Article 33

Depositary

The Director General of WIPO is the depositary of this Treaty.

Agreed Statements Concerning The WIPO Performances and Phonograms Treaty

GENEVA, DECEMBER 20, 1996

Concerning Article 1

It is understood that Article 1(2) clarifies the relationship between rights in phonograms under this Treaty and copyright in works embodied in the phonograms. In cases where authorization is needed from both the author of a work embodied in the phonogram and a performer or producer owning rights in the phonogram, the need for the authorization of the author does not cease to exist because the authorization of the performer or producer is also required, and vice versa.

It is further understood that nothing in Article 1(2) precludes a Contracting Party from providing exclusive rights to a performer or producer of phonograms beyond those required to be provided under this Treaty.

Concerning Article 2(b)

It is understood that the definition of phonogram provided in Article 2(b) does not suggest that rights in the phonogram are in any way affected through their incorporation into a cinematographic or other audiovisual work.

Concerning Articles 2(e), 8, 9, 12, and 13

As used in these Articles, the expressions "copies" and "original and copies," being subject to the right of distribution and the right of rental under the said Articles, refer exclusively to fixed copies that can be put into circulation as tangible objects.

Concerning Article 3

It is understood that the reference in Articles 5(a) and 16(a)(iv) of the Rome Convention to "national of another Contracting State" will, when applied to this Treaty, mean, in regard to an intergovernmental organization that is a Contracting Party to this Treaty, a national of one of the countries that is a member of that organization.

Concerning Article 3(2)

For the application of Article 3(2), it is understood that fixation means the finalization of the master tape ("bande-mère").

Concerning Articles 7, 11 and 16

The reproduction right, as set out in Articles 7 and 11, and the exceptions permitted thereunder through Article 16, fully apply in the digital environment, in particular to the use of performances and phonograms in digital form. It is understood that the storage of a protected performance or phonogram in digital form in an electronic medium constitutes a reproduction within the meaning of these Articles.

Concerning Article 15

It is understood that Article 15 does not represent a complete resolution of the level of rights of broadcasting and communication to the public that should be enjoyed by performers and phonogram producers in the digital age. Delegations were unable to achieve consensus on differing proposals for aspects of exclusivity to be provided in certain circumstances or for rights to be provided without the possibility of reservations, and have therefore left the issue to future resolution.

Concerning Article 15

It is understood that Article 15 does not prevent the granting of the right conferred by this Article to performers of folklore and producers of phonograms recording folklore where such phonograms have not been published for commercial gain.

Concerning Article 16

The agreed statement concerning Article 10 (on Limitations and

429

Exceptions) of the WIPO Copyright Treaty is applicable *mutatis mutandis* also to Article 16 (on Limitations and Exceptions) of the WIPO Performances and Phonograms Treaty.

Concerning Article 19

The agreed statement concerning Article 12 (on Obligations concerning Rights Management Information) of the WIPO Copyright Treaty is applicable *mutatis mutandis* also to Article 19 (on Obligations concerning Rights Management Information) of the WIPO Performances and Phonograms Treaty.

Appendix 7

Directive 2001/29/EC of the European Parliament and of the Council

of May 22, 2001
on the harmonisation of certain aspects of copyright and related rights in the information society

([2001] O.J. L167/10).

THE EUROPEAN PARLIAMENT AND THE COUNCIL OF THE EUROPEAN UNION,

Having regard to the Treaty establishing the European Community, and in particular Articles 47(2), 55 and 95 thereof,

Having regard to the proposal from the Commission,[1]

Having regard to the opinion of the Economic and Social Committee,[2]

Acting in accordance with the procedure laid down in Article 251 of the Treaty,[3]

Whereas:

(1) The Treaty provides for the establishment of an internal market and the institution of a system ensuring that competition in the internal market is not distorted. Harmonisation of the laws of the Member States on copyright and related rights contributes to the achievement of these objectives.

(2) The European Council, meeting at Corfu on June 24 and 25, 1994, stressed the need to create a general and flexible legal

---

[1] O.J. C108, 7.4.1998, p.6 and O.J. C180, 25.6.1999, p.6.

[2] O.J. C407, 28.12.1998, p.30.

[3] Opinion of the European Parliament of February 10, 1999 (O.J. C150, 28.5.1999, p.171), Council Common Position of September 28, 2000 (O.J. C344, 1.12.2000, p.1) and Decision of the European Parliament of February 14, 2001 (not yet published in the Official Journal). Council Decision of April 9, 2001.

framework at Community level in order to foster the development of the information society in Europe. This requires, *inter alia*, the existence of an internal market for new products and services. Important Community legislation to ensure such a regulatory framework is already in place or its adoption is well under way. Copyright and related rights play an important role in this context as they protect and stimulate the development and marketing of new products and services and the creation and exploitation of their creative content.

(3) The proposed harmonisation will help to implement the four freedoms of the internal market and relates to compliance with the fundamental principles of law and especially of property, including intellectual property, and freedom of expression and the public interest.

(4) A harmonised legal framework on copyright and related rights, through increased legal certainty and while providing for a high level of protection of intellectual property, will foster substantial investment in creativity and innovation, including network infrastructure, and lead in turn to growth and increased competitiveness of European industry, both in the area of content provision and information technology and more generally across a wide range of industrial and cultural sectors. This will safeguard employment and encourage new job creation.

(5) Technological development has multiplied and diversified the vectors for creation, production and exploitation. While no new concepts for the protection of intellectual property are needed, the current law on copyright and related rights should be adapted and supplemented to respond adequately to economic realities such as new forms of exploitation.

(6) Without harmonisation at Community level, legislative activities at national level which have already been initiated in a number of Member States in order to respond to the technological challenges might result in significant differences in protection and thereby in restrictions on the free movement of services and products incorporating, or based on, intellectual property, leading to a refragmentation of the internal market and legislative inconsistency. The impact of such legislative differences and uncertainties will become more significant with the further development of the information society, which has already

greatly increased transborder exploitation of intellectual property. This development will and should further increase. Significant legal differences and uncertainties in protection may hinder economies of scale for new products and services containing copyright and related rights.

(7) The Community legal framework for the protection of copyright and related rights must, therefore, also be adapted and supplemented as far as is necessary for the smooth functioning of the internal market. To that end, those national provisions on copyright and related rights which vary considerably from one Member State to another or which cause legal uncertainties hindering the smooth functioning of the internal market and the proper development of the information society in Europe should be adjusted, and inconsistent national responses to the technological developments should be avoided, whilst differences not adversely affecting the functioning of the internal market need not be removed or prevented.

(8) The various social, societal and cultural implications of the information society require that account be taken of the specific features of the content of products and services.

(9) Any harmonisation of copyright and related rights must take as a basis a high level of protection, since such rights are crucial to intellectual creation. Their protection helps to ensure the maintenance and development of creativity in the interests of authors, performers, producers, consumers, culture, industry and the public at large. Intellectual property has therefore been recognised as an integral part of property.

(10) If authors or performers are to continue their creative and artistic work, they have to receive an appropriate reward for the use of their work, as must producers in order to be able to finance this work. The investment required to produce products such as phonograms, films or multimedia products, and services such as "on demand" services, is considerable. Adequate legal protection of intellectual property rights is necessary in order to guarantee the availability of such a reward and provide the opportunity for satisfactory returns on this investment.

(11) A rigorous, effective system for the protection of copyright and related rights is one of the main ways of ensuring that European

433

cultural creativity and production receive the necessary resources and of safe-guarding the independence and dignity of artistic creators and performers.

(12) Adequate protection of copyright works and subject-matter of related rights is also of great importance from a cultural stand-point. Article 151 of the Treaty requires the Community to take cultural aspects into account in its action.

(13) A common search for, and consistent application at European level of, technical measures to protect works and other subject-matter and to provide the necessary information on rights are essential insofar as the ultimate aim of these measures is to give effect to the principles and guarantees laid down in law.

(14) This Directive should seek to promote learning and culture by protecting works and other subject-matter while permitting exceptions or limitations in the public interest for the purpose of education and teaching.

(15) The Diplomatic Conference held under the auspices of the World Intellectual Property Organisation (WIPO) in December 1996 led to the adoption of two new Treaties, the "WIPO Copyright Treaty" and the "WIPO Performances and Phono-grams Treaty", dealing respectively with the protection of authors and the protection of performers and phonogram pro-ducers. Those Treaties update the international protection for copyright and related rights significantly, not least with regard to the so-called "digital agenda", and improve the means to fight piracy world-wide. The Community and a majority of Member States have already signed the Treaties and the process of making arrangements for the ratification of the Treaties by the Com-munity and the Member States is under way. This Directive also serves to implement a number of the new international obliga-tions.

(16) Liability for activities in the network environment concerns not only copyright and related rights but also other areas, such as defamation, misleading advertising, or infringement of trade marks, and is addressed horizontally in Directive 2000/31/EC of the European Parliament and of the Council of June 8, 2000 on certain legal aspects of information society services, in particular electronic commerce, in the internal market ("Directive on

electronic commerce"),[4] which clarifies and harmonises various legal issues relating to information society services including electronic commerce. This Directive should be implemented within a timescale similar to that for the implementation of the Directive on electronic commerce, since that Directive provides a harmonised framework of principles and provisions relevant *inter alia* to important parts of this Directive. This Directive is without prejudice to provisions relating to liability in that Directive.

(17) It is necessary, especially in the light of the requirements arising out of the digital environment, to ensure that collecting societies achieve a higher level of rationalisation and transparency with regard to compliance with competition rules.

(18) This Directive is without prejudice to the arrangements in the Member States concerning the management of rights such as extended collective licences.

(19) The moral rights of rightholders should be exercised according to the legislation of the Member States and the provisions of the Berne Convention for the Protection of Literary and Artistic Works, of the WIPO Copyright Treaty and of the WIPO Performances and Phonograms Treaty. Such moral rights remain outside the scope of this Directive.

(20) This Directive is based on principles and rules already laid down in the Directives currently in force in this area, in particular Directives 91/250/EEC,[5] 92/100/EEC,[6] 93/83/EEC,[7] 93/98/EEC[8] and 96/9/EC,[9] and it develops those principles and rules

---

[4] O.J. L178, 17.7.2000, p.1.

[5] Council Directive 91/250/EEC of May 14, 1991 on the legal protection of computer programs (O.J. L122, 17.5.1991, p.42). Directive as amended by Directive 93/98/EEC.

[6] Council Directive 92/100/EEC of November 19, 1992 on rental right and lending right and on certain rights related to copyright in the field of intellectual property (O.J. L346, 27.11.1992, p.61). Directive as amended by Directive 93/98/EEC.

[7] Council Directive 93/83/EEC of September 27, 1993 on the co-ordination of certain rules concerning copyright and rights related to copyright applicable to satellite broadcasting and cable retransmission (O.J. L248, 6.10.1993, p.15).

[8] Council Directive 93/98/EEC of October 29, 1993 harmonising the term of protection of copyright and certain related rights (O.J. L290, 24.11.1993, p.9).

[9] Directive 96/9/EC of the European Parliament and of the Council of March 11, 1996 on the legal protection of databases (O.J. L77, 27.3.1996, p.20).

and places them in the context of the information society. The provisions of this Directive should be without prejudice to the provisions of those Directives, unless otherwise provided in this Directive.

(21) This Directive should define the scope of the acts covered by the reproduction right with regard to the different beneficiaries. This should be done in conformity with the acquis communautaire. A broad definition of these acts is needed to ensure legal certainty within the internal market.

(22) The objective of proper support for the dissemination of culture must not be achieved by sacrificing strict protection of rights or by tolerating illegal forms of distribution of counterfeited or pirated works.

(23) This Directive should harmonise further the author's right of communication to the public. This right should be understood in a broad sense covering all communication to the public not present at the place where the communication originates. This right should cover any such transmission or retransmission of a work to the public by wire or wireless means, including broadcasting. This right should not cover any other acts.

(24) The right to make available to the public subject-matter referred to in Article 3(2) should be understood as covering all acts of making available such subject-matter to members of the public not present at the place where the act of making available originates, and as not covering any other acts.

(25) The legal uncertainty regarding the nature and the level of protection of acts of on-demand transmission of copyright works and subject-matter protected by related rights over networks should be overcome by providing for harmonised protection at Community level. It should be made clear that all rightholders recognised by this Directive should have an exclusive right to make available to the public copyright works or any other subject-matter by way of interactive on-demand transmissions. Such interactive on-demand transmissions are characterised by the fact that members of the public may access them from a place and at a time individually chosen by them.

(26) With regard to the making available in on-demand services by broadcasters of their radio or television productions incorporat-

ing music from commercial phonograms as an integral part thereof, collective licensing arrangements are to be encouraged in order to facilitate the clearance of the rights concerned.

(27) The mere provision of physical facilities for enabling or making a communication does not in itself amount to communication within the meaning of this Directive.

(28) Copyright protection under this Directive includes the exclusive right to control distribution of the work incorporated in a tangible article. The first sale in the Community of the original of a work or copies thereof by the rightholder or with his consent exhausts the right to control resale of that object in the Community. This right should not be exhausted in respect of the original or of copies thereof sold by the rightholder or with his consent outside the Community. Rental and lending rights for authors have been established in Directive 92/100/EEC. The distribution right provided for in this Directive is without prejudice to the provisions relating to the rental and lending rights contained in Chapter I of that Directive.

(29) The question of exhaustion does not arise in the case of services and on-line services in particular. This also applies with regard to a material copy of a work or other subject-matter made by a user of such a service with the consent of the rightholder. Therefore, the same applies to rental and lending of the original and copies of works or other subject-matter which are services by nature. Unlike CD-ROM or CD-I, where the intellectual property is incorporated in a material medium, namely an item of goods, every on-line service is in fact an act which should be subject to authorisation where the copyright or related right so provides.

(30) The rights referred to in this Directive may be transferred, assigned or subject to the granting of contractual licences, without prejudice to the relevant national legislation on copyright and related rights.

(31) A fair balance of rights and interests between the different categories of rightholders, as well as between the different categories of rightholders and users of protected subject-matter must be safeguarded. The existing exceptions and limitations to the rights as set out by the Member States have to be reassessed in the light of the new electronic environment. Existing differences

437

in the exceptions and limitations to certain restricted acts have direct negative effects on the functioning of the internal market of copyright and related rights. Such differences could well become more pronounced in view of the further development of transborder exploitation of works and cross-border activities. In order to ensure the proper functioning of the internal market, such exceptions and limitations should be defined more harmoniously. The degree of their harmonisation should be based on their impact on the smooth functioning of the internal market.

(32) This Directive provides for an exhaustive enumeration of exceptions and limitations to the reproduction right and the right of communication to the public. Some exceptions or limitations only apply to the reproduction right, where appropriate. This list takes due account of the different legal traditions in Member States, while, at the same time, aiming to ensure a functioning internal market. Member States should arrive at a coherent application of these exceptions and limitations, which will be assessed when reviewing implementing legislation in the future.

(33) The exclusive right of reproduction should be subject to an exception to allow certain acts of temporary reproduction, which are transient or incidental reproductions, forming an integral and essential part of a technological process and carried out for the sole purpose of enabling either efficient transmission in a network between third parties by an intermediary, or a lawful use of a work or other subject-matter to be made. The acts of reproduction concerned should have no separate economic value on their own. To the extent that they meet these conditions, this exception should include acts which enable browsing as well as acts of caching to take place, including those which enable transmission systems to function efficiently, provided that the intermediary does not modify the information and does not interfere with the lawful use of technology, widely recognised and used by industry, to obtain data on the use of the information. A use should be considered lawful where it is authorised by the rightholder or not restricted by law.

(34) Member States should be given the option of providing for certain exceptions or limitations for cases such as educational and scientific purposes, for the benefit of public institutions such as

libraries and archives, for purposes of news reporting, for quotations, for use by people with disabilities, for public security uses
and for uses in administrative and judicial proceedings.

(35) In certain cases of exceptions or limitations, rightholders should
receive fair compensation to compensate them adequately for the
use made of their protected works or other subject-matter.
When determining the form, detailed arrangements and possible
level of such fair compensation, account should be taken of the
particular circumstances of each case. When evaluating these
circumstances, a valuable criterion would be the possible harm to
the rightholders resulting from the act in question. In cases where
rightholders have already received payment in some other form,
for instance as part of a licence fee, no specific or separate payment may be due. The level of fair compensation should take full
account of the degree of use of technological protection measures referred to in this Directive. In certain situations where the
prejudice to the rightholder would be minimal, no obligation for
payment may arise.

(36) The Member States may provide for fair compensation for
rightholders also when applying the optional provisions on
exceptions or limitations which do not require such compensation.

(37) Existing national schemes on reprography, where they exist, do
not create major barriers to the internal market. Member States
should be allowed to provide for an exception or limitation in
respect of reprography.

(38) Member States should be allowed to provide for an exception or
limitation to the reproduction right for certain types of reproduction of audio, visual and audiovisual material for private use,
accompanied by fair compensation. This may include the
introduction or continuation of remuneration schemes to compensate for the prejudice to rightholders. Although differences
between those remuneration schemes affect the functioning of
the internal market, those differences, with respect to analogue
private reproduction, should not have a significant impact on the
development of the information society. Digital private copying
is likely to be more widespread and have a greater economic
impact. Due account should therefore be taken of the differences

439

between digital and analogue private copying and a distinction should be made in certain respects between them.

(39) When applying the exception or limitation on private copying, Member States should take due account of technological and economic developments, in particular with respect to digital private copying and remuneration schemes, when effective technological protection measures are available. Such exceptions or limitations should not inhibit the use of technological measures or their enforcement against circumvention.

(40) Member States may provide for an exception or limitation for the benefit of certain non-profit making establishments, such as publicly accessible libraries and equivalent institutions, as well as archives. However, this should be limited to certain special cases covered by the reproduction right. Such an exception or limitation should not cover uses made in the context of on-line delivery of protected works or other subject-matter. This Directive should be without prejudice to the Member States' option to derogate from the exclusive public lending right in accordance with Article 5 of Directive 92/100/EEC. Therefore, specific contracts or licences should be promoted which, without creating imbalances, favour such establishments and the disseminative purposes they serve.

(41) When applying the exception or limitation in respect of ephemeral recordings made by broadcasting organisations it is understood that a broadcaster's own facilities include those of a person acting on behalf of and under the responsibility of the broadcasting organisation.

(42) When applying the exception or limitation for non-commercial educational and scientific research purposes, including distance learning, the non-commercial nature of the activity in question should be determined by that activity as such. The organisational structure and the means of funding of the establishment concerned are not the decisive factors in this respect.

(43) It is in any case important for the Member States to adopt all necessary measures to facilitate access to works by persons suffering from a disability which constitutes an obstacle to the use of the works themselves, and to pay particular attention to accessible formats.

(44) When applying the exceptions and limitations provided for in this Directive, they should be exercised in accordance with international obligations. Such exceptions and limitations may not be applied in a way which prejudices the legitimate interests of the rightholder or which conflicts with the normal exploitation of his work or other subject-matter. The provision of such exceptions or limitations by Member States should, in particular, duly reflect the increased economic impact that such exceptions or limitations may have in the context of the new electronic environment. Therefore, the scope of certain exceptions or limitations may have to be even more limited when it comes to certain new uses of copyright works and other subject-matter.

(45) The exceptions and limitations referred to in Article 5(2), (3) and (4) should not, however, prevent the definition of contractual relations designed to ensure fair compensation for the rightholders insofar as permitted by national law.

(46) Recourse to mediation could help users and rightholders to settle disputes. The Commission, in cooperation with the Member States within the Contact Committee, should undertake a study to consider new legal ways of settling disputes concerning copyright and related rights.

(47) Technological development will allow rightholders to make use of technological measures designed to prevent or restrict acts not authorised by the rightholders of any copyright, rights related to copyright or the *sui generis* right in databases. The danger, however, exists that illegal activities might be carried out in order to enable or facilitate the circumvention of the technical protection provided by these measures. In order to avoid fragmented legal approaches that could potentially hinder the functioning of the internal market, there is a need to provide for harmonised legal protection against circumvention of effective technological measures and against provision of devices and products or servies to this effect.

(48) Such legal protection should be provided in respect of technological measures that effectively restrict acts not authorised by the rightholders of any copyright, rights related to copyright or the *sui generis* right in databases without, however, preventing the normal operation of electronic equipment and its technological development. Such legal protection implies no obligation to

design devices, products, components or services to correspond to technological measures, so long as such device, product, component or service does not otherwise fall under the prohibition of Article 6. Such legal protection should respect proportionality and should not prohibit those devices or activities which have a commercially significant purpose or use other than to circumvent the technical protection. In particular, this protection should not hinder research into cryptography.

(49) The legal protection of technological measures is without prejudice to the application of any national provisions which may prohibit the private possession of devices, products or components for the circumvention of technological measures.

(50) Such a harmonised legal protection does not affect the specific provisions on protection provided for by Directive 91/250/EEC. In particular, it should not apply to the protection of technological measures used in connection with computer programs, which is exclusively addressed in that Directive. It should neither inhibit nor prevent the development or use of any means of circumventing a technological measure that is necessary to enable acts to be undertaken in accordance with the terms of Article 5(3) or Article 6 of Directive 91/250/EEC. Articles 5 and 6 of that Directive exclusively determine exceptions to the exclusive rights applicable to computer programs.

(51) The legal protection of technological measures applies without prejudice to public policy, as reflected in Article 5, or public security. Member States should promote voluntary measures taken by rightholders, including the conclusion and implementation of agreements between rightholders and other parties concerned, to accommodate achieving the objectives of certain exceptions or limitations provided for in national law in accordance with this Directive. In the absence of such voluntary measures or agreements within a reasonable period of time, Member States should take appropriate measures to ensure that rightholders provide beneficiaries of such exceptions or limitations with appropriate means of benefiting from them, by modifying an implemented technological measure or by other means. However, in order to prevent abuse of such measures taken by rightholders, including within the framework of agreements, or taken by a Member State, any technological

measures applied in implementation of such measures should enjoy legal protection.

(52) When implementing an exception or limitation for private copying in accordance with Article 5(2)(b), Member States should likewise promote the use of voluntary measures to accommodate achieving the objectives of such exception or limitation. If, within a reasonable period of time, no such voluntary measures to make reproduction for private use possible have been taken, Member States may take measures to enable beneficiaries of the exception or limitation concerned to benefit from it. Voluntary measures taken by rightholders, including agreements between rightholders and other parties concerned, as well as measures taken by Member States, do not prevent rightholders from using technological measures which are consistent with the exceptions or limitations on private copying in national law in accordance with Article 5(2)(b), taking account of the condition of fair compensation under that provision and the possible differentiation between various conditions of use in accordance with Article 5(5), such as controlling the number of reproductions. In order to prevent abuse of such measures, any technological measures applied in their implementation should enjoy legal protection.

(53) The protection of technological measures should ensure a secure environment for the provision of interactive on-demand services, in such a way that members of the public may access works or other subject-matter from a place and at a time individually chosen by them. Where such services are governed by contractual arrangements, the first and second subparagraphs of Article 6(4) should not apply. Non-interactive forms of online use should remain subject to those provisions.

(54) Important progress has been made in the international standardisation of technical systems of identification of works and protected subject-matter in digital format. In an increasingly networked environment, differences between technological measures could lead to an incompatibility of systems within the Community. Compatability and interoperability of the different systems should be encouraged. It would be highly desirable to encourage the development of global systems.

(55) Technological development will facilitate the distribution of

works, notably on networks, and this will entail the need for rightholders to identify better the work or other subject-matter, the author or any other rightholder, and to provide information about the terms and conditions of use of the work or other subject-matter in order to render easier the management of rights attached to them. Rightholders should be encouraged to use markings indicating, in addition to the information referred to above, *inter alia* their authorisation when putting works or other subject-matter on networks.

(56) There is, however, the danger that illegal activities might be carried out in order to remove or alter the electronic copyright-management information attached to it, or otherwise to distribute, import for distribution, broadcast, communicate to the public or make available to the public works or other protected subject-matter from which such information has been removed without authority. In order to avoid fragmented legal approaches that could potentially hinder the functioning of the internal market, there is a need to provide for harmonised legal protection against any of these activities.

(57) Any such rights-management information systems referred to above may, depending on their design, at the same time process personal data about the consumption patterns of protected subject-matter by individuals and allow for tracing of on-line behaviour. These technical means, in their technical functions, should incorporate privacy safeguards in accordance with Directive 95/46/EC of the European Parliament and of the Council of October 24, 1995 on the protection of individuals with regard to the processing of personal data and the free movement of such data.[10]

(58) Member States should provide for effective sanctions and remedies for infringements of rights and obligations as set out in this Directive. They should take all the measures necessary to ensure that those sanctions and remedies are applied. The sanctions thus provided for should be effective, proportionate and dissuasive and should include the possibility of seeking damages

---

[10] O.J. L281, 23.11.1995, p.31.

and/or injunctive relief and, where appropriate, of applying for seizure of infringing material.

(59) In the digital environment, in particular, the services of inter-mediaries may increasingly be used by third parties for infringing activities. In many cases such intermediaries are best placed to bring such infringing activities to an end. Therefore, without prejudice to any other sanctions and remedies available, right-holders should have the possibility of applying for an injunction against an intermediary who carries a third party's infringement of a protected work or other subject-matter in a network. This possibility should be available even where the acts carried out by the intermediary are exempted under Article 5. The conditions and modalities relating to such injunctions should be left to the national law of the Member States.

(60) The protection provided under this Directive should be without prejudice to national or Community legal provisions in other areas, such as industrial property, data protection, conditional access, access to public documents, and the rule of media exploitation chronology, which may affect the protection of copyright or related rights.

(61) In order to comply with the WIPO Performances and Phono-grams Treaty, Directives 92/100/EEC and 93/98/EEC should be amended,

HAVE ADOPTED THIS DIRECTIVE:

CHAPTER I

OBJECTIVE AND SCOPE

Article 1

Scope

1. This Directive concerns the legal protection of copyright and related rights in the framework of the internal market, with particular emphasis on the information society.

2. Except in the cases referred to in Article 11, this Directive shall

445

leave intact and shall in no way affect existing Community provisions relating to:

(a) the legal protection of computer programs;

(b) rental right, lending right and certain rights related to copy-right in the field of intellectual property;

(c) copyright and related rights applicable to broadcasting of programmes by satellite and cable retransmission;

(d) the term of protection of copyright and certain related rights;

(e) the legal protection of databases.

CHAPTER II

RIGHTS AND EXCEPTIONS

Article 2

Reproduction Right

Member States shall provide for the exclusive right to authorise or prohibit direct or indirect, temporary or permanent reproduction by any means and in any form, in whole or in part:

(a) for authors, of their works;

(b) for performers, of fixations of their performances;

(c) for phonogram producers, of their phonograms;

(d) for the producers of the first fixations of films, in respect of the original and copies of their films;

(e) for broadcasting organisations, of fixations of their broadcasts, whether those broadcasts are transmitted by wire or over the air, including by cable or satellite.

Article 3

Right of Communication to the Public of Works and Right of Making Available to the Public other Subject-Matter

1. Member States shall provide authors with the exclusive right to authorise or prohibit any communication to the public of their works, by wire or wireless means, including the making available to the public of their works in such a way that members of the public may access them from a place and at a time individually chosen by them.

2. Member States shall provide for the exclusive right to authorise or prohibit the making available to the public, by wire or wireless means, in such a way that members of the public may access them from a place and at a time individually chosen by them:

(a) for performers, of fixations of their performances;

(b) for phonogram producers, of their phonograms;

(c) for the producers of the first fixations of films, of the original and copies of their films;

(d) for broadcasting organisations, of fixations of their broadcasts, whether these broadcasts are transmitted by wire or over the air, including by cable or satellite.

3. The rights referred to in paragraphs 1 and 2 shall not be exhausted by any act of communication to the public or making available to the public as set out in this Article.

Article 4

Distribution Right

1. Member States shall provide for authors, in respect of the original of their works or of copies therof, the exclusive right to authorise or prohibit any form of distribution to the public by sale or otherwise.

2. The distribution right shall not be exhausted within the Community in respect of the original or copies of the work, except where

the first sale or other transfer of ownership in the Community of that object is made by the rightholder or with his consent.

Article 5

Exceptions and Limitations

1. Temporary acts of reproduction referred to in Article 2, which are transient or incidental [and] an integral and essential part of a technological process and whose sole purpose is to enable:

(a) a transmission in a network between third parties by an intermediary, or

(b) a lawful use

of a work or other subject-matter to be made, and which have no independent economic significance, shall be exempted from the reproduction right provided for in Article 2.

2. Member States may provide for exceptions or limitations to the reproduction right provided for in Article 2 in the following cases:

(a) in respect of reproductions on paper or any similar medium, effected by the use of any kind of photographic technique or by some other process having similar effects, with the exception of sheet music, provided that the rightholders receive fair compensation;

(b) in respect of reproductions on any medium made by a natural person for private use and for ends that are neither directly nor indirectly commercial, on condition that the rightholders receive fair compensation which takes account of the application or non-application of technological measures referred to in Article 6 to the work or subject-matter concerned;

(c) in respect of specific acts of reproduction made by publicly accessible libraries, educational establishments or museums, or by archives, which are not for direct or indirect economic or commercial advantage;

(d) in respect of ephemeral recordings of works made by broadcasting organisations by means of their own facilities and for their own broadcasts; the preservation of these recordings in official archives may, on the grounds of their exceptional documentary character, be permitted;

(e) in respect of reproductions of broadcasts made by social institutions pursuing non-commercial purposes, such as hospitals or prisons, on condition that the rightholders receive fair compensation.

3. Member States may provide for exceptions or limitations to the rights provided for in Articles 2 and 3 in the following cases:

(a) use for the sole purpose of illustration for teaching or scientific research, as long as the source, including the author's name, is indicated, unless this turns out to be impossible and to the extent justified by the non-commercial purpose to be achieved;

(b) uses, for the benefit of people with a disability, which are directly related to the disability and of a non-commercial nature, to the extent required by the specific disability;

(c) reproduction by the press, communication to the public or making available of published articles on current economic, political or religious topics or of broadcast works or other subject-matter of the same character, in cases where such use is not expressly reserved, and as long as the source, including the author's name, is indicated, or use of works or other subject-matter in connection with the reporting of current events, to the extent justified by the informatory purpose and as long as the source, including the author's name, is indicated, unless this turns out to be impossible;

(d) quotations for purposes such as criticism or review, provided that they relate to a work or other subject-matter which has already been lawfully made available to the public, that, unless this turns out to be impossible, the source, including the author's name, is indicated, and that their use is in accordance with fair practice, and to the extent required by the specific purpose;

(e) use for the purposes of public security or to ensure the proper performance or reporting of administrative, parliamentary or judicial proceedings;

(f) use of political speeches as well as extracts of public lectures or similar works or subject-matter to the extent justified by the informatory purpose and provided that the source, including the author's name, is indicated, except where this turns out to be impossible;

(g) use during religious celebrations or official celebrations organised by a public authority;

(h) use of works, such as works of architecture or sculpture, made to be located permanently in public places;

(i) incidental inclusion of a work or other subject-matter in other material;

(j) use for the purpose of advertising the public exhibition or sale of artistic works, to the extent necessary to promote the event, excluding any other commercial use;

(k) use for the purpose of caricature, parody or pastiche;

(l) use in connection with the demonstration or repair of equipment;

(m) use of an artistic work in the form of a building or a drawing or plan of a building for the purposes of reconstructing the building;

(n) use by communication or making available, for the purpose of research or private study, to individual members of the public by dedicated terminals on the premises of establishments referred to in paragraph 2(c) of works and other subject-matter not subject to purchase or licensing terms which are contained in their collections;

(o) use in certain other cases of minor importance where exceptions or limitations already exist under national law, provided that they only concern analogue uses and do not affect the free circulation of goods and services within the Community, without prejudice to the other exceptions and limitations contained in this Article.

4. Where the Member States may provide for an exception or

limitation to the right of reproduction pursuant to paragraphs 2 and 3, they may provide similarly for an exception or limitation to the right of distribution as referred to in Article 4 to the extent justified by the purpose of the authorised act of reproduction.

5. The exceptions and limitations provided for in paragraphs 1, 2, 3 and 4 shall only be applied in certain special cases which do not conflict with a normal exploitation of the work or other subject-matter and do not unreasonably prejudice the legitimate interests of the rightholder.

CHAPTER III

PROTECTION OF TECHNOLOGICAL MEASURES AND RIGHTS-MANAGEMENT INFORMATION

Article 6

Obligations as to technological measures

1. Member States shall provide adequate legal protection against the circumvention of any effective technological measures, which the person concerned carries out in the knowledge, or with reasonable grounds to know, that he or she is pursuing that objective.

2. Member States shall provide adequate legal protection against the manufacture, import, distribution, sale, rental, advertisement for sale or rental, or possession for commercial purposes of devices, products or components or the provision of services which:

(a) are promoted, advertised or marketed for the purpose of circumvention of, or

(b) have only a limited commercially significant purpose or use other than to circumvent, or

(c) are primarily designed, produced, adapted or performed for the purpose of enabling or facilitating the circumvention of,

any effective technological measures.

3. for the purposes of this Directive, the expression "technological measures" means any technology, device or component that, in the

normal course of its operation, is designed to prevent or restrict acts, in respect of works or other subject-matter, which are not authorised by the rightholder of any copyright or any right related to copyright as provided for by law or the *sui generis* right provided for in Chapter III of Directive 96/9/EC. Technological measures shall be deemed "effective" where the use of a protected work or other subject-matter is controlled by the rightholders through application of an access control or protection process, such as encryption, scrambling or other transformation of the work or other subject-matter or a copy control mechanism, which achieves the protection objective.

4. Notwithstanding the legal protection provided for in paragraph 1, in the absence of voluntary measures taken by rightholders, including agreements between rightholders and other parties concerned, Member States shall take appropriate measures to ensure that rightholders make available to the beneficiary of an exception or limitation provided for in national law in accordance with Article 5(2)(a), (2)(c), (2)(d), (2)(e), (3)(a), (3)(b) or (3)(e) the means of benefiting from that exception or limitation, to the extent necessary to benefit from that exception or limitation and where that beneficiary has legal access to the protected work or subject-matter concerned.

A Member State may also take such measures in respect of a beneficiary of an exception or limitation provided for in accordance with Article 5(2)(b), unless reproduction for private use has already been made possible by rightholders to the extent necessary to benefit from the exception or limitation concerned and in accordance with the provisions of Article 5(2)(b) and (5), without preventing right holders from adopting adequate measures regarding the number of reproductions in accordance with these provisions.

The technological measures applied voluntarily by rightholders, including those applied in implementation of voluntary agreements, and technological measures applied in implementation of the measures taken by Member States, shall enjoy the legal protection provided for in paragraph 1.

The provisions of the first and second subparagraphs shall not apply to works or other subject-matter made available to the public on agreed contractual terms in such a way that members of the public may access them from a place and at a time individually chosen by them.

When this Article is applied in the context of Directives 92/100/EEC and 96/9/EC, this paragraph shall apply *mutatis mutandis*.

Article 7

Obligations Concerning Rights-management Information

1. Member States shall provide for adequate legal protection against any person knowingly performing without authority any of the following acts:

(a) the removal or alteration of any electronic rights-management information;

(b) the distribution, importation for distribution, broadcasting, communication or making available to the public of works or other subject-matter protected under this Directive or under Chapter III of Directive 96/9/EC from which electronic rights-management information has been removed or altered without authority,

if such person knows, or has reasonable grounds to know, that by so doing he is inducing, enabling, facilitating or concealing an infringement of any copyright or any rights related to copyright as provided by law, or of the *sui generis* right provided for in Chapter III of Directive 96/9/EC.

2. For the purposes of this Directive, the expression "rights-management information" means any information provided by rightholders which identifies the work or other subject-matter referred to in this Directive or covered by the *sui generis* right provided for in Chapter III of Directive 96/9/EC, the author or any other rightholder, or information about the terms and conditions of use of the work or other subject-matter, and any numbers or codes that represent such information.

The first subparagraph shall apply when any of these items of information is associated with a copy of, or appears in connection with the communication to the public of, a work or other subject-matter referred to in this Directive or covered by the *sui generis* right provided for in Chapter III of Directive 96/9/EC.

CHAPTER **IV**

COMMON PROVISIONS

Article 8

Sanctions and Remedies

1. Member States shall provide appropriate sanctions and remedies in respect of infringements of the rights and obligations set out in this Directive and shall take all the measures necessary to ensure that those sanctions and remedies are applied. The sanctions thus provided for shall be effective, proportionate and dissuasive.

2. Each Member State shall take the measures necessary to ensure that rightholders whose interests are affected by an infringing activity carried out on its territory can bring an action for damages and/or apply for an injunction and, where appropriate, for the seizure of infringing material as well as of devices, products or components referred to in Article 6(2).

3. Member States shall ensure that rightholders are in a position to apply for an injunction against intermediaries whose services are used by a third party to infringe a copyright or related right.

Article 9

Continued Application of Other Legal Provisions

This Directive shall be without prejudice to provisions concerning in particular patent rights, trade marks, design rights, utility models, topographies of semi-conductor products, type faces, conditional access, access to cable or broadcasting services, protection of national treasures, legal deposit requirements, laws on restrictive practices and unfair competition, trade secrets, security, confidentiality, data protection and privacy, access to public documents, the law of contract.

Article 10

Application Over Time

1. The provisions of this Directive shall apply in respect of all works and other subject-matter referred to in this Directive which are, on December 22, 2002, protected by the Member States' legislation in the field of copyright and related rights, or which meet the criteria for protection under the provisions of this Directive or the provisions referred to in Article 1(2).

2. This Directive shall apply without prejudice to any acts concluded and rights acquired before December 22, 2002.

Article 11

Technical Adaptations

1. Directive 92/100/EEC is hereby amended as follows:

(a) Article 7 shall be deleted;

(b) Article 10(3) shall be replaced by the following:

"3. The limitations shall only be applied in certain special cases which do not conflict with a normal exploitation of the subject-matter and do not unreasonably prejudice the legitimate interests of the rightholder."

2. Article 3(2) of Directive 93/98/EEC shall be replaced by the following:

"2. The rights of producers of phonograms shall expire 50 years after the fixation is made. However, if the phonogram has been lawfully published within this period, the said rights shall expire 50 years from the date of the first lawful publication. If no lawful publication has taken place within the period mentioned in the first sentence, and if the phonogram has been lawfully communicated to the public within this period, the said rights shall expire 50 years from the date of the first lawful communication to the public."

However, where through the expiry of the term of protection granted pursuant to this paragraph in its version before amendment by Directive 2001/29/EC of the European Parliament and of the Council of May 22, 2001 on the harmonisation of certain aspects of copyright and related rights in the information society[11] the rights of producers of phonograms are no longer protected on December 22, 2002, this paragraph shall not have the effect of protecting those rights anew.

Article 12

Final Provisions

1. Not later than December 22, 2004 and every three years thereafter, the Commission shall submit to the European Parliament, the Council and the Economic and Social Committee a report on the application of this Directive, in which, *inter alia*, on the basis of specific information supplied by the Member States, it shall examine in particular the application of Articles 5, 6 and 8 in the light of the development of the digital market. In the case of Article 6, it shall examine in particular whether that Article confers a sufficient level of protection and whether acts which are permitted by law are being adversely affected by the use of effective technological measures. Where necessary, in particular to ensure the functioning of the internal market pursuant to Article 14 of the Treaty, it shall submit proposals for amendments to this Directive.

2. Protection of rights related to copyright under this Directive shall leave intact and shall in no way affect the protection of copyright.

3. A contact committee is hereby established. It shall be composed of representatives of the competent authorities of the Member States. It shall be chaired by a representative of the Commission and shall meet either on the initiative of the chairman or at the request of the delegation of a Member State.

4. The tasks of the committee shall be as follows:

---

[11] O.J. L167, 22.6.2001, p.10.

(a) to examine the impact of this Directive on the functioning of the internal market, and to highlight any difficulties;

(b) to organise consultations on all questions deriving from the application of this Directive;

(c) to facilitate the exchange of information on relevant developments in legislation and case-law, as well as relevant economic, social, cultural and technological developments;

(d) to act as a forum for the assessment of the digital market in works and other items, including private copying and the use of technological measures.

Article 13

Implementation

1. Member States shall bring into force the laws, regulations and administrative provisions necessary to comply with this Directive before December 22, 2002. They shall forthwith inform the Commission thereof.

When Member States adopt these measures, they shall contain a reference to this Directive or shall be accompanied by such reference on the occasion of their official publication. The methods of making such reference shall be laid down by Member States.

2. Member States shall communicate to the Commission the text of the provisions of domestic law which they adopt in the field governed by this Directive.

Article 14

Entry into Force

This Directive shall enter into force on the day of its publication in the *Official Journal of the European Communities*.

Article 15

Addressees

This Directive is addressed to the Member States.

Done at Brussels, May 22, 2001.

Bibliography

Books and Publications

Bailey H.S., *The Art and Science of Book Publishing* (Ohio University Press, 1970) (3rd ed. 1990)

Ball H., *The Law of Copyright and Literary Property*, (Banks, Albany, N.Y., 1944)

Berthold F.J. & H. von Hartlieb, *Filmrecht—ein Handbuch*, (C.H. Beck'sche Verlagsbuchhandlung, Munich-Berlin, 1957)

Bertrand A., *Le droit d'auteur et les droits voisins*, 2nd ed., (Masson, Paris, 1999)

Birrell A., *Seven Lectures on the Law and History of Copyright in Books* (Cassell, London, 1899)

Bugbee B.W., *Genesis of American Patent and Copyright Law* (Public Affairs Press, Washington, 1967)

Colombet C., *Propriété littéraire et artistique*, 8th ed., (Dalloz, Paris, 2001)

Cornish W.R., *Intellectual Property: Patents, Copyright, Trade Marks and Allied Rights*, 4th ed., (Sweet & Maxwell, London, 1999)

Davies G. & H.H. von Rauscher auf Weeg, *Challenges to Copyright and Related Rights in the European Community* (ESC Publishing Limited, Oxford, 1983)

Davies G. & M.E. Hung, *Music and Video Private Copying, An International Survey of the Problem and the Law* (Sweet & Maxwell, London, 1993)

Dellebeke M. (ed.), *Copyright in Cyberspace*, Proceedings of the ALAI Study Days Amsterdam, June 1996, (Otto Cramwinckel, Amsterdam, 1997)

Derieux E. & P. Trudel, *"L'intérêt public, principe du droit de la communication"*, (Victoires Editions, 1996)

Desbois H., *Le Droit d'auteur en France*, 3rd ed., (Dalloz, Paris, 1978)

Desbois H., A. Françon & A. Kerever, *Les conventions internationales du droit d'auteur et des droits voisins* (1976)

Dietz A., *Copyright Law in the European Community* (Alphen aan den Rijn, Sijthoff & Noordhoff, 1978)

Dock M.-C., *Etude sur le droit d'auteur*, (Libraire générale de droit et de jurisprudence, Paris, 1963)

Dworkin G. & R.D. Taylor, *Blackstone's Guide to the Copyright, Designs and Patents Act 1988*, (Blackstone Press Ltd, London, 1989)

Eddy J.P., *The Law of Copyright* (Butterworths, London, 1957)

Edelman B., *Droits d'auteur, droits voisins. Droit d'auteur et marché*, (Dalloz, Paris, 1993)

Erdmann W., W. Gloy & R. Herber, *Festschrift for H. Piper*, (Beck, Munich, 1996)

Escarra J., J. Rault & F. Hepp, *La Doctrine française du droit d'auteur* (Editions Bernard Grasset, Paris, 1937)

Fechner F., *Geistiges Eigentum und Verfassung*, (Mohr Siebeck, Tübingen, 1999)

Ficsor M., *The Law of Copyright and the Internet*, (Oxford University Press, Oxford, 2002)

Françon A., *Cours de propriété littéraire, artistique et industrielle*, (Les Cours de droit, Paris, 1996–1997, updated 1999)

Fromm K.-F. & W. Nordemann, *Urheberrecht*, 9th. ed., (Verlag W. Kohlhammer, Stuttgart/Berlin, 1998)

von Gamm O.-F., *Urheberrechtsgesetz, Kommentar*, (C.H. Beck'sche Verlagsbuchhandlung, Munich, 1968)

Ganea P., C. Heath & G. Schricker (eds), *Urheberrecht Gestern-Heute-Morgen, Festschrift für Adolf Dietz zum 65. Geburtstag,* (Verlag C.H. Beck, Munich, 2001)

Garnett K., J. Rayner James & G. Davies, *Copinger and Skone James on Copyright*, 14th ed., (Sweet & Maxwell, London, 1999)

Garnett K., J. Rayner James & G. Davies, *Copinger and Skone James on Copyright, Supplement to the 14th ed.*, (Sweet & Maxwell, London, 2002)

Gautier P.-Y., *Propriété littéraire et artistique*, 4th ed., (coll. Droit fondamental, PUF, Paris, 2001)

Geiger C., *Droit d'auteur et droit du public à l'information, approche de droit comparé*, Mémoire de DEA, (Université de Montpellier, E.R.C.I.M., 1998)

Gervais D., *La notion d'oeuvre dans la Convention de Berne et en droit comparé*, (Librairie Droz, Geneva, 1998)

Gervais D., *The TRIPs Agreement—Drafting History and Analysis*, (Sweet & Maxwell, London, 1998)

Ginsburg J. & Y. Gaubiac, "Private Copying in the Digital Environment", in *Intellectual Property and Information Law*, Essays in Honour of Herman Cohen Jehoram, (Kluwer Law International, The Hague, London, Boston, 1998)

Goldstein P., *Copyright Principles, Law and Practice*, (Little Brown and Company, Boston, Toronto, London, 1989)

Goldstein P., *Copyright's Highway—The Law and Lore of Copyright from Gutenberg to the Celestial Jukebox*, (Hill and Wang, New York, 1994)

Goldstein P., *International Copyright, Principles, Law and Practice*, (Oxford University Press, Oxford, 2001)

Hanson H., ed., *U.S. Intellectual Property: Law and Policy*, (Sweet & Maxwell, London, 2000)

Hemmer J.J., *The Supreme Court and the First Amendment*, Praeger Special Studies, Vol.XV (Praeger, New York, 1986)

Heymann E., *Die Zeitliche Begrenzung des Urheberrechts* (Prussian Academy of Sciences, Berlin, 1927)

Hubmann H., *Das Recht des schöpperischen Geistes*, (Walter de Gruyter & Co., Berlin, 1954)

Hugenholtz B. ed., *The Future of Copyright in a Digital Environment*, (Kluwer, The Hague, 1996)

Hummel M., *Die volkswirtschaftliche Bedeutung des Urheberrechts*, (IFO-Institut für Wirtschaftsforschung, Duncker & Humblot, Berlin-Munich, 1989)

Hummel M., *Die volkswirtschaftliche Bedeutung des Urheberrechts*, Gutachten im Auftrag des Bundesministers der Justiz, No. 125 in der Schriftenreihe des IFO—Instituts für Wirtschaftsforschung, Information Highway Advisory Council, Final Report, *The Challenge of the Information Highway*, (Canada, 1995) (Duncker & Humblot, Berlin/Munich, 1989)

Kaplan B., *An Unhurried View of Copyright*, (Columbia University Press, New York & London, 1967)

Kase F.J., *Copyright Thought in Continental Europe*, (Fred B. Rothman, South Hackensack, N.J., 1967)

Kirchhof P., *Der Gesetzgebungsauftrag zum Schutz des geistigen Eigentums gegenüber modernen Vervielfältigungstechniken* (Decker & Müller Verlag, Heidelberg, 1988)

Kleinke Y., *Pressedatenbanken und Urheberrecht; Zur urheberrechtlichen Bewertung der Nutzung von Zeitungsartikeln in Pressedatenbanken*, Köln, etc. (Carl Heymanns Verlag, 1998)

Kleinke Y., *Pressedatenbanken und Urheberrecht*, Köln, etc. (Carl Heymans Verlag, 1999)

Laboulaye L. & G. Guiffrey, *La propriété littéraire au XVIII siècle*, (Hachette, Paris, 1859)

Ladas S.P., *The International Protection of Literary and Artistic Property*, 2 Vols (Macmillan, New York, 1938)

Lehmann M., ed., *Internet- und Multimediarecht* (Cyberlaw), (Schöpfer-Poeschel Verlag, Stuttgart, 1997)

Locke J., *Two Treatises of Government* [1690], edited by: Laslett P., (Cambridge University Press, 1988)

Lucas A. & H.-J.: *Traité de la Propriété Littéraire & Artistique, Litec*, 2nd ed., (Librairie de la Cour de Cassation, Paris, 2001)

Lucas A., *Droit d'auteur et numérique*, (Litec, Paris, 1998)

MacQueen H.L., *Copyright, Competition and Industrial Design*, 2nd ed., Hume Papers on Public Policy: Vol.3, No.2, (Edinburgh University Press, 1995)

Masouyé C., *Guide to the Berne Convention*, (WIPO, 1978), para.1.15.

Möhring P. & K. Nicolini, *Urheberrechtsgesetz*, Kommentar, 2nd. ed., (Vahlen, Munich, 2000)

Morgan C., *The House of Macmillan*, (Macmillan, London, 1944)

Neumann T., *Urheberrecht und Schulgebrauch*, UFITA Vol.115 (Baden-Baden, Nomos, 1994)

Nimmer M.B., *Nimmer on Copyright. A Treatise on the Law of Literary, Musical and Artistic Property and the Protection of Ideas*, (Matthew Bender, New York, 2001 ed.)

Nordemann W., K. Vinck & P. Hertin, *International Copyright and Neighboring Rights Law* (VCH, Weinheim, 1990)

Owens R., *"Digital Rights Management (DRM)—A Look Ahead"*, (paper delivered at Fordham University School of Law Ninth Annual Conference on International Intellectual Property Law and Policy, April 19–20, 2001)

Patterson L.R., *Copyright in Historical Perspective*, (Vanderbilt University Press, Nashville, 1968)

Patterson L.R., and Lindberg S.W., *The Nature of Copyright—A Law of Users' Rights*, (The University of Georgia Press, Athens & London, 1991)

Phillips J., *The Economic Importance of Copyright* (CLIP, 1985)

Plaisant R., "La Durée du droit pécuniaire de l'auteur et de son évolution", *Mélanges A. Françon*, (Dalloz, Paris, 1995)

Plaisant R., *Propriété littéraire et artistique*, (Delmas, Paris, 1985)

Plant A., *Selected Economic Essays and Addresses* (Routledge and Kegan

Paul, London & Boston, 1974)

Posner R.A., *Economic Analysis of Law*, 2nd ed., (Little, Brown & Co., Boston, 1977)

Pouillet E., *Traité théorique et pratique de la propriété littéraire et artistique*, 3rd ed., (Marchal et Billard, Paris, 1908)

Price T., *The Economic Importance of Copyright*, (Common Law Institute of Intellectual Property (CLIP), London, 1993))

Putnam G.H., *The Question of Copyright*, 2nd ed., (The Knickerbocker Press, New York, 1896)

Putnam, G.H., *Books and their Makers During the Middle Ages, 1476–1600* (New York & London, 1896)

von Rauscher auf Weeg H.H., *Das Aufführungsrecht der Interpreten und Schallplattenhersteller nach geltendem deutschen Recht*, (W. Kohlhammer Verlag, Cologne, 1960)

Rehbinder M., *Urheberrecht*, 11th ed., (C. Beck'sche Verlagsbuchhandlung, Munich, 2001)

Reinbothe J. & S. von Lewinski, *The WIPO Treaties 1996*, (Butterworths, London, 2002)

Renouard A.-C., *Traité des droits d'auteur dans la littérature, les sciences et les beaux-arts* (Jules Renouard et Cie. Libraires, Paris, 1838)

Ricketson S., *The Berne Convention for the Protection of Literary and Artistic Works: 1886–1986*, (Centre for Commercial Law Studies, Queen Mary College, London, 1987)

Rose M., *Authors and Owners, the Invention of Copyright*, (Harvard University Press, 1994)

Schack H., *Urheber- und Urhebervertragsrecht*, 2nd ed., (Mohr Siebeck, Tübingen, 2001)

Schricker G., *Urheberrecht*, Kommentar, 2nd. ed. (C.H. Beck'sche Verlagsbuchhandlung, Munich, 1999)

Seville C., *Literary Copyright Reform in Early Victorian England (the Framing of the 1842 Copyright Act)*, (Cambridge University Press, 1999)

Sherman B. & A. Strowel, *Of Authors and Origins, Essays on Copyright Law*, (eds.) (Clarendon Press, Oxford, 1994)

Siwek S.E. & H. Furchtgott-Roth, *Copyright Industries in the US Economy 1977–1993*, (International Intellectual Property Alliance, January 1995)

Siwek S.E. & H. Furchtgott-Roth, *Copyright Industries in the US Economy*, (Reports prepared for the International Intellectual Property Alliance (IIPA), November 1990, September 1992, October 1993 and January 1995)

Siwek S.E. & G. Mosteller, (Reports prepared for the International Intellectual Property Alliance (IIPA), 1996 & 1998)

Siwek S.E., *Copyright in the US Economy* (Reports prepared for the International Intellectual Property Alliance (IIPA), Washington, 1999, 2000 & 2002)

Sirinelli P., ed., *Code de la Propriété intellectuelle,* 3rd ed., (Dalloz, Paris, 2002)

Sirinelli P., *Propriété littéraire et artistique et droits voisins,* (Dalloz, coll. Mementos, Paris, 1992)

Skilbeck J., *The Economic Importance of Copyright* (International Publishers' Association, London, 1988)

Skilbeck J., *The Export Performance of the Copyright—Dependent Industries* (CLIP, 1988)

Skone James E.P., J.F. Mummery & J. Rayner James, *Copinger and Skone James on Copyright* (Sweet & Maxwell, London, 1980)

Stamatoudi I.A. & P.L.C. Torremans, *Copyright in the New Digital Environment,* (Sweet & Maxwell, London, 2000)

Sterling J.A.L., *World Copyright Law,* (Sweet & Maxwell, London, 1998)

Stewart S.M., *International Copyright and Neighbouring Rights,* 2nd ed., (Butterworths, London, 1989)

Strowel A., *Droit d'auteur et copyright—Divergences et convergences,* (Bruylant, Bruxelles, 1993)

Strowel A., "Convergences entre droit d'auteur et copyright dans la société de l'information", in Intergu (ed), *Schutz von Kultur und geistigem Eigentum in der Informationsgesellschaft,* Baden-Baden, (Nomos Verlag, 1998)

Strowel A. and J.-P. Trialle, *Le droit d'auteur, du logiciel au multi-média,* (Bruylant, Brussels, 1997)

Symonds M., *"The dot.com imperative",* The World in 2000, (The Economist Group, London, 1999)

Ulmer E., *Urheber-und Verlagsrecht,* 3rd. ed., (Springer Verlag, Berlin, Heidelberg, New York, 1980)

Vithlani H., *The Economic Impact of Counterfeiting,* (OECD, Paris, 1998)

Vogel M., *Deutsche Urheber- und Verlagsrechtsgeschichte zwischen 1450 und 1850,* (AGB XIX, Frankfurt a.m., 1978)

Walker D.M., *Oxford Companion to Law* (Oxford, 1980)

Wand P., *Technische Schutzmaßnahmen und Urheberrecht—Ein Vergleich des international, europäischen, deutschen und US-amerikanischen Rechts,* (Munich, Beck, 2001)

Wittenberg P., *The Protection of Literary Property* (The Writer Inc, Boston, 1986/1978, revised ed. 1978)

Articles

Abrams H. B., "Historic Foundation of Copyright Law", [1983] 29 Wayne Law Review 1119

Adelstein A. & Peretz S., "The Competition of Technologies in Markets for Ideas: Copyright and Fair Use in Evolutionary Perspective", (1985) 5 Int. Rev. of Law and Economics 209

Adams J.N. & Edenborough M., "The Duration of Copyright in the United Kingdom after the 1995 Regulations", [1996] E.I.P.R. 590

Adams J.N., " 'Small Earthquake in Venezuela': The Database Regulations 1997", [1998] E.I.P.R. 129

Adams J.N., "The Reporting Exception: Does it Still Exist", [1999] E.I.P.R. 383

Alberstat P., "Copyright Extension in the United States: The Mouse that Roared", [1999] ENT.L.R., 61

Bechthold B., "From Copyright to Information Law—Implications of Digital Rights Management", in *Security and Privacy in Digital Rights Management*, (Sander T., ed., Heidelberg, Springer, Berlin, 2001)

Becourt D., "La Révolution française et le droit d'auteur pour un nouvel universalisme", [1990] 143 R.I.D.A. 231

Begue S. & Cohen-Tanugi L., "Droit d'auteur et copyright face aux technologies numériques: comparaisons transatlantiques", (2001) 178 *Léqipresse* 1

Benabou V.-L. & Varet V., "*La Codification de la propriété intellectuelle*", IRPI, La Documentation française, (Paris, 1998)

de Boor H.O., "Lettre d'Allemagne", [1954] *Le Droit d'Auteur*, 203

de Boor H.O., "Lettre d'Allemagne", [1955] *Le Droit d'Auteur*, 180

de Boor H.O., "Lettre d'Allemagne", [1955] *Le Droit d'Auteur*, 154

Bornkamm J., "Copyright and the Public Interest—The Three-Step Test in International Copyright", (paper delivered at the Fordham University School of Law 10th. Annual Conference on International Intellectual Property Law and Policy, New York, April 4 & 5, 2002)

Boutet M., "General Considerations", [1958] XIX R.I.D.A. 13

Brennan D.J., "The Three-Step Test Frenzy—Why the TRIPs Panel

Decision might be considered Per Incuriam", [2002] I.P.Q. 2, 212

Breyer S., "The Uneasy Case for Copyright: A Study of Copyright in Books, Photocopies, and Computer programs", (1970) 84 Harv. L. Rev. 281

Breyer S., "Copyright A Rejoinder", (1972) 20 U.C.L.A. L. Rev. 75

Brown Hon. H. & Miller D., "Copyright Term Extension: Sapping American Creativity", [1996] 44 Journal, Copyright Soc. of the USA 94

Burrell R., "Defending the Public Interest", [2000] E.I.P.R. 394

Burrell R., "Reining in Copyright Law: Is Fair Use the Answer", [2001] 4 I.P.Q. 361

Caron C., "Abuse of Rights and Authors' Rights", [1998] 176 R.I.D.A. 3

Caron C., "La loi du ler août 2000 relative à la liberté de communication et la propriété intellectuelle", *CEE* 2000, n.9–10

Caron C., "Les droits de l'homme réconciliés avec le droit d'auteur", [2001] *D.*, Jurisprudence, 2504

Chafee Z. Jr., "Reflexions on the Law of Copyright", I & II, [1945] 45 Columbia Law Rev. 503 and 719

Chalton S., "The Effect of the EC Database Directive on United Kingdom Law in relation to Databases: A Comparison of Features", [1997] E.I.P.R. 278

Chalton S., "The Copyright and Rights in Databases Regulations 1997: Some Outstanding Issues on Implementation of the Database Directive", [1998] E.I.P.R. 178

Christie A. "Reconceptualising Copyright in the Digital Era", [1995] 11 E.I.P.R. 522

Correa C.M., "TRIPs Agreement: Copyright and Related Rights", (1994) 25 I.I.C. 543

Clark C., "The Copyright Environment for the Publisher in the Digital World", (International Publishers' Association, March 1996)

Clark C., 'The Answer to the Machine is in the Machine", in *The Future of Copyright in a Digital Environment*, B. Hugenholtz, ed. (Kluwer, The Hague, 1996)

Cohen Jehoram H., "Critical Reflections on the Economic Importance of Copyright" (1989) 20 I.I.C. 485

Cornish G. P., "Libraries and the Harmonisation of Copyright", [1998] E.I.P.R. 241

Cornish W.R., "Intellectual Property", in (1994) Yearbook of European Law 485

Cornish W.R., "The Notions of Work, Originality and Neigh-bouring Rights from the Viewpoint of Common Law Traditions", in *WIPO World-wide Symposium on the Future of Copyright and Neighbouring Rights*, (WIPO, Geneva, 1994)

Cornish W.R., "Recent Changes in British Copyright Law", [1997] 172 R.I.D.A. 151 at 157

Costes L., "Le nouveau régime de la protection juridique des bases de données", in *Cahiers Lamy Informatique* 1998, no.107 (Part I) & 108 (Part 2)

Cottier T., "The value and effects of protecting intellectual property rights within the World Trade Organisation", (*ALAI Geneva study session 1994*, Groupe suisse de l'ALAI et les auteurs, Berne, 1994)

Davies G., "New Technology and Copyright Reform", [1984] 12 E.I.P.R. 335

Davies G., "The Public Interest in Collective Administration of Rights", [1989] Copyright 82

Davies G., "The Convergence of Copyright and Authors' Rights—Reality or Chimera?", (1995) 26 I.I.C. 964

Davies G., "Technical Devices as a Solution to Private Copying", in I.A. Stamatoudi and P.L.C. Torremans, *Copyright in the New Digital Environment: The Need to Redesign Copyright*, 163, (Sweet & Maxwell, London, 2000)

Davies G., "Copyright in the Information Society—Technical Devices to Control Private Copying", in Ganea P., Heath C., & Schricker G., eds., *Urheberrecht Gestern-Heute-Morgen, Festschrift für Adolf Dietz zum 65. Geburtstag,* 307, (Verlag C.H. Beck, Munich, 2001)

Davison M., "Geographical Restraints on the Distribution of Copyright Material in a Digital Age: Are they Justified?" [1996] 9 E.I.P.R. 477

Derieux E., "Bases de données et droit du public à l'information", *Les Petites Affiches*, 1998, no.21

de Freitas D., "Economic Arguments for Protecting Intellectual Property", (1990) 2 Intellectual Property in Business 26

Desbois H., "La loi française du 11 mars 1957", [1957] *Le droit d'auteur* 84

Desbois H., "The Moral Right", [1958] XIX R.I.D.A. 121

von Diemar U., "Kein Recht auf Privatkopien-Zur Rechtsnatur der gesetzlichen Lizenz zu Gunsten de Privatverfielfältigung", (2002) 7 G.R.U.R. 587

Dietz A., "Letter from Germany", [1973] Copyright 93

Dietz A., "Letter from the Federal Republic of Germany, The Development of Copyright between 1984 and the beginning of 1989", [1990] Copyright 58

Dietz A., "Copyright in the Modern Technological World: a Mere Industrial Property Right?", (1991) 39 Journal of the Copyright Society of the USA 83

Dietz A., "Copyright Law Developments in Germany from 1993 to Mid-1997" [1998] 175 R.I.D.A. 96 & [1998] 176 R.I.D.A. 167

Dixon A.N., and Self L.C., "Copyright Protection for the Information Superhighway", [1994] 11 E.I.P.R. 465

Dock M.-C., "Genèse et évolution de la notion de propriété littéraire", [1974] LXXIX R.I.D.A. 165

Dreier T., "Copyright Law and Digital Exploitation of Works—the Current Copyright Landscape in the Age of the Internet and Multimedia", 1997, (available online at *www.ipa-uie.org* (English translation of original German text))

Dreier T., *Urheberrecht im Zeitalter von Internet und Multi-media*, (Friedrich-Ebert-Stiftung, Bonn, 1997)

Dreier T., "Authorship and New Technologies from the Viewpoint of Civil Law Traditions", (paper presented at the WIPO Worldwide Symposium on the Future of Copyright and Neighbouring Rights, Paris, June, 1994)

Dusollier S., "Electrifying the Fence: The Legal Protection of Technological Measures for Protecting Copyright", [1999] E.I.P.R. 285

Edelman B., Note re CA Versailles, Ch. réun. (November 20, 1991), D. 1992

Edelman B., "Du mauvais usage des droits de l'homme D. 2000, Chronique, 455

Edelman B., "Les bases de données ou le triomphe des droits voisins", D. 2000, 89

Elster A., "Die wettbewerbliche und die immanente Begrenzung des Urheberrechts", [1926] 31 G.R.U.R. 493

Elster A., "Der Schutz des Geisteswerkes als Ausgleich zwischen Urheber und Allgemeinheit", [1931] 4 U.F.I.T.A. 215

Ermecke G. "The Social Significance of Intellectual Property", (lecture given at the Congress of the International Copyright Society, Berlin, September 16, 1962)

Escarra, J., "Le projet de loi française sur la propriété littéraire et artistique", (1954) V RIDA 3

Espinel V.A., "Harmony on the Internet: The WIPO Performances and Phonograms Treaty and United Kingdom Copyright Law", [1998] ENT.L.R. 21

Evans L.H., "Copyright and the Public Interest", (1949) 53 *Bulletin of the New York Public Library*, 3 at 4 (also published in (1949) II 1 *Bulletin du droit d'auteur* 2 (Unesco, Paris))

Fabiani M., "A Profile of Copyright in Today's Society", [1982] Copyright 154

Fabiani M., "The Geneva Diplomatic Conference on Copyright and the Rights of Performers and Phonogram Producers", [1997] ENT.L.R. 98

Feather J., "Authors, Publishers and Politicians: The History of Copyright and the Book Trade", [1988] 12 E.I.P.R. 377

Fernay R., "Grandeur, misère et contradictions du droit d'auteur", [1979] Il Diritto di Autore, Anno L 419, [1981] 109 R.I.D.A. 138

Fichte J.-G., "Beweis der Unrechtmäßigkeit des Büchernachdrucks", in *Berlinische Monatsschrift*, (1793) Vol.21, 443 at 451

Ficsor M., "How much of What? The "Three-Step Test" and its application in two recent WTO dispute settlement cases", (2002) 192 R.I.D.A. 110

Ficsor M., "Disquieting Report from the Maginot Line of Authors", [1982] Copyright 104

Finkelstein T., "La loi américaine de 1790 sur le droit d'auteur", (1963) XXXVII RIDA 35

Françon A., "Letter from France", [1986] Copyright 359

Françon A., "Letter from France", [1991] Copyright 283

Françon A., "Le Droit d'auteur au-delà des frontières: une comparaison des conceptions civiliste et de common law", [1991] 149 R.I.D.A. 2

Françon A., "Observations sur l'arrêt Chiavarino", [1991] *RTD com.* 592

Françon A., "Propriété littéraire et artistique", in *Chroniques de législation et de jurisprudence françaises*, [April–June 1997], *RTD com.*, 50

Friedman B., "From Deontology to Dialogue: The Cultural Consequences of Copyright", [1994] 13 Cardozo Arts and Entertainment 157

Fry R., "Rental Rights Derailed: Performers and Authors Lose out on Rental Income for Old Productions", [1997] 2 ENT.L.R. 31

Galloux J-C, "L'exclusivité de télédiffusion des évènements face au droit du public à l'information", *JCP* 1997, ed. G., I, 4046

Garloff P., "Copyright and Kunstfreiheit—zur Zulässigkeit ungenehmigter Zitate in Heiner Müllers letztes Theaterstücks", [2001]

6 G.R.U.R. 476

Garrigues C., "Databases: A Subject-Matter for Copyright or for a Neighbouring Rights Régime?", [1997] E.I.P.R. 3

Gaubiac Y., "Freedom to Quote from an Intellectual Work", [1997] 171 R.I.D.A. 2

Gaubiac Y., "Les exceptions au droit d'auteur: un nouvel avenir", [2001] 6 *Communication Commerce Electronique*, 12

Gaudrat P., "Loi de transposition de la directive 96/9 du 11 mars 1996 sur les bases de données: dispositions relatives au droit d'auteur", [July–Sept. 1998], *RTD com.* 51(3),

Geiger C., "Die Informationsfreiheit als Schranke des Urheberrechts-Anmerkung zur Entscheidung des TGI Paris vom 23. Februar 1999", [2001] 3 G.R.U.R. Int. 252

Geiger C., "Zum zweispältigen Verhältnis von Urheberrecht und Informationsfreiheit-Anmerkung zum Urteil der Cour d'Appel de Paris vom 30. Mai 2001", [2002] 4 G.R.U.R. Int., 329

Geiger C., "Les exceptions au droit d'auteur à des fins d'enseignement et de recherche en droit allemand", (October 2002) *PI*

Geller P.E., "Case Note", [1991] 150 R.I.D.A. 99

Geller P.E., "The Universal Electronic Archive: Issues in International Copyright", (1994) 25 I.I.C. 54

Geller P.E., "Can the GATT Incorporate Berne Whole?", [1990] 4 WIPR 193

Geller P.E., "New Dynamics in International Copyright", [1993] 16 Colum.-VLA J.L. & Arts 461

Gendreau Y., "Digital Technology and Copyright: Can Moral Rights Survive the Disappearance of the Hard Copy?", [1995] 6 ENT.L.R. 214

Ginsburg J.C., "Recent Developments in U.S. Copyright Law", [1987] 133 R.I.D.A. 111

Ginsburg J.C., "A Tale of Two Copyrights: Literary Property in Revolutionary France and America", [1989] 147 R.I.D.A. 125

Ginsburg J.C., "Developments in U.S. Copyright Law Since 1990", [1993] 158 R.I.D.A. 133

Ginsburg J.C., Case note [1994] 162 R.I.D.A. 349

Ginsburg J.C., "News from US (I)", [1999] 179 R.I.D.A. 143

Ginsburg J., "Copyright Use and Excuse on the Internet", [2000] 24 Colum—VLA J.L. & Arts

Ginsburg J. & Gaubiac Y., "L'avenir de la copie privée numérique en Europe", (2000) *Communication Commerce électronique*, Chron. N. 1

Ginsburg J.C., "Toward Supranational Copyright Law? The WTO

Panel Decision and the 'Three-Step Test' for Copyright Exceptions", [2001] 187 R.I.D.A. 3

Ginsberg J.C., "The Last Ten Years in US Copyright: Overreaching or Reaching Out?", (paper presented at Fordham University School of Law, 10th Annual International Intellectual Property Conference, New York, April 4–5, 2002)

Ginsburg J. & Kernochan J.M., "One Hundred and Two Years Later: the United States Adhere to the Berne Convention", [1989] 141 R.I.D.A. 57

Ginsburg J. & Gaubiac Y., "Private Copyright in the Digital Environment", in *Intellectual Property and Information Law*, Essays in Honour of Herman Cohen Jehoram, (Kluwer Law International, The Hague, London, Boston, 1998)

Gladney H.M., "Digital Intellectual Property: Controversial and International Aspects", [2000] 24 Colum—VLA J.L. & Arts 47

Goldberg D. & Bernstein R.J., "The Prohibition on Circumvention and the Attack on the DVD", [2001] E.I.P.R. 160

Goldmann B.C., "Victory for Songwriters in WTO Music-Royalties Dispute Between U.S. and EU", [2001] 4 I.I.C. 412

Goldstein P., "Copyright: The Donald C. Brace Memorial Lecture", (1991) 38 *Journal of the Copyright Society of the USA*, 3

Goldstein P., "Copyright and Authors' Right in the XXIst Century", (paper delivered at the WIPO World-wide Symposium on the Future of Copyright and Neighbouring Rights, Paris, June, 1994)

Goodenough O.L., "Pointillism, Copyright and the Droit d'auteur: Time to See a Bigger Picture", [1994] 2 ENT.L.R. 35

Gordon W., "Fair Use as Market Failure: A Structural and Economic Analysis of the *Betamax* Case and its Predecessors", [1982] 82 Colum.L.Rev. 1600

Gordon W. "An Enquiry into the Merits of Copyright: The Challenges of Consistency, Consent, and Encouragement Theory", 41 Stanford L.Rev. 1343 (1989)

Goutal J.-L., "The WIPO Treaty of 20 December 1996 and the French Conception of Author's Rights", (2001) 187 R.I.D.A. 66

Griffiths J., "Copyright and Public Lending in the United Kingdom", [1997] E.I.P.R. 499

Griffiths J., "Copyright in English Literature: Denying the Public Domain", [2000] E.I.P.R. 150

Haftke M., "Pro Sieben Media AG v. Carlton UK Television Ltd. and Twenty-Twenty Vision Ltd.", [1999] ENT.L.R. 118

Hauert R., "Control and limits of the moral right of the artist",

[1959] XXIII R.I.D.A. 50

Heide T., "Copyright in the E.U. and United States: What "Access Right'? [2001] E.I.P.R. 469

Hesse C., "Enlightenment Epistemology and the Laws of Authorship in Revolutionary France 1777–1793", [1990] 30 *Representations* 109

Hirsch-Ballin E.D., "Authors' rights compared with those of the community" [1956], X R.I.D.A. 18

Hugenholtz B., "Why the Copyright Directive is Unimportant, and Possibly Invalid", [2000] E.I.P.R. 499

Hummel M., "The Economic Importance of Copyright", 12 IFO-Digest, No. 4/89, at 32 (IFO Institute for Economic Research, Munich)

Hummel M., "The Economic Importance of Copyright", UNESCO Copyright Bulletin, Vol. XXIV, No.2, at 14 (1990)

Hurt R.M. and Schuchman R.M., "The Economic Rationale of Copyright", (1966) 56 Am. Econ. Rev. 426

Jolibois C., Report of the Commission (Doc. Sénat No. 350) [1986] 127 R.I.D.A. 278 *et seq.*

Kamina P., "Le droit du public à l'information peut-il justifier une exception au droit d'auteur?" *D.* 1999, Jurisprudence, 580

Karjala D.S., *et al.*, "Comment of US Copyright Law Professors on the Copyright Office Term of Protection Study", [1994] 12 E.I.P.R. 531

Kasdan J., "The Economics of Copyright with Applications to Licensing", (Working Paper, Columbia Law School, October 1966)

Kastenmeier R.W. & Remington M.J., "The Semiconductor Chip Protection Act of 1984: *A Swamp or Firm Ground?*" 70 Minnesota L. Rev. 417 (1985)

Kastenmeier R.W., The 1989 Horace S. Manges Lecture—"Copyright in an Era of Technological Change: A Political Perspective", 14 Colum.-VLA J.L. & Arts, 1 (1989)

Kauffmann G., "Exposing the Suspicious Foundations of Society's Primacy in Copyright Law: Five Accidents", 10 Colum.-VLA Journal of Law and the Arts, 381 (1986).

Kerever A., "Is Copyright an Anachronism?", [1983] Copyright 368

Kerever A., "One Aspect of the Law of July 3, 1985: Modernisation of the Law of March 11, 1957", [1986] 127 R.I.D.A. 22

Kerever A., "The French Revolution and Authors' Rights", [1989] 141 R.I.D.A. 9

Kerever A., "Copyright: The Achievements and Future Development of European Legal Culture", [1990] *Copyright* 130

Kreile R., "The 1989 Amendment to the German Copyright Act", [1990] 10 Copyright World 24

Kreile R., "Collection and Distribution of the Statutory Remuneration for Private Copying with Respect to Recorders and Blank Cassettes in Germany", [1992] 23 I.I.C. 449

Kretschmer F., "Gesetzentwurf zur Regelung des Urheberrechts in der Informationsgesellschaft," [2002] G.R.U.R. 501

Ladd D., "To Cope with the World Upheaval in Copyright", [1983] *Copyright* 289

Laddie H., "Copyright: Over-strength, Over-regulated, Over-rated?", [1996] E.I.P.R. 253

Lai S., "Database Protection in the United Kingdom: The New Deal and Its Effects on Software Protection", [1998] E.I.P.R. 32

Lai S., "Digital Copyright and Watermarking", [1999] E.I.P.R. 171.

Laligant O., "The French Revolution and Authors' Rights or Perenniality of the Subject Matter for Protection", [1991] 147 R.I.D.A. 36

Landau M., "Digital downloads, copy code and U.S. Copyright Law", (paper delivered at the Ninth Annual Conference on International Intellectual Property Law and Policy, Fordham University School of Law, New York, April 19 & 20, 2001)

Landes W.M. and Posner R.A., "An Economic Analysis of Copyright Law", (1989) 18 Journal of Legal Studies 325

Lang J., "The law of 3 July 1985", [1986] 127 R.I.D.A. 6

Lang J. "Exposé des motifs" [1986] 127 R.I.D.A. 168

Lassen B.S., "Collectivism and Individual Rights in Norwegian Copyright Law", (1963) Scandinavian Studies in Law, 79

Latreille A., "La protection des dispositifs techniques, Entre suspicion et sacralisation", (2002) 2 *Propriétés intellectuelles* 35

Lefranc D., "Le nouveau public (réflexions comparatistes sur les décisions 'Napster' et 'MP3.com')", [2001] 1 *D.* 107

von Lewinski S., "EC Proposal for a Council Directive Harmonizing the Term of Protection of Copyright and Certain Related Rights", (1992) 23 I.I.C. 785

Light S.N., Parody, Burlesque and the Economic Rationale for Copyright, [1979] 11 Connecticut Law Review, No.4, 615

Litman J., "Copyright and Information Policy", (1992) 55 Law and Contemporary Problems, 196

Ljungman S., "Nogot om Verkshöjd", [1972] N.I.R. 35

Ljungman S., "The Function of Copyright in Present Day Society: Some Reflections with Reference to the Nordic Situation", [1976] 88 R.I.D.A. 51

Löffler M., "Das Grundrecht auf Informationsfreiheit als Schranke des Urheberrechts", [1980] 5 N.J.W., 201

Löwenheim U., "Copyright in Civil Law and Common Law Countries: A Narrowing Gap", (paper presented at the Conference on the Economics of Intellectual Property Rights, University of Venice, October 1994)

McCarthy J.T., "Intellectual Property—America's Overlooked Export", (1996) 28 Intellectual Property L. Rev. 315

Mann R., "New Aspects of the Right of Reproduction and the Use of Archives in Germany", [2000] E.I.P.R. 93

Marks D.S. & Turnbull B.H., "Technical Protection Measures: The Intersection of Technology, Law and Commercial Licences", [2000] E.I.P.R. 198

Masouyé C., "Droit d'auteur: Horizon 2000", [1979] Il Diritto di Autore 163

Masouyé C., "Towards a Prolongation of the General Duration of Protection", (1959) XXIV R.I.D.A. 93

Matthyssens J., "Copyright Law Schemes in France during the Last Century", [1954] IV R.I.D.A. 15

Metzger A., "Germania 3, Gespenster am toten Mann oder Welchen Zweck darf ein Zitat gemäss s.51 Nr.2 UrhG verfolgen", [2000] 11 Z.U.M. 924

Möller M., "The Reform of the Copyright Law of the Federal Republic of Germany" [1986] Copyright 271

Monti M., Opening Speech, (International Conference on Intellectual Property Rights, Vienna, July 1998) (see European Commission DG Internal Market website: www.europa.eu.int)

Mosawi A., "Some Implications of the New Regulations Regarding Rental Rights", [1995] 8 ENT.L.R. 307

Müller-Katzenburg A., "Offener Rechtsstreit um verhüllten Reichstag", [1996] N.J.W. 2341

Nimmer D., "The Impact of Berne on United States Copyright Law",[1989] 8 Carduzo Arts & Entertainment Law Journal 27

Nimmer M.B., "Does Copyright Abridge the First Amendment Guarantees of Free Speech and Press?", [1970] 17 UCLA Law Rev. 1180

Nordemann W., "The 1972 Amendment of the German Copyright Act", [1973] I.I.C. 179

Noguier P., "Le Pillage de l'écrit, photocopies, télécopies et copies différées; la gestion collective obligatoire, une solution juridique", [1994] Légicom No.3

Nordemann W., "A Right to Control or Merely to Payment?—Towards a Logical Copyright System", [1980] 1 I.I.C. 49

Oakes J.E., "Copyright and the First Amendment: Where Lies the Public Interest?", [1984] 59 Tulane Law Rev. 135

von Olenhausen A.G., "Ewiges geistiges Eigentum und Sozialbindung des Urheberrechts in der Rechtsentwicklung und Diskussion in 19. Jahrhundert in Frankreich und Deutschland, Herschel W., Hubmann H. & Rehbinder M., eds.: Festschrift für Georg Roeber zum 10. Dezember 1981 (HochschulVerlag, Freiburg, 1982)

Olivier F. & Barbry E., "Aperçu rapide relatif à la loi n.97–283 du 27 mars 1997—Quelles dispositions pour la diffusion des oeuvres par cable et satellites?", *J.C.P.* 1977, èd. G. n.22, *Actualités*

Olson T.P., "The Iron Law of Consensus: Congressional Responses to Proposed Copyright Reforms since the 1909 Act", (1989) 36 Journal, Copyright Soc. of the USA 109

Olsson H., "Copyright in the National Economy", [1982] Copyright 130

Olswang S., "Accessright: An Evolutionary Path for Copyright into the Digital Era?" [1995] 5 E.I.P.R. 215

Oman R., "Berne Revision: the Continuing Drama", (1993) 7 *World Intellectual Property Report* 160.

Oman R., "The Role of the United States in International Copyright", speech at the Finnish Copyright Society in Helsinki, August 22, 1989, [1989] 58 NIR 243

Palmer T.G., "Are Patents and Copyrights Morally Justified? The Philosophy of Property Rights and Ideal Objects", (1990) 13 Harvard Journal of Law and Public Policy 816

Pares P., "La conception française du droit d'auteur", [1954] II R.I.D.A. 3

Parrinder P., "The Dead Hand of European Copyright", [1993] E.I.P.R. 391

Patterson L. R., "The Statute of Anne: Copyright Misconstrued", [1966] 3 Harv. J. Legis 223

Patterson L.R., "Copyright and Authors' Rights: A Look at History", [1968] XVI Harvard Library Bulletin, No.4, 370

Patterson L.R., "Private Copyright and Public Communication: Free Speech Endangered", [1975] 28 Vanderbilt Law Rev. 1161

Patterson L.R.: "Free Speech, Copyright and Fair Use", [1987] 40 Vanderbilt Law Rev. 1

Philips J., "Copyright: Towards a Positive Approach?", [1974] LXXXII R.I.D.A. 34

Philips J., "The Berne Convention and the Public Interest", [1986] 11 Colum.-VLA J. L. and A. 165

Phillips J., "Fair Stealing and the Teddy Bear's Picnic", [1999] ENT.L.R. 57

Phillips J., "When is a Fact", [2000] ENT.L.R. 116

Plaisant M., "Welcome to the Law", [1958] XIX R.I.D.A. 9

Plaisant R., "La protection du logiciel par le droit d'auteur", [1983] G.P. 2.348

Plaisant R., "La Durée du droit pécuniaire de l'auteur et son évolution", Mélanges A. Françon, 351 (Dalloz, 1995)

Plant A., "The Economic Aspects of Copyright in Books", (1934) 1 *Economica* (n.s.) 167

Plant A., "The New Commerce in Ideas and Intellectual Property", (Stamp Memorial Lecture 1953, Athlone Press, University of London, 1953)

Pollaud-Dulian F., "Abus de droit et droit moral", *D.* 1993, Chronique

Pollaud-Dulian F., "Brèves Réflexions sur la loi n.97–283 du 27 mars 1997", *J.C.P.* 1997, éd. G. Chronique, 4024

Pollaud-Dulian F., "The Duration of Copyright", [1999] 176 R.I.D.A. 83

Poppelmann B.-H., "Verhüllter Reichstag", [1996] 4 Z.U.M. 293

Prager F.D.A., "History of Intellectual Property From 1545 to 1787", [1944] 26 Journal of the Patent Office Society, No.11

Pratt E.T., "Intellectual Property Role in US Trade Policy", [1988] Rev. of the LES 159

Recht P., "Copyright, a New Form of Property", [1969] Copyright 94

Reinbothe J., "Digital Rights Management: The Legal Framework", (paper delivered at the Fordham University School of Law 10th Annual Conference on International Intellectual Property Law and Policy, New York, April 4 & 5, 2002)

Richard A., Report, (1986) 127 R.I.D.A. 176

Ricketson S., "Duration of Term of Protection Under the Berne Convention", [1991] Copyright 88.

Ricketson S., "The Copyright Term", [1992] 23 I.I.C. 753 & 755.

Ringer B., "Renewal of Copyright", Study No.1 (Vol.1, *Studies in Copyright*, 1963)

Ringer B., "The Role of the United States in International Copyright—Past, Present and Future", [1968] 56 Georgetown Law Journal 1050

Ringer B., "Copyright in its Historical and Philosophic Setting", from records of a meeting of the Information Industry Association, July 18–19, 1969 (published by Information Industry Association, 1970)

Ringer B., "Copyright and the Future of Authorship", [1976] Copyright 156

Ringer B., "Two Hundred Years of American Copyright Law", Bicentennial Symposium of the American Bar Association, 1976

Ringer B., "The Demonology of Copyright", Bowker Memorial Lecture, (US Publisher's Weekly, November 18, 1974)

Ringer B., "Copyright in the 1980's", [1976] *Bulletin of the Copyright Society of the USA*, 299.

Ringer B., "First Thoughts on the Copyright Act of 1976", [1977] *Copyright* 187

Ringer B., "Authors' Rights in the Electronic Age: Beyond the Copyright Act of 1976", (1981) 1 Loyola Entertainment Law Journal 1

Robinson A., "The Life and Terms of U.K. Copyright in Original Works", [1997] 2 ENT. L.R. 60

Roeber G., "Urheberrecht oder Geistiges Eigentum", [1956] 21 U.F.I.T.A. 150

Romatka G., "Bild-Zitat und ungenehmigte Übernahme von Lichtbildern", [1971] 1 AfP 20

Rosenfield H.N., "The Constitutional Dimension of Fair Use in Copyright Law", [1975] 50 Notre Dame Law Rev. 790

Ruete M., "The Kirchenmusik Judgment—Constitutional and Intellectual Property Rights", [1980] E.I.P.R. 198

Rumphorst W., "Comment on the School Book Case", (1972) 3 I.I.C. 401

Samnadda J., "Technical Measures, Private Copying and Levies: Perspectives on Implementation", (paper delivered at the Fordham University School of Law 10th Annual Conference on International Intellectual Property Law and Policy, New York, April 4 & 5, 2002)

Samuelson P., "Digital Media and the Changing Face of Intellectual Property Law", (1990) 16 Rutgers Computer and Technology Law Journal 323

Sander T., ed., *Security and privacy in digital rights management*, (Heidelberg, Springer, Berlin, 2001)

Saunders D., "*Purposes or Principle? Early Copyright and the Court of*

Chancery", [1993] E.I.P.R. 452

Sayal M., "Copyright and Freedom of the Media: A Balancing Exercise?" [1995] 7 ENT.L.R. 263

Schippan M., "Codification of Contract Rules for Copyright Owners—The Recent Amendment of the German Copyright Act", [2000] E.I.P.R. 171

Schwarz M., "Copyright in Compilations of Facts: Feist Publications, Inc. v. Rural Telephone Service Co., Inc.", [1991] E.I.P.R. 178

Schricker G., "Hundert Jahre Urheberrechtsentwicklung", in Festschrift zum hundertjährigen Bestehen der Deutschen Vereinigung für gewerblichen Rechtschutz und Urheberrecht und ihrer Zeitschrift, Weinheim, VCH, (1991) Part 4, 1095

Simon E., "The Integration of Intellectual Property and Trade Policy", *Economy and authors' rights in the international conventions*, (ALAI Geneva study session 1994, *Groupe Suisse de l'ALAI et les auteurs*, Berne, 1994)

Sirinelli P., "Le Droit d'auteur à l'aube du 3ème Millénaire", J.C.P. 2000, ed. G. n.1–2

Silbertson A., "The Economic Importance of Copyright", *Creativity and Intellectual Property Rights: Evolving Scenarios and Perspectives*, EU International Conference, Vienna, July 1998, European Commission DG Internal Market)

Siwek S.E., *Copyright in the US Economy, Reports*, (prepared for the IIPA, Washington, 1999, 2000 & 2002)

Siwek S.E., & Furchtgott-Roth H., *Copyright Industries in the U.S. Economy*, (Reports prepared for the IIPA, November 1990, September 1992, October 1993 & January 1995)

Slaughter J., "TRIPS: The GATT Intellectual Property Negotiations Approach their Conclusion", (1990) 11 E.I.P.R. 418

Stewart S.M., "Two Hundred Years of English Copyright Law", [1977] Copyright 228

Stewart S.M., "International Copyright in the 1980s", Geiringer Memorial Lecture 1980, [1981] 28 Bulletin of the Copyright Soc. of the USA 351

Stojanovic M.N., "The *raison d'être* of Copyright", [1979] 102 R.I.D.A. 124

Strowel A., "Considérations sur le droit d'auteur à la lumière des intérêts sous-jacents", *Droit positif, droit comparé et histoire du droit*, Vol.3 in the series *Droit et Intérêt* (Facultés universitaires Saint Louis, Vol. 49, Brussels, 1990)

Strowel A., "Licences non volontaires et socialisation du droit d'auteur: un danger ou une nécessité?", [1991] Cahiers de propriété intellectuelle

Strowel & Dusollier, "La protection légale des systèmes techniques", in WIPO Workshop on Implementation Issues of the WIPO Copyright Treaty (WCI) and the WIPO Performances and Phonograms Treaty (WPPT), WIPO doc. WCT-WPPT/IMP/2

Thomas A., "DVD Encryption-DeCSS", [2000] ENT.L.R. 135; "MP3 Wars: The Battle for Copyright in Cyberspace", [2000] ENT.L.R. 165

Tompson R.S., "Scottish Judges and the Birth of British Copyright", The Juridical Review, Part 1 [1992] 1

Tournier A., "An Appraisal of the Law", [1958] XIX R.I.D.A. 79

Tournier J.-L., "Le droit exclusif du compositeur de musique: réalité ou fiction" (The Sole Rights of the Composer: Reality or Fiction?), [1961] XXXIII RIDA 20

Turkewitz N., "Authors' Rights are Dead", (1990) 38 Journal of the Copyright Society of the USA 45

Tyerman B.W., "The Economic Rationale for Copyright Protection for Published Books: A Reply to Professor Breyer", (1971) 18 U.C.L.A. Law Rev. 1100

Uchtenhagen U., "The Economic Significance of Copyright", [1989] Copyright 280

Ulmer E., "Lettre d'Allemagne", [1955] Le Droit d'Auteur 154

Ulmer E., "Lettre d'Allemagne", [1956] Le Droit d'Auteur 180, at 182.

Ulmer E., "Vom deutschen Urheberrecht und seiner Entwicklung", [1957] 23 U.F.I.T.A. 257

Ulmer E., "Lettre d'Allemagne", [1957] Le Droit d'auteur 14

Ulmer E., "Lettre d'Allemagne", [1961] Le Droit d'auteur 14

Ulmer E., "Letter from Germany" [1965] Copyright 275

Varet V., "Droit d'auteur et liberté d'expression", [2001] Légipresse, 184

Vaver D. "Intellectual Property Today: of Myths and Paradoxes", (1990) LXIX The Canadian Bar Review 98

Vilbois J., "Historical Account", [1958] XIX R.I.D.A. 41

Vinje T.C., "A Brave New World of Technical Protection Systems: Will there Still be Room for Copyright?" [1996] 8 E.I.P.R. 431

Vinje T.C., "The New WIPO Copyright Treaty: A Happy Result in Geneva", [1997] E.I.P.R. 230

Vinje T.C., "Should we Begin Digging Copyright's Grave", [2000] E.I.P.R. 551

Vivant M., "Pour une compréhension nouvelle de la notion de courte citation en droit d'auteur", J.C.P. 1989, I, 3372

Vivant M., "Pour une épure de la propriété intellectuelle", in Mélanges A. Françon, p.415 (Dalloz, Paris, 1995)

Vivant M., "Entre droit d'auteur et Copyright—L'Europe au carrefour des logiques", [1997] 10 Cahiers de Propriété intellectuelle 41

Vogel M. "Die Geschichte des Urheberrechts im Kaiserreich", [1987] 12 G.R.U.R. 873

Vogel M., "Die Entfaltung des Übersetzungsrechts im deutschen Ürheberrecht des 19. Jahrhunderts", [1991] G.R.U.R. 16 at 21

Vogel M. "Urheberrecht in Deutschland zwischen Aufklärung und Vormärz", in Buchhandelsgeschichte [1989], 1 Beilage zum Bbl. Nr. 77

Vogel M. "Urheberpersönlichkeitsrecht und Verlagsrecht im letzten Drittel des 19. Jahrhunderts", [1994] 8/9 G.R.U.R. 587

Wandtke A., "Zur kulturellen und sozialen Dimension des Urheberrechts", [1993] 123 U.F.I.T.A. 5

Woodmansee M. "The Genius and the Copyright: Economic and Legal Conditions of the Emergence of the Author", [1984] 17 Eighteenth Century Studies 425

Yen A.C., "Restoring the Natural Law: Copyright as Labor and Possession", [1990] 51 Ohio State Law Journal, No.2

Zissu R.L., "Fair Use: From Harper and Row to Acuff Rose", [1994] 42, 1 Journal, Copyright Soc. of the USA, 7

Other Material—Governmental Reports & Parliamentary Proceedings

United Kingdom

Hansard, Vol.56, February 5, 1841

Hansard, Parliamentary Debates, Third Series, Vol.61, April 6, 1842

Report of the Commissioners of the Copyright Commission, 1878 [C–2036]

Report of the Committee on the Law of Copyright, 1909, Cmnd 4976

Copyright and Designs Law, Report of the Committee to consider the Law on Copyright and Designs, Chairman—The Hon. Mr Justice

Whitford, March 1977, HMSO, Cmnd 6732

Reform of the Law relating to Copyright, Designs and Performers' Protection, Cmnd 8302, HMSO, July 1981.

Intellectual Property Rights and Innovation, Cmnd 9117, HMSO, December 1983

The Recording and Rental of Audio and Video Copyright Material. A Consultative Document. (Green Paper) February 1985, HMSO, Cmnd 9445

Information Society: Agenda for Action in the UK, Report of the House of Lords Select Committee on Science and Technology, HL Paper 77, Session 1995–96, 5th Report, July 1996

Report from the Intellectual Property Group of the Government's Creative Industries Task Force, March 2000

Creative Industries Mapping Document 2001, (Department of Culture, Media and Sport (DCMS), London, 2001)

United States of America

Report of the Register of Copyrights on the General Revision of the US Copyright Law, 87th Congress, 1st session, July 1961

Duration of Copyright, report prepared for the Subcommittee on Patents, Trade Marks and Copyrights of the Committee on the Judiciary, US Senate, 86th Congress, 2nd Edition, Washington 1961

Supplementary Report of the Register of Copyrights on the General Revision of the US Copyright Law, 89th Congress, 1st Session, May 1965

House of Representatives Report No.94–1476 to the 94th Congress, 2nd session, dated September 3, 1976

An Analysis of Computer and Photocopyright Copyright Issues from the Point of View of the General Public and the Ultimate Comsumer, National Commission (USA) of New Technological Uses of Copyright Works (CONTU) (June 1977)

Performance Rights in Sound Recordings, House Committee on the Judiciary (Print No.15), 95th Congress, 2nd Session (1978)

The Impact of Copyright Law on the Economy, study prepared by the US Central Bureau of Statistics, February 26, 1982

Report of the US Copyright Office to the Subcommittee on Patents, Copyright and Trademarks of the Committee on the Judiciary, US

Senate, on the size of the Copyright Industries in the United States, December 1984

National Information Infrastructure Task Force, Working Group on Intellectual Property Rights, Chair: *Bruce A. Lehman*, September 1995

Senate Judiciary Committee Report, S.Rep.No.104–315, 104th Congress 2nd Session (1996).

"The Digital Millenium Copyright Act of 1998", US Copyright Office Summary, December 1998

Report of the Committee, US Senate, 105th Congress, 2nd Session, May 11, 1998

France

Archives Parlementaires de 1787 à 1860, Première Série, Tome xxii, January 13, 1791

Commission de la propriété littéraire, collection des procès-verbaux, chairman, le Vicomte de la Rochefoucauld (Paris, Imprimerie de Pillet Ainé, 1826)

Commission de la propriété littéraire et artistique, Rapports à l'Empereur, Décrets, Collection des procès-verbaux (Imprimerie Impériale, Paris, 1863).

Exposé des motifs du projet de Loi sur la propriété littéraire et artistique, annexed to the Minutes of the session of the *Assemblée nationale*, held on June 9, 1954 (doc. no.8612) [1954] V R.I.D.A. 150

"Industrie Culturelle et Nouvelle Technique", Report of the Committee chaired by Pierre Sirinelli, Ministère de la Culture et de la Francophonie, Paris, 1994

IRPI—Institut de recherche en propriété intellectuelle Henri Desbois, Dossier documentaire, Travaux préparatoires, Loi no.57-298 du 11 mars 1957 sur la propriété littéraire et artistique, Université Pantheon-Assas (Paris II), Paris

IRPI—Institut de recherche en propriété intellectuelle Henri Desbois, Dossier documentaire, Travaux préparatoires, Loi no.85-660 du 3 juillet 1985 relative aux droits d'auteurs et aux droits des artistes interprètes, des producteurs de phonogrammes et de vidéogrammes et des entreprises de communication audiovisuelle, tomes 1 et 2, Université Pantheon-Assas (Paris II), Paris

Revue international du droit d'auteur (R.I.D.A.): special issues on the French law (July 3, 1985, January 27, 1986 & April 28, 1986)

Germany

Entwurf eines Gesetzes betreffend das Urheberrecht an Werten der Literatur und der Tonkunst) presented to the Reichstag on December 8, 1900, Reichstag doc. No. 97, 10th legislative period, II Session 1900/1901

Bericht der XI. Kommission über den Entwurf eines Gesetzes, betreffend das Urheberrecht an Werken der Literatur und der Tonkunst, No.214, Reichstag, 10. Legislatur Periode, II. Session 1900/1901 (Report of the X1th Parliamentary Commission on the Draft Law)

Report in 1901 Le Droit d'Auteur 94

Report in 1927 Le droit d'auteur 101

Ministerialentworf (Departmental bill) 1959

Referentenentworf (Ministerial draft bill) 1954

Regierungsentworf (Government bill) 1962

L'Union internationale au seuil de 1935, Étude générale, 1935 Le Droit d'Auteur 4

Vergütungsbericht of July 5, 2000

Reichsgesetzblatt II Partie, No. 61, December 19, 1934, at 1395

Other

Competition Policy and Intellectual Property Rights, OECD (Organisation for Economic Cooperation and Development) Study, 1989

The Challenge of the Information Highway, Final Report of the Information Highway Advisory Council, Canada, 1995

Documents of the Committee of Experts on a Possible Protocol to the Berne Convention, 1st–6th Sessions, 1991–96

Documents of the Committee of Experts on a Possible Instrument for the Protection of the Rights of Performers and Producers of Phonograms, 1st–5th Sessions, 1991–96

Europe's Way to the Information Society, An Action Plan, Communication of the Commission to the Council and the European Parliament, (COM (94) 347 final) July 19, 1994

European Commission Green Paper on Copyright and Related Rights in the Information Society, July 19, 1995

Report of the Committee of Experts on a Possible Protocol to the Berne Convention for the Protection of Literary and Artistic Works, 2nd Session, Geneva, February 10–18, 1992

OECD (Trade Division), *Economic Arguments for Protecting Intellectual Property* (Paris, November 1990)

Index